Real Writing

Argumentation, Reflection, Information

Walter H. Beale
University of North Carolina, Greensboro

Scott, Foresman and Company Glenview, Illinois
Dallas, Tex. Oakland, N.J. Palo Alto, Cal.
Tucker, Ga. London, England

To Sarah, Stella, and Louise

Also available:

Real Writing: Argumentation, Reflection, Information with Stylistic Options: The Sentence and the Paragraph

Stylistic Options: The Sentence and the Paragraph

Instructor's Manuals

These may be obtained through a local Scott, Foresman representative or by writing to English Editor, College Division, Scott, Foresman and Company, 1900 E. Lake Avenue, Glenview, IL 60025.

Acknowledgments

CHAPTER ONE "A Sears Suit: Call for clarification" from *Time,* February 5, 1979, vol. 113, no. 6. Reprinted by permission from *Time,* The Weekly Newsmagazine; Copyright Time Inc. 1979. From "Mrs. Eisenhower," *The Atlanta Journal,* November 2, 1979. Reprinted by permission. "Abolish the Corporate Income Tax," *The New York Times,* September 11, 1977. Copyright © 1977 by The New York Times Company. Reprinted by permission. From "Creeping Sanity" by Daniel Oliver, *National Review,* October 26, 1979. Copyright © 1979 by National Review, Inc., 150 East 35th Street, New York, N.Y. 10016. Reprinted by permission. From "Unreforming the Parties" by J. Patrick Dobel and Ronald R. Stockton, *Commonsense,* Summer 1979, vol. 2, no. 2. Copyright © 1979 by the Republican National Committee. Reprinted by permission. Excerpt from "Greensboro Knows Grim Struggles, Not Fatal Ones" by Mark I. Pinsky from *The New York Times,* January 13, 1980. Copyright © 1980 by The New York Times Company. Reprinted by permission. "Participants, Not Patients" from *Close to Home* by Ellen Goodman. Copyright © 1979 by The Washington Post Company. Reprinted by permission of Simon & Schuster, a Division of Gulf & Western Corporation. **CHAPTER TWO** From "Marijuana Therapy" by David Blum, *The New Republic,* September 16, 1978, vol. 179, no. 12. Reprinted by permission of *The New Republic,* © 1978 The New Republic, Inc. "Is the Public Interested in the Public Interest?" From *Keeping Your Eye on Television* by Les Brown, Pilgrim Press, 1979. Reprinted by permission of the author. From "Feeding the Hungry" by Nick Kotz, *The New Republic,* November 25, 1978, vol. 179, no. 22. Reprinted by permission of *The New Republic,* © 1978 The New Republic, Inc. From "Best Agent for Courtroom Reform: Televised Trials" by Evelle J. Younger from *Los Angeles Times,* January 6, 1980. Reprinted by permission of the author. From "Can the American Family Survive?" by Margaret Mead, *Redbook,* February 1977, vol. 148, no. 4. Copyright © 1977 by The Redbook Publishing Company. Reprinted by permission. From "The Free Market at Work in Hong Kong" by Alvin Rabushka. Reprinted by permission of *The Wall Street Journal,* © Dow Jones & Company, Inc. 1980. All Rights Reserved. From "Zionism: A 'Cultural Affinity'" by George F. Will from *The Washington Post,* October 29, 1975. Copyright © 1975, The Washington Post Company. Reprinted with

All other literary credits appear on pages 339–340, which constitute a legal extension of the copyright page.

Library of Congress Cataloging in Publication Data.

Beale, Walter H.
Real writing.

Includes index.
1. English language—Rhetoric. I. Title.
PE1408.B465 808'.042 81-14429
ISBN 0-673-15446-7 (pbk.) AACR2

2 3 4 5 6-VHJ-86 85 84 83 82

Preface

I believe, and hope others believe, that writing well is not only a personal accomplishment but also a valuable form of social participation and leadership. For this reason *Real Writing* focuses upon writing that is public and non-specialized, writing directed at the common and immediate concerns of individuals and communities. Advantages of this focus are that it gives students direct access to subjects and situations through their interests and experiences, and that it provides a broad range of purposes and strategies.

Composition is frequently taught on the basis of formal patterns, a practice that can reduce student writing to academic exercises. Although most of the familiar materials of modern composition teaching are here, along with much from classical rhetoric, I have concentrated on writing in *real* situations, using positive strategies for achieving *real* goals of writing in our society. In developing and class-testing the materials of this book over many years, I have always used the principle of real writing in both their design and detail.

Design and Uses of the Book

The three parts of the book cover three major types of writing: *Deliberative,* also known as *argumentative; Reflective/Exploratory;* and *Informative.*

Real Writing opens with and concentrates on argumentation for a special reason—argumentation deals directly with choice and value, basic dimensions of all writing. It focuses upon the problems of individuals and communities. The study of argumentative writing can awaken in students a sense of the purposes and functions of writing in the wider society.

I have tried to make the art of argument, covered in the first six chapters, more approachable and useful than it is in most textbooks. Avoiding the usual textbook concentration on what *not* to do—what forms of proof to avoid, what fallacies to shun—I have used a positive approach. Given a particular purpose and situation, what *can* you do? What arguments *can* you use? Also, I have tried to relate argumentation to the writer—in each of these chapters, I have included "special" strategies for use in argumentation, particularly those which involve narrative, irony, and satire.

The first three chapters include finding and narrowing topics, developing a thesis, argumentative method, form, and the larger process of deliberation. The next three deal in turn with the three major kinds of issue in deliberative writing—*policy, value,* and *interpretation.* Any of these three chapters can follow from Chapter 3, and the three chapters may be taught in any order. The arrangement reflects my sense of their increasing difficulty. But there are good arguments for other arrangements, and it is possible to use only one of them before going on to other things.

Parts 2 and 3 on *Reflective/Exploratory* and *Informative Writing,* though shorter than Part 1, are just as concerned with purpose and situation, and with writing as an instrument of public communication. Part 2 emphasizes that reflective writing is more than private expression, and it recommends strategies for transforming personal insights into interesting and provocative communication. Part 3 emphasizes that informative writing is more than the organization of facts, that it has specific purposes with learnable strategies for fulfilling these purposes.

Where to Begin

Real Writing may be used in a variety of ways. Each of the three parts is independent, and each begins with an exploration of purpose. Instructors who wish to concentrate on argumentation and persuasion can follow the book as arranged, using Chapters 4–6 as needed to suit their courses.

Instructors who wish to begin with more familiar material on arranging and developing information, including some paragraph practice with standard modes—description, definition, cause and effect, comparison and contrast—can begin with Part 3, *Informative Writing.* An advantage of beginning here is that students can be encouraged to seek out and compile information for use in argumentative essays later on.

Instructors who wish to have students use personal narrative can start immediately with Part 2, *Reflective/Exploratory Writing.*

Readings, Exercises, and Writing Assignments

The professional and student essays at the end of each chapter and elsewhere are integral to the book, illustrating the purposes, situations, and strategies discussed in each unit. The large number of these readings should eliminate the need for a separate reader.

The exercises are placed strategically throughout the chapters. They have been designed as integral parts of the text rather than as supplementary additions to it.

The writing assignments reflect the possibilities outlined and demonstrated in their chapters. These assignments are, of course, suggestions that can be adapted and supplemented. Most of them are assignments that have been used with success in the classroom.

A Personal Word

At every stage of its development *Real Writing* received critical readings from Francis Hubbard, Cleo McNelly, Robert Perrin, and David Skwire. Through their suggestions and encouragement, these people made the book much better than I could have on my own, and I am grateful to them. Special thanks to Robert S. Rudolph for a thorough reading of the entire manuscript. I have been unusually fortunate in having such good editors, and good friends, at Scott, Foresman: Harriett Prentiss, Amanda Clark, Jane Steinmann, and Andrea Coens, especially Jane and Andrea, who worked closely with the manuscript and improved it in countless ways. Closer to home, Karen Meyers and Laurie White, my friends, colleagues, and collaborators in *Stylistic Options,* provided constant encouragements and many valuable suggestions.

Walter H. Beale

Overview

Contents

Essays

To the student

I need not tell you that writing is an important skill or dwell upon how central it will be to your success in college. I probably need not remind you that writing is a marketable skill—one that will serve you well in almost any profession. I would, however, like to discuss two reasons why writing is important and essential, especially to you, especially now.

First of all, writing is not merely a method of communicating; it is a method of knowing and of coming to know. This may seem like an outlandish idea, but it is widely testified to by people who write extensively. You begin with an idea, an insight, or a body of information. But in the process of working the idea or information into a coherent and convincing presentation, you produce new orderings and discover new relationships. There is a very real sense in which your understanding is not complete—it remains half-formed and untested—until you have communicated it in writing.

Second, writing is an important form of social participation and leadership. And because it is a special way of understanding *as well as* a way of communicating, no amount of technological innovation will alter that fact. The modern revolution in electronic communication has not diminished the importance of writing; it has increased it. There is more writing and publication going on right now than at any time in history.

Communities and organizations, like individuals, need good writing. They need it for communicating information, for solving problems, for sharing insights and experiences, for building consensus about what they love and value, and for increasing and refining their understanding of themselves. In learning to write well, you are becoming an educated person and cultivating a central human art. At the same time, you are learning to contribute something vital to the communities and organizations to which you belong.

This conviction about the dual importance of writing informs both the title and the method of this book. It asks you to do "real writing," and it attempts to guide you in that task. It concentrates on three of the most prominent types of public, non-specialized writing: *Deliberative, Reflective/Exploratory,* and *Informative.*

These different types of writing involve different purposes, situations, and forms and strategies. Each, however, offers the challenge of finding as well as communicating insights. And in each type, the needs of individuals and communities converge.

Part One

Deliberative Writing

1 Getting Started

Chapter Overview

This chapter introduces deliberative writing by comparing it with some other kinds of rhetorical writing and by describing some of its important characteristics. It also provides the writer with some powerful tools for getting started on a deliberative essay—methods for discovering topics, for narrowing topics, and for formulating thesis statements.

• What Is Deliberative Writing?

Some definitions and comparisons

We all recognize, on the basis of intuition and experience, that there are different kinds of writing—for different purposes, with different author-audience relationships and different "rules of the game." It's difficult to define in short space a type of writing, but its nature may become clear when compared with other types. We begin, then, with a definition of deliberative writing and some comparisons.

> Deliberative writing is writing whose main purpose is to support a conclusion or opinion about some problem or question of human experience. Its usual method is argumentation.

This is not a complete definition but a starting point. Following are three short essays. As you read each of them, ask yourself these questions: What does it "amount to"—that is, what kind of *action* does it perform? Does it suggest, propose, report, complain, promise, accuse (or defend), endorse, or perform some other action? How does it perform this action? What is its principal method and where is the author in all of it? Finally, which of the three essays is an example of deliberative writing?

Essay 1: A Sears Suit

Call for clarification

Normally, companies are on the receiving end of lawsuits about discrimination against workers on the basis of sex and race. But last week Sears, Roebuck, the world's largest retailer (annual sales: more than $17 billion), upset that pattern.

In a sweeping class action filed in the Washington, D.C., Federal District Court, Sears blamed the Government for whatever employment imbalances exist in the retail industry. The suit, prepared by veteran Civil Rights Attorney Charles Morgan Jr., charges that the Justice Department, the Labor Department, the Equal Employment Opportunity Commission and seven agencies have built up an absurd number of conflicting goals for different minorities. Sears maintains that it is not company employment practices that have held back integration but the Government's failure to press vigorously for equality in housing, education and craft training.

Sears, the leader in an industry that employs more than 15% of the labor force, has long been at odds with the EEOC. Indeed, some thought the suit was designed to steal thunder from an anti-Sears suit still pending at EEOC.

Sears officials deny this, but they make no secret of their frustrations with Washington. In 1973 the EEOC charged that Sears, which has about 417,000 people on its payroll, had followed discriminatory hiring and promotion practices. The company added a new dimension to its affirmative action program: Sears units were to hire one minority group member for every white hired until the payroll reflected the composition of the local area; women were to be hired for jobs that were traditionally men's, and vice versa. But in 1977, after an investigation, the EEOC decided that there was still "reasonable cause" to believe that the company was discriminating, and Sears and the commission have been wrangling ever since.

In its suit, Sears asks the courts to declare its existing affirmative action program to be in full accord with the law. Insists Ray Graham, Sears' director of equal opportunity: "We've made a tremendous effort to comply." He notes that since 1966 the company proportion of women managers has risen from 20% to 36%; of women craftworkers from 3.8% to 8.1%; of black managers from 4% to 7.2%; and of black craftworkers from 2.8% to 8.9%. But the EEOC now demands that 50% of new management positions and 33% of new craft openings be given to women and Sears officials protest that these goals are arbitrary.

Though Government attorneys consider the suit to be mainly a public relations gesture, it will strike a chord among many businessmen who maintain that the "discrimination" problem lies with the cumulative bad effects over the years of the many changes, contradictions and lack of coordination in federal employment regulations. The suit notes that some of Sears' present difficulties stem from postwar years, when Washington urged companies to hire veterans, who were then predominantly white and male. The later imperative to hire more women and minorities not only conflicted with this earlier priority but also resulted in hiring policies being reviewed by ten different agencies and departments. Now, Sears notes, the 1978 ban on mandatory retirement at 65 leaves fewer job openings for other minorities. A good many businessmen would agree with Sears Chairman Edward Telling when he says that his suit is a needed effort "to cut through conflicting regulation and to force a clarification of irreconcilables."—*Time*

Essay 2: Mrs. Eisenhower

Many Americans will mourn the death of Mamie Eisenhower, particularly those old enough to remember the era of World War II. She was a living reminder of the hero general who was her husband, and as such a symbol of the thousands of wives who waited at home in hope of ultimate victory and the safe return of a loved one.

Mrs. Eisenhower was also a popular first lady during her husband's presidency. She was not as controversial as Eleanor Roosevelt had been, nor as much on display as her successors Jacqueline Kennedy and Lady Bird Johnson. Mrs. Eisenhower was in the White House at a time when a quiet, self-effacing first lady was not subject to the criticism that later came to Mrs. Richard Nixon.

Like Ike himself, Mrs. Eisenhower came out of a simpler age and measured up to its values well. We will miss her.—*The Atlanta Journal*

Essay 3: Abolish the Corporate Income Tax

Nothing infuriates taxpayers more than watching business executives live well at public expense. Abuse of corporate expense account deductions—conferences at plush resorts, golf club dues, three-martini lunches—is thus, justifiably, a prime target for tax reformers, especially as the Administration now readies its tax reform program. In economic terms, though, a far more important issue in business tax reform is whether we ought to tax corporations in the first place.

Taxing corporate income is a convenient and popular means of collecting revenue. The unfortunate side effects of the tax, however, have led economists to question its value. By lowering the net return on investment, the tax may reduce expenditures for plant and equipment, and thereby slow economic growth. The corporate income tax, moreover, gives businesses a powerful incentive to raise their capital by borrowing, rather than by selling new stock. Interest payments on bonds are counted as a business expense, and taxed only as personal income for the recipient. By contrast, regular corporate income is taxed twice—once, when the money is earned by the corporation, then again as personal income, when it is paid out as dividends. Such arbitrary advantage favors one class of investors (bondholders) over another (stockholders), and one kind of enterprise (unincorporated partnerships) over another (corporations). More important, the incentive tempts corporations to go deeply into debt to reduce tax liability, thus increasing their financial vulnerability in lean times.

Numerous schemes for righting the balance have been proposed—Brookings economist Joseph Pechman catalogues six major alternatives. Everyone would like to eliminate the bias in favor of debt capital and increase investment without sacrificing government revenue. We favor the most straightforward way: outright abolition of the corporate income tax—what is known in tax jargon as "full integration." After abolition, corporations would continue to transmit funds to the Treasury. But these payments would serve as withholding against the personal income tax liability of individual stockholders.

The big virtue of full integration is that it would end government influence over the way business is financed. Stock and bond income would be treated equally. And because corporate profits would be subject to personal income tax when they were earned, rather than when they were paid as dividends, the revenue loss to the Treasury would be modest. In addition, the tax cut would be distributed progressively; stockholders in low personal income tax brackets would get proportionately more, those in high brackets proportionately less.

What full integration might not do very well is to encourage investment. At present the tax laws "punish" corporations by taxing away a good portion of their earnings. Those same laws, however, give corporations a reason to retain and reinvest what they have left. Profits paid out as dividends are immediately taxed again as personal income, while retained profits escape this second bite indefinitely. Once the corporation tax was abolished, firms would earn more after taxes, but have no special tax incentive to plow those earnings back into the business. Stockholders might or might not choose to do for themselves what corporations do for them now.

The effect of abolishing the corporation tax on investment is in any event of secondary importance. If investment needs to be spurred—as it very well might—other incentives, not linked to the tax system, are available. A good tax system raises revenue with minimal impact on the behavior of individuals or businesses. The corporate income tax has no place in such a system.—*The New York Times*

Even if you have never studied writing or rhetoric formally, you probably already recognize important differences among the three essays, and you probably already identified "Abolish the Corporate Income Tax" as the deliberative essay. Even without considering the question of method, it is clear that this essay comes closest to meeting the definition—*writing whose main purpose is to support a conclusion or opinion about some problem or question of human experience.* In this essay the problem is how to reform our federal tax system, and the conclusion is given in the title—abolish the corporate income tax. The essay "amounts to" a proposal that this be done.

The basic method of this essay is *argumentation,* the process of supporting conclusions with facts and reasoning. But argumentation is not the only method of deliberation. Deliberation is a larger process, involving a number of methods, whereby a community of people discusses and decides what is true, valuable, worth doing, and expedient or necessary. "Abolish the Corporate Income Tax" proposes a particular solution to a particular problem, but deliberative writing can cover a wider range of functions. It can also offer insights into and urge certain understandings of human affairs.

Briefly consider the other two essays. The first, "A Sears Suit," is not a deliberative essay but rather an *informative* one. The essay does more, of course, than merely present the facts. The pun on "suit" provides a momentary, though irrelevant, bit of humor. The first paragraph provides a "framing generalization," and the last paragraph speculates about the significance of the suit. But these things are clearly secondary to what the essay "amounts to" —*an arrangement and presentation of information* about an important legal event. Accordingly, the author-audience relationship is different from that of the deliberative essay. In "Abolish the Corporate Income Tax," the author is an "advocate" of a certain position, attempting to influence public opinion; in "A Sears Suit" the author is a "reporter"—someone commissioned to discover and organize information about public events.

If you didn't choose "Abolish the Corporate Income Tax" as the deliberative essay, chances are you chose "Mrs. Eisenhower." You might have done so because the essay offers opinions about and evaluations of Mrs. Eisenhower's life and character. But these opinions and evaluations do not really contribute to a process of deliberation. The author makes no attempt to support these opinions and no direct attempt to persuade you that they are true; he merely voices them. And he doesn't really need to support them, because they are opinions that few people would argue about, especially under the circumstances of Mrs. Eisenhower's death. This essay is neither deliberative nor informative; it is a type of writing called *occasional* or *commemorative.* The essay "amounts to" a public commemoration or recognition. Note too that the role of the author is different; he stands neither as advocate nor reporter but as a spokesman for the community.

These three essays certainly do not exhaust the types of writing or rhetoric. (One important type not represented, *reflective/exploratory* writing, is treated at length in Part Two.) But by now it should be fairly clear that the deliberative essay is one that *participates in a larger process of decision making by supporting a conclusion or opinion about some question or problem of human experience.*

Deliberative writing as a form of leadership

People hold different images of deliberative writing, and some of these images are not as useful as others. One particularly unfortunate image is that of deliberation as a kind of combat, with opposing sides slugging it out, both seeking to win the argument. This conception overlooks the fact that deliberative writing is almost never addressed to the opposition, but rather to an uncommitted or "lukewarm" middle group. Of course in many situations—such as a political election—opposing sides struggle for the allegiance of that middle group; but the image of combat does not really grasp what is going on. In deliberative writing you are not "bringing out the big guns" against your enemies; you are addressing an audience of potential friends or followers.

Another unfortunate image of deliberation is that of a kind of missionary activity, in which you are supposed to "convert" people or "win them over" to your point of view. This image is closer to reality than the image of combat, but it still overlooks the fact that most people do not completely change their minds or allegiances after reading a deliberative essay, or even a deliberative book. And they usually wouldn't admit it even if they did.

The process of conversion or turning completely around in one's thinking is usually either very gradual, involving a long period of thinking and reacting, or very dramatic, involving deeply emotional experiences and reactions to events. The purposes of deliberation are much more limited. The deliberative writer is less interested in converting people to a way of life or a way of thinking about life than in offering good reasons for thinking or acting one way or another in a specific situation.

For this reason the best image for deliberative writing is neither that of combat nor of missionary activity but of *leadership.* A deliberative writer is concerned with a particular question or problem, seeking to attract the attention and commitment of people who may be less knowledgeable, less aware, or less committed. An educated person should be able to assume such a role of leadership when necessary. This is one of the reasons that rhetoric has played a central role in education since the beginning of our civilization.

EXERCISE 1.1

Examine the editorial page and the page opposite the editorial page of a national newspaper such as the *New York Times,* the *Washington Post,* or the *Los Angeles Times.* Scan all the editorials and signed columns. Which of these writings would you call deliberative? What other kinds of writing do you find? What actions or functions do these essays perform? What methods do they use?

• Writing the Deliberative Essay: Four Initial Steps

The first step: Finding subjects for deliberation

One of the most troublesome problems of students in writing classes is that of finding interesting and workable subjects. Often the problem is aggravated by the artificiality of the situation. Actual deliberation is not designed to fulfill composition assignments but to help solve human problems. A person writes a deliberative essay because he or she wants to clarify some misunderstanding, answer some important question, support some cause or candidate, call attention to some threat to the community, or criticize some public action or spectacle. In a writing course, the situation is often reversed, making the principal reason for writing the essay the need to answer an assignment.

Consequently, students often find themselves writing only to please an instructor and on topics they don't know or care much about. There are no fool-proof solutions to this problem, but there are a number of things that you can do to make your writing more purposeful and interesting.

Two general suggestions

1. Try to use "real-world" situations as much as possible. Write about subjects that you really care about and that relate to organizations or communities that you have a stake in. You don't have to write about earthshaking political or moral issues; you can write about matters of local interest, or about matters of personal ethics and decision making. The only requirement of deliberative writing in this respect is that you relate these matters to the actual or potential concerns of a specific community of readers. Write to this community, and remember that the community includes, and may be restricted to, people of your own age and circumstances.
2. Keep in mind that casting about for a subject and then producing an essay before a certain day is not as artificial or unrealistic a task as it might seem. A good deal of deliberative writing is produced by professional writers, columnists, and editorialists, who are often on the prowl for interesting topics, and who nearly always face deadlines.

Four methods for locating subjects

Method 1: Keep an eye out for focusing events. A good deal of deliberative writing is focused upon events, developments, or interesting circumstances:

- A train derailment involving the explosions of several carloads of deadly gas spurs an editorialist to propose stricter government regulations on the shipment of dangerous substances.
- A proponent of gun-control legislation seizes the occasion of a well-publicized domestic shooting to call for a renewed effort to outlaw a certain class of handguns.
- A violent clash between two extremist groups at a public rally causes a columnist to examine the possible limits of "free speech" in public demonstrations.
- A series of movies about the Vietnam War causes a commentator to speculate about the continuing effects of the war on the consciences of most Americans.

The possibilities, as you can imagine, are endless. Events and circumstances inspire new debates and resurrect old ones. Sometimes a single event can spur many different kinds of deliberative responses. For instance, one of the grisliest events of recent history was the "Jonestown Massacre" of 1978, in which almost a thousand members of a radical religious cult living in Guyana committed suicide, under the direction and coercion of their "savior" leader. As you might well suppose, the event was followed by a wide range of deliberative responses:

- some calling for tighter restrictions on religious organizations;
- others suggesting ways of identifying and dealing with religious madmen;
- others criticizing certain government agencies which had warnings but did not act on them;
- others viewing the event as a sign of the stupidity and irrationality of all religious beliefs;
- others using the event to discuss the differences between "authentic" and "false" religious beliefs.

Keep an eye on events and circumstances. Develop the habit of asking yourself what problems or questions about human experience they pose, serve as an example of, or offer an answer or solution to. Remember that such events and circumstances do not have to be of the national or global sort. They can be things going on in your own community, campus, dorm, or family—perhaps even in your own composition class.

Method 2: Listen to what people are saying. It's amazing how full of complaints, sharped-tongued criticism, and value judgments ordinary conversation is. Since deliberative discourse nearly always centers on problems and questions concerning the way things are, the way things are run, and what things are good and bad, the conversation around you can provide ample topics for deliberation. Pay attention to it and learn to analyze it; it can lead you to pose questions that could, after some thinking or investigation, lead to a deliberative response.

Some examples: a) **Overheard:** general griping about the University meal plan.
Possible questions: Is this the best possible plan?
Are there adjustments that could easily be made?
Are the complaints well founded?
Possible deliberative response: a proposal for changing the plan;
a defense of the current plan.

b) **Overheard:** a casual discussion of a national political or religious figure.

Possible questions: Why is Senator x (or Reverend y) such a popular figure?
How can people be so uninformed about political or religious issues?

Possible deliberative response: An explanation (either positive or negative in its assessment) of the person's popularity;
an essay in defense of some scorned figure or personality;
an essay correcting irrational or misinformed views of the person.

You can think of other more timely examples of your own, on the basis of the conversation around you. Step back occasionally and examine the things people are saying. What problems and questions do they raise? How do the problems or questions relate specifically to organizations or communities? Keep notes on what you hear; they may provide good subjects for essays.

Method 3: Read! If you look at a representative sampling of the deliberative essays in newspapers and magazines, you find that many of them are responses, either direct or indirect, to other pieces of writing. There's a good reason for this. Deliberation is an overall process of finding good reasons—a process in which individual essays participate. Writer 1 criticizes some policy or draws attention to some serious problem; writer 2 contends that writer 1 is uninformed. Writer 3 shows that writer 2 is not entirely sincere or impartial and that writer 1 is really on to something. Writer 4 proposes a solution; writer 5 rejects it, but proposes another. Writer 6 compares the solutions of writers 4 and 5 and finds that 5 has the better answer. The process of deliberation goes on. Meanwhile, in the world of action, opinions are being formed, actions are being taken, votes are being cast. In a rational society one can hope that the process of deliberation has been influential and beneficial, assuring the validity, workability, and acceptability of these solutions.

Get in the habit of reading something besides textbooks. Every week examine a couple of national newspapers. Look for items of interest (as well as pieces of deliberation) in national weeklies such as *Time* and *Newsweek;* examine the deliberative essays in such magazines as *The New Republic, National Review, Commentary, Commonweal,* and *Christian Century;* read your local and campus newspapers, especially the editorial pages. Any of these sources will supply you with ample opportunity to become part of a larger process of deliberation. Remember that other pieces of writing can provide "focusing events" as well as ideas for subjects.

Method 4: Keep a record of your own feelings, insights, reactions. Every day, amid countless sensations, trivial decisions about what to wear or eat or write with, snatches of memory, feelings of boredom or contentment, each of us has momentary insights, finds something puzzling, reacts with strong emotion to some action or statement, wonders if a certain course of action is wise or moral. Any of these would make an interesting subject for deliberation, provided you think it through, and provided you relate it to the interests and needs of an audience.

Most of the time, however, you forget such things completely, unless you jot them down somewhere. Keep a special notebook (small enough to carry in a pocket) in which you record momentary insights, questions you had never thought of before, reactions to what you see, hear, and read about. When you look back over your notes, some will embarrass you. Others will make you wonder why you ever wrote them down in the first place. But something in the notes may strike the right chord, and you have the beginnings of an essay.

EXERCISE 1.2

The following passages are introductions to several deliberative essays. Examine the particular ways in which events and circumstances are used to focus deliberation. Consider these possibilities:

- **focusing event (or circumstance) as the problem;**
- **focusing event as symptom of a larger problem;**
- **focusing event as solution or clue to solution;**
- **focusing event as example of a problem;**
- **focusing event as controversy to be settled.**

A. Reprinted from *U.S. News & World Report,* December 24, 1979: Few will quarrel with the idea behind the 1964 Wilderness Act—to protect from overzealous development the unspoiled gems of nature still remaining in this country. But when protecting land brings hardship to people who live nearby, who use the land and depend on it for their livelihood, perhaps it is time to take another look.

A case in point is what is happening in Minnesota's Boundary Waters Canoe Area, the largest—and most visited—officially protected wilderness area east of the Rocky Mountains.

Congress voted last year to ban the use of motor boats on all but 23 of the 1,063 lakes within the existing Boundary Waters. Environmentalists argued that this was necessary to protect the deep, clear lakes and forests . . . from man's destructions.

Many of the 25,000 residents of northeastern Minnesota heatedly disagree. They insist that the environmentalists' concern . . . is largely a matter of aesthetics. . . . They say the new restrictions have had a devastating impact on tourism, the backbone of their economy.—Marvin Stone, "Wilderness—and People." Copyright © 1979 by U.S. News & World Report, Inc. Reprinted by permission.

B. The Episcopal Church, described by W. H. Auden before he died as having gone "stark, raving mad" . . . underwent shock treatment at its most recent General Convention in Denver. And there are now some signs that recovery from its malaise of the Sixties impends. . . .

The significant actions in Denver, on the traditional prayer book, the issue of the homosexuals, and on the Equal Rights Amendment, suggest that the Episcopal Church may have slowed or even stopped the flight from sanity.—Daniel Oliver, "Creeping Sanity"

C. Something is clearly wrong with our political system. The symptoms of malfunction are obvious: individual participation has dropped precipitously; factionalism has increased and wields greater impact; political debate has shifted from substantive issues to issues of symbolism or of ad hoc self-interest . . . ; faith in public institutions declines in a rapid spiral.—J. Patrick Dobel and Ronald R. Stockton, "Unreforming the Parties"

D. A racial quota in the allotment of on-the-job training opportunities among competing employees, instituted by management-union agreement, was held lawful by the Supreme Court in the recent case of *Steelworkers* v. *Weber.* This was an important decision, and a very bad one. Its badness lies not only in the substantive result, upholding preference in employment by race, but also in the reasons given by the Court in defending that result, and in the abuse of judicial discretion manifested.—Carl Cohen, "Justice Debased: The Weber Decision"

E. Greensboro, N. C.—On Nov. 3, Sandra Smith became the latest victim in a half-century struggle between those who spin Carolina cotton and those who own the textile mills and sell the finished product to the world. The pregnant, 29-year-old, black woman was killed in Greensboro along with four fellow members of the Communist Workers Party by a group of white men claiming membership in the Ku Klux Klan and the American Nazi Party.—Mark I. Pinsky, "Greensboro Knows Grim Struggles, Not Fatal Ones"

EXERCISE 1.3

Below is a list of possible, actual, or hypothetical events or circumstances. For each, make a list of possible deliberative responses. State your responses in one of these forms:

- **an essay which addresses the question (or problem) of _____**
- **an essay which proposes _____**
- **an essay which criticizes (or defends) _____**
- **an essay which attempts to explain _____**

A. A local citizens group is staging a protest against the showing of a movie which parodies the life of Christ. They claim that the movie is offensive and blasphemous.

B. A friend of yours is dropping a course. She has a B average in the course, likes the subject, and says she is learning a great deal. But she can't stand the way the professor berates the students, using such terms as "silly," "superficial," and "mindless" to describe their written work and class comments. Twice she has come out of the class crying.

C. A movie or book that you had found moving and insightful is dismissed by a critic or some of your friends as "trashy sentimentality."

D. A local high school decides to discontinue the tradition of electing an annual beauty queen, on the grounds that the tradition is sexist and undignified.

E. An article in a medical journal recently concluded that nonsmokers who regularly work in the company of smokers suffer lung damage amounting to nearly 50 per cent of the damage suffered by the smokers themselves.

The second step: Narrowing your topic

A common problem with student essays is that they take on subjects that are too broad—subjects that involve so many questions and issues that they cannot be effectively treated in a short essay. It is difficult to say what is going to be too broad a subject and what isn't, but there is a good chance that you are taking on more than you can handle effectively if you are thinking about writing an essay: a) for or against abortion; b) for or against pornography; c) criticizing or defending capitalism, existentialism, or Christianity.

This does not mean that short essays have to deal with trivial topics. It does mean that short deliberative essays need to address limited questions and fulfill limited purposes. Remember that it is hardly ever the purpose of a deliberative essay to solve a problem or settle a question completely. The deliberative essay makes a contribution to the larger process of finding good reasons. Any of the broad topics listed above would do as general areas of deliberation, but in order to make a good, short deliberative essay based on any of them, you need to discover a specific contribution that you can make. Here are some possibilities relating to these general topics:

a) **On abortion:** Is the question of when a fetus actually becomes a "human person" relevant to the abortion debate?

Under what circumstances (if any) should elective abortions be financed by Medicare or Medicaid payments?

Is the argument that women have the "right to control their own bodies" a valid one?

b) On pornography: Is all erotic art pornographic? What is the difference?

Should the makers and purveyors of "kiddie porn" (movies involving minors in sexual acts) enjoy protection under the "Freedom of Speech" amendment?

As with finding adequate subjects, there are no sure-fire ways to achieve the right degree of narrowness or particularity. Throughout this book you will find additional suggestions for finding and particularizing topics. Here are four methods that may help.

Method 1: Make lists of questions. State your topic in the form of a question or a problem at the top of a blank sheet of paper. Then, without making any attempt at organization or system, write out as many related questions as you can think of. When you have finished, go back over the list. Some questions will not seem very relevant. Cross them out. Others will not seem to fit the category of deliberation—they may concern facts (things you could look up, and may need to), or matters so personal and subjective that it would be foolish to deliberate about them.

Now consider the remaining questions. How do they compare in particularity with your original question? Which do you think you could make a better essay from?

This method will not only help you narrow your topic; it will also help you plan your essay, by revealing some of the issues you will need to consider.

Method 2: Think of your essay as performing an action. When we think about writing, we think of *saying* something; but good deliberative writers often characterize their work as *doing* something. Deliberative writers hope to serve some purpose, to accomplish some end through discourse. There is a good chance that your essay is properly conceived if it accomplishes some particular task, such as the following:

- *supporting* (or criticizing) a position;
- *correcting* a misconception;
- *alerting an audience* to a problem;
- *defending* (or criticizing) a policy, person, or condition;
- *clarifying* a misunderstanding;
- *answering an important question* about a human problem.

This list does not exhaust the possibilities of what a deliberative essay can *do.* The important thing is for you to think of your essay as *doing* some particular thing.

EXERCISE 1.4

Read two editorials in a recent newspaper. What does each of them *do* (in the sense described here)?

Method 3: Cast your essay as a response to a single event, development, or set of circumstances. You will recognize that this method of narrowing corresponds closely to one of the methods of finding subjects—watching for "focusing events." Most of mankind's serious problems and questions are very old, have rich traditions of study and debate behind them, and probably will never be fully resolved. But events give these problems particularity and often lead to temporary resolutions, common understandings, and partial solutions. If you have done a good job of casting about for "focusing events," chances are that you've already particularized your topic and made it manageable.

EXERCISE 1.5

Choose one of the general topics listed below, and produce a list of particular questions that might lead to a deliberative essay. For each, try to think of actual or hypothetical "focusing events" or circumstances.

A. The divorce rate.
B. The parking problem on campus.
C. The attitudes of your generation toward established religion, national politics or sexual morality.
D. The Equal Rights Amendment.

Method 4: Narrow your topic by narrowing your audience. Some audiences are much narrower than others. A good deal of deliberative writing is published in journals and newspapers that have special constituencies or points of view. For instance, the magazine *Christian Century* focuses on matters of special interest to Protestant Christians. *Commonweal,* on the other hand, appeals primarily to Roman Catholics. *Commentary,* though broader in appeal than the other two, has a special focus on Jewish concerns. The readership of a magazine like the *New Republic* is generally politically liberal, while that of the *National Review* is generally conservative. And many publications are devoted to special subject matters, encompassing almost any special interest you can imagine.

An advantage of writing for specific audiences is that it helps make the purpose and context of what you write more specific and concrete—you speak to the needs of a specific group of people. This allows you to choose arguments and examples that appeal specifically to that group. Part of your task in bringing in that "real-world" situation referred to earlier might be to designate an audience for your deliberative essay, perhaps even to specify the place where it might be published.

But how about that "general audience"—the one that is addressed by so many of the deliberative essays appearing in magazines and newspapers? Even here there should be a narrowing principle. Remember that deliberative writing is not a form of combat and not a missionary effort but a form of leadership, and you can't lead everybody. In any situation, subject, and argument, there are limitations on whom you can or need to reach. On the one hand, there are potential readers who are simply unreachable—they either have no interest in the subject or they are already totally committed to an opposing viewpoint. On the other hand, there are likely to be people who agree with you and feel just as strongly as you do about the issue.

The group you want to try to reach is in the middle. These are the people who have not made up their minds; or the people who may be leaning one way or the other, but with reservations; or the people who would agree with you but haven't thought about it much; or the people who agree but who don't feel strongly enough to act on their beliefs. You want to draw a circle around this group and give them good reasons for supporting your position.

The third step: Formulating a good thesis statement

Every deliberative essay puts forward a number of claims, positions, or opinions. But usually, in a clear and unified essay, we can identify a single important claim to which all the others are subordinated and which the various elements of the essay support. That one important claim is called the *thesis* of the essay.

The meaning of *unity*—an important quality of successful writing—is oneness. To insure that your essay will be unified, first formulate a *thesis statement*—the one claim that all other elements of your essay will be designed to help support.

Many writing teachers ask students to incorporate thesis statements directly into the introductory sections of their essays, at least in their first essays. This procedure helps inexperienced writers keep control over what they are doing. On the other hand, it is not always necessary to do this—different circumstances call for different writing strategies, and there are many different ways of making the basic claim or claims clear. Nevertheless, whether you incorporate your thesis statement directly or not, be sure that you have one, at least in your head. If you have a clear sense of what you want your essay to do and a clear formulation of what you want your essay to say, you're in a better position to accomplish your goals than if you begin with only a vague notion. Spending some time formulating and elaborating a thesis statement is also valuable as a way of investigating your topic, of anticipating the major lines of your argument, and of adjusting your claims to an audience.

The discussion of the thesis statement in this unit is different from those you have studied in other books. In most books, the thesis statement is treated as a short statement, usually a single sentence, which identifies the main point or main argument of an essay. Students are asked to devise thesis statements to insure that they write essays with a single main point or argument in mind. Here you are asked to go beyond that simple goal by elaborating your thesis statement in various ways. You will find that the formulation of thesis statements is a powerful prewriting device—one that will help you explore your subject matter, test its workability as a deliberative topic, and devise ways of reaching and persuading an audience.

A thesis statement need not be restricted to a single sentence, but it should be short—not more than two or three sentences. It must contain a statement of the major *point or claim* that your essay is going to make, and it may incorporate a number of subordinate statements. These statements refer to important elements of audience or situation, to arguments your essay deals with, to points supporting your major claim, or to qualifications of or restrictions on your thesis.

A good thesis statement reflects some of the general qualities of good deliberative writing. The following are five qualities to consider as you formulate your thesis statement:

1. argumentative edge
2. timeliness, relevance, significance
3. support, documentation
4. account taken of opposing viewpoints
5. novelty, surprise

Argumentative edge. Deliberative writing cannot succeed unless the audience is aware (or can be persuaded) that the point needs to be argued—there is opposition to or there is a common lack of awareness about some important problem; or there are serious misconceptions that need to be corrected, important questions to be answered.

In some cases, providing an *argumentative edge* (a phrase coined by Sheridan Baker) is no problem. A statement such as, "The United States has seriously erred in granting diplomatic recognition to communist China," is argumentative on the face of it. On the other hand, a statement such as, "Most students at this university are actively concerned about political issues," needs more of an edge. Give it one by making the context of the argument explicit, with an introductory clause:

> Contrary to the widespread notion that today's college students are indifferent to politics . . .
>
> Students at this university may seem to be politically indifferent, but . . .
>
> Although in recent years students have tended to lose interest in politics, at this university . . .

Timeliness, relevance, significance. A good deliberative essay is not necessarily devoted to a "hot topic." But the farther removed from current controversy or practical concern a topic is, the more energy needed to indicate its significance to your audience. Impart a sense of timeliness and relevance with an introductory clause or sentence in your thesis statement:

Boring thesis statement: An educated person enjoys both pop and classical music.

Better: Most people think of pop and classical music as appealing to two entirely different cultures, but this is a serious misconception.

Support and documentation. A good argument is well supported with reasoning and with facts. Indicate the kind of support that you intend to give your thesis with a subordinate clause or another sentence:

> Contrary to the widespread feeling that today's college students are politically indifferent, many students at this university are deeply concerned about political issues. The most important sign of this is that . . .
>
> The free-agent draft is ruining major league baseball by . . .
>
> The makers and purveyors of "kiddie porn" should not enjoy protection under the freedom-of-speech amendment because . . .

Account taken of opposing viewpoints. A good argument anticipates objections, conceding as much as it can to opposing views without damaging or undermining its own point and finding ways either to refute the opposing views or to show that its own *view* is a stronger one. Anticipate and deal with objections and opposing views by incorporating into your thesis statement a clause or a sentence that indicates your awareness of other points of view. Your basic claim then becomes something that refutes or overrides these views:

> It may be true that today's college students do not actively participate very much in political organizations. Nevertheless . . .
>
> While no one doubts that the older system exploited the players at times, the current free-agent draft is ruining major league baseball by . . .
>
> It is true and it is distressing that churches today are among society's most racially distinct institutions. This does not mean, however, that most Christians are racists or that Christianity is a racist faith. What critics fail to understand is . . .

Novelty, surprise. Good deliberative writing does not simply rehash things. It has something new to say, something to add to current understandings. You shouldn't pursue novelty for its own sake, and you shouldn't be contrary just for the sake of being contrary, but here are some questions you should ask about your thesis statement. If you answer *yes* to at least one of them, you're probably on the right track.

Does your thesis statement:

1. Take a dissenting view, an unpopular viewpoint?
2. Introduce a new problem, or one that has received little notice?
3. Find a new angle on an old problem—a new solution, a new or different way of looking at the problem, a new argument one way or the other?
4. Discuss a little-known cause of a well-known effect?
5. Discuss a little-known effect of a well-known cause?
6. Establish a connection between two areas of experience that seem quite different?
7. Discover important differences between things that seem quite similar?
8. Incorporate an element of paradox or apparent contradiction? Example:

   "Most political liberals are really quite traditionalist in their basic attitudes."

   "Many civil libertarians favor legislation that is repressive in nature."
9. Show that something is really more important than it seems?
10. Show that something is really less important than it seems?

Finally, there is probably no way that any single thesis statement can take account of all the qualities mentioned here. But you should consider all of them, test your thesis against the qualities mentioned, and make your thesis statement a promise of good things to come.

EXERCISE 1.6

Each of these thesis statements needs improvement. Elaborate each with clauses and /or extra sentences, taking into account this chapter's discussion of what makes a good thesis statement.

A. If a woman is doing what she wants to, as a matter of free and educated choice, then she is "liberated."
B. Fraternities are useful campus institutions.
C. Marijuana is not a dangerous drug.
D. Most college students believe in about the same things that their parents believe in.
E. Banning all smoking in public places would be unrealistic and unfair.

The fourth step: Developing a strategy for persuasion

Actually all six units in the "deliberative" section of this book concern helping you develop "strategies for persuasion," and there is no way that we can cover everything at once. Furthermore, in anybody's writing, some strategies develop in the process of writing itself. At the beginning, though, you should establish the practice of working out an overall strategy in advance.

There are four kinds of strategies to consider in planning an essay—logical strategies, the author's image, formal strategies, and special strategies of presentation.

Logical strategies. These are your good reasons, the principal arguments that support your thesis. Draw up a list of good reasons and then select the most powerful and the most appropriate for a given audience or situation. In a short deliberative essay the best strategy is to support your thesis with a few—two or three—supporting arguments.

The author's image. An author persuades an audience partly by projecting a favorable image to that audience. This doesn't mean that you should pretend to be someone or something that you're not. Aside from being dishonest, such a strategy can backfire if readers detect your duplicity. It does mean that it's important how you come across to a reader. A reader who perceives, rightly or wrongly, that you are immature, hysterical, irrational, or in pursuit of some merely private gain may discount a great deal of what you have to say, or perhaps even stop reading. On the other hand, a reader who perceives that you are well informed, concerned, well intentioned, and reasonable will probably read on.

Although it's impossible to say that any one image will be more successful than another in every situation, you will always want to come across as well informed, well intentioned, and reasonable. It may be effective to indicate your deep involvement in a cause or situation. Or perhaps the role of the impartial judge, with no particular involvement, may be more appropriate. If you are writing to a special audience of college students, it may be effective to establish your identity as a student or professor (assuming, of course, that you happen to be one of these); on the other hand, under certain circumstances the neutral role of the well-informed observer might be more effective.

Remember that as you write you tend to characterize yourself in a particular way to people who do not know you personally. All they know is what you reveal of yourself and the stance you assume in your essay. Be sure to send out the right kinds of signals.

You can get a good idea of the mistakes writers sometimes make in projecting themselves by observing the "letters-to-the-editor" section of an average newspaper, where people sometimes dash off their ideas and grievances without much planning. Which of these two examples projects the better image?

> To the editor:
>
> I can't get over the fact that the school board has "closed" all the high school campuses at lunch time just because a few students were buying drugs. This is

just plain crazy! Don't they have any sense? Don't they realize that not all students do this? It's not fair. Why can't we get some justice in this town?

To the editor:

I am deeply concerned over the school board's recent decision to "close" local high school campuses during lunch time. I realize that drug-dealing is a serious problem and that something must be done to stop it; but it hardly seems fair to punish the majority of law-abiding students for the actions of a few renegades. I hope the school board will reconsider its action and seek a fairer solution to this problem. The present solution is grossly unfair and in fact is working severe hardships upon many students.

Formal strategies. You need to plan an organization (form) for your essay. What's the best way to begin? What would make the most effective arrangement of your arguments? How can you make an effective ending?

Special strategies of presentation. Special strategies of presentation include any departure an essay makes from the straightforward presentation of argument. "Straightforward" refers to the kind of presentation in which the writer appears to be standing before an audience in a lecture hall, presenting an argument in a calm, dignified way, and moving logically from one point to the next. The straightforward method is that of argumentation—the process of supporting conclusions with facts and reasoning. State a judgment and back it up with facts and good reasons. Describe a situation or an incident and make explicit comments or evaluations.

Sometimes, however, the medium of writing affords a more effective way of making a point than would a lecture-hall style of presentation using straightforward argumentation. For instance, instead of explicitly criticizing an action or a set of practices, an author might present them in the form of a description or a story which casts them in an unfavorable light, allowing readers to draw obvious conclusions for themselves. Sometimes an author adopts a certain pose or mask, pretending to say one thing but implying another. In one of the most famous essays ever written, Jonathan Swift, the eighteenth century satirist, delivered a strong denunciation of the treatment of poor Irishmen by their British landlords. He did not criticize the British directly, but made a "modest proposal" for solving the problem of Irish poverty by slaughtering and eating Irish babies, like livestock. (This essay appears at the end of Chapter Three.) Another kind of special strategy is found in Ellen Goodman's essay, "Participants, Not Patients," at the end of this chapter.

• Checklist: Preparing an Essay

The following outline summarizes the basic material of this chapter. Use it as a checklist in preparing your essay assignment.

I. **Subject**

A. Is it a suitable topic for deliberation?

B. Is the subject narrowed sufficiently? Does it address a particular problem or set of circumstances?

C. Do I have a clear conception of the particular audience, or the particular segment of a general audience addressed by this essay?

II. **Thesis**

A. Do I have a clear notion of what particular *action* is performed by this essay? What in particular do I wish to accomplish?

B. Does the thesis meet one or more of the requirements for a good deliberative thesis?

1. "Argumentative edge"
2. Timeliness, relevance
3. Support, documentation
4. Account taken of opposing viewpoints
5. Novelty, surprise

III. **Strategy**

A. Do I have a strong, short list of "good reasons" to support the thesis?

B. What is the most effective image of myself that I can (truthfully) present in this essay?

C. Do I have a plan for organizing the essay?

D. Are there special ways of presenting the subject that might be effective?

ESSAY ASSIGNMENTS

1. Assume that you have been hired by the local campus or city newspaper as a weekly columnist. Your assignment each week is to produce a deliberative essay that uses as a "focusing event" some story or article that has appeared in the previous week. Write the column for this week. Turn in with your essay a clipping or photocopy of the article that provided your focusing event.

2. Write a deliberative essay that makes use of any focusing event or circumstance from your own experience or reading. Assume that the essay will appear as a "Guest Column" in your local campus or city newspaper.

3. Write a deliberative essay in which you question the validity of some popular or widely held opinion. Indicate on a separate sheet the audience to which your essay is directed and where the essay might be published.

4. Write an essay in which you explain and defend an important personal decision that you have made in your life. Assume an audience of people who may be facing or may have faced similar decisions.

Essays for Analysis

Our Youth Should Serve*

by Steven Muller

Steven Muller is the president of Johns Hopkins University. This essay first appeared in Newsweek *in 1978.*

1 Too many young men and women now leave school without a well-developed sense of purpose. If they go right to work after high school, many are not properly prepared for careers. But if they enter college instead, many do not really know what to study or what to do afterward. Our society does not seem to be doing much to encourage and use the best instincts and talents of our young.

2 On the one hand, I see the growing problems of each year's new generation of high-school graduates. After twelve years of schooling—and television—many of them want to participate actively in society; but they face either a job with a limited future or more years in educational institutions. Many are wonderfully idealistic: they have talent and energy to offer, and they seek the meaning in their lives that comes from giving of oneself to the common good. But they feel almost rejected by a society that has too few jobs to offer them and that asks nothing of them except to avoid trouble. They want to be part of a new solution; instead society perceives them as a problem. They seek a cause; but their elders preach only self-advancement. They need experience on which to base choice; yet society seems to put a premium on the earliest possible choice, based inescapably on the least experience.

Necessary Tasks

3 On the other hand, I see an American society sadly in need of social services that we can afford less and less at prevailing costs of labor. Some tasks are necessary but constitute no career; they should be carried out, but not as anyone's lifetime occupation. Our democracy profoundly needs public spirit, but the economy of our labor system primarily encourages self-interest. The Federal government spends billions on opportunity grants for post-secondary education, but some of us wonder about money given on the basis only of need.

*"Our Youth Should Serve" by Steven Muller from *Newsweek,* July 10, 1978.

We ask the young to volunteer for national defense, but not for the improvement of our society. As public spirit and public services decline, so does the quality of life. So I ask myself why cannot we put it all together and ask our young people to volunteer in peacetime to serve America?

4 I recognize that at first mention, universal national youth service may sound too much like compulsory military service or the Hitler Youth or the Komsomol. I do not believe it has to be like that at all. It need not require uniforms or camps, nor a vast new Federal bureaucracy, nor vast new public expenditures. And it should certainly not be compulsory.

5 A voluntary program of universal national youth service does of course require compelling incentives. Two could be provided. Guaranteed job training would be one. Substantial Federal assistance toward post-secondary education would be the other. This would mean that today's complex measures of Federal aid to students would be ended, and that there would also be no need for tuition tax credits for post-secondary education. Instead, prospective students would *earn* their assistance for post-secondary education by volunteering for national service, and only those who earned assistance would receive it. Present Federal expenditures for the assistance of students in post-secondary education would be converted into a simple grant program, modeled on the post-World War II GI Bill of Rights.

Volunteers

6 But what, you say, would huge numbers of high-school graduates do as volunteers in national service? They could be interns in public agencies, local, state and national. They could staff day-care programs, neighborhood health centers, centers to counsel and work with children; help to maintain public facilities, including highways, rail beds, waterways and airports; engage in neighborhood-renewal projects, both physical and social. Some would elect military service, others the Peace Corps. Except for the latter two alternatives and others like them, they could live anywhere they pleased. They would not wear uniforms. They would be employed and supervised by people already employed locally in public-agency careers.

7 Volunteers would be paid only a subsistence wage, because they would receive the benefits of job training (not necessarily confined to one task) as well as assistance toward post-secondary education if they were so motivated and qualified. If cheap mass housing for some groups of volunteers were needed, supervised participants in the program could rebuild decayed dwellings in metropolitan areas.

8 All that might work. But perhaps an even more attractive version of universal national youth service might include private industrial and commercial enterprise as well. A private employer would volunteer to select a stated number of volunteers. He would have their labor at the universally applied subsistence wage; in return he would offer guaranteed job training as well as

the exact equivalent of what the Federal government would have to pay for assistance toward post-secondary education. The inclusion of volunteer private employers would greatly amplify job-training opportunities for the youth volunteers, and would greatly lessen the costs of the program in public funds.

Direct Benefits

9 The direct benefits of such a universal national-youth-service program would be significant. Every young man and woman would face a meaningful role in society after high school. Everyone would receive job training, and the right to earn assistance toward post-secondary education. Those going on to post-secondary education would have their education interrupted by a constructive work experience. There is evidence that they would thereby become more highly motivated and successful students, particularly if their work experience related closely to subsequent vocational interests. Many participants might locate careers by means of their national-service assignments.

10 No union jobs need be lost, because skilled workers would be needed to give job training. Many public services would be performed by cheap labor, but there would be no youth army. And the intangible, indirect benefits would be the greatest of all. Young people could regard themselves as more useful and needed. They could serve this country for a two-year period as volunteers, and *earn* job training and/or assistance toward post-secondary education. There is more self-esteem and motivation in earned than in unearned benefits. Universal national youth service may be no panacea. But in my opinion the idea merits serious and imaginative consideration.

FOR DISCUSSION

1. What does this essay do? (Refer to the list of possibilities in Exercise 1.3, pp. 14–15.)

2. What is the focusing event or circumstance of this essay? What function does it serve? (Refer to the list of possibilities in Exercise 1.2, pp. 13–14.)

3. What is the thesis of this essay? In what way is the thesis qualified or elaborated upon? (See paragraph 4.)

4. Steven Muller, the author, is president of Johns Hopkins University, and readers of *Newsweek,* where the essay originally appeared, were informed of this fact on the same page where the essay was printed. Do you find any evidence within the essay itself that Muller calls attention to his own special role, as a way of projecting an "image" of authority?

5. A number of Muller's specific points are highly tentative, and he leaves open a number of possibilities. Is this appropriate? How do you think that this essay might function in a larger process of deliberation?

6. In what specific instances does Muller try to anticipate objections to his argument?

Participants, Not Patients

by Ellen Goodman

Ellen Goodman's weekly column, which she writes for The Boston Globe, *appears in more than two hundred American newspapers. This essay, which first appeared there in May, 1976, is reprinted from her collection,* Close to Home.

1 Ten years ago, when Marilyn was twenty-six, she became pregnant with her first child in a midwestern university town. She was excited and anxious when she went to the clinic to ask the doctor what he thought about natural childbirth.

2 His answer was pretty succinct. She remembers it vividly, and, in truth, bitterly. He said, "I think about natural childbirth the way I think about natural appendectomy." So when Marilyn's son "was delivered by the doctor" (that's the way she talks about it), her role was simple: She was a patient. Her son came into the world upside down and howling at the cold bright light of the operating room. He was, first of all, a patient.

3 About a year ago, Marilyn's father died. He was, of course, in a hospital, in the cardiac unit of what's called "a major metropolitan teaching hospital." He, too, was a patient, a good one, who took his medicine on time, without complaint. He died during the day shift.

4 During the months that followed, Marilyn's mother said, over and over, until it became her mantra, "Well, he had the best of care, didn't he? We did everything we could." Since then, Marilyn has been thinking about it, all of it. It seems to come together, these bits and pieces of her life.

5 She thought about her hospitalized delivery when she read Suzanne Arm's *Immaculate Deception,* a book that reported on the ways in which medicine—with the best of intentions, mind you—has turned maternity into an illness and childbirth into a medical crisis.

6 She thought about her son's birth when she heard the gentle French obstetrician, Dr. Frederick Leboyer, say that he believes infants should have a "birth without violence," a quiet, warm, bathed entry into the world of the family.

7 And, of course—how could she help it?—she thought about her father's death during the horrendous Karen Ann Quinlan case. The thing that impressed her about the Quinlan case wasn't whether the girl was legally alive or dead but that she was, she is, indisputably a medical patient. Her existence is a question of medical technology.

8 So it's not surprising that, this month, when she read a quote from Ivan Illich, the former priest and sociologist, in *Psychology Today,* she memorized

it. "Death that was once viewed as a call from God, and later as a natural event, has become an untimely event that is the outcome of our technical failure to treat a disease."

9 Marilyn has joined a growing number of Americans concerned about the effect of medical technology on our lives. Not the lack of technology—the intrusion of it. Our well-being is now thought of as a medical question, and the stages of our lives are marked by passages from the pediatrician to the obstetrician to the geriatrician. Through them we avoid pain and treat death pathologically.

10 Have we given up birth and death to medicine? If they are abnormal, certifiable sicknesses and we send them to the hospital to be dealt with, don't we also lose our emotional involvement with each other and with the critical moments of our lives? If we become passive and patient and seek only the absence of pain, aren't we missing the passages of life instead of experiencing them? What does it do to us when we treat death as a technical error? When someone dies, will we sue for malpractice?

11 Marilyn is not the type to rail against doctors. She is not for dismantling hospitals and closing down medical schools. She doesn't want to give birth in a rice paddy or have a natural appendectomy. She uses Novocain at the dentist's. But she thinks, as many do, that we have to distinguish between a disease and a process of life. We all are born and die of "natural causes."

12 She would like the medical establishment to concentrate more on helping us do this in our own time and our own beds. She would like them to use their technology more judiciously, more skeptically. After all, with all the fetal monitors in the obstetrics wards, we are still eighteenth in infant mortality in the world. With all the fancy cardiac units, there is new evidence that home care may be just as effective.

13 Right now, she says the patients and the doctors conspire in a medical delivery system whereby the patient delivers himself or herself up to be "cured" from life and death. She wants to remind us to be participants, not patients. More and more she has been thinking, just thinking, mind you, that the important questions about the way we live and die aren't medical ones at all.

FOR DISCUSSION

1. This essay employs a "special strategy of presentation" (see p. 23). What precisely is the strategy? What are its effects?

2. As far as this essay is concerned, what are the special advantages of using a special strategy? What are the possible disadvantages? What does the author have to give up in using it?

3. What is the effect of the last sentence in paragraph 3: "He died during the day shift"?

4. Identify the points at which Goodman comes closest to engaging in straightforward argumentation. Are these passages effective? Are they necessary?

Student Essay: Child Pornography and the First Amendment

by Don King

1 Child pornography does not deserve protection under the First Amendment. Recently I read an article convincing me that such protection is no longer a matter of freedom of speech and press. The article ("What Pornographers Are Doing to Children: A Shocking Report," *Redbook,* August, 1977, pp. 86–90, by Judianne Densen-Gerber) opens dramatically. The author narrates her trip through an adult bookstore in New York City. She bought *Lollitots,* a magazine containing pornographic photographs of girls aged eight to fourteen, and *Moppets,* a magazine with pornographic pictures of children aged three to twelve. She continues:

> I bought a deck of playing cards that pictured naked spread eagled children. I looked at a film showing children violently deflowered on their first Communion day at the feet of a crucified priest replacing Jesus on the cross. I saw a film showing an alleged father engaged in bizarre sexual practices with his four-year-old daughter. Of 64 films presented for viewing, 35 showed children: 16 of these involved incest.

2 After reading that opening paragraph, I was not only repulsed, but also, quite frankly, on the verge of tears. Not being one very often given to rage, I since have analyzed my reactions and have determined their cause. My moral indignation is a result of my belief that child pornography destroys innocence, perverts social morality, and, most importantly, attacks the basic fiber of humanity. To protect pornographers in the name of freedom of the press is to commit societal suicide.

3 For various reasons children run away from home. In a short time, they find themselves without money, food, shelter. Pornographers prey on these lonely, homeless children. Many times the first friendly words spoken to these children are by the pornographer. Once he gains their confidence, it is not long before they are willing to do anything he asks. Consequently, innocence, an attribute every child should enjoy, is soon stripped from him by the pornographer who exploits the child for profit. And even if the child feels a twinge of his developing conscience when asked to perform, he has no real alternative. How else can an eight-year-old child support himself? However, more often than not the child's conscience is not developed when he begins to perform; as a result it never does. Therefore, that fragile innocence he is born with is ravaged beyond repair. And sex, for most people an activity related to love,

delight, and marriage, becomes for the abused child just another mechanical act analogous to shaking hands. That certain special and mystical quality of sex is replaced by a cold mechanistic commercialism.

4 Although the mutation of a child's innocence is horrible, the perversion of social morality is of greater consequence. A society willing to tolerate such abuse to its children is certainly suspect, if not, indeed, desperately sick. The obvious point is this: someone out there must be buying this filth. How else can we explain the proliferation of such titles as *Nudist Moppets, Chicken Delight, Lust for Children, Naughty Horny Imps, and Child Discipline?* (Densen-Gerber documents at least 264 different boy and girl porn magazines sold nationwide.) Curiosity might explain an initial purchase but the great number of titles indicates a deeper fascination and psychological commitment. To me it smells of death. For an organism to die, it must be the result of either disease, murder, or execution. A society like ours so morally diseased that it freely permits the murder of its children's innocence is executing itself.

5 Destruction of innocence and perversion of social morality aside, the greatest danger of child pornography is its attack on the basic fiber of humanity. By basic fiber of humanity I mean those instincts we all share—those instincts that appreciate beauty, goodness, truth, rightness, and love as well as those that understand ugliness, evil, falsehood, wrongness, and sorrow. I argue that every human, unless deprived or abused early in life, has the capacity, desire and fight to experience such instincts. They are what help make us human. Furthermore, though it may sound trite, a child is the most precious of all human treasures. Our children are our leaders of tomorrow. They are our future school board members, doctors, lawyers, preachers, mayors, judges, and so on. Are we going to allow their humanity to be devastated and in many cases completely destroyed by a freedom so diametrically opposed to their healthy development?

6 Those who offer constitutional arguments in defense of child pornographers are misguided. The men who framed the Constitution would never have tolerated pornography (though it must be admitted it existed even then). Freedom of speech and press means the right to speak out on matters of political and public debate; it does not mean the right to open mental sewers. It is the right to "agree to disagree"; it is not the right to disembowel the mind.

7 Child pornography does not deserve governmental protection because it only serves to undermine society, a society seemingly so obsessed with unconditional freedom that it is permitting itself to rot from within.

FOR DISCUSSION

1. What is the focusing event of this essay? How does the author use it?
2. Discuss King's "image" as an author. Does he seem to be pursuing any particular strategy? What might be the advantages and disadvantages of the way King comes across in the essay?

3. King states his thesis in the first sentence of the essay, but he does not really get into the question of first amendment rights until the last paragraph. Is anything gained by this strategy? Is anything lost?

4. What evidence is there that the author sees this essay as fitting into a larger process of deliberation? Do you think the essay goes far enough or is specific enough in this respect?

5. In a class discussion of this essay, it was suggested that King might have done more to anticipate and deal with possible objections to his arguments. What do you think some of these objections might be? How might they be dealt with?

2 A Form for Argumentation

Chapter Overview

This chapter introduces an adaptation of the classical scheme of organization for the deliberative essay. This scheme is useful not merely for organizing your essay but also for discovering what you are going to say and how you are going to reach and persuade your audience.

- **The Classical Scheme and Its Uses**
  - **The classical scheme**
  - **A form for written deliberation**
  - **A model student essay**
  - **The organizational scheme as a prewriting device**
- **Composing the Deliberative Essay**
  - **The introduction**
  - **The confirmation**
  - **The concession/refutation**
  - **The conclusion**
- **Alternative Forms of Arrangement**
- **Essay Assignments**
- **Essays for Analysis**

• The Classical Scheme and Its Uses

The classical scheme

One of the oldest teaching devices in the field of rhetoric is a formula for organizing and composing a piece of discourse. Classical—that is, Greek and Roman—teachers of rhetoric, who dealt mainly with speechmaking, often recognized five parts of a discourse:

1. **Introduction:** The orator begins by warming up to the audience, establishing rapport, and announcing the general theme or thesis of the speech.

2. **Narration:** Next the orator presents specific circumstances or issues to be dealt with, a summary of relevant background material, and a discussion of what is at stake.

3. **Confirmation:** Here the orator gives the principal arguments of the speech —the "good reasons" for accepting the thesis or point of view of the speech.

4. **Refutation:** Now the orator takes a look at opposing viewpoints, conceding as much as can be conceded without damaging the thesis of the speech, and *refuting* conflicting views. This is also a good place to anticipate and attempt to deal with possible objections to the speech.

5. **Conclusion:** Finally, the orator wraps up the various arguments into a summary statement, and amplifies the force of arguments already made.

The ancient teachers of rhetoric recognized that not all pieces of discourse were put together in exactly this way; they also recognized that some situations call for radical departures from the formula. But they often prescribed this order to students, not because it was absolutely ideal, but because using the scheme encouraged the writer to take account of some of the most important elements of composing—begin in an interesting way, provide background or context to the particular audience, state arguments clearly and forcefully, take account of opposing viewpoints and anticipate objections, and, finally, conclude in a satisfying and effective way.

A form for written deliberation

Although the classical scheme of organization was designed specifically for speechmaking, it can serve for written deliberation as well, particularly if adapted to the special needs and circumstances of a writer.

For written discourse, the first two sections, "Introduction" and "Narration," often run together into a single unit, which we will call "Introduction/Narration." The reason for this has to do with the differences between speechmaking situations and writing situations. When you give a speech, the audience is right there. Real people are looking at you, waiting for you to begin. A speaker generally feels the need to break the ice a bit, using various devices and formulas such as:

- thanking the introducer, pretending that such lavish praise isn't deserved;
- indicating feeling happy and honored;
- telling a self-revealing or self-deprecatory anecdote.

These devices create a sense of identification with the audience, put the audience in a receptive frame of mind, and settle the nerves of the speaker as well.

Writing is different; the author does not have direct contact with an audience. The time and place of *delivery* and the time and place of *reception* are not the same. This may be better for the author's nerves, but it creates different problems of communication, as well as different opportunities. A writer's initial problem is not breaking the ice as much as grabbing and focusing attention. Whereas ice-breaking devices seem necessary in most speaking, they seem tedious, boring, and self-centered in most writing. A speech maker cannot launch directly into an argument or the presentation of a focusing event without seeming abrupt or overly dramatic, but a writer can do precisely this as a way of catching interest and focusing attention at once.

Another important consequence of the separation of author and audience in writing is that the author must do a more thorough job of anticipating audience response. Something unclear or offensive can be detected on the spot, when making a speech, in the facial expressions, movements, and audible responses of the audience. Corrections can be made on the spot, with phrases such as, "Now what this really means is . . .," or "Of course I don't mean to imply that. . . ." Moreover, many situations of speech making allow for spontaneous questions or objections from members of the audience, or at least for a question-answer period at the end. The speech maker, consequently, gets several chances to clarify statements and to answer objections.

A writer obviously does not get this kind of on-the-spot feedback. This makes the "refutation" part of a discourse doubly important. A writer must deal with opposing views and possible objections the first time around. Both writers and speakers must also make whatever concessions they can to opposing viewpoints. In general, the more you can concede, the more reasonable you seem and the better chance your argument will have of standing up to objections. This is the reason that, in this book, this part is renamed "Concession/Refutation."

With these two modifications—the merger of "introduction" and "narration," and the renaming of the "refutation" section—our organizational scheme looks like this:

Part 1: Introduction/Narration
Part 2: Confirmation
Part 3: Concession/Refutation
Part 4: Conclusion

Not every essay you read in magazines and newspapers will conform exactly to this design. However, for most deliberative writing, it is a workable design, and it can help assure a moderate degree of success, especially for the inexperienced writer.

A model student essay

The following student essay by Linda Woolard successfully uses the modified classical scheme.

Analysis

All the Time? Forget It!

Part 1: Introduction/Narration
a) Presentation of issue

The student legislature has recently proposed a campus-wide referendum on the issue of twenty-four hour visitation in the dormitories. Even though the referendum will be non-binding, I hope that those students who value their privacy and study time will come out and send student government and the university administration a message by voting NO.

b) Statement of thesis

Although twenty-four hour visitation in the dorms would be convenient for some individuals at times, it would cause problems that far outweigh these conveniences.

Part 2: Confirmation
a) First argument

Certainly the biggest problem would be the resulting lack of privacy for dorm students. Most college students like to relax in nightgowns, T-shirts, or underwear in their rooms and halls, when they're studying late at nights, or in the mornings when they've just gotten out of bed. No matter how "liberated" we are, not many of us are going to feel comfortable doing that in the presence of members of the opposite sex. If twenty-four hour visitation is allowed, there will be both males and females in the dorms at all times of the day and night. No one will be able to venture outside her room, even for a minute or two, in nightgown or pajamas. How would you like to get dressed every time you want to go to the bathroom?

b) Second argument

Consider also the problems that are going to arise between roommates. Suppose a girl has her boyfriend in her room late at night. What's the roommate going to do about undressing to go to bed or doing other personal things? Suppose she wants to study. What then? It's no use saying, "Well, people can work things out." The fact is, there's going to be friction and hard feelings. Who needs it?

c) Third argument

The level of noise in the halls is already bad enough. Every night there are always some people who have big tests to study for or papers to write, and of course there are always others who have no work to do for the next day. These people don't always *mean* to be nuisances—they just don't remember that the noise they produce makes it hard for others who want to work or sleep. With twenty-four hour visitation, you can bet your boots it'll be a lot worse.

d) Fourth argument

Not very many people seem to have thought of it yet, but twenty-four hour visitation would make the dormitories less secure. The doors would always be unlocked, making it easy for people who do not belong in the dorms to enter them. These people might be anything from pranksters to criminals, but anyone leaving a room unlocked would be taking a chance of being robbed or seriously harmed. This is a bit risky, just for the privilege of having twenty-four visitation.

Part 3: Concession/Refutation
a) Refute opposing views (concede a point)

The people clamoring for change are saying that we don't have to have any of these problems, that we can have strict rules and security procedures, and that disputes can be settled by arbitration committees. I'm sure that some problems can be prevented in this way, but I don't believe that most of them will. We have rules and security procedures now, and everybody knows how much fudging goes on. Things are bound to get worse with twenty-four hour visitation. And the problem with arbitration is that it always comes *after* the fact—after things have gotten nasty between roommates, after somebody couldn't sleep and flunked a test or didn't finish a paper. Furthermore, you know who always comes out looking bad, don't you? It's the poor drag who wanted to sleep or study. Not the ones who wanted to party all night—they were just trying to have a little fun!

b) Anticipate objections

I hope you won't get me wrong. I am not a sleepaholic and I don't consider myself a wallflower. I like to go out, I like to have guys up to my room occasionally, and I don't mind my roommate to get into arguments and hurt each others' feelings.

Part 4: Conclusion

I just don't think it's worth it. College students have to put up with the rush and noise of classes all day long. Keeping things the way they are would at least allow us a few hours of peace and quiet at night. Of course not everybody wants peace and quiet all the time, least of all me. But I think the right to have it some of the time should be protected.

(Return to wording of title)

The organizational scheme as a prewriting device

The classical scheme does more than help you organize an essay. Like the device for formulating and testing thesis statements in Chapter 1, the classical scheme can help you discover your subject more fully and devise a strategy for persuading your audience. This is a good reason for having the classical scheme in mind, whether you decide to organize an essay that way or not. Each section of the scheme should remind you of questions you need to ask yourself before and as you write.

1) Introduction/Narration

What is the situation that this essay responds to?
What elements of background or context need to be presented?
What are the principal issues?
What is the best way to capture and focus the audience's attention?
What tone should I establish? What image of myself should I project?

2) Confirmation

What are the best "good reasons" or supporting points for my thesis?
How can I demonstrate that these are valid points?
What important facts or testimony will support these points?

3) Concession/Refutation

What are the most important opposing arguments? What concessions can I make and still support my thesis?
How can I refute opposing arguments or minimize their significance?
What are the possible objections to my own argument?
What are the possible misunderstandings of my own argument?
How can I best deal with these objections and misunderstandings?

4) Conclusion

How can I best leave a strong impression of the rightness and importance of my view?
How can I best summarize or exemplify the most important elements of my argument?

How can I best summarize or exemplify the most important elements of my argument?
What is the larger significance of the argument? What long-range implications are there?
How can I make an effective sense of closing?

• Composing the Deliberative Essay

In this section we will consider each of the four parts of a classical essay in detail.

The introduction

An effective introduction is crucial to most deliberative writing. It can mean the difference between the essay's being read and taken seriously or its being passed over for something else. Most people are reluctant to walk out on a speech, but a reader can simply stop reading. Moreover, in writing you have a special need to clarify your subject and your own role as advocate or spokesman. You don't have someone to introduce you and explain what your topic is. Finally, remember that, under most circumstances, people are not exactly lined up waiting to hear what you have to say. It's your job to make it interesting and worthwhile.

Sometimes, by the time you get ready to put pen to paper, you already have a clear idea of how you want to begin. Other times you know pretty much what to say, but you grope about for the right opening. In either case, keep in mind the functions of a good introduction, and consider some alternatives.

There are basically four things an introduction should do, and they can be summed up in four words—interest, background, thesis, and role.

1. The introduction should attract a reader's attention and focus it on the subject.
2. The introduction should provide necessary background information for a particular audience. It should identify the general problem as well as the particular issues.
3. The introduction should clearly signal your own point of view or the *direction* of your argument. In a short essay this usually means a statement of your thesis.
4. The introduction should establish or clarify any special relationship you have to the subject or audience, and it should establish the image of yourself that you wish to project to the audience.

Sometimes a single statement or opening device can perform several of these tasks simultaneously. Usually, however, you can't do all of these things at once, and the situation will call for stressing one or two of them at the expense of others. Consider all four and use common sense.

If your subject is already a matter of concern to an audience, if you are dealing with a well-established controversy, or if your thesis is a particularly strong or striking one, then a straightforward announcement of the topic is sufficient. On the other hand, if your topic is not one of immediate concern or controversy, you may have to catch your reader's attention, and you may have to provide background information. There are a number of conventional openers, sometimes called "hooks," that you can use to stimulate interest and establish your purposes. The following examples illustrate a few of the possibilities.

Thesis opening. The strategy here is to concentrate attention by stating your thesis right at the beginning, sometimes in a bold and provocative way.

> Man will never conquer space. Such a statement may sound ludicrous, now that our rockets are already 100 million miles beyond the moon and the first human travelers are preparing to leave the atmosphere. Yet it expresses a truth which our forefathers knew, one we have forgotten—and our descendants must learn again, in heartbreak and loneliness.—Arthur C. Clark, "We'll Never Conquer Space"

> We Americans are on the verge of doing ourselves what our worst enemies have been unable to do: destroy our intelligence services.—Melvin R. Laird, "Let's Stop Undermining the CIA"

Focusing event. The strategy here is to present (or recall) a particular situation or set of circumstances. The essay either addresses the event head-on, as a problem in itself, or indirectly, as symptomatic of a larger problem. This is one of the most common types of openers in deliberative writing.

> Government doctors are rolling exquisite marijuana cigarettes for a 28-year-old Washingtonian named Bob Randall, placing them in a prescription jar with an adults-only hard-to-twist-off cap and delivering them to him through a government pharmacy. He smokes eight cigarettes a day (he says they don't affect him), then devotes the remainder of his time to fighting the very bureaucrats who set up the program. The reason: Randall has acute glaucoma, and if he did not take marijuana daily, his eye would swell with painful pressure. At least two million other Americans have the same disease, but are forbidden to use Randall's pain-killing tool. If they asked the government for a similar arrangement, they would be turned down.—*The New Republic,* "Marijuana Therapy"

A small news article in 1953 reported that a man with no criminal record went for his gun and shot his TV set. It was the first known instance of videocide, although not the last, and it bespoke the frustrations of viewers around the country—in those early days when television was young—who sat before their sets unable to resist the talking images but helpless to answer back. . . .

Undiminished after a quarter century, that general frustration is mixed now in many households with anxieties about what television may be doing to children, the political system or the moral fabric of the society. Some writers, cursing television as a drug, have advised discarding the television set, as if that would solve all the problems. The idea is as myopic and unrealistic as the notion held by many people that they can make their statement against television simply by not watching it.—Les Brown, "Is the Public Interested in the Public Interest?"

A police car silently moves through the streets of Goldsboro. The policeman is looking for a 14-year-old who ran away from home because she couldn't take any more of her mother's comparisons between her and her "multi-talented" sister. At home, it is not the mother who is feeling totally at fault, but rather the sister, who knows she is the exact reason why the girl ran away. Of course, the mother is finally beginning to realize what she has done.

This situation may not sound as common as one where the child runs away because of child-abuse, but it is very real and it is a problem that parents should become more aware of. Although it is good to let them know that you are pleased with their accomplishments, giving excessive praise to children does more harm than good.—Lavoris Brinson, "Is It Always Good to Praise Children?" Student Essay

Focusing quotation. This opener uses a quotation as a kind of focusing event. Where do you get quotations? You either 1) remember them; 2) get them from any reading or research you have been doing on your subject; or 3) look them up in a book of quotations. Here are two good sources of quotations on a variety of subjects: Bartlett, John. *Familiar Quotations* and Simpson, James B. *Contemporary Quotations.*

"Wherever we went and wherever we looked," the doctors retorted, "we saw children in significant numbers who were hungry and sick, children for whom hunger is a daily fact of life, and sickness in many forms an inevitability. The children we saw were more than just malnourished. They were hungry, weak, apathetic. Their lives are being shortened. They are visibly and predictably losing their health, their energy, their spirits. They are suffering from hunger and disease, and directly or indirectly, they are dying from them—which is exactly what 'starvation' means."

The physicians were describing conditions not in Biafra or the Sahel, but right here in America in 1967.—Nick Kotz, "Feeding the Hungry"

Focusing question. The strategy here is to attract interest by posing a question. Your thesis will generally be the answer to the question.

Do more Americans want inflation to keep roaring along than want it to abate? —Alfred L. Malabre, Jr., "Why Worry About Inflation?"

Will machines destroy emotions, or will emotions destroy machines? This question was suggested long ago by Samuel Butler in *Erewhon,* but it is growing more and more actual as the empire of machinery is enlarged. Bertrand Russell, "Machines and the Emotions"

Problem or controversy. The strategy here is to present (or recall) an important problem or controversy. The essay will either explain something about the problem or suggest solutions.

A criminal trial in California is a circus in which even a mediocre lawyer can delay a case to death, thanks to absurd rules of criminal procedure. In Los Angeles County, the length of criminal jury trials has increased 24% in the past three years.

Television coverage of trials, in appropriate cases and with careful judicial supervision, could do more to improve this situation than judges and lawyers have been able to do in 50 years.—Evelle J. Younger, "Best Agent for Courtroom Reform: Televised Trials"

All over the United States, families are in trouble. It is true that there are many contented homes where parents are living in harmony and raising their children responsibly, and with enjoyment in which the children share. Two out of three American households are homes in which a wife and husband live together, and almost seven out of ten children are born to parents living together in their first marriage.

However, though reassuring, these figures are deceptive. A great many of the married couples have already lived through one divorce. And a very large number of the children in families still intact will have to face the disruption of their parents' marriage in the future. The numbers increase every year.—Margaret Mead, "Can the American Family Survive?"

Rebuttal. The strategy here is to "come out swinging." Clarify and draw attention to your own point of view by contrasting it with an opposing point of view, sometimes a more popular one.

Dogma has it that only government taxes can produce the capital required to transform a less developed country into a modern industrial economy, replete with national airline, shipping line, steel mills, petrochemical plants and other symbols of economic independence.

Dogma also asserts that massive governmental intervention is required to prevent inequitable distribution of wealth and income as a country develops.

One notable challenge to these dogmas is found in the modern city-state of

Hong Kong—a story of capitalist economic achievement from a virtual starting point of zero. Hong Kong's success is due to human response to economic freedom and personal incentives; it has materialized on a near resourceless slab of barely inhabitable granite under extremely adverse circumstances.—Alvin Rabushka, "The Free Market at Work in Hong Kong"

Most Americans believe that our society of consumption-happy, fun-loving, jet-traveling people creates the greatest happiness for the greatest number. Contrary to this view, I believe that our present way of life leads to increasing anxiety, helplessness, and eventually, to the disintegration of our culture. I refuse to identify fun with pleasure, excitement with joy, busyness with happiness, or the faceless, buck-passing "organization man" with an independent individual.—Erich Fromm, "Our Way of Life Makes Us Miserable"

Analogy or parallel case. The strategy here is to begin with the description or presentation of a situation that is analogous or parallel to the one you are writing about. Analogy can be particularly effective when your purpose is to criticize or pass judgment against some act or development.

In the mid-seventeenth century, Oliver Cromwell contemplated exterminating the Irish and settling Ireland with Europe's persecuted Jews. Regarding the Irish, the plan appealed to Cromwell's passionate side. Regarding the Jews, the plan appealed to his common sense.

It acknowledged that the Jewish people were, indeed, a "people." Possessing a common past and culture, they lacked only land, which is not the essence of a nation. The Jews were a nation in need of a home.

More than 300 years later the Jewish people and the legitimacy of their nationalism are under attack in the organization misleadingly named the United Nations. A U.N. committee has voted 70-29 to declare that Zionism is a form of racism. This move was sponsored by Arab regimes and was supported primarily by dictatorial regimes—China and Chile, the Soviet Union and Spain.—George Will, "Zionism and Legitimacy"

Confession or personal introduction. Sometimes the situation is right for this. Your subject concerns you in such a personal way that your best strategy is to explain your own involvement in it.

For most of my adult life I have thought of myself as a Social Democrat, and I still do, but I have also tried to be observant and to learn from experience. Two lessons have especially impressed me: 1) that the practice of socialism—as exemplified in a majority of the world's nations—is far more authoritarian and inhumane than its idealistic thinkers of the past predicted, or its proponents of the present have the honesty to observe; and 2) that the practice of democratic capitalism—now observed in barely two dozen nations of the world—is far more humane than any theory about it. It dismays me, moreover, that many of my fellow theologians have not awakened from their dogmatic slumbers when it comes to economics.—Michael Novak, "The Grand Inquisitor, Born Again"

Introductions to Avoid

The Creaky, Mechanical Opener
"The purpose of this essay is to . . ."
"The thesis of this essay is . . ."

The Grandiose Opener
"All through the ages mankind has sought to . . ."

The Cliché Opener
"In today's modern world . . ."

The Dramatic Soap Opera Opener
"Thump . . . thump . . . there was a noise on the front porch . . ."

EXERCISE 2.1

Examine the following introductions from student essays. Indicate what specific methods they use for focusing reader interest and for establishing their own points of view. Which of them could be improved? How?

A. "Uhh, excuse me, Miss, do you have an extra punch?" "No, I'm sorry." "Well, _____ you, then!" he said, storming off. This is a typical scene in the college cafeteria and the language is typical of the vulgarity that our generation uses. Profanity has been used for generations and generations, but it is used most frequently today. Today's teenagers have almost made it the "universal language," stripping Latin of its title. The young generation is making considerable progress—getting college educations, making new discoveries, shaping the pathway to a better tomorrow. With so much knowledge and optimism, it can be said that the young people of the '80's are a very intelligent group of people, but their frequent use of intolerable profanity makes them seem ignorant.—Lavoris Brinson, "Profanity and Today's Teenager"

B. Student government has always been a part of the college, but recently students have become critical of its usefulness. Since the decline in the popularity of student government, some colleges have taken it upon themselves, through the means of a school vote, to abolish their student government. This is not right. I feel that a school's government is a vital asset because it works for protecting our rights as students, and it makes the long work-and-study process of college life more enjoyable.—Ralph Gurkin, "Student Government Is Working"

C. Much has been written touting the benefits of a college education particularly in today's world of specialization. I am in total agreement with this, as I am sure the majority of the people are; however, I advocate delaying college for several years after high school graduation, taking this time to work and learn first hand about life.—Jennifer Pardu, "College Delayed—Pros and Cons"

D. By now, Columbus Countians, especially those living in the Whiteville-Chadbourn area, are bound to be aware of the issue that has recently caused so much turmoil: should the seven mile section of Highway 130 between Whiteville and Chadbourn be widened to include four lanes instead of the present two lanes? Supporters of the project claim that widening the road will attract new industry as well as provide a safer route for travelers. Detractors view this proposed project as an unwarrantable waste of money. Although action has already been taken by the area Chambers of Commerce and the county Board of Commissioners to aid in guaranteeing the expansion, it would be a wise idea for the residents of the county to examine this "beneficial" improvement project and let their voices be heard! Taxpaying citizens must realize that it is not too late to prevent this extravagant expenditure of funds. Spending an estimated $5.7 million on a project that should not even exist is certainly not a logical thing to do.—Lisa Elvington, "A $5.7 Million Waste"

E. What teenager can get in his/her car without turning on the radio? The degree to which the songs around us are played, or perhaps overplayed, is phenomenal. Walk in any clothing store and one is instantly a victim. But what are these trite unoriginal songs telling us? Why do we continue to buy these records since we are undoubtedly endorsing what is being said? These songs which we are listening to are mere reprints of one another, dealing with the same love-sick subjects, which provide an unrealistic view of life.—Sandy Crowe, "Pop Music Blues"

The confirmation

The nature of argument

Usually this is the most important section of a deliberative essay, the one where the writer backs up or substantiates the thesis of the essay. This process of substantiating a thesis is generally known as *argumentation,* and the best way to understand it is by examining first what an argument is.

An *argument* is a statement that is supported by other statements. The back-up or support statements are usually called *premises,* and the statement that they support is called the *conclusion* or *claim* of the argument:

Jack will never be a great pianist because he has short fingers.

It's easy to see in this example that the claim or conclusion is the statement, "Jack will never be a great pianist," and that the other statement, "He has short fingers," is a premise. But there is something else here that you don't see, an unspoken statement that joins the other two. The unspoken link between the claim (Jack will never be a great pianist) and the specific premise (He has short fingers) is another, more general premise:

People who have short fingers cannot become great pianists.

In scientific or mathematical argumentation authors are expected to state their premises along with their conclusions. However, public deliberation is less formal. Authors tend to follow the natural habit of leaving some premises (and sometimes conclusions also) unstated, and they often find it quite effective to do so.

Every argument, then, has three parts, whether all are stated or not—a conclusion and two premises. One of the premises is a general statement (sometimes called a *warrant*), and the other is a more specific statement (sometimes called a *datum*).

Example: Jack will never be a great pianist. *(Conclusion* or *Claim)*
People with short fingers cannot be great pianists. (Unstated *General Premise* or *Warrant*)
Jack has short fingers. *(Specific Premise* or *Datum)*

When one of the premises of an argument is left unstated, it is referred to as an *assumption.* The general premise in the example above is an assumption because it is left unstated. In the argument, "Jack will never be a great pianist because he is too lazy to practice," the unstated premise—the assumption—is that without practice no one can become a great pianist. Sometimes assumptions are fairly safe like this one, but sometimes they are questionable. There have been great pianists with comparatively short fingers.

EXERCISE 2.2

For each of the arguments listed below, identify the claim and the unstated premise or assumption. Is the assumption a safe one or is it open to question?

A. Notre Dame is sure to beat Purdue, because Michigan won over Purdue and Notre Dame has already beaten Michigan by a wide margin.

B. Marijuana should be legalized, since so many people are smoking it anyway.

C. The Russians have cheated on every treaty agreement they have ever signed with the United States. Why won't they cheat if this treaty is ratified?

D. A liberal arts education is a waste of time. There is no job that it prepares you to perform.

E. We must reinstitute the draft in this country because the volunteer army is just not working.

F. Harrison would make a terrible Superior Court Judge. He's spent his entire legal career as a tax consultant, and he has never argued a case in court.

G. Of course there should be more sex education in the schools. Look at the number of teen-age pregnancies just this year!

H. Because of the strict need to maintain standards of excellence, universities should not be compelled to engage in "affirmative action" when hiring faculty.

I. Obviously Americans are getting flabby; we win fewer gold medals in the Olympics every year.

J. Of course women should be given preferential treatment in hiring. For centuries men have exploited and discriminated against women, and now they must pay for it.

Combining arguments: The chain of support

Fortunately, informal argumentation is a natural process for most people, and you don't have to memorize a lot of rules or terminology in order to engage in it. On the other hand, knowing something about the process helps you argue in a more effective way. One important thing to understand about the process is how arguments link together, forming a "chain of support," in an extended piece of writing.

A single argument, with its claim and two premises, hardly ever settles anything by itself. One reason is that people want to consider a number of different arguments in making a decision. Another reason is that, although the premises may supply adequate support for the conclusion or claim, the premises themselves may need support. For example, if you wanted to argue that a proposal for 24-hour visitation in dormitories is unwise because it would jeopardize security, you would spend most of your effort supporting the idea that security would actually be jeopardized. The premise of your larger argument becomes a claim in a smaller one, and that claim must be supported also.

We can illustrate this process by examining the student essay on 24-hour visitation (pp. 36–38). In this essay the student urges other students to vote against the policy because it will cause problems that "far outweigh the conveniences." *Assuming* that most students will vote against a policy that causes such problems, the author devotes the whole essay to supporting the notion that the problems will be caused by the policy. She uses four basic arguments: 1) that it will result in a lack of privacy; 2) that it will cause friction between roommates; 3) that it will increase the level of noise and disturbance at night; and 4) that it will make the dorms less secure. Each of these statements becomes, in turn, a claim which must be supported with still other statements. The process can be diagrammed this way:

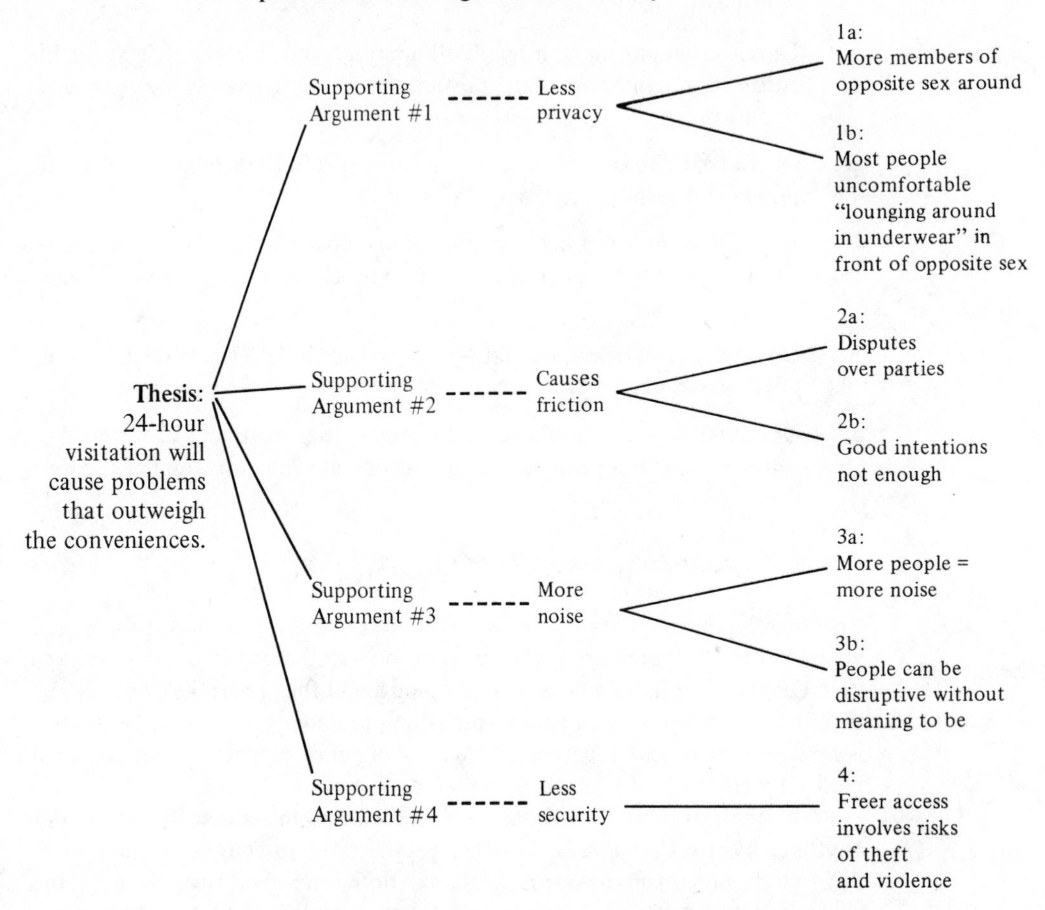

The chain of support must end somewhere, especially in deliberative writing, where arguments become too lengthy if you try to prove everything you say. The deliberative writer must choose arguments very carefully, selecting the ones that are most powerful and most readily supportable with reasoning, examples, and facts.

The deliberative writer also must be able to make judgments about which statements require a good deal of support and which statements can stand on their own. For example, the author of the visitation essay supported the statement that the policy would cause a loss of privacy (Argument #1 on the chart) with the statement that most students are not liberated enough to lounge around in underwear in front of members of the opposite sex. But notice that she does not try to support the statement that most students are not liberated enough; she merely states it. Should she have? Under the circumstances she probably made the right decision. In the first place, most of her audience will probably accept it as true, and those who don't accept it wouldn't be "reachable" by any part of her essay. Moreover, the thesis of the essay doesn't depend upon everyone agreeing on this point. The probability that some students feel this way supports the general idea. At most, she could be accused of overstating the case rather than being wrong.

EXERCISE 2.3

Which of the following statements need support, and which stand on their own, at least in support of other statements? Assume an audience of students at your college or university.

A. Most Americans do not object to the playing of "The Star Spangled Banner" at athletic contests.

B. If it could be demonstrated that a particular policy was unfair to women, then most people would be against that policy.

C. Most professors care only about money.

D. Most people would disapprove of an action that they thought was dishonest.

E. Most students would cheat on exams if they thought they could get away with it.

F. Some students would cheat on exams if they thought that they could get away with it.

G. As a group, lawyers, doctors, and professors are more educated than businessmen.

H. As a group, lawyers, doctors, and professors are more honest than businessmen.

I. The best way to improve your writing is to take courses in composition.

J. Something natural is better than something artificial.

Three ways to support arguments: Reasoning, facts and examples, testimony

There is no way to learn the complete art of argumentation at once, though you will learn more about it in the remaining chapters of this book. Fortunately, you already know a great deal, by intuition. For now, keep in mind that there are three basic ways to support arguments—with "good reasons," with facts and examples, and with testimony.

Good reasons are the basic supporting arguments for your thesis. You are in favor of certain things because they will make life better in some specific way; you're against certain things because they will make life worse. You approve of certain things because they meet certain standards; you disapprove of them because they don't.

Facts and examples are often the best support you can give for good reasons. If you accuse some policy of being unfair, then readers want to know in what ways it is unfair. What particular example of unfair treatment or results can you supply? If you claim that adopting a certain policy (like 24-hour visitation in the dorms) will lead to problems, then readers want to know what you mean in concrete terms. What actual events might occur? Have such events occurred elsewhere, under similar conditions?

Testimony is the report of what other people have written or said, or the author's own report of personal experience. It is especially effective in argumentation when it comes from people who are considered authorities on a specific subject, or when it comes from people who have a special involvement in the activities concerned. Usually testimony is not the most powerful kind of argument in deliberative writing (in contrast with court cases), and it is best used in support of secondary points. For these points, it is the next best thing to actual facts or statistics. If you claim that many people are dissatisfied with the service they receive from automobile dealerships, testimony from the right person serves as well as actual statistics.

Two important steps in preparing the confirmation section

Make a list of "good reasons" that will support your thesis. If possible, make a design similar to the one on p. 48. Then choose the ones that will have the most powerful effect on your audience. Discard arguments that seem less effective or difficult to support. Examine the assumptions that might be involved in any particular argument. Are these assumptions reasonable? Do they bring up questions that you may need to answer?

Gather facts, examples, and testimony. The student who wrote the essay on 24-hour visitation gathered all her examples from her experience and from her projections of what might happen. This strategy served her well, although the argument might have been stronger if she had used examples of what actually happened in dorms with 24-hour visitation. If you are writing on a more public issue, arm yourself with some background information and pertinent facts. This doesn't mean doing a lot of research. There are painless ways of getting pertinent information on practically any subject, if you have access to a library. Here are a few sources of information:

1) For information on current events and controversies:

The Readers' Guide to Periodical Literature. 1900–date

(Indexes essays and articles by topic and author. Usually up-to-date within 3 months)

The New York Times Index. 1913–date
(Indexes by topic and by author's of signed pieces. Usually up-to-date within 6 months)

Facts on File: Weekly World News Digest with Cumulative Index. 1940–date
(Usually up-to-date within about 1 month)

2) For information on contemporary personalities:

Current Biography. 1940–date (monthly)
Who's Who in America (Annual)
International Who's Who (Annual)

3) For general information and statistics:

The New Encyclopedia Britannica
Statistical Abstract of the United States (annual)
The card catalogue of your library

4) When you're stuck

Ask for help from the *reference librarian* in your library. Reference librarians are highly trained information seekers, and they can be very helpful.

5) Local information and controversy

Use the telephone to call local agencies, departments, or individuals. If necessary and possible, set up personal interviews. (Identify yourself and your specific reason for calling; be brief and polite.)

EXERCISE 2.4

The following quotations are from an essay by Marvin Maurer. Identify the type of support that is being used in each of the passages.

A. The format of television news requires the news program to emphasize sensational events. Newspapers, too, report sensational news. With their more flexible format, however, they can afford to include background and historical data as well as news about average people and successful events. Readers are able to select items of interest to read, and unlike the television viewer, reject material that is disagreeable or uninteresting.

B. Television news must capture and hold far larger and diverse audiences than the printed press to pay its way. An NBC executive lamented that "a newspaper . . . can easily afford to print an item of conceivable interest to only a small percentage of its readers. A television news program must be put together with the assumption that each item will be of some interest to everyone that watches."

C. While the networks are among the staunchest defenders of free expression . . . they will compromise principles in order to enhance their audience ratings. In an astonishing article *The New York Times* described how ABC subordinated its news division's integrity to an outside influence. Soviet officials were permitted to censor and monitor ABC news stories about life in Russia. Some Soviet officials actually sat in ABC's New York offices reviewing its network reporting. *The Times* article contended that these startling concessions to the Russians were part of the network's effort to secure coverage rights for the 1980 Olympics.

D. The ever-increasing pace to secure higher audience ratings impels the networks to compromise standards of objectivity to the point where they will cooperate with extremist groups seeking publicity. . . . For example, in January 1975, NBC presented a dramatic view of a grocery store exploding in Belfast. Obviously, television crews had been notified in advance of the action.

E. Television, then, is by no means a neutral reporting instrument. Michael Robinson's study of the impact of CBS's film, *The Selling of the Pentagon,* led him to conclude that television is able to alter once positively held views about American institutions. . . .

F. Television news has a greater impact on, and influence over, audiences than newspapers because of the difference in format. Print takes up "space" while television uses up "time." A newspaper reader may easily bypass all the political news and rush right on to the sports section, but not the television viewer. . . . The viewer, then, is a captive of the entire TV news program.—Marvin Mauer, *Point-Counterpoint: Readings in American Government*

EXERCISE 2.5

List the exact place or places where answers to the following questions are found.

A. How many people died in automobile accidents in 1945?
In 1975?

B. Where does most of the world's industrial chrome come from?

C. What was the average price of a gallon of regular gasoline in the United States in 1965?

D. Identify the following people:
Willy Brandt
Joan Didion
Randall Jarrell

E. A recent essay, which has appeared in an American magazine or journal, on one of the following topics:
The financial plight of private colleges
Heart disease
Intercollegiate sports

The concession/refutation

There is always another side, another point of view. And no matter how strong your own arguments are, it is always dangerous to ignore the other side. In the first place, you might be wrong about some things. By adjusting your views to account for whatever is valid in the other point of view—and there's bound to be something that is valid—you emerge with more valid and defensible views of your own. Second, by examining the other side you learn what you're up against in argumentation. By acknowledging the other side, by incorporating what is valid in it into your own view, and by attempting to demonstrate to an audience that your own view is a better one, you emerge with a more persuasive argument.

Keep in mind the process of reading. Most readers will be making judgments about what you are saying—and about you—while they are reading. If you can anticipate some of these judgments, then you can adjust your writing to deal with them. Using a concession/refutation is just one way of doing this.

Also keep in mind the larger process of deliberation. It is almost never the purpose of a deliberative essay to convert opponents, or to turn people completely around in their thinking; very few deliberative essays could achieve that purpose. A deliberative writer might hope to "plant a seed," to have some long-range effect on the thinking of opponents; but the immediate goal of the deliberative essay is to persuade an uncommitted middle group. (Another purpose of the deliberative essay is to intensify the allegiances of people who are inclined to agree with you but may still need good reasons for acting or making a stand of their own.)

As you prepare this section of your essay, direct your remarks to this middle group. Concede as much as you can to other points of view, but come back strong with reasons that opposing views are inadequate. It is not necessary to disprove opposing views absolutely. Demonstrate that your own good reasons outweigh them. Essentially, you need to do two things:

1. Make a list of opposing arguments and points of view. Choose the most important of these and devise counter-arguments or reasons why they are less compelling than your own.
2. Look back over your own arguments. What weaknesses are there? What possible objections could someone make? In what ways might someone get the wrong idea about your own character or motives?

The author of the student essay on 24-hour visitation has done both of these things, in two separate paragraphs. First she argues against the notion that strict rules and procedures will prevent the problems she is predicting (paragraph 6). Then in the next paragraph she considers the possibility that some readers might dismiss her arguments as those of a wallflower or spoil-sport. She effectively forestalls these impressions by saying she is as fun-loving as the next person and that she is not opposed to the idea of visitation within limits.

The conclusion

It is less easy to talk about endings in the abstract than it is about beginnings, mainly because the conclusion of an essay so often takes its substance from what has already been written. Nevertheless, conclusions do perform certain valuable functions, and there are certain things to keep in mind while composing them.

Tying things together. Create a sense of closure or finality. One way to do this is to make sure you have fulfilled all the expectations you set up in earlier sections of the essay. Another is to use such signaling phrases as "finally," "in conclusion," and so on. You shouldn't overdo this, however, and such phrases shouldn't be used obtrusively or mechanically.

Another way of concluding is to refer back to the beginning of the essay, creating a kind of closed circle. Work in a final reference to the opening focusing event; if the essay began with a question, bring up the question again and answer it. Reiterate a phrase or concept that was used in the title or the first paragraph. The student essay does this by referring back to the phrase "all the time" in the title.

Summary and reiteration of principal arguments. You don't have to get long-winded, but it can be useful to reiterate your strongest points, particularly when the conclusion follows a Concession/Refutation section in which you have been dealing mainly with opposing arguments. The conclusion is a good place to come back strong, making sure that your best arguments will stick. The student essay does this effectively, reiterating the main point that 24-hour visitation simply isn't worth the trouble it will cause.

The final blast. Sometimes authors like to reserve a clincher for the very end, a powerful argument or piece of testimony, usually of greater significance than others. Such devices help the essay end on a note of conviction and high-mindedness, sometimes warning of grave consequences or predicting glorious results. These endings are usually more appropriate in speech making than in writing. Listen to Patrick Henry, in 1775:

> Why stand we here idle? What is it that gentlemen wish? What would they have? Is life so dear, or peace so sweet, as to be purchased at the price of chains and slavery? Forbid it, Almighty God! I know not what course others may take; but as for me, give me liberty, or give me death!

Such eloquence as this surely is out of place in an essay on 24-hour visitation —or almost any essay for that matter—and the author of our sample essay has wisely avoided it. On the other hand, there are occasions when the "high-minded" final blast, appropriately toned down, would serve well. But don't overdo it.

• Alternative Forms of Arrangement

The beauty of the classical scheme of arrangement is not that it always dictates the best way to put together an essay, but rather that it gives the deliberative writer a kind of home base from which to gather thoughts and arguments and to make judgments about both form and subject matter. Since all essays have to begin and end in some way, most departures from classical arrangement come in the in-between sections, particularly Concession/Refutation. In fact, many essays do not have a separate Concession/Refutation section at all. Some authors handle opposing arguments right at the beginning. Others counter possible objections or take up opposing arguments at various points along the way, in the Confirmation section. In any case, a good essay anticipates objections and opposing viewpoints in some way.

In the long run, the greatest value of knowing about classical arrangement and using it as a pre-writing device is that it helps you assess the advantages and disadvantages of whatever formal strategy you hit upon. For most deliberative writing, it's a good standard plan.

The most radical departures from classical arrangement also involve departures from the standard method of argumentation. These are the "special strategies of presentation" discussed on p. 23 in Chapter 1, and exemplified by Ellen Goodman's essay (pp. 28–29). In this case, the author chose to emphasize a single general point or to leave a single impression in a highly striking way. At the same time, using such a strategy, the author gave up the opportunity to present a comprehensive argument with an impressive chain of support. Whether the choice is a good one depends entirely upon the circumstances. But once again, knowing about classical arrangement will help you make the choice.

ESSAY ASSIGNMENTS

1. Attack some common misconception about your generation, students at your college or university, college students in general, or some other group you know. Support your argument with reasoning, facts, examples, and testimony. Use the modified classical scheme of arrangement.

2. Write an essay in which you propose changes in the orientation and reception of new students on your campus. In your *introduction,* make sure that you explain and illustrate what is wrong with the current

practices. In your *confirmation* section, present your proposed changes and explain how they will improve things. In your *concession/refutation* section, try to anticipate possible objections to your plan. Consider contacting some appropriate officials, either in the administration or in student government, for information and reactions to your ideas.

3. Using the general strategy as outlined in assignment #2, write an essay in which you make a proposal of any kind.

4. Argue either the pro or con side of any local or campus controversy. If appropriate, assume that your audience will be participating in a referendum or "straw vote" on the subject.

Essays for Analysis

The Truth About the Black Middle Class*

Vernon E. Jordan, Jr.

Vernon E. Jordan, Jr. is former executive director of the National Urban League. This essay first appeared in Newsweek, *July 8, 1974.*

1 Recent reports of the existence of a vast black middle class remind me of daring explorers emerging from the hidden depths of a strange, newly discovered world bearing tales of an exotic new phenomenon. The media seem to have discovered, finally, black families that are intact, black men who are working, black housewives tending backyard gardens and black youngsters who aren't sniffing coke or mugging old ladies.

2 And out of this "discovery" a new black stereotype is beginning to emerge. Immaculately dressed, cocktail in hand, the new black stereotype comes off as a sleek, sophisticated professional lightyears away from the ghetto experience. As I turn the pages of glossy photos of these idealized, fortunate few, I get the feeling that this new black image is all too comforting to Americans weary of the struggle against poverty and racism.

3 But this stereotype is no more real than was the old image of the angry, fire-breathing militant. And it may be just as damaging to black people, for whom equal opportunity is still a theory and for whom a national effort to bring about a more equitable distribution of the fruits of an affluent society is still a necessity. After all, who can argue the need for welfare reform, for guaranteed jobs, for integrated schools and better housing, when the supposed beneficiaries are looking out at us from the pages of national magazines, smiling at the camera between sips from their Martinis?

Ballyhoo

4 The "new" black middle class has been seen recently in prime time on a CBS News documentary; it has adorned the cover of The New York Times Magazine, and it has been the subject of a Time cover story. But its much ballyhooed emergence is more representative of wishful thinking than of reality. And important as it is for the dedication and hard work of countless black

families finally to receive recognition, the image being pushed so hard may be counterproductive in the long run.

5 The fact is that the black middle class of 1974, like that of earlier years, is a minority within the black community. In 1974, as in 1964, 1954 and in the decades stretching into the distant past, the social and economic reality of the majority of black people has been poverty and marginal status in the wings of our society.

6 The black middle class traditionally included a handful of professionals and a far larger number of working people who, had they been white, would be solidly "working class." The inclusion of Pullman porters, post-office clerks and other typical members of the old black middle class was due less to their incomes—which were well below those of whites—than to their relative immunity from the hazards of marginal employment that dogged most blacks. They were "middle class" relative to other black people, not to the society at large.

7 Despite all the publicity, despite all the photos of yacht-club cocktail parties, that is where the so-called black middle class stands today. The CBS broadcast included a handyman and a postal worker. Had they been white they would be considered working class, but since they were black and defied media-fostered stereotypes, they were given the middle-class label.

Income

8 Well, is it true that the black community is edging into the middle class? Let's look at income, the handiest guide and certainly the most generally agreed-upon measurement. What income level amounts to middle-class status? Median family income is often used, since that places a family at the exact midpoint in our society. In 1972 the median family income of white's amounted to $11,549, but black median family income was a mere $6,864.

9 That won't work. Let's use another guide. The Bureau of Labor Statistics says it takes an urban family of four $12,600 to maintain an "intermediate" living standard. Using that measure, the average black family not only is *not* middle class, but it earns far less than the "lower, non-poverty" level of $8,200. Four out of five black families earn less than the "intermediate" standard.

10 What about collar color? Occupational status is often considered a guide to middle-class status, and this is an area in which blacks have made tremendous gains, breaking into occupations unheard of for non-whites only a decade ago. When you look at the official occupation charts, there is a double space to separate higher-status from lower-status jobs such as laborer, operative and service worker. That gap is more than a typographical device. It is an indicator of racial separation as well, for the majority of working whites hold jobs above that line, while the majority of blacks are still confined to the low-pay, low-status jobs below it. At the top of the job pinnacle, in the elite categories of the professions and business, the disparity is most glaring, with one out of four whites in such middle-class jobs in contrast to every tenth black worker.

Tenuous Gains

11 Yes, there are black doctors, dentists and lawyers, but let no one be fooled into thinking they are typical—these professions include only 2 per cent blacks. Yes, there are black families that are stable, who work, often at more than one job, and who own cars and homes. And yes, they are representative of the masses of black people who work the longest hours at the hardest jobs for the least pay in order to put some meat on the table and clothes on their backs. This should be emphasized in every way possible in order to remind this forgetting nation that there is a dimension of black reality that has never been given its due.

12 But this should not blind us to the realization that even with such superhuman efforts, the vast majority of blacks are still far from middle-class status. Let us not forget that the gains won are tenuous ones, easily shaken from our grasp by an energy crisis, a recession, rampant inflation or nonenforcement of hard-won civil-rights laws.

13 And never let us fall victim to the illusion that the limited gains so bitterly wrenched from an unwilling nation have materially changed the conditions of life for the overwhelming majority of black people—conditions still typified by discrimination, economic insecurity and general living conditions inferior to those enjoyed by the majority of our white fellow citizens.

FOR DISCUSSION

1. Assuming that this essay follows the modified classical scheme described in this chapter, identify each of the sections. Where does each section begin and end?

2. Examine the introduction to this essay. Does it fit one of the types represented on pages 39–43? Or does it combine more than one type?

3. In a sense, this entire essay is a refutation, but it does have a Concession/ Refutation section. What particular points does Jordan concede? What in particular does he do to show that the conceded points do not undermine his thesis?

4. What is Jordan's larger reason for wanting to correct misperceptions about the black middle class? What are the practical implications of Jordan's thesis? Does Jordan state these implications?

5. What is Jordan's principal method of supporting his claims? Is this the most appropriate method, given the nature of his thesis?

6. Examine the conclusion. Which of the functions of a conclusion, listed on pp. 54–55, does it fulfill?

When Rights Collide*

by Amitai Etzioni

Amitai Etzioni is a professor of sociology at Columbia University and director of the Center for Policy Research. This essay first appeared in Psychology Today, *October 1977.*

1 The viewpoint, now gaining momentum, that would allow individuals to "make up their own minds" about smoking, air bags, safety helmets, Laetrile, and the like ignores some elementary social realities. The ill-informed nature of this viewpoint is camouflaged by the appeal to values that are dear to most Americans. The essence of the argument is that what individuals wish to do with their lives and limbs, foolhardy though it might be, is their own business, and that any interference would abridge their rights.

2 Mr. Gene Wirwahn, the legislative director of the American Motorcyclist Association, which is lobbying against laws requiring riders to wear helmets, put it squarely: "The issue that we're speaking about is not the voluntary use of helmets. It's the question of whether or not there should be laws telling people to wear them." State representative Anne Miller, a liberal Democrat in Illinois, favors legalization of Laetrile. She explains that she is aware that this apricot-pit extract is useless, but insists that "the government shouldn't protect people from bad judgment. They might as well bar holy water."

3 U.S. representative Louis Wyman recently invoked much the same argument in leading the brigade that won adoption in the House of a resolution making seat belts voluntary. The 1974-model cars had been engineered not to start unless the seat belt was buckled. Wyman, a New Hampshire Republican, called the buckle-up system un-American, saying it made the government a Big Brother to auto drivers. Representative Abraham Kazen, Texas Democrat, summed it all up: "It is wrong to tell the individual what is good for him. . . . These are some of the things that the American people want to judge for themselves. Give them the equipment if they so desire, *and if they do not, let them do whatever they want.*"

4 No civil society can survive if it permits each person to maximize his or her freedoms without concern for the consequences of one's act on others. If I choose to drive without a seat belt or air bag, I am greatly increasing my chances, in case of accident, of being impaled on the steering wheel or exiting via the windshield. It is not just my body that is jeopardized; my careening auto, which I cannot get back under control, will be more likely to injure people in other autos, pedestrians, or riders in my car. (Yes, my passengers choose their own fate when they decide to ride with me, but what about the infants who are killed and injured because they are not properly protected?)

*"When Rights Collide" by Amitai Etzioni. Reprinted from *Psychology Today Magazine,* October 1977, vol. 11, no. 5.

5 American institutions were fashioned in an era of vast unoccupied spaces and preindustrial technology. In those days, collisions between public needs and individual rights may have been minimal. But increased density, scarcity of resources, and interlocking technologies have now heightened the concern for "public goods," which belong to no one in particular but to all of us jointly. Polluting a lake or river or the air may not directly damage any one person's private property or living space. But it destroys a good that all of us—including future generations—benefit from and have a title to. Our public goods are entitled to a measure of protection.

6 The individual who chooses to act irresponsibly is playing a game of heads I win, tails the public loses. All too often, the unbelted drivers, the smokers, the unvaccinated, the users of quack remedies, draw on public funds to pay for the consequences of their unrestrained freedom of choice. Their rugged individualism rapidly becomes dependency when cancer strikes, or when the car overturns, sending the occupants to hospitals for treatment paid for at least in part by the public, through subsidies for hospitals and medical training. But the public till is not bottomless, and paying for these irresponsible acts leaves other public needs without funds.

7 True, totalitarian regimes often defend their invasions of individual liberties by citing public need or "national interest." One difference is that they are less concerned with protecting public goods than they are with building national power or new world orders. Instead of insisting on protection for *some* public rights, such regimes seek to put the national interest above all individual rights. The lesson is that we must not allow any claim of public or national need to go unexplained. But at the same time, we cannot allow simple-minded sloganeering (from "creeping Communism" to "Big Brother") to blind us to the fact that there are needs all of us share as a community.

8 Last but not least, we must face the truth about ourselves. Are we the independent, self-reliant individuals the politicians like to tell us we are? Or are we a human combination of urges and self-controls, impulses and rational judgments? Can we trust ourselves to make wise judgments routinely, or do we at times have to rely on the laws our elected representatives have fashioned, with our consent, to help guide us? The fact is that driving slowly saves lives, lots of lives; but until we are *required* to do so, most of us drive too fast. The same holds true for buckling our seat belts, buying air bags, and so on. Similarly, we need protection from quack cures. It sounds very libertarian to argue that each person can make up his or her own mind about Laetrile. But the fact is that when confronted with cancer and fearful of surgery, thousands of Americans are tempted to try a "painless medication" first, often delaying surgery until it is too late.

9 All in all, it is high time the oversimplifications about individual freedom versus Big Brother government were replaced by a social philosophy that calls for a balance among the rights of *various* individuals, between individual rights and *some* public rights, and that acknowledges the support we fallible individuals need from the law.

FOR DISCUSSION

1. This essay departs slightly from the modified classical scheme in the way it handles the element of Concession/Refutation. Explain the nature of the departure.

2. What kind of introduction does Etzioni use? Do you think it is strong enough?

3. Etzioni's principal method of supporting his claims is different from Jordan's in the preceding essay. What is that method? What is it about the nature of this essay that makes this particular method more appropriate?

4. What is the function of Etzioni's conclusion? How does it differ from Jordan's?

5. Make a list of Etzioni's principal "good reasons."

3 Propositions and Problem Solving

Chapter Overview

This chapter introduces different kinds of argumentative propositions and their relation to a larger framework of problem solving. These concepts are important to deliberative writing in two ways: 1) They sharpen your thinking and focus your pre-writing investigations about a subject; and 2) They help you understand the particular role you are playing, or the particular task you are attempting to accomplish, in the larger process of deliberation.

• Introduction

In deliberative writing it is important to know where you stand, in at least two related ways. One is in the particular kind of claim you are setting forth in your thesis, and the other is in the particular role your essay is playing in a larger process of decision making. Different kinds of claims and different stages in the process of decision making imply different tasks for the writer. These claims and stages lead to different strategies for accomplishing the tasks.

Suppose, for instance, that your thesis is a statement of policy—a statement of the form "We should do X":

- We should allow 24-hour visitation in the dorms.
- We should ban smoking in the classrooms.

Here you face goals, obstacles, and opportunities that are different from those you would face if your thesis were a statement of interpretation, one that made a claim about the nature or causes of some event or problem:

- The overall economic position of blacks has not improved very much in the last decade.
- Students today are much less career-oriented than they were a decade ago.

In one case you encourage people to *act* in a certain way; in the other you encourage them to *believe* in a certain way. Your own role as a writer is different in each case.

Where you stand in the overall process of decision making is equally important. If your thesis stands near the beginning stages of problem solving or decision making—where people are trying to understand the nature and causes of a problem—you have a task and situation that is different from those at the final stages—where specific solutions are being chosen and implemented. We can examine these areas separately by exploring first some different kinds of propositions and then the process of problem solving.

• Propositions: Basic Units of Deliberation

Some kinds of statement

A *proposition*—as opposed to a question, a command, or a greeting—is a statement that can be affirmed or denied. Propositions are the basic units of deliberation, serving either as the claims of argument or as the premises of argument. One of the most important things to understand about propositions is that they can perform different roles and say different things, even though they may look alike. A good way to remember this is to think about the ambiguity of the verb "to have." Examine the following sentences, and consider some of the differences in what they say.

1. George has a chainsaw.
2. George has a drinking problem.
3. George has an article in *Reader's Digest.*
4. George has great parties.
5. George has a mean streak.

If the differences among these propositions are not obvious to you, ask the question, "What does he do with it?" after each one. It becomes clear that the only one he can "do" anything with is the chainsaw. Only proposition 1 is about George's actually "having" or owning anything. Proposition 2 makes a statement about George's condition, while proposition 3 makes a statement about something George has done. Proposition no. 4 makes a statement about something George does regularly, and proposition 5 makes a statement about one of George's qualities or attributes.

There are many other ways propositions differ. Look at them in comparison with one another and ask, "What different kinds of statements do they amount to?" Consider, for instance, these two propositions:

1. San Diego is in southern California.
2. San Diego is a lovely city.

It's clear that proposition # 1 states a *fact* about San Diego, whereas proposition # 2 states a *judgment* about San Diego. This is an important distinction, and we will return to it later in this chapter.

"One of these things doesn't belong here"

One way to test and refine your understanding of different kinds of propositions is to play a game similar to the one played on *Sesame Street.* The name of the game is "One of These Things Doesn't Belong Here," and it's played by presenting a group of objects or pictures, several of which are equal but one of which is different. For instance, when presented with an apple, an orange, a banana, and a glass of milk, a child is expected to choose the glass of milk as "the thing that doesn't belong there." They are all types of food, but three of them are solid (fruits) and one is liquid (not a fruit).

Here is an example of the "One of These Things Doesn't Belong Here" game, using propositions. See if you can pick out the proposition that doesn't belong in each group before reading the answers that follow.

a. Bunker College has a 24-hour visitation policy in the dorms.
Bunker College used to have a 24-hour visitation policy.
Bunker College needs a 24-hour visitation policy.

b. Bunker College could have a 24-hour visitation policy if it wanted one.
Students at Bunker College would favor a 24-hour visitation policy.
Students at Bunker College should vote for a 24-hour visitation policy.

c. Dress codes are sets of rules dictating what the members of a group should wear at given times.
Dress codes are ways of governing the allowable range of variation in clothing for a given community.
Dress codes are ways of preserving power for school officials by stifling the creativity of students.

In group **a,** the proposition that doesn't belong is the last one, "Bunker College needs a 24-hour visitation policy." It amounts to a judgment about what ought to be done, whereas the other two are statements of fact.

In group **b,** all three statements are judgments rather than statements of fact, but the one that doesn't belong is the last, "Students at Bunker College should vote for a 24-hour visitation policy." The other two statements are interpretations or statements about probabilities. The third amounts to a recommendation, a statement urging that a certain action be taken.

In group **c,** the first two propositions are *definitions.* They explain the nature and purposes of dress codes. The third, while it may look like a definition, is really a judgment about dress codes, attributing covert motives to the enactors of dress codes and harmful effects upon those who are subject to them.

EXERCISE 3.1

Identify the proposition that "doesn't belong" in each of the groups of propositions below. Explain why.

A. Religion is an organized set of attitudes and practices centered upon belief in a supreme being.
Religion is the opiate of the people.—Karl Marx
Religion is the organized suppression of natural urges by a special ruling class of the spirit.
Religion: A daughter of Hope and Fear, explaining to Ignorance the nature of the Unknowable.—Ambrose Bierce

B. The cost of going to college has become unreasonable.
The cost of going to college is definitely worth paying.
The cost of going to college should be defrayed by state governments.

C. John F. Kennedy was the only Roman Catholic President.
Millard Fillmore was the only truly religious President.
Richard Nixon was the only Quaker President.

D. 50 percent of all married people are women.
All bachelors are unmarried.
50 percent of all bachelors have warts.

E. Small liberal arts colleges deserve to survive.
Small liberal arts colleges are in financial trouble.
Small liberal arts colleges are maintaining high enrollments.

Facts, definitions, and judgments

Although there are many ways to distinguish among propositions, the distinction between statements of *fact, definition,* and *judgment* is important to deliberation. The distinction helps you identify the kinds of questions that deliberation attempts to answer.

A statement or question of *fact* concerns the identity and simple attributes of something, and whether, where, or when something exists or has occurred. The following are statements or questions of fact:

1. Are there any mummies left in Egypt?
2. Who is Thomas Aquinas?
3. America withdrew its combat forces from Vietnam in the period, 1972–76.
4. Volkswagens have 4-cylinder engines.

A statement or question of *definition* concerns what something is and its special characteristics or functions. The following are statements or questions of definition:

1. What is the difference between murder and manslaughter?
2. A deliberative essay is one whose main purpose is to support a thesis about some human question or problem.
3. What is a constitutional monarchy?

A statement or question of *judgment* concerns arriving at a conclusion or making a decision about something. The following are statements or questions of judgment:

1. Should the makers of child pornography enjoy protection under the First Amendment guarantee of free speech?
2. American athletic contests are too dominated by the spirit of "winning is everything."
3. Passage of the Equal Rights Amendment is not likely to improve the status of women.

The distinction between statements of fact, definition, and judgment seems straightforward, but actually it is very tricky. Statements of fact and definition often shade into one another and into statements of judgment without changing their form. A statement may look factual but actually include definition and judgment.

Questions of fact shade into questions of judgment when they involve an element of conjecture. When all the facts of a situation are not known, we are forced to make certain assumptions or guesses which, along with factual evidence, serve as premises to conclusions about what actually happened or why it happened. All crime mysteries work this way, and attempts to predict the future involve a great deal of conjecture and assumption.

Statements and questions of fact can also overlap with those of definition and judgment when they use terms that are either evaluative or subject to different interpretations. Here are some statements or questions that look factual but which actually overlap with definition or judgment:

1. "George murdered his wife." This could be a statement of fact, but it could also involve definition. It could be that George *killed* his wife but that the killing did not constitute "murder" in the legal sense. He might have done it in self-defense, he might have been insane, or it might have been an accident.
2. "George is a rascal, and that's a fact!" Here the word "rascal" is judgmental. It does not refer directly to any concrete action or attribute.
3. "Is the United Kingdom a constitutional monarchy?" This could be a question of fact only if there is a common understanding of "constitutional monarchy." If so, the question is whether or not the United Kingdom's government was one of that type. If not, it becomes a question of definition as well.

Statements and questions of definition also overlap those of judgment when they use evaluative or controversial terms, such as "progressive," "democratic," "liberal," and so on. Think about how well these terms go with the word "truly" and you will easily see the point: "truly progressive," "truly democratic," "truly liberal." Such terms involve much more than definitions of things and actions; they involve **evaluations** and **ideals** that amount to judgments. This is not a bad or fallacious way of conducting deliberation; it is simply one of the ways that language works. It can be deceptive, and it can be used to deceive us, unless we learn to recognize it.

EXERCISE 3.2

Which of the following statements or questions most likely involve facts, and which overlap with definition and judgment?

A. George has sensitive teeth.

B. George has a "sweet tooth."

C. George has a sweet disposition.

D. George doesn't want his children to watch television.

E. God doesn't want His children to watch television.

F. George Washington was married to Martha Washington.

G. George Washington loved Martha Washington.

H. George has a drinking problem.

I. The governor decreed a state of emergency because of the severe rainstorms.

J. The governor remained single because he was afraid of women.

EXERCISE 3.3

Which of the following statements are straightforward definitions, and which overlap with judgment?

A. A Christian is one who believes or professes to believe in the teachings of Jesus Christ.

B. A Christian is any person who acts charitably toward other people.

C. A Christian is one who follows the teachings of Christ in so far as they are not inconsistent with a life of sin.—Ambrose Bierce

D. A country in which all governmental decisions are made by a single person is not a true democracy.

E. A country in which young people can be drafted into the army against their wills is not a true democracy.

F. Common sense is the backbone of our nation.

G. Common sense is the unreflective opinion of ordinary men.

H. The U.S. Military is a system of social welfare for the fighting class.

I. Language is the music with which we charm the serpents guarding another's treasure.—Ambrose Bierce

J. Language is a system of vocal signals organized toward the end of human communication.

What's worth arguing about?

People love to argue, sometimes just for the sake of arguing. Some arguments, though, are either unnecessary or futile. Two kinds of argument are almost always useless—those involving simple matters of *fact* and those involving personal *taste* or *subjective opinion.*

Sometimes people argue heatedly about who won the World Series in 1965 or how many people died in automobile accidents last year. Such episodes can be entertaining, but as arguments they are useless since they don't involve anything that really needs to be decided. A fact exists—just look up the answer. The same is true of simple equations. If the Yankees are four games ahead in the American League East, and if there is only one game left for each team to play, then there's no use arguing over who is going to win the division title.

Arguments over matters of personal taste are also a waste of time—there is no way of settling them and no reason to do so. Subjective matters such as what food tastes best, whose spouse is the handsomest, or which President had the most charm fall into this category. This can be a troublesome area, however. An important stage in deliberation involves a discussion about whether something is legitimately arguable or a matter of personal taste or opinion. For instance, opponents of legislation restricting prostitution, pornography, and the use of alcohol argue that these are matters of personal decision; but proponents of restricting legislation claim that they involve objective issues of public health and social order.

EXERCISE 3.4

Which of the following statements provide useful subjects of deliberation, and which do not?

A. By 1800 most large ports and commercial centers in the U.S. had daily newspapers.

B. Daily newspapers do a better job of covering the news than do the television networks.

C. Older men are more desirable to the opposite sex than older women.

D. Ice cream is hazardous to your health.

E. Ice cream is better than marijuana.

F. There are no poisonous snakes east of the Mississippi.

G. Taking a composition course is not necessarily the best way to learn to write effectively.

H. Whether or not to have an abortion is a woman's private decision.

I. Even if the Cubs win the rest of their games they cannot finish higher than third place in the league standings.

J. Walking fast is more enjoyable than jogging.

Values and metaphysics

Two kinds of propositions that can be especially problematic are value judgments and metaphysical judgments. *Values* are notions about what is good or bad, right or wrong; hence, a value judgment is a statement about inherent worth or rightness. The following are straightforward value judgments:

1. *Real Writing* is an excellent textbook.
2. It is immoral to smoke while standing up.
3. Sir Laurence Olivier is a superb actor.

Metaphysical literally means "beyond the physical," and it is sometimes used to describe statements referring to abstract, non-physical concepts such as "God," "Beauty," "Truth," and so on. Metaphysical judgments cannot be confirmed or denied on the basis of factual evidence. The following are straightforward metaphysical judgments:

1. God is an infinite being.
2. Only material things have reality.
3. All men are created equal.

Some claim that value or metaphysical judgments are not worth arguing about because they are inherently subjective and nonfactual. We do accept or reject some statements on the basis of faith or intuition. "There is but one God" and "All humans have the right to liberty" fall into this category. But not all value judgments or metaphysical claims are totally subjective. Arguments in general are not based on facts, strictly speaking, but on premises. Obviously, facts alone cannot prove it is wrong to steal someone else's property. But if your audience accepts the premise that everyone has a right to own property, then you can make a case against stealing as a violation of that right.

The usefulness of an argument depends on the kind of community the argument is taking place in. What premises are accepted or established within that community? An argument about whether miracles exist, for instance, is worthwhile only within a community that had some common understandings of religious belief. You can argue value judgments, but you have to base your arguments on common agreements about what is true and false, good and bad. And you have to know your audience.

EXERCISE: 3.5

What general agreements would have to be established before arguing for the following propositions?

A. *Gone With the Wind* is an immoral movie.

B. Abortion is the same thing as murder.

C. It is a sin to eat mashed potatoes.

D. You shouldn't eat mashed potatoes because it is such a middle-class thing to do.

E. Honors programs should be abolished because they are elitist.

• Three Kinds of Theses: Interpretation, Value, Policy

You already know that a *thesis* is the principal claim an essay makes. This claim is the central proposition of the essay, the one which everything else helps support. In most deliberative essays the thesis fits into one of three basic categories—interpretation, value, or policy. Although an essay contains more than one type of proposition, the thesis proposition leads the way and determines the direction of the entire essay.

Theses of *interpretation* are judgments about what is true, what is meant or signified, why some things happen, and what may happen in the future. Essays that answer the following questions contain theses of interpretation:

1. Has the study of foreign language declined in schools and colleges in the last twenty years?
2. Why has the study of foreign languages declined?
3. Do average, educated Americans drink more than they used to? Why?

Theses of *value,* again, are judgments about what is good or bad, right or wrong. Essays that answer the following questions contain theses of value:

1. Is stealing sometimes justified?
2. Is *Mr. Rogers' Neighborhood* a good television program for children?
3. Are Americans too concerned with individual rights and freedoms?

Theses of *policy* are judgments about what actions should be taken or what plans or rules should be adopted. Essays that take stands on the following questions contain theses of *policy:*

1. If men are drafted into the military, should women also be drafted?
2. Should your college allow 24-hour visitation in the dormitories?
3. Should all freshman students be required to take English composition?

Like the earlier distinction between facts, definitions, and judgments, the distinction between theses of interpretation, value, and policy can be a tricky one. Here too, the different kinds of statement overlap with one another under some circumstances.

Theses of interpretation overlap with theses of value when there is implicit approval or disapproval in the findings. The conclusion, for instance, that the study of foreign language has declined over the last twenty years implies dismay over the situation, unless accompanied by a statement disclaiming approval or disapproval. Theses of interpretation also become evaluations when they deal with judgmental designations or definitions. The claim that a certain condition was caused by "negligence" clearly involves a negative evaluation.

Theses of value overlap with policy statements when they involve implicit recommendations for action. The claim that President X was a better statesman than President Y does not imply any such recommendation; but the claim that Candidate X is a better statesman than Candidate Y does. The judgment that court-ordered busing to achieve racial balance in the schools has not been successful overlaps with a policy thesis by implying that the practice should be changed or abandoned.

The distinction between interpretation, value, and policy is a valuable one because it clarifies the functions of whole deliberative essays. A single deliberative essay stands primarily as an interpretation, an evaluation, a statement of values, or a recommendation. When you write a deliberative essay, know "where you stand." This gives you a clearer perspective on what you need to accomplish and how to accomplish it.

EXERCISE 3.6

Make a list of the essays you have read so far in this book or in your course. For each one, indicate whether it concerns a judgment of interpretation, value, or policy.

EXERCISE 3.7

The following questions are from the headings for a book of essays on American government by Herbert M. Levine. Indicate whether essays attempting to answer these questions are statements of interpretation, value, or policy. What areas of crossover might exist?

A. Does a power elite prevent the people from ruling in the U.S.?

B. Can the United States engage in covert operations abroad and still be considered a democracy?

C. Did the founding fathers believe in democracy?

D. Will the Equal Rights Amendment improve the rights of women?

E. Do the television media distort the news?

F. Are there significant differences between the Democratic party and the Republican party?

G. Should we abolish the electoral college?

H. Are strong presidents desirable in the American political system?

I. Is the U.S. defense establishment strong enough to cope with Soviet military threats?

J. Do quota systems deny constitutional rights under the Equal Protection clause?

• Where Essays Stand: The Process of Problem Solving

Kinds of theses

Again, by distinguishing whether your essay deals primarily with a question of interpretation, value, or policy, you can understand where it stands. A way of strengthening this understanding is to relate it to the larger process of deliberation. When you do, you see the specific kind of contribution your essay can make. Good deliberative writers do this almost through intuition.

Sharpen your own intuitions about the larger process of deliberation by viewing it as a system for solving problems. Deliberative writing is usually about problems of various sorts. For instance, the purpose of a deliberative essay may be any of the following:

- to call attention to a serious problem;
- to correct misunderstandings about a problem;
- to examine the causes of a problem;
- to propose a solution to a problem;
- to argue against a proposed solution to a problem;
- to take sides on alternate solutions to a problem.

There are other possibilities, but you can view the individual essay as part of a process of problem solving that has three distinct stages. These stages relate to the three types of theses already identified:

1. Identifying and understanding the problem
   (Theses of Interpretation)
2. Establishing goals
   (Theses of Value)
3. Finding and testing solutions
   (Theses of Policy)

This set of connections is an oversimplification, but it is a good place to start. Use the following expanded model of problem solving (adapted from an article by Richard L. Larson) to examine your subject and understand where your essay stands.

The Stages of Problem Solving

Stage I: Identifying and Understanding the Problem

1. What exactly is the problem? What undesirable condition or conflict exists?
2. What are the causes of the problem? Is it a new problem or an old problem? Are there other problems like it, or is it unique?
3. How serious is the problem in relation to other problems?
4. Is this problem a basic problem, in the sense that its solution would lead to the solution of some other problems? Or is it really less important—the symptom of a larger problem?

Stage II: Establishing Goals

5. What goals and values must be served and adhered to by any solution that is offered? Are there conflicting goals? In general, what kind of solution would be acceptable?
6. If there are multiple or conflicting goals, which of these are more important? What priorities should be followed?

Stage III: Finding and Testing Solutions

7. What can we do to solve the problem?
8. What would be the results? Would a proposed solution succeed? What further problems might be caused by a particular solution?
9. Should we or should we not adopt a proposed solution? If there are multiple solutions, which are likely to be the most powerful?
10. How should an adopted solution be implemented? What procedures and safeguards should be instituted?

EXERCISE 3.8

Following are 10 deliberative statements. To what stage of the problem-solving process, as outlined in the model above, does each seem most closely related?

Example: "24-hour visitation in the dormitories would cause difficulties that outweigh the benefits." This statement relates most closely to III.8, "What further problems might be caused by a particular solution?"

A. Any solution to the energy crisis must be one that does not cause undue hardship to any particular region of the country.

B. The reason we have a shortage of oil is that we have been keeping the cost of gasoline and heating fuel artificially low.

C. We'll never solve the problem of inflation unless we first do something about the energy problem.

D. Although higher taxes on gasoline would reduce fuel consumption significantly, they would wreck the economy, and they would work undue hardships on the poor and elderly.

F. The distrust of government that so many legislators are worried about is not something that can be changed overnight; it is part of a larger distrust of all formal institutions.

F. *Gone With the Wind* is an immoral movie.

G. *Gone With the Wind* may be immoral in some sense, but certainly not to the extent that anyone should pay much attention to it.

H. The practice of child labor is still shockingly prevalent in the world today.

I. The President should impose gasoline rationing immediately.

J. Wage-price controls have never been effective and they won't be effective now.

Uses of the problem-solving model

The actual process of deliberation and problem solving is not as orderly as the model implies. Sometimes, for instance, people submit proposals for action (III.7 in the model) long before there could be any policy decision. This is done as a means of inspiring discussion of the problem in general. Almost always, several stages of the process go on at once.

The problem-solving model can be useful to the deliberative writer in a number of different ways. Following are four of the most important ones.

First, the model is useful for identifying "where you stand" with a particular essay. What contribution to the overall process can your essay make? What larger question is your thesis related to?

Second, the model is an important tool for narrowing your topic. A single essay could take a reader through the whole process, from identification and definition of a problem to the proposal and testing of solutions. But usually an essay focuses on a particular stage, playing a specific role in the larger process of public deliberation. Individual essays could be generated from any of the ten questions.

Third, the model provides a useful guide for exploring your subject. If you are doing background reading or interviewing, it helps you find the most important questions to ask. And as you narrow down a particular piece of the problem for an individual essay, it helps you have a larger frame of reference.

Fourth, the model provides a useful tool for criticizing other essays and other points of view. It could improve on what they offer or even refute them. Remember that one of the most important sources of focusing events for a deliberative essay can be another deliberative essay.

Each of the ten questions of the problem-solving model provides a critical test:

1. Is the problem accurately described? Does it really exist? (Is there really a shortage of parking, for instance?)
2. Is the problem adequately understood? Is the author well informed about how the problem began?
3. Is the problem really as serious as the author claims or implies?
4. Is the author addressing the symptoms rather than the causes of the problem?
5. Does the author have a clear sense of what general goals should be met?
6. Does the author have a clear and accurate sense of the priorities among these goals?
7. Does the proposed solution really address the problem? Does it make sense just on the face of it?
8. Does a proposed solution fulfill all important goals? Will it work? Will it have ill consequences, create new problems of its own?
9. Are there better solutions than the one proposed?
10. Has an adopted solution been implemented properly?

EXERCISE 3.9

Think of a position on any subject with which you disagree. Referring to the list of questions above for testing other points of view, what precise points of disagreement can you identify?

ESSAY ASSIGNMENTS

1. Write a deliberative essay based upon exercise 3.9.

2. Write an essay in which you identify and stress the importance of some unrecognized problem that concerns a group that you identify with. Address your essay to members of the group.

3. Write an essay, addressed either to a general or a specific audience, about some problem or set of problems that you think is being approached in the wrong way. In your essay, point out what is wrong with the approach, and then outline what you believe to be a more effective approach.

4. Write an autobiographical essay that focuses upon some important problem in your life and how you solved, are solving, or failed to solve the problem. Assume an audience of peers who may have faced similar problems.

5. Write an essay in which, in the manner of Swift's "A Modest Proposal," (pp. 81–87) you offer a bogus and outrageous solution to a real problem for the purpose of making some satirical point.

Essays for Analysis

The Fat of the Land*

by Lionel Tiger

The focusing event of the first paragraph of this essay was President Jimmy Carter's criticism, at the time, of the tax-deductible "three-martini lunch," indulged in by businessmen. This essay first appeared in Newsweek, *July 2, 1979.*

1 President Carter should have complained not only about the three-Martini lunch but also about what frequently figures in this tax-deductible bill of fare: a thick, fat-marbled, tasty steak. Delicious, yes, but also injurious, because the dose of saturated fat and cholesterol the steak contains is not deductible.

2 I recently attended an international conference of the American Health Foundation on the cholesterol and lipid levels necessary to minimize the risk of coronary heart disease. The problem addressed is a grave one—underline, I'm afraid, grave. It is estimated that some 600,000 Americans die each year as a direct consequence of coronary heart disease, while at least 2 million suffer either temporary or lingering incapacity caused by malfunction of their circulatory systems.

3 A disconcertingly large proportion of the national health bill is devoted to the care of people whose hearts give way or give up. The cost in human carnage and suffering is enormous as well; about twice as many people die each year from heart problems as from cancer.

4 While the relationship between saturated fats and heart disease is a highly complex and controversial issue, an array of carefully controlled, long-term studies by scientists in many countries persuasively suggests that while diet is only one of a number of factors affecting the disease, it clearly *is* a factor. Because we can make real and quick choices about what we eat and what we feed our children it seems to me worthwhile to make these choices knowledge ably. This is not just a private matter, but a societal one too, acted out daily in the cafeterias of schools, the military and in restaurants. Therefore, we must

*"Fat of the Land" by Lionel Tiger from *Newsweek,* July 2, 1979.

enlist the strategists of the food and agriculture industries. And it would help if the nutritional puritans who hector us and make us feel guilty would instead provide straightforward information about what to eat and why.

Meat

5 How did the crisis emerge and what can we do about it? To understand the contemporary situation we must look to our evolution as an animal species. For millions of years our ancestors lived like other members of the primate kingdom, principally eating fruits and vegetables. Only in the past 3 million to 4 million years did we add meat, and our subsequent preference for it and associated animal and dairy fats appears to be a significant element in the medical problems we are now encountering.

6 Nature endowed us with the ability to savor a wide variety of foods. This omnivorous capacity has served us well, contributing to our biological success as a species, because it enabled us to change our diet according to the available flora and fauna of a particular place and time.

7 In the remote past, we lived in small groups which cooperated to acquire and consume their food. Given the rigors of the hunt, it makes sense to suppose that an association was established between eating meat and feeling skilled and well-off. And when some 500,000 years ago we tamed fire and began to cook our meat, its attractiveness and digestibility were enormously enhanced.

8 We were "designed" to enjoy meat and need a certain amount of animal protein for our health. How much and what kind? Probably less than members of the rich societies now eat and certainly a different kind from what generally appears on our dinner plates. We simply eat far too little vegetables, fruits and grains, as a proportion of our over-all diet. There is a "protein mystique" in the culture and much of the protein we consume is high-fat, corn-fed beef which is critically different from the lean meat of the animals we hunted.

9 Our agricultural economy, our taste preferences, our notions of status foods and the convenience of meats, which in effect cook themselves in their own fat, are all attractive inducements to maintain the status quo. Can it be that that frequently dreaded solution to all our ills, government regulation, may be a necessary part of relieving our health burden?

10 For example, just as airlines were required to provide no-smoking areas for those who took seriously the Surgeon General's advice about the perils of smoking, perhaps they and others in the catering business should be obligated to provide low-calorie, low-cholesterol diets as a matter of course. An immediate first move would be to ask all such public providers of food to offer skim milk along with the "regular" high-fat-content variety. I, for one, would be persuaded of an airline's concern for its passengers' welfare if it advertised not that inevitable steak dinner, but food more appropriate to what we know about medical safety. And while airlines are happy to serve low cholesterol meals when these are ordered in advance, this is an unnecessary inconvenience to people who are simply trying to live healthily.

Challenge

11 Our concern must begin with children. Among kids aged 5 to 18, the cholesterol levels in the rich Western societies average between 160 and 180 milligrams, compared with 100 to 150 in many other areas on earth. It would be beneficial, probably necessary, to reduce these levels to 120 to 140 among our children to be able to achieve optimal levels for adults. This may seem difficult. Every parent knows how easy and gratifying it is to give children their favorite foods—hamburgers, French fries, ice cream, etc. Yet children should begin their eating careers relying on fruit as dessert, vegetables and low-saturated-fat foods as their basic diet. The restaurant industry, particularly in its fast-food incarnations, has been remarkably adroit at catering to the tastes of children—ill-advised tastes, it appears, given current medical understanding. The challenge is to restructure what is offered to children in these popular restaurants, as well as in school cafeterias, in order to reduce radically serum-cholesterol levels.

12 Among adults, there are some encouraging changes—*la cuisine nouvelle* or *cuisine minceur,* call it what you will, is a healthy effort to alter people's attitudes about what is acceptable to eat.

13 A more sensible approach to food appears to be gathering influence among the educated members of the rich societies—their coronary heart-disease rates have already begun to fall with relative rapidity. Nevertheless, the average level of blood cholesterol in affluent nations is still around 220. The reports presented at the American Health Foundation conference all agreed that 180 was the highest desirable level. Above that level the risk of coronary heart disease grows perceptibly and significantly—again, this is the major health problem in our society. There are steps we can take to solve it. Why not take them?

FOR DISCUSSION

1. This essay carries the reader through all three major stages of the problem-solving process. Referring to the detailed model on p. 75, identify various stages in the essay.
2. What particular cause does Tiger single out for treatment? Why does he concentrate upon this particular cause, even though he recognizes that it is only one of a number of causes?
3. How did the problem get to be a problem, by Tiger's account?
4. What specific goals does Tiger set for a solution to the problem? Are these goals realistic?
5. At one point Tiger calls for a restructuring of what is offered to children in fast-food restaurants. Is this a feasible solution? How might it be implemented? What further problems might be caused by this solution?

A MODEST PROPOSAL
For Preventing the Children of Poor People in Ireland from Being a Burden to Their Parents or Country, and for Making Them Beneficial to the Public

by Jonathan Swift

Jonathan Swift (1667–1745) was a famous pamphleteer and satirist in eighteenth-century England and Ireland. He was also a churchman, dean of St. Patrick's Cathedral in Dublin. His most famous work is Gulliver's Travels. *"A Modest Proposal" was first published and distributed as a pamphlet in 1729, in both Ireland and England. In the year before its publication, a famine in Ireland had aggravated the poverty caused partly by repressive English legislation and harsh treatment by English absentee landlords. These are the real targets of the essay.*

1 It is a melancholy object to those who walk through this great town or travel in the country, when they see the streets, the roads, and cabin doors, crowded with beggars of the female sex, followed by three, four, or six children, *all in rags,* and importuning every passenger for an alms. These mothers, instead of being able to work for their honest livelihood, are forced to employ all their time in strolling to beg sustenance for their helpless infants: who as they grow up either turn thieves for want of work, or leave their dear native country to fight for the pretender in Spain, or sell themselves to the Barbadoes.

2 I think it is agreed by all parties that this prodigious number of children in the arms, or on the backs, or at the heels of their mothers, and frequently of their fathers, is in the present deplorable state of the kingdom a very great additional grievance; and, therefore, whoever could find out a fair, cheap, and easy method of making these children sound, useful members of the commonwealth, would deserve so well of the public as to have his statue set up for a preserver of the nation.

3 But my intention is very far from being confined to provide only for the children of professed beggars; it is of a much greater extent, and shall take in the whole number of infants at a certain age, who are born of parents in effect as little able to support them, as those who demand our charity in the streets.

4 As to my own part, having turned my thoughts, for many years, upon this important subject, and maturely weighed the several schemes of other projectors, I have always found them grossly mistaken in their computation. It is true, a child just dropt from its dam, may be supported by her milk for a solar year with little other nourishment, at most not above the value of two shillings, which the mother may certainly get, or the value in scraps, by her lawful occupation of begging; and it is exactly at one year that I propose to provide for them in such a manner, as, instead of being a charge upon their

parents, or the parish, or wanting food and raiment for the rest of their lives, they shall, on the contrary, contribute to the feeding and partly to the clothing of many thousands.

5 There is likewise another great advantage in my scheme, that it will prevent those voluntary abortions, and that horrid practice of women murdering their bastard children, alas! too frequent among us—sacrificing the poor innocent babes, I doubt, more to avoid the expense than the shame—which would move tears and pity in the most savage and inhuman breast.

6 The number of souls in this kingdom being usually reckoned one million and a half, of these I calculate there may be about two hundred thousand couples whose wives are breeders; from which number I subtract thirty thousand couples, who are able to maintain their own children, although I apprehend there cannot be so many, under the present distresses of the kingdom; but this being granted, there will remain an hundred and seventy thousand breeders. I again subtract fifty thousand, for those women who miscarry, or whose children die by accident or disease within the year. There only remain an hundred and twenty thousand children of poor parents annually born: The question therefore is, How this number shall be reared, and provided for? which, as I have already said, under the present situation of affairs, is utterly impossible by all the methods hitherto proposed; for we can neither employ them in handicraft or agriculture; we neither build houses (I mean in the country) nor cultivate land: They can very seldom pick up a livelihood by stealing till they arrive at six years old, except where they are of towardly parts, although, I confess, they learn the rudiments much earlier; during which time they can however be properly looked upon only as *probationers;* as I have been informed by a principal gentleman in the county of Cavan, who protested to me, that he never knew above one or two instances under the age of six, even in a part of the kingdom so renowned for the quickest proficiency in that art.

7 I am assured by our merchants, that a boy or a girl before twelve years old is no saleable commodity; and even when they come to this age they will not yield above 3l. or 3l. 2s. 6d. at most on the exchange; which cannot turn to account either to the parents or kingdom, the charge of nutriment and rags having been at least four times that value.

8 I shall now therefore humbly propose my own thoughts, which I hope will not be liable to the least objection.

9 I have been assured by a very knowing American of my acquaintance in London, that a young healthy child well nursed is at a year old a most delicious, nourishing, and wholesome food, whether stewed, roasted, baked, or broiled; and I make no doubt that it will equally serve in a fricassee or a ragout.

10 I do therefore humbly offer it to public consideration that of the 120,000 children already computed, 20,000 may be reserved for breed, whereof only one-fourth part to be males; which is more than we allow to sheep, black cattle, or swine; and my reason is, that these children are seldom the fruits of marriage, a circumstance not much regarded by our savages; therefore one male will be sufficient to serve four females. That the remaining 100,000 may, at a

year old, be offered in sale to the persons of quality and fortune through the kingdom; always advising the mother to let them suck plentifully in the last month, so as to render them plump and fat for a good table. A child will make two dishes at an entertainment for friends; and when the family dines alone, the fore or hind quarter will make a reasonable dish, and seasoned with a little pepper or salt will be very good boiled on the fourth day, especially in winter.

11 I have reckoned upon a medium that a child just born will weigh 12 pounds, and in a solar year, if tolerably nursed, will increase to 28 pounds.

12 I grant this food will be somewhat dear, and therefore very proper for landlords, who, as they have already devoured most of the parents, seem to have the best title to the children.

13 Infant's flesh will be in season throughout the year, but more plentiful in March, and a little before and after, for we are told by a grave author, an eminent French physician, that fish being a prolific diet, there are more children born in Roman Catholic countries about nine months after Lent than at any other season; therefore reckoning a year after Lent, the markets will be more glutted than usual, because the number of Popish infants is at least three to one in this kingdom, and therefore it will have one other collateral advantage by lessening the number of Papists among us.

14 I have already computed the charge of nursing a beggar's child (in which list I reckon all cottagers, labourers, and four-fifths of the farmers) to be about two shillings *per annum,* rags included, and I believe no gentleman would repine to give ten shillings for the carcass of a good fat child, which, as I have said, will make four dishes of excellent nutritive meat, when he hath only some particular friend or his own family to dine with him. Thus the Squire will learn to be a good landlord, and grow popular among his tenants, the mother will have eight shillings net profit, and be fit for work till she produces another child.

15 Those who are more thrifty (as I must confess the times require) may flay the carcass; the skin of which, artificially dressed, will make admirable gloves for ladies, and summer boots for fine gentlemen.

16 As to our City of Dublin, shambles may be appointed for this purpose, in the most convenient parts of it, and butchers we may be assured will not be wanting, although I rather recommend buying the children alive, and dressing them hot from the knife, as we do roasting pigs.

17 A very worthy person, a true lover of this country, and whose virtues I highly esteem, was lately pleased, in discoursing on this matter, to offer a refinement upon my scheme. He said that many gentlemen of this kingdom, having of late destroyed their deer, he conceived that the want of venison might be well supplied by the bodies of young lads and maidens, not exceeding fourteen years of age, nor under twelve, so great a number of both sexes in every country being now ready to starve, for want of work and service: and these to be disposed of by their parents if alive, or otherwise by their nearest relations. But with due deference to so excellent a friend, and so deserving a patriot, I cannot be altogether in his sentiments; for as to the males, my

American acquaintance assured me from frequent experience that their flesh was generally tough and lean, like that of our schoolboys, by continual exercise, and their taste disagreeable, and to fatten them would not answer the charge. Then as to the females, it would, I think with humble submission, be a loss to the public, because they soon would become breeders themselves: And besides, it is not improbable that some scrupulous people might be apt to censure such a practice (although indeed very unjustly) as a little bordering upon cruelty, which, I confess, hath always been with me the strongest objection against any project, however so well intended.

18 But in order to justify my friend, he confessed that this expedient was put into his head by the famous Psalmanazer, a native of the island Formosa, who came from thence to London, above twenty years ago, and in conversation told my friend that in his country when any young person happened to be put to death, the executioner sold the carcass to persons of quality, as a prime dainty, and that, in his time, the body of a plump girl of fifteen, who was crucified for an attempt to poison the emperor, was sold to his Imperial Majesty's Prime Minister of State, and other great Mandarins of the Court, in joints from the gibbet, at four hundred crowns. Neither indeed can I deny that if the same use were made of several plump young girls in this town, who, without one single groat to their fortunes, cannot stir abroad without a chair, and appear at the playhouse, and assemblies in foreign fineries, which they never will pay for, the kingdom would not be the worse.

19 Some persons of a desponding spirit are in great concern about that vast number of poor people, who are aged, diseased, or maimed, and I have been desired to employ my thoughts what course may be taken to ease the nation of so grievious an encumbrance. But I am not in the least pain upon that matter, because it is very well known that they are every day dying, and rotting, by cold, and famine, and filth, and vermin, as fast as can be reasonably expected. And as to the younger labourers they are now in almost as hopeful a condition. They cannot get work, and consequently pine away for want of nourishment, to a degree, that if at any time they are accidentally hired to common labour, they have not strength to perform it; and thus the country and themselves are happily delivered from the evils to come.

20 I have too long digressed, and therefore shall return to my subject. I think the advantages by the proposal which I have made are obvious and many, as well as of the highest importance.

21 For first, as I have already observed, it would greatly lessen the number of Papists, with whom we are yearly over-run, being the principal breeders of the nation, as well as our most dangerous enemies, and who stay at home on purpose with a design to deliver the kingdom to the Pretender, hoping to take their advantage by the absence of so many good Protestants, who have chosen rather to leave their country than stay at home, and pay tithes against their conscience to an Episcopal curate.

22 Secondly, The poor tenants will have something valuable of their own,

which by law may be made liable to distress and help to pay their landlord's rent, their corn and cattle being already seized, and *money a thing unknown.*

23 Thirdly, Whereas the maintenance of 100,000 children from two years old and upward, cannot be computed at less than 10s. a-piece *per annum,* the nation's stock will be thereby increased £50,000 *per annum,* beside the profit of a new dish introduced to the tables of all gentlemen of fortune in the kingdom who have any refinement in taste. And the money will circulate among ourselves, the goods being entirely of our own growth and manufacture.

24 Fourthly, The constant breeders beside the gain of 8s. sterling *per annum* by the sale of their children, will be rid of the charge of maintaining them after the first year.

25 Fifthly, This food would likewise bring great custom to taverns, where the vintners will certainly be so prudent as to procure the best receipts for dressing it to perfection, and consequently have their houses frequented by all the fine gentlemen, who justly value themselves upon their knowledge in good eating; and a skilful cook who understands how to oblige his guests, will contrive to make it as expensive as they please.

26 Sixthly, This would be a great inducement to marriage, which all wise nations have either encouraged by rewards or enforced by laws and penalties. It would increase the care and tenderness of mothers toward their children, when they were sure of a settlement for life to the poor babes, provided in some sort by the public, to their annual profit instead of expense. We should see an honest emulation among the married women, which of them would bring the fattest child to the market. Men would become as fond of their wives during the time of their pregnancy as they are now of their mares in foal, their cows in calf, their sows when they are ready to farrow; nor offer to beat or kick them (as is too frequent a practice) for fear of a miscarriage.

27 Many other advantages might be enumerated. For instance, the addition of some thousand carcasses in our exportation of barreled beef, the propagation of swine's flesh, and improvement in the art of making good bacon, so much wanted among us by the great destruction of pigs, too frequent at our table; which are no way comparable in taste or magnificence to a well-grown, fat, yearling child, which roasted whole will make a considerable figure at a lord mayor's feast or any other public entertainment. But this and many others I omit, being studious of brevity.

28 Supposing that 1,000 families in this city would be constant customers for infants' flesh, besides others who might have it at merry-meetings, particularly at weddings and christenings, I compute that Dublin would take off annually about 20,000 carcasses; and the rest of the kingdom (where probably they will be sold somewhat cheaper) the remaining 80,000.

29 I can think of no one objection that will possibly be raised against this proposal, unless it should be urged that the number of people will be thereby much lessened in the kingdom. This I freely own, and it was indeed one principal design in offering it to the world. I desire the reader will observe, that

I calculate my remedy for this one individual *Kingdom of Ireland and for no other that ever was, is, or I think ever can be upon earth.* Therefore let no man talk to me of other expedients: *of taxing our absentees at 5s. a pound: of using neither clothes nor household furniture except what is of our own growth and manufacture: of utterly rejecting the materials and instruments that promote foreign luxury: of curing the expensiveness of pride, vanity, idleness, and gaming in our women: of introducing a vein of parsimony, prudence, and temperance: of learning to love our country, in the want of which we differ even from Laplanders and the inhabitants of Topinamboo: of quitting our animosities and factions, nor acting any longer like the Jews, who were murdering one another at the very moment their city* was taken: of being a little *cautious not to sell our country and conscience for nothing: of teaching landlords to have at least one degree of mercy toward their tenants: lastly, of putting a spirit of honesty, industry, and skill into our shopkeepers; who, if a resolution could now be taken to buy only our native goods, would immediately unite to cheat and exact upon us in the price, the measure, and the goodness, nor could ever yet be brought to make one fair proposal of just dealing, though often and earnestly invited to it.*

30 Therefore I repeat, let no man talk to me of these and the like expedients, till he has at least some glimpse of hope that there will be ever some hearty and sincere attempt to put them in practice.

31 But as to my self, having been wearied out for many years with offering vain, idle, visionary thoughts, and at length utterly despairing of success, I fortunately fell upon this proposal, which as it is wholly new, so it hath something solid and real, of no expense and little trouble, full in our own power, and whereby we can incur no danger in disobliging England. For this kind of commodity will not bear exportation, the flesh being of too tender a consistence, to admit a long continuance in salt, *although perhaps I could name a country, which would be glad to eat up our whole nation without it.*

32 After all, I am not so violently bent upon my own opinion, as to reject any offer, proposed by wise men, which shall be found equally innocent, cheap, easy, and effectual. But before something of that kind shall be advanced in contradiction to my scheme, and offering a better, I desire the author or authors, will be pleased maturely to consider two points. *First,* as things now stand, how they will be able to find food and raiment for a hundred thousand useless mouths and backs. And *Secondly,* there being a round million of creatures in human figure throughout this kingdom, whose whole subsistence put into a common stock would leave them in debt two millions of pounds sterling, adding those who are beggars by profession, to the bulk of farmers, cottagers and labourers, with their wives and children, who are beggars in effect; I desire those politicians, who dislike my overture, and may perhaps be so bold to attempt an answer, that they will first ask the parents of these mortals, whether they would not at this day think it a great happiness to have been sold for food at a year old, in the manner I prescribe, and thereby have avoided such a perpetual scene of misfortunes as they have since gone through,

by the oppression of landlords, the impossibility of paying rent without money or trade, the want of common sustenance, with neither house nor clothes to cover them from the inclemencies of the weather, and the most inevitable prospect of entailing the like, or greater miseries, upon their breed for ever.

33 I profess in the sincerity of my heart, that I have not the least personal interest in endeavouring to promote this necessary work, having no other motive than the *public good of my country, by advancing our trade, providing for infants, relieving the poor, and giving some pleasure to the rich.* I have no children by which I can propose to get a single penny; the youngest being nine years old and my wife past child-bearing.

FOR DISCUSSION

1. This essay is a famous example of how the problem-solving process, as well as the classical scheme of arrangement (see Chapter Two), can be turned into a "special strategy of presentation." The essay is highly entertaining, but it makes a serious point as well. What do you think Swift hoped to gain by presenting matters in this way?
2. This kind of special strategy may be more effective in some situations than others. Can you generalize about the kind of situation in which such a strategy can be most effective?
3. Refer to item #5 in the problem-solving model on page 75. What goals does this essay set forth as requirements of any particular solution?
4. Swift does something interesting with the Concession/Refutation section of this essay. What is it?
5. What is the author's image in this essay?
6. In paragraph 17 the author rejects the notion of slaughtering and eating teenagers, on the grounds that the practice might be criticized as "a little bordering upon cruelty." What strategy of ordinary deliberation does this passage mimic? What is its actual effect in this context?

Student Essay: Old News and New Problems: No Changes in Format, Please

by Lisa Brown

The Carolinian *is the student newspaper at UNC-Greensboro, and its editor is chosen by general election.*

1 Almost annually, it seems, around election time, one or more of the candidates for Editor of *The Carolinian* propose changes in format for the

paper. Sometimes these changes seem reasonable enough, but in some cases the proposals are simply not very well thought out. This is certainly the case with what seems to be the most popular suggestion, that of changing *The Carolinian's* format to tabloid. The present staff of *The Carolinian* would do well to study any changes suggested by whoever is elected editor, as the staff was forced to do last year at this time.

2 Most of us working at *The Carolinian* last spring had never considered the possibility of changing the paper's format. However, we were forced to consider it when one candidate for the editorship promised that, if elected, he would push to change the paper from the standard twice-weekly broad format to a once-weekly tabloid. After some thought and experimentation, those of us on the staff realized the shortcomings of the proposed change. It was obvious that a once-weekly tabloid paper would reduce advertising potential, allow less flexibility in layout, and aggravate the ever-present problem of printing old news.

3 The person who proposed the change felt that the new arrangement would ease the staff's extracurricular workload and make a more readable, more convenient size of newspaper. There is little doubt that it would do that, but one wonders, in light of all the other difficulties we face, if these are really problems worth addressing at this school. Staff members do complain rather persistently about the amount of time they're spending on the newspaper; but the fact that nearly all of them last year were opposed to the change should tell you how important that problem really is. All the staff members are paid, many are getting valuable experience for careers in journalism, and few would be willing to scrap a whole issue per week in exchange for the time that would be saved. As for the convenience of the format, this is really a problem for big-city newspapers, where many of the readers are mass-transit commuters, or where the papers themselves have to be bundled and shipped over long distances. It's simply no issue for a campus newspaper.

4 The changeover to tabloid, while not solving any important problems, would create some new ones—problems of printing old news, of training people in a new format, and of advertising.

As a twice-weekly paper, we cannot even now avoid printing *some* old news. If something newsworthy happens on campus on a Thursday, it won't appear in print until the next Tuesday. Wouldn't it be a good deal worse if there were a whole week between printings? Actually, we would be reduced to a sort of announcement sheet.

5 There would be a layout problem as well. Layout is not an easy task for the beginner. It is certainly well and good for students to sharpen layout skills as much as possible, but they shouldn't be expected to begin their training with a difficult format. With a tabloid-size paper, the more highly skilled students would probably end up doing layout every time, and the beginners might be discouraged from ever learning.

6 What makes the tabloid format so much more difficult? There are more pages in a tabloid paper, and the pages are smaller. This means that oftentimes

an article will have to be continued on a back page, and an excess of "continued" articles is very confusing for the people who must lay the things out.

7 Even more importantly, a tabloid-size paper makes advertising more difficult than it has to be. With a broad format, an ad salesman can place a full-page ad for a substantial sum of money—sometimes on a continuing basis, as *The Carolinian* has done with several beer distributers. With a tabloid paper, however, the unfortunate ad salesman would have to sell *two* full-page ads (perhaps to two different businesses) to make as much money and take up as much space as one full-page ad in a broad format.

8 And what if the advertiser did happen to buy a two-page spread? The paper would still come out once a week. In order to match the ideal advertising capability of the present format—a full page in each issue is the most that can be reasonably expected—the advertiser would have to buy *four* full pages in the tabloid paper each week. It is almost absurd to hope for such a thing.

9 There is a final, less tangible problem. Psychologically, the changeover to tabloid would make *The Carolinian* seem to be a kind of *National Enquirer* scandal sheet rather than a respectable newspaper. The tabloid format is usually reserved for magazines or magazine-type publications. Most newspapers just aren't done that way, and the format really might have a negative effect on attitudes towards *The Carolinian* as a "real" paper (a status that is not always granted this student publication as it stands).

10 Most of us at *The Carolinian* were quite relieved when the candidate who had proposed the tabloid format lost the election, although we realized that the issue would probably come up again this year. There are many areas where the newspaper could use improvement, but this is simply not one of them. We hope that this year's new editor will learn from last year's debate. Changes come best in small doses, and only when they are truly needed.

FOR DISCUSSION

1. Is this essay's thesis one of policy, value, or interpretation?

2. Look again at the problem-solving model on p. 75. What particular points are touched upon most persistently in this essay?

3. This essay does not contain a Concession/Refutation section. Does it need one?

4. Look at the list of questions, on p. 77, for critiquing proposed solutions to problems. Which of these does the author of this essay use?

4 Problems of Policy: What Shall We Do?

Chapter Overview

This chapter introduces the process of deliberating about policies. The model for solving problems, from the previous chapter, will contribute to the discussion since we are dealing with some real or potential difficulty in a community. Issues and strategies in this kind of deliberation are the need for change, the causes and cures of problems, and the acceptability of policies.

• What Is Policy Deliberation?

In any community, decisions have to be made about matters of policy—whether or not to build this bridge, close that school, pass this ordinance. In some cases these decisions are made by public referendums; in other cases they are made by executives (presidents, deans, managers) or executive committees, after hearing opinions from experts and interest groups.

In either case, the process of deliberation is vital in two ways. First, it helps insure that the best possible decisions are made; all sides are heard and all options are considered. Second, it helps build public support for whatever policy eventually is adopted; it enlightens the public about problems and solutions and allows individuals and groups to contribute to the effort.

A tenet of our democratic heritage is that educated and concerned citizens have the responsibility to participate in this process of deliberation. You do not have to be an expert or a technical wizard, although you should be as well informed as possible about your subject. However, your ability to reason, your common sense, and your sense of morality are equally important. Also important is your understanding of the way in which all of these things come together in a situation that calls for deliberative writing.

Matters of policy include proposals and decisions about what actions to take, what procedures to follow, or what rules govern these actions and procedures. The examples and explanations in this chapter concern the actions taken or procedures adopted by communities of people—towns, universities, states, clubs—any group of people, formally organized or not, who have some common interest or purpose. However, the basic principles and strategies of policy deliberation can apply to personal decisions as well, particularly where a variety of factors are taken into account.

Consider the question of whether or not to use drugs or alcohol. An essay on the morality of the practice would fall under the heading of values deliberation rather than policy, and it would use the special principles and strategies of values deliberation (see Chapter 5). However, an essay which considered the question from different angles—the costs, benefits, and dangers, as well as the moral question—would be a policy statement and would use the strategies of policy deliberation.

In most controversies about personal conduct there is disagreement over how much weight should be given to practical and situational considerations, as opposed to moral ones. Often the two kinds of considerations cannot be separated. There are cases in which a practice is acceptable morally but inadvisable for practical reasons. There are opposite cases as well—a practice is wrong morally but necessary under certain circumstances, perhaps as the lesser of two evils. In any case, in order to consider personal conduct using the strategies of policy deliberation, your audience must agree that a variety of factors are important.

The direct focus of policy deliberation is usually on specific cases and decisions rather than general principles. Policy decisions usually answer specific questions, such as: "Should the federal government require auto makers to install air bags in all new automobiles?" The more general question—"Does the federal government have the right to interfere in the production and consumption of legal goods and services?"—is clearly related and would have to be considered in any thorough discussion of the air-bag question. There are other considerations as well, such as how effective the requirement would be in saving lives, whether it would create new problems, and what the alternatives might be.

EXERCISE 4.1

Turn back to Exercise 1.3 in Chapter 1, pp. 14–15. Do the exercise again, this time making each of your answers a hypothetical essay that contains a thesis of policy.

EXERCISE 4.2

Look back through all the essays reprinted in Chapters 1–3. Which are clearly policy essays?

EXERCISE 4.3

If you have read Jonathan Swift's "A Modest Proposal" (see Chapter 3), consider this question: What role does the relationship between moral and practical questions play in the essay? What use does Swift make of the potential conflict between the two?

• Some Types and Functions of Policy Deliberation

It may have occurred to you that the problem-solving model in Chapter 3, p. 75, relates directly to policy deliberation. It does, since most policies (actions or procedures adopted by communities and individuals) are designed to solve, prevent, or lessen the severity of problems. (It might be useful to review the various stages in the problem-solving model at this point.)

Although every stage of the problem-solving process is relevant to matters of policy, the set of questions given with Stage III, "Finding and Testing Solutions," is most useful to identify the specific functions that policy essays normally perform. A reprint of this section follows.

Stage III: Finding and Testing Solutions

7. What can we do to solve the problem?

8. What would be the results? Would a proposed solution succeed? What further problems might be caused?
9. Should we or should we not adopt a proposed solution? If there are multiple solutions, which are likely to be most powerful?
10. How should an adopted solution be implemented? What procedures and safeguards should be instituted?

The questions from this section of the model point to different types of policy essays and to the different functions that individual policy essays might perform. Here are some specific possibilities:

1. Propose a new solution to a well-known problem. Offer a new set of actions or regulations.
2. Emphasize the importance or severity of some problem and offer some tentative solutions.
3. Support or criticize a specific policy that has already been proposed. Either point to alternate solutions or make a case for no action being taken.
4. Make a case for one among a number of proposed policies.
5. Criticize an existing policy. Either call for a better policy or propose an alternate policy.
6. Defend an existing policy against criticisms.
7. Call for adjustments in an existing policy.
8. Call for better implementation of a current policy.

Identifying one point in the problem-solving process as the focus for a policy essay does not mean that you can ignore other points. In fact, you can build a case by referring to the other points. For instance, in making a case against a new policy—prohibiting alcoholic beverages in dormitories, for instance—you can locate points of weakness by asking these questions:

1. Is there a serious problem addressed by the policy? Is there any real need for a change?
2. Is the proposed policy based on an adequate understanding of the problem?
3. Are the goals of the proposed policy worthy ones?
4. Will the policy work? Will it fulfill its goals?
5. Are the costs too high? Will there be new problems as a result?
6. Are there alternate policies that would achieve the same results and be more acceptable?

By identifying a specific function associated with a specific stage of the problem-solving process, you give your policy essay a clear and manageable goal. You increase the possibility that your essay will be understood and appreciated.

• Basic Issues and Strategies in Policy Deliberation

Whenever a decision has to be made, a number of specific questions or disputes arise. The ways in which these questions are answered often determines the decision. These questions are known as *issues*—the important questions decisions are based on. One of your first jobs in policy deliberation is to discover what the most important issues are.

It is difficult to predict what the crucial issues are going to be for any particular policy question. Sometimes a single, overriding issue dominates. Other times a variety of issues are important. The process of deliberation itself may weed out or settle minor issues, leaving a few crucial ones to be settled; on the other hand, people often discover new issues along the way. And almost always, certain issues are more important to some groups and audiences than others. You have to assess the situation, exercising your judgment about what the important issues are, to you and to your audience.

Even though we can't predict the crucial issues, we can come up with a list of what the crucial issues might be. In writing an essay on a question of policy you can use this list to find issues. For any policy question, one or more of the following issues will be crucial:

1. The Need for Change
2. Cause and Cure
3. Workability and Feasibility of Policies
4. Acceptability of Policies
5. Available Alternatives

All policy deliberation begins with identification of a problem and establishment of a *need* for change. Then you can examine *causes* and suggest *cures.* These cures must be examined to see if they will *work* and if they can be *implemented.* To have any chance of being adopted, they must be *acceptable* to the community affected by them. Finally, *alternative* and *competing* cures must be compared and evaluated.

Once you find the important issues for your policy essay, devise strategies for dealing with them. Each of the five issues is discussed as follows.

The need for change

In policy argumentation, there is a maxim that, "Presumption rests with the *status quo.*" This means that if you're proposing a change, you have to show that there is a real need for change; the burden of proof is on you. There is a kind of built-in inertia and resistance to change in human affairs, a tendency to "leave well enough alone."

If you are not dealing with a threat (like open warfare or a tornado), most people will opt for "the way things are" (the *status quo*), unless they can be persuaded, through deliberation, that the consequences of not acting are more threatening than the disruption from a change. For instance, experts and political leaders have been exhorting us for years about the need for energy conservation. But not until recently were most Americans persuaded that the problem was real. It took several periods of long lines, shortages, and soaring energy prices to bring home the point that deliberation failed to make.

This built-in resistance to change is dangerous in many respects, but it is also a source of stability. Not all problems are as great as people think, especially in comparison with other problems. Any society or organization that tried to attend to everything at once—or to change too fast—would be a shambles. Sometimes things need to be changed, sometimes they don't, and sometimes they can't be changed. In any case, it is never enough for the proponents of change to say, "Well, why not?" If the need for change is not immediately apparent to your audience, you must demonstrate that need.

Cause and cure

Just as any call for change must come from a real and important problem, any persuasive proposal must be based on an analysis of the causes of the problem and the best ways of dealing with them.

In the simplest cases, the best solution is to remove the causes of a problem. If your car doesn't start easily, rides like a bucking horse, and stalls at every stop sign, you know you have a problem, and you begin to look for the cause. You (or your mechanic) checks the carburetor and gasline, and you don't find anything wrong. You check out the firing system, and you discover the probable cause—filthy and corroded spark plugs. The solution? New spark plugs. But suppose the spark plugs were changed last month? Now you've got a "real problem." You still need new plugs, but you also know that you're only treating the symptoms of the problem. If you don't find the real cause, you'll be spending a fortune for spark plugs and repairs for your car.

Or suppose you notice that the oil is low every several days of driving? Common sense tells you that just putting in more oil is no real solution, so you take it to a mechanic, who informs you that the engine seals and piston rings are shot. For $600 he can remove the causes of the problem with an engine overhaul. But you don't have $600 of ready cash, and besides, the car is already ten years old. Since treating the causes of the problem does not seem feasible, you are faced with a number of options:

1) Do nothing. Drive the car until it drops. A quart of oil every 200 miles is cheaper than the alternative. You wouldn't use up $600 worth in four years. You have bigger problems to worry about.

2) Alleviate the effects; muddle through. Change to a heavier grade of oil to keep it from leaking so fast. Buy it by the case at the discount store. Keep a bag of cat litter in the trunk to soak up oil spills on your friends' driveways. Drive less.

3) Revolutionize the system! a) Buy a new car. This is going to mean real hardship; it also means you'll have to postpone some other plans. But you just have to have reliable transportation and, besides, a new car will get much better gasoline mileage, need fewer repairs, and save you money in the long run.

b) (Even more revolutionary.) Forget about a car. Sell the car and buy a bicycle. Save some of the money for public transportation fares. Use the rest to buy gifts for all of your friends who own cars.

Unfortunately, the problems that we face are almost never simple. The causes of problems are varied and difficult to ascertain; even when they are properly understood, it is not always possible to do much about them. On the other hand, many problems do get solved, at least temporarily, and human beings have a remarkable capacity for muddling through. In any case, the alternatives are likely to be one of those already mentioned:

1. Eliminate the Cause
2. Alleviate the Effects
3. Do Nothing and Hope for the Best
4. Revolutionize the System

Not all of these options are available for every problem. In most cases there is a good deal of debate about which is the best alternative.

Workability and feasibility of policies

Any solution to a problem should have a chance of succeeding in one of the ways mentioned, and those who propose the solution must show that it will. There are three strategies for making a case for a solution:

1. Develop a Scenario
2. Find Similar or Analogous Cases
3. Consider Costs

Developing a scenario

A scenario is the plot of a story or a drama that hasn't been played out yet. When using a scenario as a strategy for your case, make a projection of what is likely to happen if your proposal is adopted. Emphasize the likelihood of a happy ending. If you are arguing against a proposal, develop a scenario that ends in, at best, no change, and, at worst, a catastrophe.

Finding similar or analogous cases
Two related kinds of arguments are possible in this strategy—the *argument by comparison* and the *argument by analogy.* We'll consider them separately.

Argument by comparison. Support your proposed policy by showing a situation where a similar policy succeeded. Conversely, you can make a devastating argument against a proposal by showing that it was tried somewhere and failed.

If City A is considering adopting an ordinance allowing drivers to turn right on red lights after coming to a full stop, proponents of the idea will be delighted to discover that City B, a town of similar size, passed the same ordinance two years ago with good results. There are fewer traffic jams, less air pollution from idling automobiles, and there has been no rise in the accident rate. No one has been killed or seriously injured as a result of the new policy. If the results were different, however, opponents would use the case as an example against the policy.

A defense against this kind of argument is to show that the cases are not as similar as they seem. In the instance of the "right-on-red" proposal, opponents might point out that City B had serious congestion problems to begin with, whereas City A does not. The thoroughfare system in City B is completely different from that in City A, and there are far more hazardous intersections in City A. On the other hand, if you support a policy that has failed previously, you can argue that the circumstances in your case are different. People weren't ready for it before and didn't give it a chance to work; special interests blocked it or incompetent administration corrupted it. Now, however, circumstances have changed.

Argument by analogy. In an argument by analogy you compare the situation and the proposed policy not to a situation with the same problem and solution but rather to a situation that is only similar in some way. For instance, some economists are fond of comparing the problem of inflation to a kind of sickness in which the patient (the economy) must take some bitter medicine (high unemployment, recession, cuts in social services) in order to recover. Opponents of the policies that lead to unemployment and cuts in social services point out that the analogy between inflation and the sick patient is very inexact—there is no single "patient" (the "economy" is an abstraction), and that the situation is more like asking some patients to get sicker so that others can recover.

Analogies can be powerful devices in deliberation. They dramatize complex problems, and they offer popular appeal, as when the relationship between businesses and regulatory agencies is referred to as an example of "foxes guarding the henhouse." Because analogies are inexact and can oversimplify matters, however, there is always a strong defense against them—they are inexact and they oversimplify.

Considering costs

Closely related to a policy's ability to work is its cost and what additional problems might be caused by implementing it. The $600 auto repair is a good example of a policy that will work but is too costly. The student essay in Chapter 2 pp. 36–38 argues against a proposal for 24-hour visitation in dormitories, on the grounds that the new policy would cause problems that outweigh the possible benefits. The basic argument, then, is that the costs of the policy would be too high.

Acceptability of policies

Ends and means

A policy may be both workable and feasible, in strictly economic or operational terms, but still be unacceptable because it conflicts with established beliefs, customs, or constitutional principles. It may do so in one of two ways.

First, the goals of the policy may seem wrong. For instance, almost everyone now regards segregation statutes, which for many years prevented black citizens from sharing the same public facilities with white citizens, as both unconstitutional and immoral. The same is true of child labor practices and any form of involuntary servitude.

Second, the means of attaining goals may seem wrong. The goals of Swift's "A Modest Proposal"—to reduce poverty in Ireland—are acceptable, but the means obviously are not. One solution to a group of health-care problems is for hospitals to refrain from using artificial life-support systems for all terminally ill patients. But this solution is not acceptable on ethical grounds for many people, and there are legal difficulties as well. A frequently proposed solution to the problem of teenage unemployment is to suspend minimum-wage laws in certain cases, thus allowing employers to hire more unskilled young people, giving them a chance to gain skills and employment experience. But this proposal is often resisted because of a general commitment to the notion of a "living wage" and also because of a fear of exploitative labor practices.

Argument by definition

When people argue for or against policies on the grounds of acceptability, they argue *by definition.* They are measuring proposed or existing policies against certain ideals or principles, often embodied in such terms as "fair," "equal," "democratic," "progressive," and so on. The term "exploitative labor practice" is an example. People who favor suspending the minimum wage laws would never respond to the charge of favoring the exploitation of workers by saying something like, "Well, what's so bad about exploitation when it produces results?" They would instead maintain that such a policy is not really "exploitative," though they would need a definition of "exploitation" that excludes reducing the minimum wage.

The argument might go like this:

> *Exploitation* in wage policies refers to the payment of wages that are disproportionately lower than the value of the services performed. But a reduced minimum wage for unskilled adolescent workers would not be *exploitation.* The fact that so many such workers remain unemployed is a sign that the current cost of their labor is actually higher than its value in the marketplace. Indeed, it is difficult to see how any system that would allow for the gainful employment of citizens who cannot otherwise find work could be called *exploitation,* unless there were a conspiracy among employers to keep the wages too low. We can prevent such conspiracies.

Available alternatives

Comparing policies

Finally, in order to make a successful case for a proposed policy, supporters must demonstrate that the policy is better than available alternatives. To make a case against the competition, you can argue in the following ways:

- Your proposal is based on a better understanding of the problem.
- Your proposal is more feasible, costs less, and involves fewer harmful side-effects.
- Your proposal is acceptable to more people, in accord with ethical and constitutional principles.

Suppose you favor taking no action at all. In this case, you might argue that the situation is uncertain now and that we should keep the options open. No one completely understands the problem yet; any immediate action may be rash. We should try to "buy time" or "muddle through" until the time is right or a more attractive alternative is discovered. *Look before you leap!*

But suppose you're on the other side of this question. You might argue for the urgency of the situation and warn of dire consequences if something isn't done soon. *He who hesitates is lost!*

The argument by division

One of the most effective strategies for weighing alternatives in policy deliberation is the argument *by division.* Reduce the alternatives to two or three, and discuss them, reserving your proposal to the end. Present this alternative as the best after exposing the defects of the other plans.

> There are three ways that we can solve the parking problem on this campus. The first, that of building more parking lots or garages, is simply not feasible. They are too expensive, and there is not enough land to build them on. The second, that of restricting parking on campus, would certainly reduce the severity of the

problem, but it is unacceptable. This university is committed to making higher education available to a wide range of traditional and non-traditional students, and as long as the automobile is the primary mode of transportation in this region we must accommodate it. The third solution, that of creating an efficient busing system from remote parking centers, is the most logical and feasible. It will be less costly than new parking garages, serve a larger number of people, and be only a little less convenient for most people.

"The Federalist," reprinted at the end of this chapter, is a classic example of the effective use of argument by division.

• Existing Policies: Some Lines of Attack and Defense

The discussion so far has focused on making cases for or against *proposed* policies. But the five basic issues we discussed apply to all policy situations, not merely to those involving new proposals. Here, in capsule form, are some of the strategic possibilities for deliberation about existing policies.

Attacking a Current Policy	**Defending a Current Policy**
1. The goals of the policy are unacceptable today, even though they may have been acceptable at one time.	**1.** The goals of the policy are valid, even though some people have supported it for the wrong reasons, or even though the results have not always been praiseworthy.
2. From the beginning the policy was based upon a flawed perception of the problem.	**2.** With all of its flaws, the policy remains the best long-term response to the underlying causes of the problem.
3. The policy was an adequate response to the problem at one time, but now the situation has changed.	**3.** Although the policy may need to be adjusted somewhat to account for changing circumstances, the basic plan is a good one.
4. The policy is no longer necessary.	**4.** If you think that the policy is no longer necessary, just consider these facts. . . . Then consider what might happen if the policy is rescinded.
5. The policy is not working. It has not achieved its goals.	**5.** There have been some problems in implementing the policy.

Slowly but surely the policy is working; it just needs more time.

The policy has been sabotaged by special interests.

Detractors have not given the policy a chance to work.

6. The policy is, or has become, too expensive. It is causing other problems that outweigh the benefits.

6. In the long run, this policy will be the least costly.

   Compared to the acceptable alternatives, the costs are not exorbitant.

   Although there have been some unfortunate side effects, it would be better to deal with these on a one-to-one basis than to abandon a policy that is working.

   It's a matter of commitment—some things are worth what you have to pay for them.

   We have no choice. This is what we have to do, no matter what the costs.

7. Although the goals of the policy are laudable, its methods conflict with basic values, rights, or principles.

7. We believe in these basic values and principles, but opponents of the policy are defining them too narrowly (or too loosely). Seen in the proper perspective, these methods are fully compatible with values and principles in question.

   Nothing is perfect. In any working situation there must be some compromise. The compromises in this case are not dangerous ones. Opponents are too idealistic.

8. There are better ways to do it.

8. In spite of the flaws in the current policy, there is no proof that alternative policies would be any better.

   It would be dangerous and costly to change things now.

• A Final Word About Narrowing the Topic

Some policy statements, such as those prepared by national commissions and study groups, attempt to cover all issues and alternatives in a single document. Such documents are often long and tedious. The usual process of deliberation resembles an on-going conversation more than a corporate effort. There are different arguments and issues from different individuals in separate statements or essays, and each makes a limited contribution to the overall discussion.

Think of your own policy essay as limited in this way. You don't have to cover every possible issue—although you should try to anticipate all objections in your pre-writing. Find those crucial issues that seem most relevant, and concentrate upon them. Let your essay serve a specific function.

EXERCISE 4.4

Place each of the following arguments under the heading of ***need, cause & cure, workability & feasibility, acceptability,*** **or** ***alternatives.*** **Also identify special arguments such as argument** ***by analogy, by comparison, by definition,*** **or** ***by division.***

A. Taxing corporate income is a convenient and popular means of collecting revenue. The unfortunate side effects of the tax, however, have led economists to question its value. By lowering the net return on investment, the tax may reduce expenditures for plant and equipment, and thereby slow economic growth.—"Abolish the Corporate Income Tax," *The New York Times*

B. A good tax system raises revenue with minimal impact on the behavior of individuals or businesses. The corporate income tax has no place in such a system.—"Abolish the Corporate Income Tax"

C. Reprinted from *U.S. News & World Report,* December 24, 1979: Few will quarrel with the idea behind the 1964 Wilderness Act—to protect from overzealous development the unspoiled gems of nature still remaining in this country. But when protecting land brings hardship to people who live nearby, who use the land and depend on it for their livelihood, perhaps it is time to take another look.—Marvin Stone, "Wilderness—and People." Copyright © 1979 by U.S. News & World Report, Inc. Reprinted by permission.

D. The men who framed the Constitution would never have tolerated pornography. Freedom of speech and press means the right to speak out on matters of political and public debate; it does not mean the right to open mental sewers. It is the right to "agree to disagree." It is not the right to disembowel the mind.—Don King, "Child Pornography and the First Amendment," Student Essay

E. The wholesale distribution of contraceptives by a social agency could well be construed as an enticement towards, or at least an endorsement of pre-marital sex by teenagers. One must take into account the perspective of the teenage girl who, in trying to decide whether to "do it," learns how readily available contraceptives are—and more importantly, that her parents need never know. That, I submit, is the clincher. I feel confident that if receiving contraceptives hinged on parental approval, more girls would resort to a more effective method of birth control—abstinence.—Michael Gough, "Parents, Children, and Contraception," Student Essay

F. We are going to make very little real progress in solving the problem of pollution until we recognize it for what, primarily, it is: an economic problem, which must be understood in economic terms. Of course there are *noneconomic* aspects of pollution . . . , but all too often, . . . secondary matters dominate discussion. Engineers, for example, are certain that pollution will vanish once they find the magic gadget or power source. Politicians keep trying to find the right kind of burearcracy. . . . But . . . all such approaches are bound to have disappointing results, for they ignore the primary fact that pollution is an economic problem.—Larry E. Ruff, "The Economic Common Sense of Pollution"

G. In contrast to the United States' penchant for [corporal punishment of school children], only West Germany and England retain corporal punishment in Western Europe. It is also outlawed in the Scandinavian countries, the Soviet Union and all other Communist bloc countries, Japan, Israel, and Jordan.

Indeed, foreigners . . . are appalled at such indices of American civilization as the practice in a section of rural Oklahoma. There children with learning disabilities are now being mainstreamed into "regular" classes and then are beaten daily for not keeping up. School officials helpfully point out that they not only whip for disciplinary purposes but also for "motivation."—Nat Hentoff, "Spare the Rod, Save the Child"

• Special Strategies of Presentation

In Chapter 1 we defined special strategies of presentation as methods of presentation that were different from the "normal" methods of argument. By "normal" we meant the orderly presentation of arguments, as if before an audience in a lecture hall. Essays that represent or contain special strategies of presentation are found throughout this book. Two such essays have already appeared—Ellen Goodman's "Participants, Not Patients" and Jonathan Swift's "A Modest Proposal."

In "Participants, Not Patients" the special strategy consists of focusing on the problems of one person, letting the reader draw conclusions about the general problem her case represents. In "A Modest Proposal," by contrast, British policies are criticized by what looks like straightforward argumentation in favor of an absurdly cruel proposal, highlighting the absurdity and cruelty of policies already in effect.

Swift's essay uses the special strategies of *satire*—criticizing practices or people by making them seem ridiculous—and *irony*—in which the reader understands that what is actually said is not really meant to be taken at face value. Both of these strategies are used in the following essay by Art Buchwald. It was originally printed in *The Washington Post,* in June, 1968. At the time there was a bill before Congress requiring the registration of firearms. The bill was being fiercely opposed by the powerful American Rifle Association, which was maintaining that registration violated the Constitutional principle of the "right to bear arms."

> "The Committee to Abolish the Registration of Automobiles and the Licensing of Drivers" has just opened up a lobby in Washington and I was happy to visit with Roger Crash, their spokesman.
>
> Mr. Crash said, "We have formed this organization because the constitutional rights of all automobile drivers are at stake. There is no reason why anybody should not be allowed to own and drive an automobile in this country without his rights being infringed by local, state and Federal authorities."
>
> "Obviously you're against registration of vehicles, then?"
>
> "We certainly are. Most people who drive should not be inconvenienced by some bureaucrat who wants to know what they intend to use a car for. There is a conspiracy in this country to get everyone to register their automobiles, so they eventually can be taken away from them."
>
> "Who is behind the conspiracy?"
>
> "The Communists. They know that America would collapse overnight if their automobiles were confiscated. This country is going through an hysterical period right now. They blame all the automobile deaths and accidents on the drivers. But you're not going to prevent accidents by asking people to register their vehicles. If somebody wants a car to kill somebody, he'll find it, no matter how many laws you have."
>
> "You're also against driver's tests, aren't you?"
>
> "We certainly are. Why should you penalize the law-abiding average driver by making him take a driver's test just to catch a few nuts who are outside the law?
>
> "By asking someone to take a driver's test, you are subjecting him to indignity and guilt by association. You cannot punish the car-loving citizen who only uses his automobile for pleasure, in order to prevent accidents caused by lawless elements of our society."
>
> "Mr. Crash, one of the arguments for registering automobiles and making people take a driver's test is that it prevents the vehicles from getting into the hands of children, criminals, and unstable people who might cause accidents."
>
> "The bleeding hearts and do-gooders use this argument all the time. But the automobile is part of our American birthright. Has it ever occurred to you that in every police state the dictators make their people register their automobiles and take driver's tests?"
>
> "Is your society for doing away with traffic laws as well?"
>
> "We are against anything that would inconvenience a driver in any way. People must be free to do what they want with their automobiles. Our economy

depends on motor vehicles. Every time you pass a traffic law you discourage someone from buying a car. Traffic laws do not prevent accidents, people prevent accidents."

"How do you propose to repeal the registration and driving test laws that are now on the books?"

"By launching a mammoth letter campaign. We're going to ask everyone who owns a car to write his Congressman and Senator demanding the repeal of all laws having to do with motor vehicles. This is an election year and I assure you, our legislators are paying attention to their mail."

"I must admit you make a strong case against automobile controls. Do you think you have a chance?"

Mr. Crash replied, "There is now a big hue and cry about automobile accidents in this country, but it will die down soon. And then our lobby will really be able to go into action. We're tax-free, you know."—"A Crash Program for the Right to Drive"

The intent of this "fake interview" is fairly obvious—to reveal the absurdity of the argument that registration will violate any essential right to bear arms. It relates the argument to a comparable situation—the registration of automobiles, which is widely accepted. In its own way, this essay amounts to an extended version of the argument *by analogy* (see pp. 97–98).

The potential advantages and disadvantages of special strategies are readily apparent. What you gain is the ability to make a point in an especially striking way. You give up the opportunity to present a thorough, rational case for or against something. There is also the possibility that the strategy might fall flat—readers might not find the presentation as amusing as you expect them to. But these strategies can work especially well in writing, as opposed to speechmaking. Don't be afraid to try them, especially in a composition course.

ESSAY ASSIGNMENTS

1. Explore a specific problem of a community, organization, or interest-group that you belong to. (Possibilities: school, student government, local community, church or synagogue, dormitory, apartment dwellers, fan club, composition class.) Assume that your audience is other members of that group, and write an essay that fulfills one of the specific functions listed on p. 93.

2. Criticize a current policy or state of affairs through the use of a mocking form such as the "fake proposal" (as in "A Modest Proposal," p. 81), the "fake interview" (as in "A Crash Program for Right to Drive," pp. 104–105), or a "fake defense" of the policy.

3. Develop a policy thesis about a personal decision or action. Discuss it from a social and pragmatic point of view as well as from an ethical one. Assume an audience of students on your campus.

Essays for Analysis

Let's Not Get Out the Vote

by Robert E. Coulson

Most Americans feel obliged to believe that everyone should get out and vote in every election, but rather large numbers of them don't bother to do so when the time comes. Robert Coulson suggests that this is not as catastrophic a fact as most people seem to think. This essay is as provocative today as it was in November 1955, when it first appeared in Harper's *magazine.*

1 Three years ago anyone who failed to vote had to face the combined scorn of both political parties, the schoolteachers, boy scouts, war veterans, chambers of commerce, and leagues of women voters. Last year bar associations, girl scouts, tavern keepers, President Eisenhower, radio and TV stations, and junior chambers of commerce joined the crusade. There is every prospect that in future elections, nonvoters will face jail sentences or fines, or be called to testify before investigating committees.

2 Before this happens, someone should come to their defense. Non-voters are often more intelligent, more fair-minded, and just as loyal as voters. The right not to vote is as basic as the right to. If voting is made a duty, it ceases to be a privilege.

3 Let's look at the voting behavior of Mr. and Mrs. Whipcord and Mrs. Whipcord's brother Harold, on the day of the local school-board election. Mrs. Whipcord says, "I have studied the candidates and have made up my mind. I will vote for Jones." Mr. Whipcord says, "I know nothing about the candidates or the issues. I will stay home, and allow the election to be decided by the votes of those who have made a study and formed an opinion." Harold says, "I don't know anything about the candidates or the problems, but by golly, I'm going to vote. It's my duty. I'll pick the fellows with the shortest names."

4 If there is a bad citizen among these three, which one is it? Whose procedure is least likely to bring good government to the school district?

5 Non-voting, multiplied by the thousands, is said to mean voter apathy, and this is supposed to be a sin. Have we lost our sacred American right to be apathetic? Suppose Mr. Whipcord studied the candidates carefully and

concluded that Candidate Jones was a boob and Candidate Smith was a thief. Is it un-American to refuse to choose between them? Or suppose he is satisfied that Jones and Smith are equally qualified, equally able, and that the school's problems are in good hands no matter which man wins. He is not apathetic; he is satisfied. Why should he be forced to choose between candidates on some esoteric basis?

6 The notion that "getting out the vote" makes for better election results is neither non-partisan, patriotic, nor logical. It is a device to favor the machines of both parties. It handicaps independent candidates, unfairly burdens the party in power, makes elections more expensive to conduct, greatly slows the tallying, and—worst of all—places the emphasis on the ritual of voting rather than the thought behind the vote.

7 If you fill in all the blank spaces on the ballot, the political machines will steal three-fourths of your vote. Let's see how this works, in a typical primary election.

8 Here are seven offices to be filled by nomination, with two or three candidates for each office. Citizen Stringfellow is interested in seeing Jones win for Auditor. He has no information about the candidates for Attorney General, Treasurer, Superintendent of Schools, or the others. He votes for Jones and then looks on down the list. He has been persuaded that it is his duty to vote for *somebody* for each office. So for six of the seven offices, he marks an X opposite the name best known to him, or the name on top, or the name suggested by his committeeman. These are machine candidates, and Citizen Stringfellow has given away six-sevenths of his vote.

9 After him, comes Citizen Stalwart, who knows the candidates for two of the seven offices. He also fills in all the blanks, letting the machine steal five-sevenths of his vote. One of his blind votes cancels out the intelligent vote cast by Citizen Stringfellow. At this rate, during a day's balloting, the candidates backed by the strongest machines with the biggest publicity budgets will win, even though not a single voter had an intelligent preference for them.

10 Is this what Thomas Jefferson had in mind?

11 "Getting out the vote" is always partisan. A calm and dignified effort benefits the party in power. An excited or hysterical effort benefits the party out of power. The Republicans were very happy to use the pressure of "neutral" groups in the 1952 elections. But they had better learn that this is a two-edged sword. Next time, the girl scouts, veterans' groups, radio stations, newspapers, and community funds may be out needling the Republicans with propaganda.

12 "Vote this time or your vote may be gone forever." "This may be your last chance." "Vote now or never." Anyone who is led to the polls by such arguments is going to vote against whoever brought us to the edge of this crevasse. As the pressure on the public increases, the party out of power is most likely to benefit in direct proportion to it.

13 All public-opinion surveys show that a certain proportion of the electorate has no opinion about many vital issues, does not know who is running for

office, and does not care. A gentle campaign to bring a submissive one-third of the apathetic sheep to the polls gets out a voting majority for the candidates who have had the greatest amount of publicity—who usually belong to the party in power. A rip-snorting effort to get out all the ignoramuses tends to turn them into the rebel column, and thus benefits the outs.

14 In either event, the girl scouts should wash their hands of it. The job of getting out the vote is a partisan effort which belongs to the professionals.

15 The silliest idea of all is the notion that it is un-American or unpatriotic not to vote. "A plague on both your houses" is a fair American attitude—all too often a logical one. Stupidity does not become wisdom by being multiplied.

16 In every election not more than one-third of the people care very much how it comes out. A certain percentage may have some sort of belief or opinion without feeling very strongly about it; another percentage may have studied the matter a little without forming an opinion; another percentage may not even have studied it; and so on, until we come to the people who are not even aware that an election is being held. The more we urge these people to clutter up the polling place, the more delay there is in voting, the more the cost of ballots and clerks, and the slower the returns.

17 If Candidate Jones would normally have won by 3,000 votes to 1,000, and we corral 10,000 more people into the polling places, won't Candidate Jones still win, by 8,000 to 6,000? Mathematically the last-minute coin flippers may make the election look close, but what patriotic purpose is accomplished?

18 And if the coin-flippers should happen to defeat the will of the informed majority, the cause of good government would emphatically not have been served.

19 Our city had a referendum recently in which the people voted for a tax increase to build an incinerator and against a tax increase to operate it. Every one of your communities has probably known referendums where the voters approved the bonds for a school but disapproved the sites, or voted for the site and against the bonds. All those voters who marked in opposite directions on the same afternoon were unwisely pressured into voting.

20 You have also seen primary elections where the boob with the catchy name ran away from the able man whose publicity was colorless. You have seen final elections where the straight party voters and the blank fillers smothered any discriminating choices which the thoughtful voters had made. You may have noticed with distress some of the undignified didos, cruel epithets, pompous verbosities, and Shakespearean gestures with which even good men become burdened early in their campaigns. All of these are caused in large measure by "get out the vote" efforts which emphasize putting a cross in half the squares.

21 Instead of urging people to vote, we ought to be urging them to study and form opinions. If thought and inspection of the candidates do not create a real desire to vote, then the citizen should be encouraged to stay at home on election day. A low vote is part of the public record and itself a significant

voter reaction which ought to be preserved. Maybe neither of the candidates was worth voting for.

22 Certainly the right to vote is important and should not be curtailed. A fool who is willing to walk all the way to the polling place should be given every freedom to record every stupid impulse he feels, for these will tend to cancel each other out. But no one should pretend that marking X in a square is any proof of patriotism or even intelligence. It is not your duty to vote, but, if you choose to, then it should be your duty to be intelligent about it.

FOR DISCUSSION

1. Look at the list of possible functions for policy essays on page 93. Which of these does Coulson's essay come closest to fulfilling?
2. Briefly look back at the section on "the author's image" in Chapter 1, pp. 22–23. What sort of image is Coulson projecting? How would you characterize the tone of the piece? Is this a successful strategy? Why or why not? (Consider especially the first three paragraphs, where the tone is established.)
3. After refreshing your memory on the basic issues and strategies listed and discussed on pp. 94–100 of this chapter, identify the basic issue and/or strategy evident in paragraphs 4, 5, 14, 19, and 20.

The Federalist: No. X

by James Madison

This essay is one of a series of essays designed to educate the public and urge adoption of the new Constitution of the United States. It is a classic example of rational argumentation and an enduring document in the theory of democratic government. The essay first appeared in The New York Packet *on November 23, 1787.*

TO THE PEOPLE OF THE STATE OF NEW YORK

1 Among the numerous advantages promised by a well-constructed Union, none deserves to be more accurately developed than its tendency to break and control the violence of faction. The friend of popular Governments never finds himself so much alarmed for their character and fate, as when he contemplates their propensity to this dangerous vice. He will not fail, therefore, to set a due value on any plan which, without violating the principles to which he is attached, provides a proper cure for it. The instability, injustice, and confusion introduced into the public councils, have, in truth, been the mortal diseases under which popular Governments have everywhere perished; as they continue to be the favorite and fruitful topics from which the adversaries to liberty derive their most specious declamations. The valuable improvements made by

the American Constitutions on the popular models, both ancient and modern, cannot certainly be too much admired; but it would be an unwarrantable partiality, to contend that they have as effectually obviated the danger on this side, as was wished and expected. Complaints are everywhere heard from our most considerate and virtuous citizens, equally the friends of public and private faith, and of public and personal liberty, that our Governments are too unstable; that the public good is disregarded in the conflicts of rival parties; and that measures are too often decided, not according to the rules of justice, and the rights of the minor party, but by the superior force of an interested and overbearing majority. However anxiously we may wish that these complaints had no foundation, the evidence of known facts will not permit us to deny that they are in some degree true. It will be found, indeed, on a candid review of our situation, that some of the distresses under which we labor have been erroneously charged on the operation of our Governments; but it will be found, at the same time, that other causes will not alone account for many of our heaviest misfortunes; and, particularly, for that prevailing and increasing distrust of public engagements, and alarm for private rights, which are echoed from one end of the continent to the other. These must be chiefly, if not wholly, effects of the unsteadiness and injustice, with which a factious spirit has tainted our public administrations.

2 By a faction, I understand a number of citizens, whether amounting to a majority or minority of the whole, who are united and actuated by some common impulse of passion, or of interest, adverse to the rights of other citizens, or to the permanent and aggregate interests of the community.

3 There are two methods of curing the mischiefs of faction: the one, by removing its causes; the other, by controlling its effects.

4 There are again two methods of removing the causes of faction: the one, by destroying the liberty which is essential to its existence; the other, by giving to every citizen the same opinions, the same passions, and the same interests.

5 It could never be more truly said than of the first remedy, that it was worse than the disease. Liberty is to faction, what air is to fire, an aliment without which it instantly expires. But it could not be less folly to abolish liberty, which is essential to political life, because it nourishes faction, than it would be to wish the annihilation of air, which is essential to animal life, because it imparts to fire its destructive agency.

6 The second expedient is as impracticable, as the first would be unwise. As long as the reason of man continues fallible, and he is at liberty to exercise it, different opinions will be formed. As long as the connection subsists between his reason and his self-love, his opinions and his passions will have a reciprocal influence on each other; and the former will be objects to which the latter will attach themselves. The diversity in the faculties of men, from which the rights of property originate, is not less an insuperable obstacle to an uniformity of interests. The protection of these faculties is the first object of Government. From the protection of different and unequal faculties of acquiring property,

the possession of different degrees and kinds of property immediately results; and from the influence of these on the sentiments and views of the respective proprietors, ensues a division of the society into different interests and parties.

7 The latent causes of faction are thus sown in the nature of man; and we see them everywhere brought into different degrees of activity, according to the different circumstances of civil society. A zeal for different opinions concerning religion, concerning Government, and many other points, as well of speculation as of practice; an attachment to different leaders ambitiously contending for preëminence and power; or to persons of other descriptions whose fortunes have been interesting to the human passions, have, in turn, divided mankind into parties, inflamed them with mutual animosity, and rendered them much more disposed to vex and oppress each other, than to coöperate for their common good. So strong is this propensity of mankind to fall into mutual animosities, that where no substantial occasion presents itself, the most frivolous and fanciful distinctions have been sufficient to kindle their unfriendly passions, and excite their most violent conflicts. But the most common and durable source of factions has been the various and unequal distribution of property. Those who hold, and those who are without property, have ever formed distinct interests in society. Those who are creditors, and those who are debtors, fall under a like discrimination. A landed interest, a manufacturing interest, a mercantile interest, a moneyed interest, with many lesser interests, grow up of necessity in civilized nations, and divide them into different classes, actuated by different sentiments and views. The regulation of these various and interfering interests forms the principal task of modern Legislation, and involves the spirit of party and faction in the necessary and ordinary operations of the Government.

8 No man is allowed to be a judge in his own cause; because his interest would certainly bias his judgment, and, not improbably, corrupt his integrity. With equal, nay with greater reason, a body of men are unfit to be both judges and parties at the same time; yet what are many of the most important acts of legislation, but so many judicial determinations, not indeed concerning the rights of single persons, but concerning the rights of large bodies of citizens? and what are the different classes of Legislators, but advocates and parties to the causes which they determine? Is a law proposed concerning private debts? It is a question to which the creditors are parties on one side, and the debtors on the other. Justice ought to hold the balance between them. Yet the parties are, and must be, themselves the judges; and the most numerous party, or, in other words, the most powerful faction, must be expected to prevail. Shall domestic manufactures be encouraged, and in what degree, by restrictions on foreign manufactures? are questions which would be differently decided by the landed and the manufacturing classes; and probably by neither, with a sole regard to justice and the public good. The apportionment of taxes on the various descriptions of property is an act which seems to require the most exact impartiality; yet there is, perhaps, no legislative act in which greater opportu-

nity and temptation are given to a predominant party, to trample on the rules of justice. Every shilling, with which they overburden the inferior number, is a shilling saved to their own pockets.

9 It is in vain to say, that enlightened statesmen will be able to adjust these clashing interests, and render them all subservient to the public good. Enlightened statesmen will not always be at the helm: Nor, in many cases, can such an adjustment be made at all, without taking into view indirect and remote considerations, which will rarely prevail over the immediate interest which one party may find in disregarding the rights of another, or the good of the whole.

10 The inference to which we are brought is, that the *causes* of faction cannot be removed; and that relief is only to be sought in the means of controlling its *effects.*

11 If a faction consists of less than a majority, relief is supplied by the republican principle, which enables the majority to defeat its sinister views by regular vote. It may clog the administration, it may convulse the society; but it will be unable to execute and mask its violence under the forms of the Constitution. When a majority is included in a faction, the form of popular Government, on the other hand, enables it to sacrifice to its ruling passion or interest both the public good and the rights of other citizens. To secure the public good, and private rights against the danger of such a faction, and at the same time to preserve the spirit and the form of popular Government, is then the great object to which our inquiries are directed: Let me add, that it is the great desideratum, by which alone this form of Government can be rescued from the opprobrium under which it has so long labored, and be recommended to the esteem and adoption of mankind.

12 By what means is this object attainable? Evidently by one of two only. Either the existence of the same passion or interest in a majority, at the same time, must be prevented; or the majority, having such coexistent passion or interest, must be rendered, by their number and local situation, unable to concert and carry into effect schemes of oppression. If the impulse and the opportunity be suffered to coincide, we well know that neither moral nor religious motives can be relied on as an adequate control. They are not found to be such on the injustice and violence of individuals, and lose their efficacy in proportion to the number combined together; that is, in proportion as their efficacy becomes needful.

13 From this view of the subject, it may be concluded, that a pure Democracy, by which I mean a Society consisting of a small number of citizens, who assemble and administer the Government in person, can admit of no cure for the mischiefs of faction. A common passion or interest will, in almost every case, be felt by a majority of the whole; a communication and concert results from the form of Government itself; and there is nothing to check the inducements to sacrifice the weaker party, or an obnoxious individual. Hence it is, that such Democracies have ever been spectacles of turbulence and contention; have ever been found incompatible with personal security, or the rights of property; and have in general been as short in their lives, as they have been

violent in their deaths. Theoretic politicians, who have patronized this species of Government, have erroneously supposed, that by reducing mankind to a perfect equality in their political rights, they would, at the same time, be perfectly equalized and assimilated in their possessions, their opinions, and their passions.

14 A Republic, by which I mean a Government in which the scheme of representation takes place, opens a different prospect, and promises the cure for which we are seeking. Let us examine the points in which it varies from pure Democracy, and we shall comprehend both the nature of the cure, and the efficacy which it must derive from the Union.

15 The two great points of difference, between a Democracy and a Republic, are, first, the delegation of the Government, in the latter, to a small number of citizens elected by the rest: Secondly, the greater number of citizens, and greater sphere of country, over which the latter may be extended.

16 The effect of the first difference is, on the one hand, to refine and enlarge the public views, by passing them through the medium of a chosen body of citizens, whose wisdom may best discern the true interest of their country, and whose patriotism and love of justice will be least likely to sacrifice it to temporary or partial considerations. Under such a regulation, it may well happen, that the public voice, pronounced by the representatives of the People, will be more consonant to the public good, than if pronounced by the People themselves, convened for the purpose. On the other hand, the effect may be inverted. Men of factious tempers, of local prejudices, or of sinister designs, may by intrigue, by corruption, or by other means, first obtain the suffrages, and then betray the interests of the people. The question resulting is, whether small or extensive Republics are most favorable to the election of proper guardians of the public weal; and it is clearly decided in favor of the latter by two obvious considerations.

17 In the first place, it is to be remarked that however small the Republic may be, the Representatives must be raised to a certain number, in order to guard against the cabals of a few; and that however large it may be, they must be limited to a certain number, in order to guard against the confusion of a multitude. Hence, the number of Representatives in the two cases not being in proportion to that of the Constituents, and being proportionally greatest in the small Republic, it follows, that if the proportion of fit characters be not less in the large than in the small Republic, the former will present a greater option, and consequently a greater probability of a fit choice.

18 In the next place, as each Representative will be chosen by a greater number of citizens in the large than in the small Republic, it will be more difficult for unworthy candidates to practise with success the vicious arts, by which elections are too often carried; and the suffrages of the People, being more free, will be more likely to centre in men who possess the most attractive merit, and the most diffusive and established characters.

19 It must be confessed, that in this, as in most other cases, there is a mean, on both sides of which inconveniences will be found to lie. By enlarging too

much the number of electors, you render the representative too little acquainted with all their local circumstances and lesser interests; as by reducing it too much, you render him unduly attached to these, and too little fit to comprehend and pursue great and National objects. The Federal Constitution forms a happy combination in this respect; the great and aggregate interests being referred to the National, the local and particular to the State Legislatures.

20 The other point of difference is, the greater number of citizens and extent of territory which may be brought within the compass of Republican, than of Democratic Government; and it is this circumstance principally which renders factious combinations less to be dreaded in the former, than in the latter. The smaller the society, the fewer probably will be the distinct parties and interests composing it; the fewer the distinct parties and interests, the more frequently will a majority be found of the same party; and the smaller the number of individuals composing a majority, and the smaller the compass within which they are placed, the more easily will they concert and execute their plans of oppression. Extend the sphere, and you take in a greater variety of parties and interests; you make it less probable that a majority of the whole will have a common motive to invade the rights of other citizens; or if such a common motive exists, it will be more difficult for all who feel it to discover their own strength, and to act in unison with each other. Besides other impediments, it may be remarked, that where there is a consciousness of unjust or dishonorable purposes, communication is always checked by distrust, in proportion to the number whose concurrence is necessary.

21 Hence, it clearly appears, that the same advantage which a Republic has over a Democracy, in controlling the effects of faction, is enjoyed by a large over a small Republic,—is enjoyed by the Union over the States composing it. Does the advantage consist in the substitution of Representatives, whose enlightened views and virtuous sentiments render them superior to local prejudices, and to schemes of injustice? It will not be denied, that the Representation of the Union will be most likely to possess these requisite endowments. Does it consist in the greater security afforded by a greater variety of parties, against the event of any one party being able to outnumber and oppress the rest? In an equal degree does the increased variety of parties, comprised within the Union, increase this security. Does it, in fine, consist in the greater obstacles opposed to the concert and accomplishment of the secret wishes of an unjust and interested majority? Here, again, the extent of the Union gives it the most palpable advantage.

22 The influence of factious leaders may kindle a flame within their particular States, but will be unable to spread a general conflagration through the other States. A religious sect may degenerate into a political faction in a part of the Confederacy; but the variety of sects dispersed over the entire face of it, must secure the National Councils against any danger from that source. A rage for paper money, for an abolition of debts, for an equal division of property, or for any other improper or wicked project, will be less apt to

pervade the whole body of the Union, than a particular member of it; in the same proportion as such a malady is more likely to taint a particular county or district, than an entire State.

In the extent and proper structure of the Union, therefore, we behold a Republican remedy for the diseases most incident to Republican Government. And according to the degree of pleasure and pride we feel in being Republicans, ought to be our zeal in cherishing the spirit, and supporting the character, of Federalists.

PUBLIUS.

FOR DISCUSSION

1. Much of the early part of this essay is devoted to the topic of Cause and Cure, making an especially effective use of the argument *by division.* Make a diagram of the alternatives as Madison presents them.
2. What are the specific causes of faction? What are the proposed cures?
3. What other examples of the argument *by division* can you find in this essay?
4. Examine the *comparison* in paragraphs 13–16. What is the function of the comparison?
5. Madison presents his argument mainly in theoretical terms and does not mention specifically the Constitution of the United States. What general, unstated premise makes this essay basically a policy statement in favor of ratifying the new constitution? Why do you suppose Madison presented the argument in this way?

Student Essay: Ban Baggies?

by Barbara Marrs

1 A mother is picking up her sixteen-year-old daughter at a record shop in the local shopping mall. Looking around the store, she wanders into the back room, where she sees a display of brightly colored "bongs," "carburetor pipes," and spoons, obviously intended for use with illegal drugs. Horrified at finding her daughter studying a book on the pleasures of cocaine, she notices that she has already purchased a pack of rolling papers. Time for action!

2 Situations like this have prompted some parents to take organized legal action against owners of shops that sell drug-related paraphernalia. Parents complain that the open sale of these accessories creates an atmosphere that encourages drug use by legitimizing and glamorizing it in the minds of young people. The owners of head shops—establishments that either specialize in drug related products or feature them as a sideline—point out rather sleazily

that the items in question are not in themselves illegal. Parents respond with organized efforts to make them illegal, by sponsoring local ordinances against them.

3 Will this be an effective response to the problems of drug abuse? Or does it merely divert attention and energy away from the real causes of the problem? While I am not a parent or a head shop owner, I am concerned about drug abuse, and I have made an effort to find out about the relation of paraphernalia sales to the problem. After hearing the views of parents, head shop owners, drug-abuse counselors, and attorneys, I have become skeptical about laws against selling the stuff. I think that the people selling it deserve all the bad publicity that can be drummed up against them; but I have concluded that legal action against drug-related paraphernalia is not a solution to the problems of drug abuse.

4 It is highly questionable that ordinances against head shops would do much actually to reduce the levels of drug abuse. The drugs themselves are illegal; and yet government statistics show that one in five Americans has tried marijuana, that one in ten uses it regularly, and that one in twenty-two has tried cocaine. If the fact of their being illegal has such little effect against the drugs themselves, is it likely that laws against the gadgets that go with them will be any more effective?

5 Head shop owners, bless their civic hearts, bring up another point worth considering. There are dozens of items that you can buy in any supermarket that regularly serve quite well as makeshift drug accessories. Plastic sandwich bags, commonly used to package and store various kinds of food, can be bought openly in grocery stores, but their sale is not threatened. There are plastic "Star Wars" space guns that are great for blasting marijuana smoke into your lungs. Baby bottles, straws, ballpoint pens, and "Catch-a-Buzz" frisbees double quite nicely as pot-smoking devices. McDonald's coffee spoons are just right for snorting cocaine.

6 Most people who use drugs know about these items, and they know that the sophisticated gadgets available at the head shops amount to luxury gimmicks. Moreover, these items are going to continue to be available, just as drugs are going to continue to be available, whether illegal or not.

7 But that's beside the point, some parents would contend. The head shops are bad, not so much for making drug paraphernalia available as for promoting the mystique of drug use. All those brightly designed gadgets gathered together and sold openly in special boutiques have the effect of drawing a constituency to drugs, similar to the constituencies that are drawn to skiing and backpacking by other kinds of speciality shops. If it were illegal to ski, one parent pointed out to me, we wouldn't allow the selling of skis on the open market.

8 I think the point about building up the mystique of drug use is a valid one, although I think the skiing analogy may be inexact. I'm sure that if skiing were illegal the sale of skis would also be illegal, just as is the sale of drugs. But I'm not sure that we would also rush to outlaw the sale of heavy knit sweaters with Alpine designs, thermal underwear, and mountain lodges with

huge fireplaces, even if there developed a class of businessman who specialized in such items, just because we felt that the sale of these items promoted the mystique of skiing.

9 I don't mean to make light of a serious problem. The head shops are clearly promoting the use of drugs, either directly or indirectly, and as such they constitute an embarrassment and a threat. (How much of a threat is not clear. One local drug counselor pointed out that most young people make their contacts for drugs at school rather than at head shops.) And there's another problem—local ordinances against head shops may be unconstitutional. The Drug Enforcement Administration has drafted a model law to help communities curtail the sale of drug related items; but Justice Department officials warn that the constitutionality of such a law is still in question. Backed by lawyers and civil liberties groups, shop owners have already won rulings over such laws in court—often on the grounds that people cannot be punished on the mere assumption of intent to use drugs.

10 Even if constitutional laws prohibiting the sale of drug paraphernalia could be passed, drug counselors and lawyers (as well as our ever-astute head shop owners) contend that a ban on these items will do little to stunt the growth of drug use. And one begins to wonder if parents might not more usefully place their efforts elsewhere, perhaps at a more personal level, considering all the energy that is bound to be absorbed in court battles.

11 At best, restricting the sale of these items may alter the atmosphere of permissiveness that concerns some parents, and more informal publicity campaigns might achieve the same effect. But it is unrealistic to expect a ban on paraphernalia even to begin to solve the problem of drug abuse—anymore than a ban on shot glasses would solve the problem of alcoholism.

FOR DISCUSSION

1. Look at the list of possible functions for policy essays on page 93. Which of these does Marrs' essay come closest to fulfilling?

2. Marrs uses deprecatory phrases to describe the owners of head shops (see paragraphs 2, 5, 10), even though her argument does not go against them. Is some particular rhetorical strategy at work here?

3. Review the five basic issues listed on p. 94 of this chapter. What does Marrs identify as the basic issue? Which others does she bring up?

4. Examine Marrs' use of the argument *by analogy* in paragraphs 7 and 8. Marrs questions the exactness of an opposing analogy and then substitutes one of her own. Is this analogy more exact than the one it replaces?

5. What effort does Marrs make to present herself as a mature, responsible deliberator?

5 Problems of Value: What Is It Worth?

Chapter Overview

This chapter introduces the functions and strategies of deliberation focused upon matters of *value.* Essays with theses of value concern the worth or acceptability of individual acts and products as well as general cultural tendencies. They also concern the principles we use to guide and evaluate individual acts.

- **What Is Values-Deliberation?**
  - **Theses of value and the process of problem solving**
  - **The evaluation of acts and products**
  - **Cultural criticism**
  - **Discussions of principle**
- **Some Specific Functions of Values-Deliberation**
- **Basic Issues in Values-Deliberation**
  - **The nature of evaluation**
  - **Value standards**
  - **Sources of value standards**
  - **Conflicting standards**
  - **Finding the appropriate standard**
- **Persuasive Strategies: Association and Dissociation**
  - **Logical forms of association**
  - **Verbal association**
- **An Outline of Defensive Strategies**
- **Special Strategies of Presentation**
- **Essay Assignments**
- **Essays for Analysis**

• What Is Values-Deliberation?

Theses of value and the process of problem solving

Essays with theses of value concern the worth or acceptability of actions and things. Many evaluative terms are used in value judgments—good and bad, right and wrong, beautiful and ugly. Since important choices are seldom clear cut, this type of deliberation deals with questions of *priorities* and assessments of *comparative worth.* Given that things can be good in some ways but not so good in others, what criteria or general principles are most important? And given that nothing is perfect, what things are better (or less harmful) than others?

Evaluation is an essential human activity. Discussions of values are essential to the process of decision making as well. Consider once again the problem-solving model in Chapter 3 (p. 75). Questions of value appear at crucial stages.

One stage is the identification of problems. This often involves questions of value, because it can determine that something isn't as it should be. Another crucial stage determines what goals are met by any solution to a problem. This involves judgments (and sometimes disputes) about what ought to be. And remember that, in discussions of policy, one of the important issues is the acceptability of a plan in terms of principles and values, as well as those of feasibility and cost. Any of these points in the process of problem solving could be the basis of an essay focused on a values problem.

The evaluation of acts and products

Essays focused on values and evaluation have other important uses not directly related to the processes of problem solving. In a free society, any event or act of public interest is subject to *assessments* or *criticisms.* These often take the form of published essays—primarily reviews and commentaries. Unlike value-discussions that seek to influence policy decisions, reviews and commentaries focus on events that have already happened—decisions already made, actions already taken, or books already written.

Public commentary (especially political commentary) is more often negative than positive—disapproval spurs writing more than approval does. But negative commentaries are often answered by positive defenses. Commentary comes from different quarters, representing different interests and different standards of judgment. In an atmosphere of freedom and truthfulness, public values-deliberation is a useful and beneficial process. It informs the public, guides the choices of individuals, and sometimes helps win public acceptance for the unfamiliar or unorthodox. It improves the overall performance of individuals and institutions by upholding standards.

Cultural criticism

Sometimes criticism and commentary turn away from specifics and toward general tendencies of thought and behavior. Such writing, commonly known as *cultural criticism,* differs from other kinds of evaluation by treating individual troubles as symptoms of larger problems. These problems are broadly called "materialism," "Puritanism," "elitism," and so on. This sort of writing is useful as a way for communities and organizations to see where they are headed. It is also a way for individuals to take stock of themselves within larger communities. The essay by Michael Novak, at the end of this chapter, is a good example of cultural criticism.

Discussions of principle

Finally, because criticism and evaluation use certain standards of goodness or rightness, they lead into debates about these standards themselves. For instance, suppose that someone criticized a program as being "elitist." One defense against the charge is to claim that the program is not *really* elitist. But another is to call for an examination of the standard of evaluation itself. This leads to questions such as the following:

- What is "elitism," exactly?
- Is it really a bad thing? Why or why not?
- Is it bad under all circumstances, or are there cases in which it is justified or necessary?
- Are there different kinds of "elitism"? Are they all bad?

Answering these questions might lead to an essay defending instances of elitism. It might also lead to an essay clarifying the notion of elitism itself, as a possible guide for future evaluations.

Discussions of evaluations need definitions of basic values, principles, or rights—any standard of value—and their applications to concrete circumstances. Such discussions keep alive an awareness of guiding principles and help clarify the application of principles to new circumstances. They also help expose shabby ideas and values.

EXERCISE 5.1

Look briefly at the essays reprinted in Chapters 1–3. Which focus on matters of value?

EXERCISE 5.2

Why is it important to do the right things for the right reasons? Can you think of an example in which the right thing was done for the wrong reasons? What are the possible dangers there? Consider the issue of premarital sex, for instance. Are there wrong reasons for doing the right thing?

EXERCISE 5.3

Think about the following statement: "Modern societies must decide what their loves truly are—or else technology itself will entrap them in what is merely feasible." —Michael Novak, *Ascent of the Mountain, Flight of the Dove.* Can you think of specific instances, either public or private, that illustrate this point?

• Some Specific Functions of Values-Deliberation

The material in this chapter will be more meaningful if you yourself use values-deliberation while writing an evaluative essay. As you search for an essay-topic or as you choose among the suggested topics on pp. 201–205, the following list may be useful. Here are some of the specific functions of evaluative essays:

Criticize, praise, or defend some product, person, practice, or organization. The object of your criticism (or praise or defense) could be a consumer product (a book, movie, or play), a controversial local or national figure, an action of some organization or community, or an organization itself (a club, student government, or union).

Recommend the best among several alternatives. Compare two or more of the items listed above.

Criticize or defend a characteristic of a community or group. Characteristics are usually given labels such as industriousness, snobbishness, enthusiasm, apathy.

Question some commonly approved value. For instance, honesty may not always be the best policy. Some people are taking sincerity too far. There can be too much openness.

Defend some commonly disapproved value. For instance, materialism is not such a bad thing after all. Hypocrisy has distinct social advantages. Lying can be a moral and courageous art.

Define or re-interpret some value standard (see pp. 123–126) which you believe is misapplied in a certain case. For instance, we all believe in such things as freedom of speech, freedom of religion, and individual rights. But we don't always agree on what these things mean or how they apply to particular cases. Perhaps a person or group is using the term "freedom of speech" too loosely or in the wrong context, in defending certain actions or products.

• Basic Issues in Values-Deliberation

The nature of evaluation

In any evaluation or discussion of values there are two fundamental elements—something to be evaluated and a principle or standard by which to judge it. The process of evaluation is one of measuring or assessing items in relation to value standards.

Even the most casual conversation reveals this process. "I don't like this peanut butter; it's stale and it doesn't taste much like peanuts." The person who made this comment has, in a very informal way, made an evaluation, by measuring the peanut butter against the standards of "freshness" and "tasting like peanuts."

Consider the processes involved in values-deliberation by examining some of the casual responses that might be made to the peanut-butter comment, in an idle conversation.

Measurement or assessment of the individual item

1. "I don't agree. It really tastes fresh and peanutty to me." This rebuttal *disputes the assessment or measurement.* There is no disagreement about what the standards are, only about how well the item meets the standards.

Definition of the standard

2. "Well, it seems fresh enough to me, for peanut butter. You can't expect peanut butter to be 'fresh' in exactly the same way that vegetables are fresh. Peanut butter is fresh if it doesn't taste rancid." The disagreement is not over the qualities of the individual item but over the *definition* of the value standard.

Relevance or relative importance of the standard

3. "Who cares about freshness? It's the texture that counts. Besides, peanut butter is not supposed to taste like peanuts—it's supposed to taste like peanut butter." The dispute is over the *importance* and *relevance* of standards applied to the case.

Circumstances; comparison to alternatives

4. "Well, it's not great. But it's still about the best you can get around here." There is little or no disagreement about the item or the standards of judging it. The question is one of *comparative value.* This is often an important consideration in a world where nothing is perfect. It is also a last resort in defense of something that is patently flawed.

Disputes about questions of value usually follow the lines of argument illustrated here in a trivial way:

1. the measurement or assessment of individual items;
2. the definition of value standards;
3. the determination of which value standards are most relevant in a given situation;
4. the consideration of circumstances and alternatives.

Value standards

Any evaluation involves value standards—criteria by which individual items can be measured or assessed. Some value standards, such as those we use to decide which peanut butter is best, are extremely subjective. You are not likely to get widespread agreement about what the most important qualities are, or about how these qualities could be measured. Primarily matters of taste, these decisions involve little of real importance. Extended deliberation about them would be pointless, except in small talk.

Sometimes it is claimed that debates about other kinds of decisions—especially moral and aesthetic decisions—are also pointless, that right or wrong in personal conduct or good or bad in the arts are individual, subjective matters. In a limited sense, this claim has some validity. In a free society, no individual should be forced to agree with others. But this claim overlooks one fact—people form their opinions and styles of behavior not in isolation but in communities. They interact with one another and exercise various kinds of influence upon one another. One person's decision inevitably affects other people. Moreover, the formal actions and policies of communities generally reflect some consensus about what is valuable and what is right or wrong. The ongoing process of evaluation and criticism in a community builds that concensus and changes it from time to time, to meet new needs.

However, deliberation about values is sometimes subjective and pointless. In fact, it is certain to be that way unless you as a writer appeal directly to or establish common understandings about value standards with your readers. You cannot hope to persuade an audience about the worth of some action on the basis of value standards that you hold but they do not. You have to find or establish some common ground of value with an audience.

For instance, if you disapprove of a certain practice on the basis of your religious belief, while others with that same belief favor the practice, you have a common ground for deliberation—a common religious faith. On the other hand, if you want to reach a larger audience, an audience that includes people who don't share your religious belief, you need some broader basis of understanding to win your point—a principle that most religions share or some broad humanitarian goal. In a civilization as diverse as ours, this can be difficult and frustrating. But it is not impossible, and it is definitely worth the effort.

Sources of value standards

Any values-deliberation may involve a variety of value standards, deriving from different sources of understanding and belief and from different areas of experience. One of the reasons discussions about values sometimes go around in circles is that people are talking at cross purposes—judging the same item but employing different standards of value. They never approach a common ground of value.

Suppose that Person A likes a certain movie because of its "realistic portrayal of social problems," but Person B objects that the movie is "much too long, and the dialogue is flat and uninteresting." These two people are clearly judging the movie by two different standards of value. Person A has standards that are called "social"; Person B has standards that are called "aesthetic"—referring to artistic beauty or effectiveness.

So far the discussion between A and B has been potentially useful. A made some good points ignored by B, and B pointed out some flaws ignored by A. But any further discussion is going to go nowhere, unless these two people agree upon some standard of value. Listed below are some of the common sources of value standards:

Cultural and community standards. These are the general beliefs of a community, as reflected in the basic attitudes and statements of its people. The beliefs may apply to an entire nation or to some smaller community. Americans, for instance, generally agree on basic notions of fair play, respect for individual rights, justice, and equality, to name a few. They do not always practice them, of course, and they differ sharply on how they should be interpreted or applied in individual cases. But they do agree on the values themselves, at least in the abstract.

EXERCISE 5.4

Examine several magazine or television advertisements for consumer products such as soft drinks, beer, or cigarettes. What images of personal happiness do the advertisers want their products to be associated with? Do the ads seem directed at any specific group of people? Explain your answer.

Constitutional and codified standards. These are the general principles, rights, and guidelines that have been formulated and that usually bind the members and leaders of any organization or political unit. Examples include the Constitution of the United States and the various codes of ethics that govern professional groups, such as doctors and lawyers. In the cases that come before the United States Supreme Court, the relevant value standards are the rights and constraints set forth in the Constitution. What is almost always in dispute is how a particular right or constraint applies in a given situation.

Philosophies and schools of thought. Philosophies and schools of thought have comprehensive and systematic viewpoints on subjects they are principally concerned with—politics, economics, the arts—and these viewpoints provide instruments of criticism. Most of the major religions have comprehensive systems of values providing fairly systematic criteria for the evaluation of human action. The doctrines of "charity," or "love of God," are familiar standards of value derived from a religious system.

Performance standards. These are standards used in judging products or organizations designed for specific purposes—bicycles, stereo headsets, baseball teams, and the like. The standards assess how well the products perform (and sometimes how convenient and safe they are) in comparison with other products of the same type. Standards of this sort translate into certain tests which can be performed upon equivalent products under similar circumstances.

Conflicting standards

Human existence would be much simpler (and much duller) if every evaluation could be based on a single test supplied by a single value standard. But human choices are extremely complicated; in almost any situation of evaluation or ethical choice, several different standards come into play, and these may well conflict with one another. Such conflicts make it necessary to establish priorities—commitments about which standards are most important—and even then we may have to compromise.

Even in the cases judged by performance standards—usually the easiest to deal with—we run into complications and conflicts. In choosing a new car, for instance, you find that A gets excellent gasoline mileage but has little cargo space, while B has lots of room but guzzles gasoline; C has the room you need and gets good mileage but has a terrible repair record. You have to decide what your priorities are and then find an acceptable compromise.

Another source of complexity is conflict between different types of value standards. The most common of these is the conflict between performance standards and cultural or moral standards. For instance, medical scientists may develop machinery capable of sustaining indefinitely the lives of comatose or terminally ill patients. But inevitably conflicts about the moral and social value of such machinery will arise, as well as legal and ethical conflicts about its proper and humane use.

Finding the appropriate standard

Good evaluations pay attention to particular circumstances and ways in which standards might be relevant to them. Weak evaluations apply standards that are somehow inappropriate to what is being evaluated.

It would be rather silly and futile to judge a children's book by the same standards that you apply to a best selling novel. It is more useful and sensible to understand that you are dealing with a distinct type of literature—a type that has special features, limitations, and purposes. You judge it as a children's book, not as something else. Some children's books, of course, are great literature at the same time, but we should not expect all children's books to be this way. The best evaluation of anything should be based on how well it fulfills its purposes within its own limitations.

Any criticism or evaluation should consider these questions:

1. What kind of item are you dealing with? What are the special characteristics and limitations of this category?
2. What is (or was) its particular purpose? How well does it fulfill that purpose?
3. What are the special circumstances under which the item was produced or the action took place? What particular opportunities, difficulties, or conflicts were inherent in the situation?
4. How does the item or action compare with other items or actions with similar aims and under similar circumstances?

After asking these questions you may find that you disapprove of the kind of item you are dealing with or with its purposes—in which case you would disapprove of it no matter how well executed it was. If so, you at least have clarified your own thinking.

EXERCISE 5.5

What objections might be made to the following evaluative comments?

A. This is a terrible physics book—too full of mathematical formulas and scientific jargon.

B. This is excellent pornography—lots of exciting action and really splendid camera angles.

C. Hitler has been maliciously credited with the deaths of six million Jewish civilians during World War II. Most reliable historians put the number at closer to four million, and some estimates run as low as two hundred thousand.

D. I didn't think that *Star Wars* was very realistic.

E. So what if Senator Fussmund misdirected a few measly thousand dollars from operating expenses. At least he's not like those welfare chiselers that misdirect millions of the taxpayers' dollars every year. Who ever brings charges against them?

• Persuasive Strategies: Association and Dissociation

The simplest and most straightforward evaluations of individual items are those involving product testing in magazines like *Consumer Reports.* The typical procedure is to identify the appropriate standards for particular products, to conduct tests based on those standards, and then to compare the results. The criteria for new automobiles, for instance, include such things as safety, fuel economy, passenger comfort, and estimated frequency-of-repair. Although some criteria (such as "passenger comfort") may involve subjective judgment, most of the tests are *empirical*—they rely on factual information and measurement.

However, most of the important judgments we make cannot be based on statistical and empirical measurements. Questions involving moral, aesthetic, and even some kinds of performance standards call for judgments of a different sort. These judgments involve making reasonable connections or associations between individual objects being judged and general standards of value, such as fairness, justice, and integrity. If your judgment is favorable, you try to show a positive association between the individual item and the standard. If the judgment is unfavorable, you do the opposite.

On the other hand, when we make value judgments we do more than associate objects and actions with abstract standards. We also make associations between the item being judged and other items that we already believe to be either "good" or "bad." Abstract value standards may be implicit in such judgments, but the direct focus is on the object or attribute that represents the standard.

Some of these associations are irrational, as when we don't like a particular book just because we despise the person who wrote it. Others are clearly fraudulent, as when a prosecutor or a journalist attempts to discredit a person through "guilt-by-association"—pointing out that the person's friends have been criminal types.

Other associations are logical and can provide reliable guides for evaluation. To make a positive judgment you seek a logical association between the item and items already considered good and a dissociation from items already considered bad. To make a negative judgment you seek the opposite, a dissociation from items considered good and an association with items considered bad. The following illustrates some logical forms of association.

Logical forms of association

Several different types of reasoning serve as strategies of association and dissociation. In the formulas accompanying each description and example, the **X** stands for the item being evaluated and the **Y** stands for the item of association or dissociation. Most of these logical forms occur in all types of deliberation. These examples illustrate some specific ways in which they operate in values-deliberation.

By definition **X** is a type of **Y**; **X** is not a type of **Y**
X has the essential characteristics **Y**; **X** does not . . .
X is a part of **Y**; **X** is not a part of **Y**
X is essentially the same as **Y**; **X** is not . . .

You define a concept by placing it in a larger class of concepts, by identifying its essential characteristics or functions, and by comparing and contrasting it with related or apparently similar concepts. As a strategy in values-deliberation, definition places an item in a class of things considered good, attributes good characteristics to it, and shows that the item is a part of or the same as something already considered good. Conversely, you dissociate the item from things considered bad.

In the first example of argument by definition, the author argues that journalism has been corrupted, becoming a kind of *paralogical rhetoric* and a kind of *fiction.*

> Everyone knows that journalism has been transformed in recent years, especially in the news magazines, from reportage into new forms of paralogical rhetoric: political argument disguised as dramatic reporting. It would be fun to spend the rest of my hour simply describing the new rhetorical devices, and the new twists on old devices, that *Time* magazine . . . exhibits from week to week, all in the name of news. Mr. Ralph Ingersoll, former publisher of the magazine, has described the key to the magazine's success as the discovery of how to turn news into fiction, giving each story its own literary form, with a beginning, a middle, and an end, regardless of whether the story thus invented matches the original event. Everyone I know who has ever been treated by *Time*—whether favorably or unfavorably—has been shocked by the distortion of fact for effect, and the more they know about a subject the more they are shocked.—Wayne C. Booth, *Now Don't Try to Reason With Me*

In the next example, the author protests what she feels is the misuse of a particular value standard, the notion of *equality.* What she is saying, in effect, is the idea of everyone being the same is not part of the definition of this value standard:

> "All men are created equal" does not mean that all men are the same. What it does mean is that each should be accorded full respect and full rights as a unique human being—full respect for his humanity *and* for his differences from other people.—Margaret Mead, "The Egalitarian Error"

By example **X** is an example of **Y; X** is not an example of **Y**
X is a sign of **Y; X** is not a sign of **Y**

In the following passage, the author uses the typical New Year's party as a sign of a more general condition that he deplores—the deterioration of true festivity and fantasy in modern times.

> Both our enjoyment of festivity and our capacity for fantasy have deteriorated in modern times. We still celebrate, but our feasts and parties often lack real verve or feeling. Take, for example, a typical American New Year's Eve. It is

a celebration, but there is something undeniably vacuous and frenetic about it. People seem anxiously, even obsessively determined to have a good time. But under the surface of Dionysiac carousing we feel something is missing. The next day we often wonder why we bothered.—Harvey Cox, *The Feast of Fools*

By cause or origin **X** was caused by **Y; X** was not caused by **Y**
X came from **Y; X** did not come from **Y**
X was motivated by **Y; X** was not motivated . . .
X is a result of **Y; X** is not a result of **Y**
X reflects **Y; X** does not reflect **Y**

Using this strategy, you argue the goodness of an object by maintaining that it has good origins or that the forces that brought it about were praiseworthy. You criticize an object by maintaining the opposite. In the following passage the author criticizes a group of institutions by pointing out that their origins are not what they seem:

> None of the mail-order writing schools was actually founded by the "famous writers" whose names are used in the advertisements. In fact, these writers have virtually nothing to do with the operation of the schools. Most of the schools were begun by hacks with a yen for fast dollars, not lovers of literature by any means. The connection with "famous writers" is an advertising gimmick, nothing more.—June Yorlig, "Mischief in the Mails," (Student Essay)

By consequences **X** will lead to **Y; X** will not lead to **Y**
X causes **Y; X** does not cause **Y**

Using this strategy, you argue that an object is good because it causes or brings about good things; conversely an object is bad because it causes or brings about bad things. The two passages below illustrate both sides of the strategy:

> Few are the individuals who have come to the United States from any other culture on this planet who do not find greater opportunity here than where they were. For their children and their grandchildren, moreover, they may with all empirical probability expect even greater opportunity than for themselves. Our system of opportunity works, as the poor seem to know better than the privileged. —Michael Novak, "Thinking About Equality"

> Perhaps sex manuals just add to the public stock of harmless pleasure.
>
> More likely, these books, which sternly warn against making love or mayonnaise by trial-and-error, produce sexual unhappiness. They turn normal lusty people into perfectionists whose fear of failure prevents them from even getting started. How many of us have ever made mayonnaise?—George Will, "The Ploy of Sex"

EXERCISE 5.6

Identify the principal method (or methods) of association or dissociation being used in each of the following passages.

A. Today he is wearing Hush Puppies (but not 'earth shoes'—he's out of uniform), argyle socks, gray denim wash pants, a suit jacket of a discordant shade of gray, a white button-down shirt, and a dollar tie no more than two inches wide. It isn't clothing; it is a costume.

It is post-Watergate haberdashery, part of the antipose pose, a sincerity gambit from Robert Hall. It is the carefully calibrated 'uncalculated' look for politicians cunningly convinced that dishevelment serves the symbolism for candor.—George Will, "Clark vs. Javits: Battle of Left Jabs"

B. What I have been trying to suggest . . . is that we live in a world in which men show little esteem for logic, little respect for facts, no faith in anyone's ability to use thought or discourse to arrive at improved judgments, commitments, and first principles. The consequences that one would expect in such a world, when honesty of observation, care with logic, and subtlety with dialectic have declined, can of course be seen wherever men try to change each other's minds. What is left to rhetoric when solid substantive argument is denied to it? Obviously only emotional appeal and appeal to the superior moral integrity and wisdom or cleverness of the rhetorician. . . . But when men are reduced to using these properly subordinate appeals as if they were the sole means of persuasion, they produce the kind of rhetoric that we now find flowing at us, left, right, and center.—Wayne Booth, *Now Don't Try to Reason With Me*

C. I think it reflects snobbery to take the position that some communities have a right to protect their culture because it is high and others do not because we refuse to accept it as valuable. A known and experienced way of life is always of value to those who have been raised in it, and a reflexive effort to defend it demands at the least sympathy and understanding, if not acquiescence.—Nathan Glazer, "The Issue of Cultural Pluralism Today"

D. Another version of false democracy is the need to deny the existence of personal advantages. Inherited wealth, famous parents, a first-class mind, a rare voice, a beautiful face, an exceptional physical skill—any advantage has to be minimized or denied. Continually watched and measured, the man or woman who is rich or talented or well educated is likely to be called "undemocratic" whenever he does anything out of the ordinary—more or less of something than others do.—Margaret Mead, "The Egalitarian Error"

E. Festivity and fantasy are not only worthwhile in themselves; they are absolutely vital to human life. They enable man to relate himself to the past and the future in ways that seem impossible for animals. The festival, the special time when ordinary chores are set aside while man celebrates some event, affirms the sheer goodness of what is, or observes the memory of a god or hero, is a distinctly human activity. It arises from man's peculiar power to incorporate into his own life the joys of other people and the experience of previous generations.—Harvey Cox, *The Feast of Fools*

EXERCISE 5.7

The following poem by John Donne is both an indictment and a spirited depreciation of "Death." What methods of association or dissociation does Donne use in the poem? Are all of them reasonable or legitimate forms of reasoning, in your opinion?

Death Be Not Proud

Death, be not proud, though some have called thee
Mighty and dreadful, for thou art not so;
For those whom thou think'st thou dost overthrow
Die not, poor Death, nor yet canst thou kill me.
From rest and sleep, which but thy pictures be,
Much pleasure; then from thee much more must flow,
And soonest our best men with thee do go,
Rest of their bones, and soul's delivery.
Thou art slave to fate, chance, kings, and desperate men,
And dost with poison, war, and sickness dwell,
And poppy or charms can make us sleep as well
And better than thy stroke; why swell'st thou then?
One short sleep past, we wake eternally
And death shall be no more; Death, thou shalt die.

Verbal association

A subtler and less logical way of producing evaluative associations and dissociations lies in the way that writers use words and phrases to produce favorable or unfavorable impressions. The fact that certain words evoke emotional, judgmental responses makes this process possible.

Connotation and denotation

Most words and phrases have *denotative* content—that is, some explicit meaning or reference. The word "dog," for instance, refers specifically to a certain species of four-legged domesticated animal. But many words and phrases have *connotative* content as well—that is, certain emotional and judgmental associations connected with the words. As a result, two different words may *denote* or refer to essentially the same thing but carry different *connotations*—different emotional or judgmental associations. Thus "statesman" and "politician" could easily refer to the same person, but "statesman" has favorable connotations, whereas "politician" may imply something unfavorable. In the same way, expressions that mean essentially the same thing may imply different levels of social status. Many people would rather "be associated with" the Widget Corporation than to "work for" the Widget Corporation.

The connotations of words and phrases may be either favorable, unfavorable, or neutral, depending upon the words and circumstances in which the words are used. "Public servant" is favorable; "government employee" is neutral; "bureaucrat" is unfavorable.

EXERCISE 5.8

The name of this game is "My Friend/Your Friend," and the object is to find favorable and unfavorable characterizations of the same thing. For instance, if the sentence begins with "My friend is the life of the party," you might complete it with "Your friend is a loud-mouthed buffoon."

A. My friend is an energetic businessman.

B. My friend has a drinking problem.

C. My friend is a highly ethical person.

D. Your friend is complacent.

E. My friend is engaging in a speculative venture.

F. My friend likes to express his opinions.

G. My friend is cautious about lending out money.

H. Your friend is nosy.

I. My friend likes to take things easy.

J. My friend is a bit shy.

Favorable, unfavorable, and neutralized characterizations

The wide range of connotations in our language and conflicting value standards make possible widely different characterizations of the same thing. Thus, as in the last exercise, what one person characterizes as an act of "courageous daring" another characterizes as an example of "foolish recklessness."

In 1979, when the Soviet Union engineered an overthrow of the government in Afghanistan and then moved about 80,000 Soviet troops into the country, there were varying responses in the United States. Some decried the Soviet action as "an act of aggression against a sovereign nation," while others dismissed it as an "intervention aimed at shoring up a friendly government."

This process comes quite naturally to most of us. We put the best or most convenient face on things. In scholarly and scientific discourse, writers labor to avoid value judgments and to neutralize descriptions of what they study. But in deliberative writing, even the process of neutralizing can serve persuasive purposes, especially if the writer attempts to defend something perceived as unsavory. The following passages illustrate the point:

1. It is obvious to most people that the coercion of young children to portray scenes of shameful sexual perversion in smut movies degrades and humiliates the the children themselves, stunting their emotional growth for the rest of their lives.
2. Many people, perhaps a majority, hold the opinion that the employment of youthful actors to portray episodes of sexual deviance in sexually explicit films has certain harmful and possibly long-term psychological effects upon the actors.

The first of the passages above may strike you as a heavy-handed attempt to prejudice the case, whereas the second may strike you as a rather devious attempt to whitewash some lurid circumstances. Most people would desire a more factual account of actual circumstances and a more logical presentation of issues.

How far should one go in using verbal and emotional associations as means of persuasion? There is no easy answer to this question, but here are some guidelines for assessing individual situations:

1. The best case is always the rational, logical case. Characterizations, whether charged with emotional and judgmental connotations or deliberately neutralized, can make an argument more emphatic and appealing, but they never prove anything.
2. There is nothing wrong with such characterizations *per se,* unless they are deceptively used to cover up the truth or befuddle the audience.
3. The excessive use of judgmental characterizations may backfire. Audiences may react negatively to them and to your argument.
4. Your own ability to detect judgmental characterizations in the writing of others (particularly that of your opponents) is an important asset. Pointing them out can be a powerful strategy of rebuttal.

EXERCISE 5.9

Write an alternate characterization for each of the passages below:

A. Jones was terminated from employment because his aggressive management tactics tended to be somewhat unsettling to his superiors.

B. These flag-waving, cliche-chanting, super patriots want to unleash the marines and the CIA everytime something happens in the world that doesn't coincide with United States policy or interests.

C. A group of pointy-headed leftist ideologues are mounting a high-pressure campaign to coerce the congress into turning loose more money for welfare chiselers.

D. He had a childlike, innocent quality that prompted him to see only the best in people.

Direct analogy and metaphor

Closely related to verbal association and the strategy of comparison is "figurative" language—direct analogy and metaphor. Both of these devices can create associations that are persuasive but not strictly logical, and may, in fact, introduce a highly emotional element.

A *direct analogy* creates an association directly, stating that one object is "like" or "similar to" another:

> "Inflation of the currency is like a cancer, which devours and ultimately destroys the very body that gave it life."

In this analogy the association is both pejorative and emotional. The basis for the association has nothing to do with economics, of course, but with the notion of something that is self-destructive and grows rapidly. It is an axiom of logic that analogies never prove anything, and this one certainly doesn't. As a statement about economics, it would surely muddle the issues. Its rhetorical value lies in its ability to provide emotional reinforcement for an argument already made.

A *metaphor* is a figure of speech in which the analogy is not stated but implied in the choice of words:

> "Our economy is being devoured by the cancer of inflation, for which the only cure is radical surgery—cutting out malignant social programs and runaway military spending."

In this metaphor there are two implied comparisons: *inflation* is compared to *cancer* and *efforts to reduce social and military spending* are compared to *radical surgery.* The metaphor produces a composite picture or image which the reader is asked to accept as a likeness of the action being described.

Like other forms of verbal association, analogy and metaphor are sometimes appropriate, and effective. Sometimes they are not. And when used in cynical or hysterical ways, they can backfire and turn your audience against you.

EXERCISE 5.10

The following statement contains metaphors. Identify the points of comparison.

Hundreds of thousands of retarded citizens are in public institutions that offer only what is decorously called custodial care, which often means the warehousing of human beings. Often the warehousing is facilitated by the heavy use of tranquilizing drugs—chemical straitjackets.—George Will, "A Village for the Handicapped"

EXERCISE 5.11

In Chapter 1 of this book the student essay, "Child Pornography and the First Amendment," (pp. 30–32) contains a number of metaphorical characterizations. Make a list of these and comment on them. Do they strike you as fair or justified?

• An Outline of Defensive Strategies

Although most of the discussion in this chapter has been about positive and negative *evaluations,* the basic strategies of values-deliberation can be adapted to the task of *defending* items under criticism or attack. Here is a brief outline of defensive strategies:

1. Recharacterize the item. Show that the item in question has been misunderstood or mischaracterized. Seen in the proper light, it does meet the standards that have been applied to it; or at least it is not as bad as it appears.

2. Redefine the standard. People have applied too broad or narrow an understanding of the standard. Once the standard itself is seen in the proper light, it is clear that the item fits the standard.

3. Reject the standard. Opponents have judged the item according to standards that don't apply. Reveal what the appropriate standards are, and then show how the item meets these standards.

4. Relax the standard. Opponents expect too much and have measured the item against impossibly idealistic and unrealistic notions. It's a matter of degree.

5. Call attention to alternative standards. Admit the shortcomings of the item, but claim that there are also good qualities, as revealed by other points of view and other standards of judgment. These good qualities outweigh the defects. Nothing can be perfect in every respect.

6. Reject the comparison. If the item has been unfavorably compared to some other item, show that the comparison is unfair. Make more appropriate comparisons of your own—ones that work in favor of the item.

7. Appeal to circumstances. This is a much weaker, last-ditch argument; it admits the truth of criticisms or accusations, but claims that whatever the defects or shortcomings may be, they are really the result of outside circumstances.

Examples: He simply had no choice; no one could have done any differently under the circumstances.

He had a very miserable childhood; this has affected his behavior as an adult.

8. Point out the absence of alternatives. This is also a last-ditch argument. Rather than refute criticisms, point out that whatever you are defending, as flawed as it may be, is still better than any available alternative.

9. Discredit the opposition. The weakest and most desperate defense of all, it is often patently fraudulent and ill-spirited because it doesn't address the criticisms in any direct way. Instead, it questions the motives, sincerity, rationality, or integrity of those who have done the criticizing.

Example: This charge of hypocrisy is strange indeed, coming from a man whose own hypocritical behavior has embarrassed us so many times in the past.

EXERCISE 5.12

Assume that you are attempting to defend a local vendor of pornographic magazines against public attacks by Church groups. Construct arguments to fit each of the nine defensive strategies.

• Special Strategies of Presentation

The flexibility of language in conveying judgmental attitudes makes values-deliberation especially fertile territory for special strategies of presentation. As for other kinds of deliberation, one special strategy for evaluation is the "fake-genre," such as the fake-proposal (Swift, Chapter 3, p. 81), the fake-interview (Buchwald, Chapter 4, p. 104), and the fake-defense (Barfalot, Chapter 5, p. 146). Another effective strategy is to present a situation or tell a story, arranging the details of the story and setting a tone to convey a critical point without engaging in direct argumentation. Sherwood Anderson's "Loom Dance" (p. 142) is an excellent example.

ESSAY ASSIGNMENTS

1. Find two reviews—one positive and the other negative—of either a movie or play you saw or of a novel you read. Write an essay in which you discuss both sides, revealing what issues of value appear to be involved. Indicate what standard of value each author uses, explicitly or implicitly. If both use the same standard, which has applied the standard more intelligently? If they use different standards, which used the more appropriate standard? Is there some other, more important, standard that neither has considered?

2. Choose an issue or controversy in which a significant number of people are favoring or doing the right thing for the wrong reasons. Write an essay in which you discuss this problem and tell what you think the right reasons are. Include as part of your argument at least one hypothetical case in which the position you favor would be a better guide for decision.

3. Write an essay in which you defend or "rehabilitate" some idea, principle, or general cultural tendency that has unfavorable associations for most people.

4. Write an essay in which you devalue or depreciate some idea, principle, or general cultural tendency that has favorable associations for most people.

5. Write an essay that fulfills any of the specific functions for evaluative essays listed on p. 121 in this chapter.

6. Write a defense of some person, item, or action that was publicly criticized but you approve of.

7. Write a criticism of some person, item, or action that was publicly praised but you disapprove of.

Essays for Analysis

Thinking About Equality

by Michael Novak

This essay is reprinted from The National Review, *October 12, 1979.*

1 If there is a new religious doctrine in the world today, it is equality. Dogmatic slumbers always injure true religion.

2 This is supposed to be the age of equality. Yet in no nation in the world today are human beings equal to one another. In every nation, perhaps most of all (ironically) in socialist nations, there are a relative few who are wealthier, more powerful, and often more intelligent, with better health, better teeth, permission to travel, perquisites of many sorts. To hold that egalitarianism is the leading ideal of our era is to live by mystification, in illusion and unreality.

3 From Oslo to Nairobi, from Moscow to Jakarta, from Havana to New York, the more powerful loom above the less powerful. Why do we allow ourselves to be deceived? Why can't we face reality as it is? Empirically, human beings are not equal. Morally, they should not be treated so except in certain crucial respects.

4 One of the great accomplishments of democratic capitalism is that, wherever it has taken root (the number of nations in which it has done so is hardly more than a score), it raises the material level of workers to a level far beyond the dire predictions of its enemies or the expectations of its own early dreamers. It is useful in this respect to read again the doomsaying of the 1930s, as for example Reinhold Niebuhr's *Reflections on the End of an Era;* the "twilights" predicted by socialists for democratic capitalism are almost as numerous as our daily sunset. In nation after nation, the proletariat has climbed upward into the middle class, acquiring homes, appliances, and automobiles at such a rate as to have caused today's "energy crisis." At any convention of truck drivers, the automobiles driven, the suits worn by the men and the gowns by the women, are scarcely distinguishable (in price if not in style) from those of professors, ordinary lawyers, or middle managers of large corporations. Statists today complain of the *embourgeoisement* of the working

class. Many cite Lordstown (falsely) as evidence that the work force—once in daily danger of grievous injury or death—now suffers most from boredom.

5 In the United States, 97.7 per cent of all households bring in an income under $49,999. For 97.7 per cent of the population, then, there is a rather realistic equality of income, embracing electricians and professors and a majority even of lawyers. It is rather shocking to see how few Americans actually make more than $50,000 in one year, and of those how many do not manage to do so over very many years.

6 Statists frequently observe that "only one out of five youngsters will do better than his father." But one in five strikes the empirical ear as about right. In perhaps half of all cases, one would expect fathers to be superior in talent and dedication to at least some of thier sons. Downward mobility is at least as frequent as upward mobility in fact, as in theory it ought to be in any free society that rewards individuals rather than families. It is not altogether easy to pass on the advantages of one generation to the next, and, at the very least, one out of five ought to fall lower, while one out of five moves higher.

7 The reality of downward mobility helps us to put into perspective, too, another dictum of the statists. (Statists most often raise the issue of inequality, because their real purpose is to expand the power of the state. They do want inequality in at least one place: between public power and multiple private powers. They want the state to impose such equality as nature and history have not imposed. They greatly esteem the moral superiority of the state over nature and history.) This dictum holds that the top 20 per cent of the American population by income (and/or wealth) is still as distant from the bottom 20 per cent as it was in 1910.

8 A moment's reflection on family experience, however, will remind millions of Americans that the *individuals* within these percentiles have certainly changed during sixty years. Some estimate that in every decade about half the individuals in the top quintile fall below that bracket, and about half the individuals in the bottom quintile rise above that bracket. In other words, the persistence of a top fifth and bottom fifth, and even their relative distance, does not immobilize the individuals within them. In any free society, individuals will be differentially distributed over a fairly broad range of talent, character, determination, education, and luck. Of each of these gifts, some will have considerably more than others, even within a single classroom. The top quintile for each of these endowments is likely to be as distant from the bottom quintile in 1980 as in 1910.

9 Empirically, great fortunes are often lost in our sort of society, as once-powerful industries become obsolete and as families, for one reason or another, lose their knack. New fortunes are regularly being made. Many of the top executives of today's Fortune 500 were born into very poor families. Not a few sons and daughters of executives of the last generation are spending, rather than adding to, such inheritance as they once received. What goes up within

two generations often, although not always, comes down within two more. A hard empirical eye, geared to observing the fate of individuals rather than statistical categories alone, discerns much churning motion.

10 In order to mask the substantive emptiness of their faith these days, many statists hold fast to inequality as a darling scandal to dwell upon; their favorite battle at the moment (they shift fronts as they lose battles) is against meritocracy. Here statists usually put forward two arguments. The first is an empirical one, namely, that individuals now in high positions did not get where they are solely by talent, effort, or character. The second is more principled: namely that, even if they did, what is the *moral standing* of having been endowed with greater talent, drive, or character? Revealed in the latter complaint is a starkly moral vision of the universe, suitable for grammar school but incredible thereafter, according to which any just social system rewards moral standing and only moral standing.

11 To the contrary, a society rewards its most talented, hardest-working, most driven, and luckiest citizens not for moral but for selfish reasons. That society is likely to survive longer and to prosper better which offers incentives to its natural leaders, and recruits these as broadly and eagerly as it can. A society rewards such leaders not because they are more moral (although one hopes they will be) but because they lead. The justification for a meritocracy is not moral but teleological—not based upon the ontological goodness of some abstract moral scheme, but based upon a drive toward raising up natural leaders from wherever on the social ladder they may be distributed. For a society well led possesses a dynamism others, less well led, lack.

12 Few are the individuals who have come to the United States from any other culture on this planet who do not find greater opportunity here than where they were. For their children and their grandchildren, moreover, they may with all empirical probability expect even greater opportunity than for themselves. Our system of opportunity works, as the poor seem to know better than the privileged. Therein lies the secret of its dynamism and its circulation of elites.

13 Religious leaders, in particular, are easily misled by words with an idealistic ring. Against this tendency, it is important for them, especially, to practice realism—biblical realism. In the real world, even as between siblings in the same family or as between students in the same classroom, there are very real inequalities of talent, interest, desire, application, and luck. (God does not distribute his graces equally.) In many respects, nothing is lovelier than an unequal, differentiated, individualistic universe, in which tree differs from tree in shapeliness, leaf from leaf. How did anyone ever imagine that equality is a moral imperative, or that a world equal in every respect would be lovelier than the world we have?

14 Of course, the impulse arose from a moral drive within the human personality for equality under the law and for equal opportunity. Here, exactly, one must not squander treasures. For these are liberal imperatives, properly understood solely within the liberal tradition. "Equal opportunity," for exam-

ple, cannot be taken to mean the cancelation of nature and history, as if at the starting line everyone were identical. If that were to be the case, then there would be no point to any contest.

15 In a real race—a foot race in track and field—it is not uncommon for the poorest, least privileged youngster to run best. Equal opportunity does not mean that each youngster who enters Harvard enters with an identical family tradition, identical financial base, identical educational preparation, identical internal drive—or leaves Harvard with identical results. It does mean that each has a shot to make of a Harvard education a spring toward the very top in whatever profession he should choose; but that, along the way, he will have to beat out quite a number of youngsters from Yale, Michigan, Texas, and Youngstown Community College. In the real world, actually, some of the latter always win.

16 The world is often unfair. No one ever said it was a morality play. Bright parents pass along advantages less bright parents cannot, but they cannot always pass on brightness. For those who love democratic capitalism it is a joy to see underdogs win, and to watch the ceaseless invasion of the places of eminence by many born poor and without privilege. That is what is meant by equal opportunity—a possibility, a shot, often enough realized so as to be a reality beyond a doubt, but with no guarantee and little permanence for one's children.

17 God, had God wished to make the world perfectly, boringly equal, could have made individuals less various and perhaps even virtuous. As the world is, however, a social system attempting to impose equality upon nature and history can do so only by force. Which is why the illusion-drenched dream of egalitarianism leads predictably to tyranny, while realistic schemes of equality under the law and equal opportunity carry forward the energies of God's mischievous creation.

FOR DISCUSSION

1. This essay is, in part, a depreciation of a certain view of "equality." What is that view? What specific methods does Novak employ in devaluing the view? (See especially paragraphs 1, 3, 13, 14, 15, 17)

2. This essay is, in part, a defense of the system that Novak terms "democratic capitalism" against attacks by those he calls "statists." Review the list of "defensive strategies" on pp. 135–136. How many of these does Novak employ in this essay. (See especially paragraphs 4, 5, 6, 7, 9, 10, 11, 12, 13, 14, 15, 16)

3. Novak presents the "statist" view of equality as a false religion. What justification does he give for this view? What are the qualities of a false religion, as implied by Novak? Would the essay be stronger if Novak had been more specific about this?

4. The theologian Paul Tillich defined religious faith as a matter of "ultimate commitment." An equivalent term is "ultimate standard of value." If, for Novak, the notion of "equality" is an inadequate standard of "ultimate commitment," with what would he replace it?

5. Do you agree or disagree with Novak that "equality" is an inadequate standard of value?

Loom Dance

by Sherwood Anderson

This essay first appeared in The New Republic *over half a century ago. It chronicles an earlier version of a conflict that is still with us in different guises—between individual human values and the values of an industrial, technocratic society. This conflict was particularly acute in the traditionally agrarian South, the setting of Anderson's story.*

They had brought a "minute-man" into one of the Southern cotton-mill towns. A doctor told me this story. The minute-men come from the North. They are efficiency experts. The North, as everyone knows, is the old home of efficiency. The minute-man comes into a mill with a watch in his hand. He stands about. He is one of the fathers of the "stretch-out" system. The idea is like this:

There is a woman here who works at the looms. She is a weaver. She is taking care, let us say, of thirty looms. The question is—is she doing all she can?

It is put up to her. "If you can take care of more looms you can make more money." The workers are all paid by the piece-work system.

"I will stand here with this watch in my hand. You go ahead and work. Be natural. Work as you always did.

"I will watch every movement you make. I will coordinate your movements.

"Now, you see you have stopped to gossip with another woman, another weaver.

"That time you talked for four minutes.

"Time is money, my dear.

"And you have gone to the toilet. You stayed in there seven minutes. Was that necessary? Could you not have done everything necessary in three minutes?

"Three minutes here, four minutes there. Minutes, you see, make hours and hours make cloth."

I said it was put up to her, the weaver. Well, you know how such things are put up to employees in any factory. "I am going to try this," he says, "do you approve?"

"Sure."

What else is to be said?

There are plenty of people out of work, God knows.

You don't want to lose your job, do you?

(The boss speaking.)

"Well, I asked them about it. They all approved.

"Why, I had several of them into my office. 'Is everything all right?' I asked. 'Are you perfectly satisfied about everything?'

" 'Sure,' they all said."

It should be understood, if you do not understand, that the weaver in the modern cotton mill does not run his loom. He does not pull levers. The loom runs on and on. It is so arranged that if one of the threads among many thousand breaks, the loom automatically stops.

It is the weaver's job to spring forward. The broken thread must be found. Down inside the loom there are little steel fingers that grasp the threads. The ends of the broken thread must be found and passed through the finger that is to hold just that thread. The weaver's knot must be tied. It is a swiftly made, hard little knot. It will not show in the finished cloth. The loom may run for a long time and no thread break, and then, in a minute, threads may break in several looms.

The looms in the weaving rooms are arranged in long rows. The weaver passes up and down. Nowadays, in modern mills, she does not have to change the bobbins. The bobbins are automatically fed into the loom. When a bobbin has become empty it falls out and a new one takes its place. A full cylinder of bobbins is up there, atop the loom. The full bobbins fall into their places as loaded cartridges fall into place when a revolver is fired.

So there is the weaver. All she, or he, has to do is to walk up and down. Let us say that twenty or thirty looms are to be watched. The looms are of about the breadth of an ordinary writing desk or the chest of drawers standing in your bedroom.

You walk past twenty or thirty of them, keeping your eyes open. They are all in rapid motion, dancing. You must be on the alert. You are like a schoolteacher watching a group of children.

But these looms, these children of the weaver, do not stand still. They dance in their places. There is a play of light from the factory windows and from the white cloth against the dark frames of the looms.

Belts are flying. Wheels are turning.

The threads—often hundreds to the inch—lie closely in the loom, a little steel finger holding each thread. The bobbin flies across, putting in the cross threads. It flies so rapidly the eye cannot see it.

That is a dance, too.

The loom itself seems to jump off the floor. There is a quick, jerky movement, a clatter. The loom is setting each cross thread firmly in place, making firm, smooth cloth.

The dance of the looms is a crazy dance. It is jerky, abrupt, mechanical. It would be interesting to see some dancer do a loom dance on the stage. A new kind of music would have to be found for it.

There are fifteen looms dancing, twenty, thirty, forty. Lights are dancing over the looms. There is always, day in, day out, this strange jerky movement, infinitely complex. The noise in the room is terrific.

The job of the minute-man is to watch the operator. This woman makes too many false movements. "Do it like this."

The thing is to study the movements, not only of the weavers but of the machines. The thing is to more perfectly coordinate the two.

It is called by the weavers the "stretch-out."

It is possible by careful study, by watching an operator (a weaver) hour after hour, standing with watch in hand, following the weaver up and down, to increase the efficiency by as much as 100 per cent. It has been done.

Instead of thirty-six looms, let us say seventy-two. Something gained, eh? Every other operator replaced.

Let us say a woman weaver makes twelve dollars a week. Let her make sixteen. That will be better for her.

You still have eight dollars gained.

What about the operator replaced? What of her?

But you cannot think too much of that if you are to follow modern industry. To every factory new machines are coming. They all throw workmen out of work. That is the whole point. The best brains in America are engaged in that. They are making more and more complex, strange and wonderful machines that throw people out of work.

They don't do it for that reason. The millowner doesn't buy for that reason. To think of millowners as brutes is just nonsense. They have about as much chance to stop what is going on as you have.

What is going on is the most exciting thing in modern life. Modern industry is a river in flood, it is a flow of refined power.

It is a dance.

The minute-man the doctor told me about made a mistake. He was holding his watch on the wrong woman.

She had been compelled to go to the toilet and he followed her to the door and stood there, watch in hand.

It happened that the woman had a husband, also a weaver, working in the same room.

He stood watching the man who was holding the watch on his wife in there. His looms were dancing—the loom dance.

And then suddenly he began to dance. He hopped up and down in an absurd, jerky way. Cries, queer, seemingly meaningless cries, came from his throat.

He danced for a moment like that and then he sprang forward. He knocked the minute-man down. Other weavers, men and women, came running. Now they were all dancing up and down. Cries were coming from many throats.

The weaver who was the husband of the woman back of the door had knocked the minute-man down, and now was dancing upon his body. He kept making queer sounds. He may have been trying to make the music for the new loom dance.

The minute-man from the North was not a large man. He was slender and had blue eyes and light, curly hair and wore glasses.

The glasses had fallen on the floor.

His watch had fallen on the floor.

All the looms in the room kept running.

Lights danced in the room.

The looms kept dancing.

A weaver was dancing on a minute-man's watch.

A weaver was dancing on a minute-man's glasses.

Other weavers kept coming.

They came running. Men and women came from the spinning room.

There were more cries.

There was music in the mill.

And really you must get into your picture the woman—in there.

We can't leave her out.

She would be trying, nervously, to arrange her clothes. She would have heard her husband's cries.

She would be dancing, grotesquely, in a confined place.

In all the mills, the women and girls hate more than anything else being watched when they go to the toilet.

They speak of that among themselves. They hate it more than they hate long hours and low wages.

There is a kind of deep humiliation in that.

There is this secret part of me, this secret function, the waste of my body being eliminated. We do not speak of that. It is done secretly.

We must all do it and all know we must do it. Rightly seen it is but a part of our relations with nature.

But we civilized people are no longer a part of nature. We live in houses. We go into factories.

These may be a part of nature, too. We are trying to adjust ourselves. Give us time.

You—do not stand outside of this door to this little room, holding a watch in your hand, when I go in here.

There are some things in this world, even in our modern mass-production world, not permitted.

There are things that will make a weaver dance the crazy dance of the looms.

There was a minute-man who wanted to coordinate the movements of weavers to the movements of machines.

He did it.

The legs of weavers became hard and stiff like legs of looms. There was an intense up-and-down movement. Cries arose from many throats. They blended strangely with the clatter of looms.

As for the minute-man, some other men, foremen, superintendents and the like, got him out of there. They dragged him out at a side door and into a mill yard. The yard became filled with dancing, shouting men, women and girls. They got him into another machine, an automobile, and hurried him away. They patched him up. The doctor who patched him up told me the story.

He had some ribs broken and was badly bruised, but he lived all right. He did not go back into the mill.

The "stretch-out" system was dropped in that mill in the South. The loom dance of the weavers stopped it that time.

FOR DISCUSSION

1. Sherwood Anderson is known primarily for his short stories. How does this fact inform the "special strategy" of presentation in this essay?
2. Examine how Anderson uses the notion of "dance" as a metaphor in the narrative. What composite set of associations does the author build around the notion of "dance?"
3. What general value or cultural tendency does Anderson criticize in this essay? What are his methods of creating unfavorable associations?
4. Anderson's style, particularly his diction and sentence structure, is extremely spare and simple—so much so that it is clearly deliberate. What is the point of it? How does it contribute to Anderson's rhetorical purpose?

Student Essay: ARA: Why Replace a *Good* Thing?

by Dr. Benji Barfalot
Foods and Nutrition Expert
President, ARA

ARA is the name of the company that provides cafeteria services at the University of North Carolina at Greensboro. "Dr. Benji Barfalot" is, of course, a fictional character who has no relationship with the ARA organization. This essay was written by Mary Lynn Eubanks in 1979, when she was a student at the University. She insists that she wrote the essay in jest and that she actually thought ARA's food and service were "not bad."

1 It is the nature of the college student to protest against anything resembling authority. Unfortunately, the ARA Food Service has not been spared the students' wild attacks. I have even heard it proclaimed the "*A*merican *R*egurgitation *A*ssociation." Nothing can be further from the truth. Those who demand that ARA be replaced argue that it is an undesirable or "bad" food service. The qualities these students ascribe to a "bad" food service are numerous. However, upon close examination one can clearly see that these are not the qualities of a "bad" food service at all.

2 One of the most frequent criticisms is that the silverware is unclean. Unclean silverware is not—I repeat *not*—"bad." When a food service provides silverware that is not clean, it is encouraging students to bring their own silverware. Thus, the food service can eventually eliminate silverware entirely and spend the excess money on more important things—like a managers' retirement fund. Unclean silverware is therefore a desirable (rather than "bad") feature.

3 Another absurd complaint is that the food is cold. Cold food is good for you, and it definitely has advantages over warm food. One important advantage is that cold food is much more filling. Take grits for example. Grits are much more filling when they are cold and solid than when they are warm.

4 Another quality that is often mistakenly ascribed to a "bad" food service is that of poor traffic patterns. Poor traffic patterns are beneficial. They have what I call a "rat-in-the-maze" effect. Scientists have known for some time that with practice rats can learn to run a complex maze when they are rewarded with food. With time these rats become more agile. The same effect is operating when a cafeteria has poor traffic patterns. In learning to dodge a variety of carts and trays the student improves overall coordination and visual/motor skills. Such skills are often useful in a variety of situations, such as Christmas shopping and fire alarms.

5 Another misconception about food services is that unsanitary or "sloppy" practices are undesirable. However, this "sloppiness" adds a homey atmosphere to a cafeteria. Did your mother ever wear a hair net or gloves when she cooked dinner? Really? We want you to feel at home here.

6 I honestly do not know why so many people complain about slow service, either. Slow service is not an undesirable quality of a food service; it makes the meal more pleasant by making your appetite keener. For example, part of what makes a Thanksgiving meal so enjoyable is the wait, isn't it? Smelling the turkey aroma while it cooks and anticipating its delicious flavor sharpens the appetite considerably.

7 As for the food itself, there are many misconceptions. Let me educate you about them:

8 Bad coffee does not make a food service undesirable. Coffee is habit forming, it turns teeth yellow, and it irritates ulcers. Coffee is harmful to the body. Bitter and burnt coffee is almost impossible to drink. By making coffee very bitter and burnt the food service is doing the drinker a favor by saving him from physical harm.

9 Flat soft drinks are more desirable than carbonated ones. Flat soft drinks prevent burping, saving you a good deal of embarrassment. No one wants to earn the reputation of being "rude and crude."

10 Many people do not recognize the advantages of eating meats that are *very* rare. Food services that provide such meats are especially good for students. The student leads a very sedentary life (studying). Trying to consume meat that fights back gives the student some much needed exercise, in an area of the body that doesn't get used much when one is studying.

11 Vegetables are another food that many people have misconceptions about. Unenlightened people feel that vegetables should be warm and lightly seasoned. They feel that cold and greasy vegetables are undesirable. Adding large amounts of grease to vegetables makes them more healthy. They perform a cathartic action, thereby preventing constipation.

12 Rational and clear-headed people all over this campus will recognize, after thinking about these matters, that what is needed is not a change of food service but a change of attitude. ARA is not a bad food service; it has all the qualities of a good food service. Why replace a *good* thing?

FOR DISCUSSION

1. This essay employs a "special strategy of presentation" to make its point. Describe the strategy. How does it work?

2. Do you think this essay would have been less successful or more successful if the author had decided to use straightforward argumentation?

3. Think about this essay in conjunction with Buchwald's "A Crash Program for Right to Drive," (Chapter 4, pp. 104–105) and Swift's "A Modest Proposal" (Chapter 3, pp. 81–87). Can you generalize about the kinds of subject and situation for which special strategies using satire and irony might be successful?

4. Review the section on "Defensive Strategies" in this unit. What line of defense does this essay use repeatedly? How many different forms of association and dissociation can you find?

6 Problems of Interpretation: What Does It Mean?

Chapter Overview

This chapter introduces the situations and strategies of deliberation about matters of interpretation—questions about the ways things happened, the way things are, causes and effects, and the meaning or significance of events. Basic issues of interpretive deliberation include fact and generalization, definition, and causation.

• What Is Interpretive Deliberation?

Interpretation and problem solving

In deliberations about policy (Chapter 4) or value (Chapter 5), the writer assesses *the way things ought to be.* In deliberation about interpretation and understanding, the writer assesses *the way things are.* An essay concerned primarily with interpretation attempts to answer questions such as the following:

1. Why have the writing abilities of college students declined in the last two decades?
2. Did Madison, Jefferson, and Hamilton have differing conceptions of democracy?
3. Has the general notion of "democracy" changed since the days of Madison, Jefferson, and Hamilton?
4. How has the women's movement changed American life?
5. What would happen if . . . ?

We can identify a special type of deliberative essay based on questions such as these, but any kind of discourse involves questions of interpretation at various points. For example, an essay criticizing a certain movie for "promoting and glamorizing the drug culture" might be mistaken in the view that the movie actually does promote and glamorize the drug culture. An essay in response might be devoted to showing how the reviewer misread or misinterpreted the the film.

Because questions of fact and interpretation are basic to all other kinds of questions, essays that are primarily interpretive often appear in the context of larger debates about value and policy, and they take implicit stands in the larger debates. A brief review of the problem-solving model in Chapter 3 (p. 75) will confirm this point:

—In Stage I, "Identifying and Understanding the Problem," almost all of the crucial questions involve interpretation or understanding:

What is the problem?
What are the causes of the problem?
Are there other problems like it, or is it unique?
Is the problem a symptom of some larger problem?

—In Stage III, "Finding and Testing Solutions," we find further questions of interpretation:

Would a proposed solution actually attain its goals?
Would would be the costs and side effects of such an action?

Questions of interpretation and understanding surround and permeate the problem-solving process. Both questions of value and policy rest on interpretations and understandings of the way things are, how they got that way, and what changes are possible. Because judgments of value and policy are always jeopardized by misunderstandings and errors, questions of interpretation arise continually in the overall process of deliberation. And because most human problems are so complicated, it is sometimes better to withhold decisions and value judgments and, instead, try to understand things more clearly. The impulse to "rush to judgment" often needs to be resisted.

The impulse to understand experience is not as strong as the impulse to evaluate it, though it is still a valuable experience. Interpretative essays need not have a direct connection with the process of problem solving in order to be interesting and useful. There is a continuing process of public evaluation and criticism, and there should also be a continuing process of definition and analysis—an attempt to understand the nature, the causes, and the significance of events.

EXERCISE 6.1

One of the deliberative essays reprinted in Chapters 1–3 of this book is primarily concerned with interpretation. Which one is it? Is this essay clearly linked to a larger process of decision making or not?

Interpretive deliberation versus "information"

On the surface, deliberative essays focusing on interpretation might appear to be like "informative" or "expository" writing. Both kinds of writing are oriented toward understanding things rather than changing or criticizing them. And interpretive essays are often highly informative. But as close as they sometimes are, the purposes and situations of the two kinds of writing are not the same. The basic difference is that the informative essay presents and explains material while the interpretive essay develops a thesis about the material it presents and explains. Informative writing often uses the same methods of explanation and presentation as does interpretive writing, particularly when it must communicate difficult ideas or subject matter. But whereas the informative essay aims chiefly at *communicating understandings,* the interpretive essay aims chiefly at *establishing understandings.* (Informative writing is treated in Part 3.)

• The Basic Functions of Interpretive Deliberation

At this point we will examine some of the specific functions interpretive essays perform. What does this type of essay do? As you plan an interpretive essay, think of your essay as doing one of the following things:

1. *Establishing certain facts, probabilities, trends, or states.*

   Is the use of "hard" drugs among high school students more widespread than a decade ago? Is it on the rise?

   Has there been a decline or devaluation of the "work ethic" in America?

2. *Defining and analyzing certain trends, states, ideas, or movements.*

   What is the "work ethic"? What are its basic features? What class or classes of people does it apply to? How does it differ from other attitudes or life-styles?

   What is meant by "the drug culture"? What does it consist of and who does it involve? Are there serious misconceptions about it?

3. *Explaining the causes and backgrounds of events, trends, ideas, or movements.*

   Why is the use of hard drugs among high school students on the rise (or decline)?

   Why has there been a depreciation of the work ethic in America?

4. *Explaining the significance of events and trends.*

   Are recent outbreaks of racial violence in several cities signs of a "new wave" of racial conflict, or are they separate and unrelated incidents?

   What does the resurgence of interest in fraternities and sororities tell us about the current generation of college students?

5. *Assessing possibilities and probabilities; predicting the future; explaining the possible and probable consequences of certain actions or events.*

   Would it be possible to stop using nuclear power and still maintain a healthy economy in the U.S.?

   How would the introduction (or elimination) of fraternities and sororities change life on your campus?

EXERCISE 6.2

Turn back to Exercise 1.3 on p. 14. Re-do the exercise, this time restricting your projected responses to matters of interpretation or understanding.

• Issues and Strategies in Interpretive Deliberation

Deliberating about matters of interpretation involves some of the same reasoning you use in other kinds of deliberation. The topics of *causation* and *definition* permeate all kinds of deliberation, and you have encountered them earlier in this book. The difference in interpretive deliberation is the purpose for which these lines of reasoning are used and the ways in which they are shaped to fulfill this purpose. In interpretive deliberation, one or more of the following may be at issue: 1.) facts and generalizations; 2.) definition and characterization; 3.) causes and backgrounds.

Facts and generalizations

A *fact* is something that has been done, something that exists, or the properties and surroundings of an item. When we say that Mount St. Helens erupted in 1980, or that poisonous snakes exist in North Carolina, or that aluminum is lighter than steel, we are talking about facts. Nothing could be simpler. However, as any historian or reporter could tell you, getting at the "bare facts" can be very troublesome. Intelligent and truthful eyewitnesses to the same event (a traffic accident, for instance) may give conflicting stories about what actually happened. And almost any event of importance is quickly infiltrated with supposition, interpretation, and outright fabrication. Clearly one function of an essay is to challenge the factual basis of some interpretation or to set the record straight about the facts.

The nature and perils of generalization

More often at issue, however, are the *generalizations* that people draw from the basis of actual or supposed facts. Examine the following statements:

- Most Americans have a low opinion of the Congress.
- The study of foreign languages is declining in American high schools.
- Doctors are no longer reluctant to perform elective abortions.

These statements seem factual, and they may be true, but they are actually generalizations—extensions of what is true of a sample to the whole class.

In most statistical generalizing, the extension from sample to entire class is exactly proportional. If 75 percent of the sample has characteristic X, then 75 percent of the whole class has characteristic X. The statement, "Three out of four American doctors prefer Brand X" is factual only if it means that exactly four doctors were asked which brand they preferred and three replied, "Brand X"—in which case the conclusion isn't significant. The statement implies that 75 percent of all American doctors prefer Brand X. But since the surveyors could not communicate with every doctor in America, the statement is a generalization based on communication with a sample (of uncertain size) of American doctors. The assumption is that what is true of a representative sample of a class is true of the whole class.

Generalizations about the natural and physical world can be remarkably accurate (when arrived at through proper means of observation), because natural and physical phenomena themselves are remarkably uniform and predictable. Similarly, generalizations about standardized products, such as particular brands of refrigerators, can be made on the basis of a limited sample (sometimes just one); unless something went wrong with the particular item you own, there's a good chance that others of the same brand and model operate exactly the same way.

However, generalizations about human behavior and attitudes are notoriously shaky, partly because humans are are so varied and unpredictable, and partly because we have only limited understandings of human nature. Moreover, generalizations about "society," "America," or "the college generation" are even more shaky because these terms—unless tightly specified—are themselves loose generalizations. Generalizations about generalizations appear in claims like "America is experiencing a crisis of confidence." Both "America" and "crisis of confidence" are generalizations.

What kinds of generalizations are valid? The only answer applying to all situations is that *a valid generalization is one that has survived prolonged and repeated scrutiny and testing.* One of the functions of public deliberation is to provide this kind of scrutiny. And one of the most useful ways of scrutinizing generalizations is to demand strict definitions of the terms of the generalization. What precisely is meant by "crisis of confidence"? Then examine the evidence to see if there is enough and if the evidence fits the conclusion.

The statistical statement quoted earlier, "Three out of four doctors prefer Brand X," is an example of the ways in which generalizations can go wrong. This statement could be invalid or misleading in any of the following cases:

1. Only a handful of doctors were surveyed—so few that they could not possibly represent the broad class "doctors."
2. All doctors surveyed might have been employed by the manufacturers of Brand X, producing a biased result.
3. The doctors may all come from the same town, or the same medical school, thus making it unlikely that they are representative of the whole class of "doctors."
4. The doctors may have been asked to choose between Brand X and Brand Y, but Brand Z (perhaps a stronger candidate than Y) might have been left out of the question. In other words, the question may have been asked in such a way as to bias the results.
5. The choice might not have anything to do with medicine. The product might have been a stereo headphone set, for instance, something that doctors have no particular expertise in judging. The evidence, in other words, might be irrelevant to the conclusion.

Rules for adequate generalization

From the previous list of possible defects we can deduce some general rules for an adequate generalization:

a. The generalization should be based upon an adequate and representative sample of evidence. The amount of evidence should be large enough to stand for the whole experience, and the evidence should be selected in such a way as to represent diverse elements of the group. A city-wide opinion survey based on a selection of names drawn from the mailing list for real estate taxes might produce a large enough sample, but the sample could still be *unrepresentative.* People who rent homes and apartments would be left out of the survey entirely.

b. Evidence should be gathered impartially and stated impartially. A claim that 80 percent favor banning the sale of pornographic literature, based on the survey question, "Do you favor laws protecting our children against smut?" is biased by the manner of gathering evidence.

c. Evidence should be directly relevant to the conclusion. The claim that the quality of foreign language study has increased, based on an increase in grade averages, would be questionable. Is there a direct relationship between the quality of foreign language study and grade averages? In framing generalizations and in assessing the generalizations of others, don't look at only the amount and selection of evidence but also the *kind* of evidence selected and the way it matches the basic terms of the generalization. Is it a relevant index to the kind of judgment being made? Are there better kinds of evidence that should be used?

Limiting your generalizations

Generalization is a deeply ingrained habit. Most of us have a tendency to generalize too hastily and too broadly. At the same time, generalization is a necessity. We could not accomplish anything without discovering and exploiting the general and predictable tendencies of our experiences. And circumstances sometimes force us to make decisions on the basis of scanty evidence. One way to limit error and lend more credibility to our generalizations is to state them modestly, to limit their range, and to be as specific as possible.

Instead of claiming that "College students these days have no interest in politics," be more specific with, "Most of the students one talks to on this campus say they have no interest in the upcoming political elections." A claim like "There is a crisis of political confidence in America" is too vague and sweeping. More specific and credible is, "Many Americans are less confident than they used to be about the ability of government to solve social problems."

Here is a generalization that you should keep in mind when you generalize about something: Don't go beyond what you need to establish your basic point. A modest contribution to general understanding is more valuable than a flamboyant, sweeping claim that you can't substantiate and that few people will believe.

EXERCISE 6.3

In each of the statements below, how well does the evidence support the generalization?

A. Students on this campus are generally affluent. A survey by the campus office of admissions shows that 54 percent of students admitted last year come from households earning $25,000 or more, while only 8.5 percent come from households earning less than $12,000. The survey reported that this year's freshman class does not differ significantly in its makeup from classes of other years.

B. The new law calling for "full disclosure" to customers by automobile mechanics is probably unworkable. An overwhelming majority of garage owners have testified that the law would seriously impede their ability to do business.

C. An analysis of pay scales clearly demonstrates that blacks, women, and other minorities are discriminated against in salary decisions. The figures reveal that the average salary for white males is $21,000, whereas the average salary for the minority groups is only $17,500.

D. Automobile dealers are dishonest. Last week when I bought my new car the salesman tried to "sell" me several options that the promotional brochure clearly listed as "standard equipment."

E. Our city's thoroughfare system is generally in good condition and is operating smoothly. A check of the system turned up potholes and worn pavement only in isolated sections and no traffic jams at major intersections. The accident rate is down from last year.

Definition and characterization

The issue in an interpretive essay may not be the *existence* of an idea, general tendency, or movement but rather its *definition*—the essential nature, characteristics, or functions. People might agree that there is a "conservative trend" or a "rebellious atmosphere" in the country or on the campus, but they may be unsure (or may disagree) about the exact nature and qualities of such a trend or atmosphere. People may sense the need for sound management in business and financial institutions, but they may have misconceptions about what a manager actually does or what "management" actually means. The function of an interpretive essay, in whole or in part, is to establish or clarify a definition or characterization about a subject.

Depending upon the subject and circumstances of the argument, writers use one or more of the following techniques of definition or characterization.

Categorizing or *Pigeonholing:* **X** Is a Kind of **Y.** This technique identifies the item or concept by placing it in a larger category of items or concepts.

> A speech-community is a group of people who interact by means of speech. All the so-called higher activities of man—our specifically human activities—spring from the close adjustment among individuals which we call society, and this adjustment, in turn, is based upon language; the speech community, therefore, is the most important kind of social group.—Leonard Bloomfield, *Language*

Listing qualities or attributes: **X** Has the Characteristics **A, B,** and **C.** This technique builds up a general impression of something and differentiates it from others in the same class by listing its particular characteristics.

Thus we find the emergence of a new kind of organization man—a man who, despite his many affiliations, remains basically uncommitted to any organization. He is willing to employ his skills and creative energies to solve problems with equipment provided by the organization, and within temporary groups established by it. But he does so only so long as the problems interest *him.* He is committed to his own career, his own self-fulfillment.—Alvin Toffler, *Future Shock*

Partition: **X** Consists of **A, B,** and **C; X** Is Made up of **A, B,** and **C; X** Has the Functions **A, B,** and **C.** This technique lists and describes the separate parts, components, or functions of a thing.

The speech-community which consists of all English-speaking people is divided into two political communities: the United States and the British Empire, and each of these is in turn subdivided; economically, the United States and Canada are more closely united than politically; culturally, we are part of a great area which radiates from western Europe. On the other hand, even the narrowest of these groups, the political United States, includes persons who do not speak English: American Indians, Spanish speakers in the Southwest, and linguistically unassimilated immigrants.—Leonard Bloomfield, *Language*

Classification: There Are Three Types of **X—A, B,** and **C.** This technique places an object into a certain class.

The men of words are of diverse types. They can be priests, scribes, prophets, writers, artists, professors, students and intellectuals in general. Where, as in China, reading and writing is a difficult art, mere literacy can give one the status of a man of words. A similar situation prevailed in ancient Egypt, where the art of picture writing was the monopoly of a minority.

Whatever the type, there is a deep-seated craving common to almost all men of words which determines their attitude to the prevailing order. It is a craving for recognition, a craving for a clearly marked status above the common run of humanity.—Eric Hoffer, *The True Believer*

Examples: **A, B,** and **C** Are All Examples of **X.**

Culture shock is the effect that immersion in a strange culture has on the unprepared visitor. Peace Corps volunteers suffer from it in Borneo or Brazil. Marco Polo probably suffered from it in Cathay. Culture shock is what happens when a traveler suddenly finds himself in a place where yes may mean no, where a "fixed price" is negotiable, where to be kept waiting in an outer office is no cause for insult, where laughter may signify anger. It is what happens when the familiar psychological cues that help an individual to function in society are suddenly withdrawn and replaced by new ones that are strange or incomprehensible.—Alvin Toffler, *Future Shock*

Comparing and Contrasting: X Is Like Y; X Is Different from Y; X Is Not Like Y but Like Z.

Where the organization man was subservient to the organization, Associative Man is almost insouciant toward it. Where the organization man was immobilized by concern for economic security, Associative Man increasingly takes it for granted. Where the organization man was fearful of risk, Associative Man welcomes it (knowing that in an affluent and fast-changing society even failure is transient). Where the organization man was hierarchy-conscious, seeking status and prestige within the organization, Associative Man seeks it without. Where the organization man filled a predetermined slot, Associative Man moves from slot to slot in a complex pattern that is largely self-motivated. Where the organization man dedicated himself to the solution of routine problems according to well-defined rules, avoiding any show of unorthodoxy or creativity, Associative Man, faced by novel problems, is encouraged to innovate. Where the organization man had to subordinate his own individuality to "play ball on the team," Associative Man recognizes that the team, itself, is transient. He may subordinate his individuality for a while, under conditions of his own choosing; but it is never a permanent submergence.—Alvin Toffler, *Future Shock*

Explaining Origins: X Was Originally Y; X Developed in the Context Y.

Until recently, the Protestant work ethic stood as one of the most important underpinnings of American culture. According to the myth of capitalist enterprise, thrift and industry held the key to material success and spiritual fulfillment. America's reputation as a land of opportunity rested on its claim that the destruction of hereditary obstacles to advancement had created conditions in which social mobility depended on individual initiative alone. The self-made man, archetypical embodiment of the American dream, owed his advancement to habits of industry, sobriety, moderation, self-discipline, and avoidance of debt. He lived for the future, shunning self-indulgence in favor of patient, painstaking accumulation; and as long as the collective prospect looked on the whole so bright, he found in the deferral of gratification not only his principal gratification but an abundant source of profits. In an expanding economy, the value of investments could be expected to multiply with time, as the spokesman for self-help, for all their celebration of work as its own reward, seldom neglected to point out.—Christopher Lasch, *The Culture of Narcissism*

Any combination of the above. Most extended definitions of important concepts, movements, or tendencies will use a variety of techniques to cover as much territory and add as much information to the discussion as possible.

The third paradox is that our highly-vaunted sexual freedom has turned out to be a new form of puritanism. I spell it with a small "p" because I do not wish to confuse this with the original Puritanism. That, as in the passion of Hester and Dimmesdale in Hawthorne's *The Scarlet Letter,* was a very different thing. I refer to puritanism as it came down via our Victorian grandparents and became allied with industrialism and emotional and moral compartmentalization.

I define this puritanism as consisting of three elements. First, *a state of alienation from the body.* Second, *the separation* of emotion from reason. And third, *the use of the body as a machine.*

In our new puritanism, bad health is equated with sin. Sin used to mean giving in to one's sexual desires; it now means not having full sexual expression. Our contemporary puritan holds that it is immoral *not* to express your libido. . . . A woman used to be guilty if she went to bed with a man; now she feels vaguely guilty if after a certain number of dates she still refrains. . . . And the partner, who is always completely enlightened (or at least pretends to be) refuses to allay her guilt by getting overtly angry at her (if she could fight him on the issue, the conflict would be a lot easier for her). . . .

This all means, of course, that people not only have to learn to perform sexually but have to make sure, at the same time, that they can do so without letting themselves go in passion or unseemly commitment—the latter of which may be interpreted as exerting an unhealthy demand upon the partner. *The Victorian person sought to have love without falling into sex; the modern person seeks to have sex without falling into love.*—Rollo May, *Love and Will*

EXERCISE 6.4

What combination of methods of definition do you find in the last example?

EXERCISE 6.5

In each of the following passages, identify the method or methods of definition being employed.

A. When you think of your "self," you probably think of your living body, complete, as it is at this moment. But biologically it is more correct to think of yourself as merely a temporary housing, a disposable container, for your genes. Your genes—the genetic material that you inherited from your parents and which you will pass on to your children—are in a sense immortal. Our bodies are merely the carriers which they use to transport themselves from one generation to the next. It is they, not we, who are the basic units of evolution. We are only their guardians, protecting them from destruction as best we can, for the brief span of our lives.—Desmond Morris, *Manwatching*

B. Though they seem at opposite poles, fanatics of all kinds are actually crowded together at one end. It is the fanatic and the moderate who are poles apart and never meet. The fanatics of various hues eye each other with suspicion and are ready to fly at each other's throat. But they are neighbors and almost of one family. They hate each other with the hatred of brothers. They are as far apart and close together as Saul and Paul. And it is easier for a fanatic Communist to be converted to fascism, chauvinism or Catholicism than to become a sober liberal.

The opposite of the religious fanatic is not the fanatical atheist but the gentle cynic who cares not whether there is a God or not. The atheist is a religious person. He believes in atheism as though it were a new religion.—Eric Hoffer, *The True Believer*

C. The meaning of celebration, we have said, is man's affirmation of the universe and his experiencing the world in an aspect other than its everyday one. Now we cannot conceive a more intense affirmation of the world than "praise of God," praise of the Creator of this very world. This statement is generally received with a discomfort formed of many elements—I have often witnessed that. But its truth is irrefutable. The most festive festival it is possible to celebrate is divine worship. And there is no festival that does not draw its vitality from worship and that has not become a festival by virtue of its origin in worship. There is no such thing as a festival "without gods"—whether it be a carnival or a marriage. That is not a demand, or a requirement; it does not mean that that is how things ought to be. Rather, it is meant as a simple statement of fact: however dim the recollection of the association may have become in men's minds, a feast "without gods," and unrelated to worship, is quite simply unknown.—Josef Pieper, *Leisure: The Basis of Culture*

D. The most visible part of the pattern is style. *Style is the President's habitual way of performing his three political roles: rhetoric, personal relations, and homework.* Not to be confused with "stylishness," charisma, or appearance, style is how the President goes about doing what the office requires him to do—to speak, directly or through media, to large audiences; to deal face to face with other politicians, individually and in small, relatively private groups; and to read, write, and calculate by himself in order to manage the endless flow of details that stream onto his desk. No President can escape doing at least some of each. But there are marked differences in stylistic emphasis from President to President. The *balance* among the three style elements varies; one President may put most of himself into rhetoric, another may stress close, informal dealing, while still another may devote his energies mainly to study and cogitation. Beyond the balance, we want to see each President's peculiar habits of style, his mode of coping with and adapting to these Presidential demands. For example, I think both Calvin Coolidge and John F. Kennedy were primarily rhetoricians, but they went about it in contrasting ways.—James David Barber, *The Presidential Character*

E. One of the environmental movement's most interesting recent campaigns has been to save the view from Zabriskie Point in Death Valley National Monument. The federal government permits mining in Death Valley and the Tenneco Corporation, which mines borax, has staked a claim in a direct line of sight from Zabriskie Point, with the intention of opening a strip mine.

This is not the first time that environmentalists have rallied around a view. . . .

What is interesting about all this is not the battles themselves, which are typical disputes pitting one group of lobbyists against another, but the vague, intangible quality of what they are being fought over. A view is not a physical "thing" in the sense that the rare, endangered species of flora and fauna which environmentalists also battle to preserve are "things." Nor is it part of the environment and its interrelationships, what we call its ecology; ecologically unbalanced, even dying environments may still attract viewers, while perfectly balanced environments may have no scenic qualities at all. A view is not, then, a functioning, integral part of the natural world; it is nothing more than a purely visual relationship among those parts, a visual relationship seen from a certain vantage point called a "viewpoint." What defines the view as a view is, of course, man. The view is a cultural artifact. Nature does not make views; *we* make them.

We make them according to certain criteria that are even more vague and intangible than the views themselves. The places we think of as being particularly agreeable as views are "beautiful," "inspiring," "sublime," "spectacular," while other parts of the world, presumably, are not. We would be hard put to define what we mean when we use these words.—Anthony Brandt, "Views"

EXERCISE 6.6

Each of the "defining and characterizing" strategies named here precedes some subjects they can be applied to. For each of these, or for as many as your instructor indicates, write a short paragraph (50–100 words) in which you utilize the strategy named. (You may substitute subjects of your own, if you wish.)

a) Categorizing Any of the essays reprinted in this book
Your college or university
The last movie you saw

b) Listing Qualities of Attributes The religious service or "ritual" of a particular religion or denomination
Horror movies

c) Partition: Parts, Components, Functions A standard stereo system
A string quartet
A college library

d) Classification Cameras
College instructors
Pianos

e) Citing Examples The political indifference of today's college students
The political activism of today's college students

f) Comparing and Contrasting Interpretive essays to policy essays

Diesel engines to gasoline engines

Any particular type of popular music to any other type of music

g) Explaining Origins Pasteurization
Your college or university
Tennis

Causes and backgrounds

Once some phenomenon has been identified and defined, people begin to speculate about its causes. Why have average SAT scores declined over the past decade? What accounts for the dramatic rise in the number of illegitimate children born to teenagers? Why does Billy Graham have such a large and devoted following?

Probably no single issue is as crucial to the larger process of deliberation as that of cause. If we know the cause (or causes) of a problem we can try to solve it, or at least learn to live with it. If we are certain about the causes of our successes, we will certainly want to use them again.

And yet reasoning and speculation about cause is very hazardous and has greater potential for error. This section presents and illustrates some of the basic features of causal reasoning. But remember—*causes are never simple.* All phenomena have multiple causes, some of which are difficult or impossible to know. Moreover, there are always "deep" causes as well as "surface" causes. Every event or circumstance is the product of a chain or sequence of causes.

The important lesson here, aside from that of general caution, is that in order to be valid and acceptable, a statement about cause—like any generalization—should stay within limits and be stated in a modest way. The statement, "X caused Y," is almost always an oversimplification. A more sensible explanation takes the form of a more qualified statement such as "X was immediately responsible for Y," or "X is one of the causes of Y," or "One of the things that may have influenced Y was X."

"Necessary" and "sufficient" cause

When we say that X caused Y, we claim that X formed a condition under which Y took place and that there is some specific connection between the two. The term "specific connection" is crucial here. To explain a lower-than-average crop of wheat, for instance, we might note two facts: a) There was a severe drought in the Midwest this year; and b) this was an election year. Both of these facts constitute conditions under which the poor harvest took place, but only one has any "specific connection" to the poor crop.

In identifying the specific connections that make for causal relationships, philosophers often use the terms necessity and sufficiency. For any X to qualify as a possible cause of Y it must satisfy one or both of these conditions. A *necessary* cause of Y is a condition without which Y could not have taken place; a *sufficient* cause of Y is a condition capable of producing Y. A necessary condition for the invention of the train was the development of the steam engine. But significant as this was, it was not a sufficient condition; there had to be other developments as well. A severe drought in the Midwest is not a *necessary* condition for a poor crop of wheat—there could be a shortage of fertilizer or a plague of locusts—but it is a *sufficient* condition. The fact that the poor crop happened in an election year, however, is neither necessary nor —barring some bizarre chain of events—sufficient to bring about a poor harvest.

Confirming relationships of cause

There are basically three strategies for confirming relationships of cause. The first two, as formulated by the nineteenth-century philosopher John Stuart Mill, are called the "Method of Agreement" and the "Method of Difference." The third, actually an extension of Mill's second principle, is called the "Method of Proportional Correlation." Mill was more interested in building a foundation for scientific proof than in the more informal probabilities of deliberative writing. It is rarely possible to set up controlled laboratory conditions in order to study human problems. However, these methods do represent forms of reasoning that are relevant to a wide range of discussion.

The method of agreement. This method looks for the single sufficient factor that occurs in every instance of the event we are trying to explain. With each outbreak of a disease or food poisoning, health officials immediately begin interviewing patients, in search of a common factor. If the only common factor among a dozen families was that each had eaten frozen scallops purchased at a local supermarket, there is a good chance that the scallops are the immediate cause—or at least that the cases are related to the scallops in some way. If other people in the city have purchased frozen scallops in other markets and there have been no cases of food poisoning among them, then the investigation is narrowed to that particular market—either to a particular batch of scallops or to that market's handling of them.

But cases of food poisoning are much more manageable than most human problems, for which it is seldom possible to isolate a single cause. Moreover, most of us have a tendency to abuse this method by jumping to conclusions—focusing on a highly visible factor which appears with each instance of the event we are studying, and overlooking the possibility of other, less visible factors. Writers of crime mysteries use this tendency to trick us by planting *red herrings*—irrelevant clues that lead us to suspect the wrong person as the culprit.

The method of difference. This method is the opposite of the Method of Agreement. Instead of looking for the common factor in successive instances of the same occurrence, here you compare two situations—one where the phenomenon does occur and the other where it doesn't—and you attempt to find the one point of difference between them. This method is used in the procedure known as the *controlled experiment,* where the researcher sets up conditions so that they are the same in every detail except one—the suspected causal agent.

A variation of this method in the field of education is *comparison-group testing.* A researcher attempts to assess the effectiveness of a new teaching method by setting up courses of instruction for two groups of students—a "target" or "experimental" group and a "control" group. The researcher attempts to make the two groups as similar as possible—in age, class size, basic subject matter, and so on—except for the teaching method used in each group. If test scores or other measures of success are significantly better in the target group at the end of the term, then there is a possibility that the new method has helped make the difference.

Unfortunately (or, perhaps, fortunately) life is not a laboratory in which all variables except one can be controlled. Even in situations such as the one just described the Method of Difference can fail because of the difficulty of controlling, or even identifying, all the variables. For instance, teachers using a new method may be enthusiastic about the possibility of having found a new way to teach a difficult subject, while teachers in the control group may lack that enthusiasm, since they were merely repeating things that had been tried before.

Still, the method of difference can be useful in informal reasoning. Business A, which sells the same product and provides the same services and at the same prices as Business B, might decide to make an informal survey to find out why Business B is thriving while A's sales are sagging. They might discover that people prefer B because it is located near a shopping center. Or they might find that while other things appear the same, B's salespeople have an outstanding reputation for courtesy, while theirs are considered rude. You can hope for reasonable success in comparisons of this sort.

Proportional correlations. The simultaneous occurrence of two conditions, or the fact that one occurred before the other, is no reliable indication of cause.

The correlation might be a matter of natural structure. There is a high statistical correlation between thunder and rain but no causal connection—they are both effects of the same pattern of causes, parts of the same overall event. Or a correlation might be merely coincidental, as was the poor crop and the election year. However, if two conditions are independent (not effects of the same cause or parts of a single process) and one condition varies *proportionally* with the other, then one might be a cause of the other.

For example, the fact that a first-grade class with 15 students scored higher on standardized tests than an equivalent first-grade class with 30 students would cause you to suspect that the difference in class size was a causal factor. And if it turned out that a class of 20 students scored somewhere between the other two classes, while a class of 10 students scored highest of all, you would have an even stronger indication of cause.

The Method of Proportional Correlations is basically a variant of the Difference method, and it shares some of the pitfalls of that method. The crucial assumption in each case is that "other things remain equal," a condition difficult to observe outside a laboratory.

Analytic and synthetic cases

In deliberative writing none of these methods of determining cause is likely to prove completely reliable or even applicable by itself. You often find yourself trying to build up one of two different types of causal explanations—analytic or synthetic. In building an *analytic* case, you discover a variety of causes for a single event; in building a *synthetic* case, you frame a causal hypothesis to explain a variety of different things, parts, or aspects of some event. In either instance, it is important to establish the credibility of your argument not so much by the particular form of reasoning you employ as through the sheer fullness of the presentation itself.

In an analytic case you attempt to explain an event—why Candidate A won this year's election, for example—by discovering, grouping, and ranking a variety of causal elements. After making a list of likely causes, you then rank them in some way, showing that some are more crucial than others, or perhaps that one is the most important factor.

In a synthetic case you do the opposite: You take a general phenomenon—the "literacy crisis" for example—and you find a single explanatory principle that helps account for various facets of the phenomenon—declining SAT scores, decreased amount of reading and writing in home and school, increased necessity for remedial writing courses at the college level, and so on. Assuming that your hypothesis has some degree of surface plausibility, the more facets of the situation that you can relate it to, the stronger your case will be. The more exceptions or unexplained elements that opponents can dig up, the weaker your case will be.

Synthetic cases are more susceptible to error than analytic ones. Analytic cases are usually at least partially right—some of the suggested causes will be on the mark—whereas a synthetic case may be so intent upon relating various details to a single explanation that it overlooks other, perhaps more important, causes altogether. (The murder conviction based upon "circumstantial evidence" is a synthetic case. There is no direct evidence or testimony that the accused person committed the crime, but every detail of the case is explained by the hypothesis; it all "adds up.")

On the other hand, synthetic explanations can be extremely provocative, and when they are on target they tend to be more powerful and satisfying accounts, because they bring large chunks of experience within the scope of a single principle or a small group of generalizations. Even where exact relationships of cause cannot be demonstrated, the discussion can be valuable in suggesting that widely disparate experiences are somehow related to one another.

• Special Strategies: Story and Scenario

Story here means a narrative about an event that took place or leads up to the present. *Scenario* is a narrative that speculates about events that have not yet taken place. Sometimes the subject and situation is such that the most believable case that you can make—either of generalization, definition, causation, or all three—is to tell a story or project a scenario. Explain things along the way, or build a general impression of how and why things developed the way they did.

This strategy is most useful in a process of development-over-time, a series of changes, or a chain of causes. Most historical writing takes this form; the historian is not merely telling the story, in the sense of presenting the facts, but is also interpreting the story by presenting a "case" about the nature and causes of the subject.

Most examples of this strategy are too long to cite here. Bruno Bettelheim's "Joey: A Mechanical Boy," at the end of this chapter, is a good example of the narrative strategy applied in the right circumstances.

EXERCISE 6.7

How might you use the special strategies of "story" or "scenario" in each of the following cases?

A. You want to explain why Candidate X won the election last year.

B. You wish to argue that gasoline rationing, whether or not it is socially or economically desirable, could be administered efficiently and would not be the bureaucratic tangle that most people think it would.

C. Your thesis is that "intelligence" and "judgment" are unrelated, and that one is not a necessary or sufficient cause of the other.

D. Your thesis is that the new honor policy at your school will bring neither the disaster that some people predict nor the new Golden Age of academic integrity that some are hoping for.

EXERCISE 6.8

Below are several claims about cause. Which of the strategies of substantiation seems to be operating in each case? What are possible points of weakness in each case?

A. Watching television appears to have a negative impact on academic performance. At Grim High School last year nearly 75 percent of students with D averages and lower reported watching television for 20 or more hours per week; about 50 percent of the C students watched television 20 or more hours per week, while only 30 percent of the B students watched that much television. Among students with A averages, fewer than 10 percent said that they watched as many as 20 hours of television per week.

B. A large percentage of National Merit Scholars over the last decade have been Episcopalians or Unitarians. Some teaching that Episcopalians and Unitarians share but which sets them apart from other religions must be responsible for this phenomenon.

C. Doctors Frank and Stein believe that they have discovered a method of increasing the immunity to colds and sore throats among elementary school children. They selected as subjects a second grade class at Transylvania Elementary School and incorporated into their schedule a routine of 15 sit-ups at half-hour intervals. The result was 30 percent fewer colds and sore throats than were reported by the same class in the previous year.

EXERCISE 6.9

Using what you have learned about causal reasoning, explain the source of the (alleged) humor in the anecdotes below:

A. Last week at a party I had fourteen martinis, and then I had a beer. Got sick as a dog. Swore I would never mix them like that again.

B. I've got it all figured out. If the South hadn't lost the Civil War, I wouldn't have broken my arm.

EXERCISE 6.10

Examine the following examples of causal explanation. For each, indicate whether a question of "necessity," "sufficiency," "agreement," "difference," or some combination of these seems to be involved.

A. To be fettered to work means to be bound to this vast utilitarian process in which our needs are satisfied, and, what is more, tied to such an extent that the life of the working man is wholly consumed in it.

To be tied in this way may be the result of various causes. The cause may be lack of property: everyone who is a propertyless wage-earner is a proletarian, everyone "who owns nothing but his power to work," and who is consequently compelled to sell his capacity to work, is a proletarian. But to be tied to work may also be caused by coercion in a totalitarian state; in such a state everyone, whether propertied or unpropertied, is a proletarian because he is bound by the orders of others "to the necessities of an absolute economic process of production," by outside forces, which means that he is entirely subject to economic forces, is a proletarian.

In the third place, to be tied to the process of work may be ultimately due to the inner impoverishment of the individual: in this context everyone whose life is completely filled by his work (in the special sense of the word work) is a proletarian because his life has shrunk inwardly, and contracted, with the result that he can no longer act significantly outside his work, and perhaps can no longer even conceive of such a thing.—Josef Pieper, *Leisure: The Basis of Culture*

B. Most crime in America is born in environments saturated in poverty and its consequences: illness, ignorance, idleness, ugly surroundings, hopelessness. Crime incubates in places where thousands have no jobs, and those who do have the poorest jobs; where houses are old, dirty and dangerous; where people have no rights. A fraction of our people live there—less than one in five—but they number 40 million, more than our total population of a century ago. More people are jammed in several city blocks today than populated our biggest city in 1787. Probably four in five of all serious crimes flow from places of extreme poverty and most are inflicted on the people who live there. Yet most who live in poverty never commit a serious crime. . . .

Every major city in America demonstrates the relationship between crime and poor education, unemployment, bad health, and inadequate housing. When we understand this, we take much of the mystery out of crime. We may prefer the mystery. If so, we are condemned to live with crime we could prevent.—Ramsey Clark, *Crime in America*

C. In the past, permanence was the ideal. Whether engaged in handcrafting a pair of boots or in constructing a cathedral, all man's creative and productive energies went toward maximizing the durability of the product. Man built to last. He had to. As long as the society around him was relatively unchanging each object had clearly defined functions, and economic logic dictated the policy of permanence. . . .

As the general rate of change in society accelerates, however, the economics of permanence are—and must be—replaced by the economics of transience.

First, advancing technology tends to lower the costs of manufacture much more rapidly than the costs of repair work. . . . It is economically sensible to build cheap, unrepairable, throw-away objects, even though they may not last as long as repairable objects.

Second, advancing technology makes it possible to improve the object as time goes by. The second-generation computer is better than the first. . . . Improved air conditioning systems in newer buildings hurt the rentability of these 'old' buildings. All things considered, it becomes cheaper to tear down the ten-year-old buildings than to modify them.

Third, as change accelerates and reaches into more and more remote corners of the society, uncertainty about future needs increases. Recognizing the inevitability of change, but unsure about as to the demands it will impose on us, we hesitate to commit large resources for rigidly fixed objects intended to serve unchanging purposes.—Alvin Toffler, *Future Shock*

D. Numerous factors contribute to the acceptability of ideas. To a very large extent, of course, we associate truth with convenience—with what most closely accords with self-interest and personal well-being or promises best to avoid awkward effort or unwelcome dislocation of life. We also find highly acceptable what contributes most to self-esteem. Speakers before the United States Chamber of Commerce rarely denigrate the businessman as an economic force. Those who appear before the AFL-CIO are prone to identify social progress with a strong trade union movement. But perhaps most important of all, people approve most of what they best understand. As just noted, economic and social behavior are complex and mentally tiring. Therefore we adhere, as though to a raft, to those ideas which represent our understanding. This is a prime manifestation of vested interest. For a vested interest in understanding is more preciously guarded than any other treasure. It is why men react, not infrequently with something akin to religious passion, to the defense of what they have so laboriously learned.—John Kenneth Galbraith, *The Affluent Society*

E. Historical evidence speaks with a single voice on the relation between political freedom and a free market. I know of no example in time or place of a society that has been marked by a large measure of political freedom, and that has not also used something comparable to a free market to organize the bulk of economic activity.

Because we live in a largely free society, we tend to forget how limited is the span of time and the part of the globe for which there has never been anything like political freedom: the typical state of mankind is tyranny, servitude, and misery. The nineteenth century and early twentieth century in the Western world stand out as striking exceptions to the general trend of historical development. Political freedom in this instance clearly came along with the free market and the development of capitalist institutions. So also did political freedom in the golden age of Greece and in the early days of the Roman era.

History suggests only that capitalism is a necessary condition for political freedom. Clearly it is not a sufficient condition. Fascist Italy and Fascist Spain, Germany at various times in the last seventy years, Japan before World Wars I and II, tzarist Russia in the decades before World War I—are all societies that cannot conceivably be described as politically free. Yet, in each, private enterprise was the dominant form of economic organization. It is therefore clearly possible to have economic arrangements that are fundamentally capitalist and political arrangements that are not free.—Milton Friedman, *Capitalism and Freedom*

ESSAY ASSIGNMENTS

1. Write an essay in which you predict the short- and long-range effects of the elimination (or the establishment) of intercollegiate sports at your college or university. Assume that tentative proposals to eliminate (or establish) intercollegiate sports have been made.

2. Does the general public have misconceptions about some organization, occupation, social or ethnic group that you belong to, identify with, or know a great deal about? Write an essay in which you enlighten the general public on this matter.

3. Write an essay which fulfills in a specific way any of the functions of interpretive essays listed on p. 152.

4. Write an essay in which you investigate and analyze some general trend or attitude on your campus. Consider these issues: a) The existence of the trend; b) different components or classifications of the trend; c) reasons for the trend.

5. Write an essay in which you question the generalizations, definitions, or causal explanations in a recent magazine article.

Essays for Analysis

Who Killed King Kong?

by X. J. Kennedy

This essay first appeared in the Spring issue of Dissent, *1960 and has been a perennial favorite in college textbooks. A poet and author of several textbooks himself, Mr. Kennedy teaches at Tufts University.*

1 The ordeal and spectacular death of King Kong, the giant ape, undoubtedly have been witnessed by more Americans than have ever seen a performance of *Hamlet, Iphigenia at Aulis,* or even *Tobacco Road.* Since RKO-Radio Pictures first released *King Kong,* a quarter-century has gone by; yet year after year, from prints that grow more rain-beaten, from sound tracks that grow more tinny, ticket-buyers by thousands still pursue Kong's luckless fight against the forces of technology, tabloid journalism, and the DAR. They see him chloroformed to sleep, see him whisked from his jungle isle to New York and placed on show, see him burst his chains to roam the city (lugging a frightened blonde), at last to plunge from the spire of the Empire State Building, machine-gunned by model airplanes.

2 Though Kong may die, one begins to think his legend unkillable. No clearer proof of his hold upon the popular imagination may be seen than what emerged one catastrophic week in March 1955, when New York WOR-TV programmed *Kong* for seven evenings in a row (a total of sixteen showings). Many a rival network vice-president must have scowled when surveys showed that *Kong*—the 1933 B-picture—had lured away fat segments of the viewing populace from such powerful competitors as Ed Sullivan, Groucho Marx and Bishop Sheen.

3 But even television has failed to run *King Kong* into oblivion. Coffee-in-the-lobby cinemas still show the old hunk of hokum, with the apology that in its use of composite shots and animated models the film remains technically interesting. And no other monster in movie history has won so devoted a popular audience. None of the plodding mummies, the stultified draculas, the white-coated Lugosis with their shiny pinball-machine laboratories, none of the invisible stranglers, berserk robots, or menaces from Mars has ever enjoyed so many resurrections.

4 Why does the American public refuse to let King Kong rest in peace? It is true, I'll admit, that *Kong* outdid every monster movie before or since in sheer carnage. Producers Cooper and Schoedsack crammed into it dinosaurs, headhunters, riots, aerial battles, bullets, bombs, bloodletting. Heroine Fay Wray, whose function is mainly to scream, shuts her mouth for hardly one uninterrupted minute from first reel to last. It is also true that *Kong* is larded with good healthy sadism, for those whose joy it is to see the frantic girl dangled from cliffs and harried by pterodactyls. But it seems to me that the abiding appeal of the giant ape rests on other foundations.

5 Kong has, first of all, the attraction of being manlike. His simian nature gives him one huge advantage over giant ants and walking vegetables in that an audience may conceivably identify with him. Kong's appeal has the quality that established the Tarzan series as American myth—for what man doesn't secretly image himself a huge hairy howler against whom no other monster has a chance? If Tarzan recalls the ape in us, then Kong may well appeal to that great-granddaddy primordial brute from whose tribe we have all deteriorated.

6 Intentionally or not, the producers of *King Kong* encourage this identification by etching the character of Kong with keen sympathy. For the ape is a figure in a tradition familiar to moviegoers: the tradition of the pitiable monster. We think of Lon Chaney in the role of Quasimodo, of Karloff in the original *Frankenstein.* As we watch the Frankenstein monster's fumbling and disastrous attempts to befriend a flower-picking child, our sympathies are enlisted with the monster in his impenetrable loneliness. And so with Kong. As he roars in his chains, while barkers sell tickets to boobs who gape at him, we perhaps feel something more deep than pathos. We begin to sense something of the problem that engaged Eugene O'Neill in *The Hairy Ape:* the dilemma of a displaced animal spirit forced to live in a jungle built by machines.

7 *King Kong,* it is true, had special relevance in 1933. Landscapes of the depression are glimpsed early in the film when an impresario, seeking some desperate pretty girl to play the lead in a jungle movie, visits souplines and a Woman's Home Mission. In Fay Wray—who's been caught snitching an apple from a fruitstand—his search is ended. When he gives her a big fee and a movie contract, the girl is magic-carpeted out of the world of the National Recovery Act. And when, in the film's climax, Kong smashes that very Third Avenue landscape in which Fay had wandered hungry, audiences of 1933 may well have felt a personal satisfaction.

8 What is curious is that audiences of 1960 remain hooked. For in the heart of urban man, one suspects, lurks the impulse to fling a bomb. Though machines speed him to the scene of his daily grind, though IBM comptometers ("freeing the human mind from drudgery") enable him to drudge more efficiently once he arrives, there comes a moment when he wishes to turn upon his machines and kick hell out of them. He wants to hurl his combination radio-alarmclock out the bedroom window and listen to its smash. What

subway commuter wouldn't love—just for once—to see the downtown express smack head-on into the uptown local? Such a wish is gratified in that memorable scene in *Kong* that opens with a wide-angle shot: interior of a railway car on the Third Avenue El. Straphangers are nodding, the literate refold their newspapers. Unknown to them, Kong has torn away a section of trestle toward which the train now speeds. The motorman spies Kong up ahead, jams on the brakes. Passengers hurtle together like so many peas in a pail. In a window of the car appear Kong's bloodshot eyes. Women shriek. Kong picks up the railway car as if it were a rat, flips it to the street and ties knots in it, or something. To any commuter the scene must appear one of the most satisfactory pieces of celluloid ever exposed.

9 Yet however violent his acts, Kong remains a gentleman. Remarkable is his sense of chivalry. Whenever a fresh boa constrictor threatens Fay, Kong first sees that the lady is safely parked, then manfully thrashes her attacker. (And she, the ingrate, runs away every time his back is turned.) Atop the Empire State Building, ignoring his pursuers, Kong places Fay on a ledge as tenderly as if she were a dozen eggs. He fondles her, then turns to face the Army Air Force. And Kong is perhaps the most disinterested lover since Cyrano: his attentions to the lady are utterly without hope of reward. After all, between a five-foot blonde and a fifty-foot ape, love can hardly be more than an intellectual flirtation. In his simian way King Kong is the hopelessly yearning lover of Petrarchan convention. His forced exit from his jungle, in chains, results directly from his single-minded pursuit of Fay. He smashes a Broadway theater when the notion enters his dull brain that the flashbulbs of photographers somehow endanger the lady. His perilous shinnying up a skyscraper to pluck Fay from her boudoir is an act of the kindliest of hearts. He's impossible to discourage even though the love of his life can't lay eyes on him without shrieking murder.

10 The tragedy of King Kong then, is to be the beast who at the end of the fable fails to turn into the handsome prince. This is the conviction that the scriptwriters would leave with us in the film's closing line. As Kong's corpse lies blocking traffic in the street, the enterpreneur who brought Kong to New York turns to the assembled reporters and proclaims: "That's your story, boys—it was Beauty killed the Beast!" But greater forces than those of the screaming Lady have combined to lay Kong low, if you ask me. Kong lives for a time as one of those persecuted near-animal souls bewildered in the middle of an industrial order, whose simple desires are thwarted at every turn. He climbs the Empire State Building because in all New York it's the closest thing he can find to the clifftop of his jungle isle. He dies, a pitiful dolt, and the army brass and publicity-men cackle over him. His death is the only possible outcome to as neat a tragic dilemma as you can ask for. The machine-guns do him in, while the manicured human hero (a nice clean Dartmouth boy) carries away Kong's sweetheart to the altar. O, the misery of it all. There's far more truth about upper-middle-class American life in *King Kong* than in the last seven dozen novels of John P. Marquand.

11 A Negro friend from Atlanta tells me that in movie houses in colored neighborhoods throughout the South, *Kong* does a constant business. They show the thing in Atlanta at least every year, presumably to the same audiences. Perhaps this popularity may simply be due to the fact that Kong is one of the most watchable movies ever constructed, but I wonder whether Negro audiences may not find some archetypical appeal in this serio-comic tale of a huge black powerful free spirit whom all the hardworking white policemen are out to kill.

12 Every day in the week on a screen somewhere in the world, King Kong relives his agony. Again and again he expires on the Empire State Building, as audiences of the devout assist his sacrifice. We watch him die, and by extension kill the ape within our bones, but these little deaths of ours occur in prosaic surroundings. We do not die on a tower, New York before our feet, nor do we give our lives to smash a few flying machines. It is not for us to bring to a momentary standstill the civilization in which we move. King Kong does this for us. And so we kill him again and again, in much-spliced celluloid, while the ape in us expires from day to day, obscure, in desperation.

FOR DISCUSSION

1. By the time you have finished paragraph 4 of this essay, you know that its main purpose is to explain why the movie remains so popular. How does the question of "Who Killed King Kong?" relate to this explanation? To what extent does Kennedy's attribution of *cause* rest upon an interpretation of the meaning of the film?

2. Kennedy's thesis is not the kind that can be either proved or disproved by any rigorous application of the conventional means of demonstrating cause. By what standard, then, should it be judged reasonable or unreasonable, convincing or unconvincing?

3. Is Kennedy's presentation analytic or synthetic? Explain.

Joey: A "Mechanical Boy"

by Bruno Bettelheim

Bruno Bettelheim was for many years head of the Sonia Shankman Orthogenic School in Chicago. This essay first appeared in Scientific American, *March 1959.*

1 Joey, when we began our work with him, was a mechanical boy. He functioned as if by remote control, run by machines of his own powerfully creative fantasy. Not only did he himself believe that he was a machine but, more remarkably, he created this impression in others. Even while he performed actions that are intrinsically human, they never appeared to be other than machine-started and executed. On the other hand, when the machine was not working we had to concentrate on recollecting his presence, for he seemed

not to exist. A human body that functions as if it were a machine and a machine that duplicates human functions are equally fascinating and frightening. Perhaps they are so uncanny because they remind us that the human body can operate without a human spirit, that body can exist without soul. And Joey was a child who had been robbed of his humanity.

2 Not every child who possesses a fantasy world is possessed by it. Normal children may retreat into realms of imaginary glory or magic powers, but they are easily recalled from these excursions. Disturbed children are not always able to make the return trip; they remain withdrawn, prisoners of the inner world of delusion and fantasy. In many ways Joey presented a classic example of this state of infantile autism.

3 At the Sonia Shankman Orthogenic School of the University of Chicago it is our function to provide a therapeutic environment in which such children may start life over again. I have previously described the rehabilitation of another of our patients ("Schizophrenic Art: A Case Study"; *Scientific American,* April 1952). This time I shall concentrate upon the illness, rather than the treatment. In any age, when the individual has escaped into a delusional world, he has usually fashioned it from bits and pieces of the world at hand. Joey, in his time and world, chose the machine and froze himself in its image. His story has a general relevance to the understanding of emotional development in a machine age.

4 Joey's delusion is not uncommon among schizophrenic children today. He wanted to be rid of his unbearable humanity, to become completely automatic. He so nearly succeeded in attaining this goal that he could almost convince others, as well as himself, of his mechanical character. The descriptions of autistic children in the literature take for their point of departure and comparison the normal or abnormal human being. To do justice to Joey I would have to compare him simultaneously to a most inept infant and a highly complex piece of machinery. Often we had to force ourselves by a conscious act of will to realize that Joey was a child. Again and again his acting-out of his delusions froze our own ability to respond as human beings.

5 During Joey's first weeks with us we would watch absorbedly as this at once fragile-looking and imperious nine-year-old went about his mechanical existence. Entering the dining room, for example, he would string an imaginary wire from his "energy source"—an imaginary electric outlet—to the table. There he "insulated" himself with paper napkins and finally plugged himself in. Only then could Joey eat, for he firmly believed that the "current" ran his ingestive apparatus. So skillful was the pantomime that one had to look twice to be sure there was neither wire nor outlet nor plug. Children and members of our staff spontaneously avoided stepping on the "wires" for fear of interrupting what seemed the source of his very life.

6 For long periods of time, when his "machinery" was idle, he would sit so quietly that he would disappear from the focus of the most conscientious observation. Yet in the next moment he might be "working" and the center of our captivated attention. Many times a day he would turn himself on and

shift noisily through a sequence of higher and higher gears until he "exploded," screaming "Crash, crash!" and hurling items from his ever-present apparatus—radio tubes, light bulbs, even motors or, lacking these, any handy breakable object. (Joey had an astonishing knack for snatching bulbs and tubes unobserved.) As soon as the object thrown had shattered, he would cease his screaming and wild jumping and retire to mute, motionless nonexistence.

7 Our maids, inured to difficult children, were exceptionally attentive to Joey; they were apparently moved by his extreme infantile fragility, so strangely coupled with megalomaniacal superiority. Occasionally some of the apparatus he fixed to his bed to "live him" during his sleep would fall down in disarray. This machinery he contrived from masking tape, cardboard, wire and other paraphernalia. Usually the maids would pick up such things and leave them on a table for the children to find, or disregard them entirely. But Joey's machine they carefully restored: "Joey must have the carburetor so he can breathe." Similarly they were on the alert to pick up and preserve the motors that ran him during the day and the exhaust pipes through which he exhaled.

8 How had Joey become a human machine? From intensive interviews with his parents we learned that the process had begun even before birth. Schizophrenia often results from parental rejection, sometimes combined ambivalently with love. Joey, on the other hand, had been completely ignored.

9 "I never knew I was pregnant," his mother said, meaning that she had already excluded Joey from her consciousness. His birth, she said, "did not make any difference." Joey's father, a rootless draftee in the wartime civilian army, was equally unready for parenthood. So, of course, are many young couples. Fortunately most such parents lose their indifference upon the baby's birth. But not Joey's parents. "I did not want to see or nurse him," his mother declared. "I had no feeling of actual dislike—I simply didn't want to take care of him." For the first three months of his life Joey "cried most of the time." A colicky baby, he was kept on a rigid four-hour feeding schedule, was not touched unless necessary and was never cuddled or played with. The mother, preoccupied with herself, usually left Joey alone in the crib or playpen during the day. The father discharged his frustrations by punishing Joey when the child cried at night.

10 Soon the father left for overseas duty, and the mother took Joey, now a year and a half old, to live with her at her parents' home. On his arrival the grandparents noticed that ominous changes had occurred in the child. Strong and healthy at birth, he had become frail and irritable; a responsive baby, he had become remote and inaccessible. When he began to master speech, he talked only to himself. At an early date he became preoccupied with machinery, including an old electric fan which he could take apart and put together again with surprising deftness.

11 Joey's mother impressed us with a fey quality that expressed her insecurity, her detachment from the world and her low physical vitality. We

were struck especially by her total indifference as she talked about Joey. This seemed much more remarkable than the actual mistakes she made in handling him. Certainly he was left to cry for hours when hungry, because she fed him on a rigid schedule; he was toilet-trained with great rigidity so that he would give no trouble. These things happen to many children. But Joey's existence never registered with his mother. In her recollections he was fused at one moment with one event or person; at another, with something or somebody else. When she told us about his birth and infancy, it was as if she were talking about some vague acquaintance, and soon her thoughts would wander off to another person or to herself.

12 When Joey was not yet four, his nursery school suggested that he enter a special school for disturbed children. At the new school his autism was immediately recognized. During his three years there he experienced a slow improvement. Unfortunately a subsequent two years in a parochial school destroyed this progress. He began to develop compulsive defenses, which he called his "preventions." He could not drink, for example, except through elaborate piping systems built of straws. Liquids had to be "pumped" into him, in his fantasy, or he could not suck. Eventually his behavior became so upsetting that he could not be kept in the parochial school. At home things did not improve. Three months before entering the Orthogenic School he made a serious attempt at suicide.

13 To us Joey's pathological behavior seemed the external expression of an overwhelming effort to remain almost nonexistent as a person. For weeks Joey's only reply when addressed was "Bam." Unless he thus neutralized whatever we said, there would be an explosion, for Joey plainly wished to close off every form of contact not mediated by machinery. Even when he was bathed he rocked back and forth with mute, engine-like regularity, flooding the bathroom. If he stopped rocking, he did this like a machine too; suddenly he went completely rigid. Only once, after months of being lifted from his bath and carried to bed, did a small expression of puzzled pleasure appear on his face as he said very softly: "They even carry you to your bed here."

14 For a long time after he began to talk he would never refer to anyone by name, but only as "that person" or "the little person" or "the big person." He was unable to designate by its true name anything to which he attached feelings. Nor could he name his anxieties except through neologisms or word contaminations. For a long time he spoke about "master paintings" and "a master painting room" (i.e., masturbating and masturbating room). One of his machines, the "criticizer," prevented him from "saying words which have unpleasant feelings." Yet he gave personal names to the tubes and motors in his collection of machinery. Moreover, these dead things had feelings; the tubes bled when hurt and sometimes got sick. He consistently maintained this reversal between animate and inanimate objects.

15 In Joey's machine world everything, on pain of instant destruction, obeyed inhibitory laws much more stringent than those of physics. When we

came to know him better, it was plain that in his moments of silent withdrawal, with his machine switched off, Joey was absorbed in pondering the compulsive laws of his private universe. His preoccupation with machinery made it difficult to establish even practical contacts with him. If he wanted to do something with a counselor, such as play with a toy that had caught his vague attention, he could not do so: "I'd like this very much, but first I have to turn off the machine." But by the time he had fulfilled all the requirements of his preventions, he had lost interest. When a toy was offered to him, he could not touch it because his motors and his tubes did not leave him a hand free. Even certain colors were dangerous and had to be strictly avoided in toys and clothing, because "some colors turn off the current, and I can't touch them because I can't live without the current."

16 Joey was convinced that machines were better than people. Once when he bumped into one of the pipes on our jungle gym he kicked it so violently that his teacher had to restrain him to keep him from injuring himself. When she explained that the pipe was much harder than his foot, Joey replied: "That proves it. Machines are better than the body. They don't break; they're much harder and stronger." If he lost or forgot something, it merely proved that his brain ought to be thrown away and replaced by machinery. If he spilled something, his arm should be broken and twisted off because it did not work properly. When his head or arm failed to work as it should, he tried to punish it by hitting it. Even Joey's feelings were mechanical. Much later in his therapy, when he had formed a timid attachment to another child and had been rebuffed, Joey cried: "He broke my feelings."

17 Gradually we began to understand what had seemed to be contradictory in Joey's behavior—why he held onto the motors and tubes, then suddenly destroyed them in a fury, then set out immediately and urgently to equip himself with new and larger tubes. Joey had created these machines to run his body and mind because it was too painful to be human. But again and again he became dissatisfied with their failure to meet his need and rebellious at the way they frustrated his will. In a recurrent frenzy he "exploded" his light bulbs and tubes, and for a moment became a human being—for one crowning instant he came alive. But as soon as he had asserted his dominance through the self-created explosion, he felt his life ebbing away. To keep on existing he had immediately to restore his machines and replenish the electricity that supplied his life energy.

18 What deep seated fears and needs underlay Joey's delusional system? We were long in finding out, for Joey's preventions effectively concealed the secret of his autistic behavior. In the meantime we dealt with his peripheral problems one by one.

19 During his first year with us Joey's most trying problem was toilet behavior. This surprised us, for Joey's personality was not "anal" in the Freudian sense; his original personality damage had antedated the period of his toilet-training. Rigid and early toilet-training, however, had certainly con-

tributed to his anxieties. It was our effort to help Joey with this problem that led to his first recognition of us as human beings.

20 Going to the toilet, like everything else in Joey's life, was surrounded by elaborate preventions. We had to accompany him; he had to take off all his clothes; he could only squat, not sit, on the toilet seat, he had to touch the wall with one hand, in which he also clutched frantically the vacuum tubes that powered his elimination. He was terrified lest his whole body be sucked down.

21 To counteract this fear we gave him a metal wastebasket in lieu of a toilet. Eventually, when eliminating into the wastebasket, he no longer needed to take off all his clothes, nor to hold on to the wall. He still needed the tubes and motors which, he believed, moved his bowels for him. But here again the all-important machinery was itself a source of new terrors. In Joey's world the gadgets had to move their bowels, too. He was terribly concerned that they should, but since they were so much more powerful than men, he was also terrified that if his tubes moved their bowels, their feces would fill all of space and leave him no room to live. He was thus always caught in some fearful contradiction.

22 Our readiness to accept his toilet habits, which obviously entailed some hardship for his counselors, gave Joey the confidence to express his obsessions in drawings. Drawing these fantasies was a first step toward letting us in, however distantly, to what concerned him most deeply. It was the first step in a year-long process of externalizing his anal preoccupations. As a result he began seeing feces everywhere; the whole world became to him a mire of excrement. At the same time he began to eliminate freely wherever he happened to be. But with this release from his infantile imprisonment in compulsive rules, the toilet and the whole process of elimination became less dangerous. Thus far it had been beyond Joey's comprehension that anybody could possibly move his bowels without mechanical aid. Now Joey took a further step forward; defecation became the first physiological process he could perform without the help of vacuum tubes. It must not be thought that he was proud of this ability. Taking pride in an achievement presupposes that one accomplishes it of one's own free will. He still did not feel himself an autonomous person who could do things on his own. To Joey defecation still seemed enslaved to some incomprehensible but utterly binding cosmic law, perhaps the law his parents had imposed on him when he was being toilet-trained.

23 It was not simply that his parents had subjected him to rigid, early training. Many children are so trained. But in most cases the parents have a deep emotional investment in the child's performance. The child's response in turn makes training an occasion for interaction between them and for the building of genuine relationships. Joey's parents had no emotional investment in him. His obedience gave them no satisfaction and won him no affection or approval. As a toilet-trained child he saved his mother labor, just as household machines saved her labor. As a machine he was not loved for his performance, nor could he love himself.

24 So it had been with all other aspects of Joey's existence with his parents. Their reactions to his eating or noneating, sleeping or wakening, urinating or defecating, being dressed or undressed, washed or bathed did not flow from any unitary interest in him, deeply embedded in their personalities. By treating him mechanically his parents made him a machine. The various functions of life—even the parts of his body—bore no integrating relationship to one another or to any sense of self that was acknowledged and confirmed by others. Though he had acquired mastery over some functions, such as toilet-training and speech, he had acquired them separately and kept them isolated from each other. Toilet-training had thus not gained him a pleasant feeling of body mastery; speech had not led to communication of thought or feeling. On the contrary, each achievement only steered him away from self-mastery and integration. Toilet-training had enslaved him. Speech left him talking in neologisms that obstructed his and our ability to relate to each other. In Joey's development the normal process of growth had been made to run backward. Whatever he had learned put him not at the end of his infantile development toward integration but, on the contrary, farther behind than he was at its very beginning. Had we understood this sooner, his first years with us would have been less baffling.

25 It is unlikely that Joey's calamity could befall a child in any time and culture but our own. He suffered no physical deprivation; he starved for human contact. Just to be taken care of is not enough for relating. It is a necessary but not a sufficient condition. At the extreme where utter scarcity reigns, the forming of relationships is certainly hampered. But our society of mechanized plenty often makes for equal difficulties in a child's learning to relate. Where parents can provide the simple creature-comforts for their children only at the cost of significant effort, it is likely that they will feel pleasure in being able to provide for them; it is this, the parents' pleasure, that gives children a sense of personal worth and sets the process of relating in motion. But if comfort is so readily available that the parents feel no particular pleasure in winning it for their children, then the children cannot develop the feeling of being worthwhile around the satisfaction of their basic needs. Of course parents and children can and do develop relationships around other situations. But matters are then no longer so simple and direct. The child must be on the receiving end of care and concern given with pleasure and without the exaction of return if he is to feel loved and worthy of respect and consideration. This feeling gives him the ability to trust; he can entrust his well-being to persons to whom he is so important. Out of such trust the child learns to form close and stable relationships.

26 For Joey relationship with his parents was empty of pleasure in comfort-giving as in all other situations. His was an extreme instance of a plight that sends many schizophrenic children to our clinics and hospitals. Many months passed before he could relate to us; his despair that anybody could like him made contact impossible.

27 When Joey could finally trust us enough to let himself become more infantile, he began to play at being a papoose. There was a corresponding change in his fantasies. He drew endless pictures of himself as an electrical papoose. Totally enclosed, suspended in empty space, he is run by unknown, unseen powers through wireless electricity.

28 As we eventually came to understand, the heart of Joey's delusional system was the artificial, mechanical womb he had created and into which he had locked himself. In his papoose fantasies lay the wish to be entirely reborn in a womb. His new experiences in the school suggested that life, after all, might be worth living. Now he was searching for a way to be reborn in a better way. Since machines were better than men, what was more natural than to try rebirth through them? This was the deeper meaning of his electrical papoose.

29 As Joey made progress, his pictures of himself became more dominant in his drawings. Though still machine-operated, he has grown in self-importance. Now he has acquired hands that do something, and he has had the courage to make a picture of the machine that runs him. Later still the papoose became a person, rather than a robot encased in glass.

30 Eventually Joey began to create an imaginary family at the school: the "Carr" family. Why the Carr family? In the car he was enclosed as he had been in his papoose, but at least the car was not stationary; it could move. More important, in a car one was not only driven but also could drive. The Carr family was Joey's way of exploring the possibility of leaving the school, of living with a good family in a safe, protecting car.

31 Joey at last broke through his prison. In this brief account it has not been possible to trace the painfully slow process of his first true relations with other human beings. Suffice it to say that he ceased to be a mechanical boy and became a human child. This newborn child was, however, nearly 12 years old. To recover the lost time is a tremendous task. That work has occupied Joey and us ever since. Sometimes he sets to it with a will; at other times the difficulty of real life makes him regret that he ever came out of his shell. But he has never wanted to return to his mechanical life.

32 One last detail and this fragment of Joey's story has been told. When Joey was 12, he made a float for our Memorial Day parade. It carried the slogan: "Feelings are more important than anything under the sun." Feelings, Joey had learned, are what make for humanity; their absence, for a mechanical existence. With this knowledge Joey entered the human condition.

FOR DISCUSSION

1. Bettelheim's purpose is not merely to explain Joey's strange behavior but also to maintain that "his story has a general relevance to the understanding of emotional development in a machine age" (paragraph 3). State in your own words what that relevance is, as Bettelheim sees it.

2. What arguments, either explicit or implicit, does Bettelheim draw upon to establish the connection between Joey's story and "emotional development in a machine age"? Is the connection a convincing one?

3. At one point Bettelheim appeals to the causal issue of "necessary" and "sufficient" conditions. Describe his use of these concepts.

4. Bettelheim's subject matter seems to demand the "special strategy" of narration. Do you think the same ideas could have been effectively presented any other way?

5. Compare Bettelheim's method of narration with that of Sherwood Anderson in "Loom Dance" (Chapter 5, pp. 142–146). How do the differences of narrative style and method relate to differences of subject and purpose in these instances?

Student Essay: The 'Revolt Against Love': Is It Real?

by June Yorlig

1 I have been a young person all my life, and I have spent a good part of this young life reading and listening to generalizations about the "new generation" of young people. I must confess that most of the time I am flabbergasted by these generalizations, because they tend to find us in such a terrible psychological fix. It's natural, I suppose, for an older generation to constantly analyze a younger one, and it's natural for them to focus on problems. It's natural for parents to worry about their children. Maybe this accounts for some of the over-generalizations, even by scientists.

2 Dr. Herbert Hendin, a psychoanalyst, has written an article about young people entitled "The Revolt Against Love" (*Harper's,* August 1975). Dr. Hendin did a study of six hundred college students and concluded that young men and women are much more antagonistic toward one another and less capable of emotional commitments to one another than they used to be. In spite of what seems to be openness and casualness, he says, there is a "rising pitch of anger between the sexes."

3 This article is very well written and it says some good things about the dilemmas that our society makes for young people. But as I read the article I couldn't help asking myself, Who are these young people? Is it possible that I'm so isolated that I don't see these terrible problems in the people around me? At a gut level I find it hard to believe that, in general, "there is a rising pitch of anger between the sexes."

4 Dr. Hendin is a trained scientist, and I'm sure that his study is based on a proper sample of young people. There do seem to be some problems, though, with the kinds of evidence he uses. Some of it does not seem relevant to his generalizations.

5 First of all, Dr. Hendin places a lot of stock in the phrases that young people use in describing members of the opposite sex, and also in their dreams about boyfriends or girlfriends. For instance, young men describe their relationships with women, using such phrases as "ripping her apart emotionally." Women often dream of being brutalized by the men they are dating. Hendin thinks that these things mean deep hostility. "Men often feel caught up in a hostility they cannot control; women feel overwhelmed by a vulnerability they fear will be fatal."

6 However, I wonder if these phrases are all that important. I hear both men *and* women using phrases like this quite a lot, and with different meanings. Sometimes they seem hostile, but sometimes they are just slang expressions. Dr. Hendin may have forgotten to notice another difference between the generations—young people use slang and vulgar expressions more in public than they used to. As for dreams, the problem is that they can be interpreted in so many ways. It occurs to me that, if you have already decided that there is a "revolt against love," then you might interpret these dreams in the way that Dr. Hendin does. If you haven't, then you might not. Haven't women always had a tendency to feel sexually vulnerable?

7 One of the most important aspects of the "revolt against love," Dr. Hendin thinks, is the "new" inability of young people to make lasting commitments to one another. The biggest piece of evidence for this, he feels, is the outbreak of "hedonism"—pursuit of pleasure without any regard for genuine sharing of emotions, and without any regard for the future. This pursuit of pleasure is a way of running away from genuine commitment, which young people have supposedly been frightened away from.

8 I have two reactions to this argument. The first is that it seems to be an over-generalization. I know people who fit Dr. Hendin's description of the person who is afraid of commitment; but I also have friends that seem to rush *too quickly* into commitments. That's when they get "ripped apart"—not because of hostility and fear but basically because they have made the wrong commitment at the wrong time. My other reaction is that I wonder, as before, how relevant the evidence is to the conclusion. It's plain that there is a great deal of pleasure-seeking in our society, but I don't see it as a special activity of young people. In movies, in books, and out on the streets you see it among all ages. Many "hedonists" seem to me to be middle-age people trying to act like young people.

9 There's another problem. Pleasure-seeking sometimes means running away from commitment, but it doesn't always have to mean specifically that. Sometimes it means that people are just not very mature, and many young people have this problem. Sometimes I think it might mean that people haven't *found* their commitments yet, or that they have lost them for some reason. Finally, it could be that modern affluence has made it possible for more young people to do things that people of all ages have been tempted to do.

10 I don't want to make light of Dr. Hendin's article, which I recommend. Dr. Hendin makes it clear that our society has all sorts of problems that make it very difficult for young people these days. It is also true that changing sex roles have created a good deal of uneasiness and uncertainty between the sexes. But Dr. Hendin over-generalizes when he translates this into a revolt against love. I think that young people are looking for love, not revolting against it.

FOR DISCUSSION

1. Review the rules for adequate generalization, on pp. 154–155. Which of these does this essay invoke to express misgivings about the "revolt against love"?
2. The introduction (paragraphs 1–3) is rather long for a short essay. Is this long introduction justified? What is the author attempting to accomplish, in addition to stating her subject and thesis? How might the introduction be shortened?
3. Look at the author's argument about dreams, in the last two sentences of paragraph 6. What specifically is she finding wrong with Hendin's generalization at this point?
4. Comment on the style and tone of this essay, specifically the author's use of the first person throughout. What are the possible advantages and disadvantages of this stylistic strategy?
5. Read Dr. Hendin's article in the August 1975 *Harper's.* Does this essay treat the article fairly? Do you think the author's objections are valid? Are there important arguments that she overlooks? (This could lead to an essay of your own. Defend Hendin's thesis against Yorlig's attack.)
6. What effort does the author make to tone down her criticism? What does this do for her essay?

Part Two

Reflective/Exploratory Writing

Overview

This part introduces some of the basic aims, subjects, and strategies of the reflective/exploratory essay—a type which is concerned with sharing and reflecting upon human experience. The reflective/exploratory essay is distinguished from the deliberative essay by its comparatively relaxed and informal tone, by the element of personal expression, and by the frequent use of special strategies of presentation.

- **What Is Reflective/Exploratory Writing?**
  - **Reflective/exploratory writing compared with deliberative writing**
  - **Distinctive features of reflective/exploratory writing**
- **Forms for the Reflective/Exploratory Essay**
  - **"Straightforward presentation"**
  - **Narrative**
  - **Dramatic presentation**
- **Themes and Strategies of the Reflective/Exploratory Essay**
  - **Paradoxes**
  - **Enigmas and puzzles**
  - **"Reversals" and contrary notions**
  - **Emblems**
  - **Characters**
  - **Irregular arts**
  - **Personal experiences**
- **312 Topics!**
- **Essay Assignments**
- **Essays for Analysis**

• What Is Reflective/Exploratory Writing?

Two centuries ago the term "essay," which we now use to describe several different kinds of writing, referred specifically to the kind of writing that we are calling "reflective/exploratory"—one of the most richly developed forms of the essay. It is a kind of essay that is more personal, less formal, and more free-wheeling and idiosyncratic than the deliberative essay. It explores, shares, and reflects upon human experience. Samuel Johnson, the great eighteenth century critic, defined it rather deprecatingly as a "loose sally of the mind", but the reflective/exploratory essay is more than that. It is an important medium for discovering and relating insights about human experience, a sophisticated and edifying form of entertainment, and, among its best practitioners, a form of literary art.

Reflective/exploratory writing compared with deliberative writing

Even though the reflective/exploratory essay is an older form, it is still best understood in comparison with deliberation. It differs from deliberation in four basic areas: 1) purpose, 2) subject matter, 3) method and form, and 4) style and tone.

Purpose

The usual purpose of deliberative writing is to support a thesis about some human problem. It contributes to a process in which problems are identified, studied, and sometimes solved. Its basic role is one of leadership within some community or institution.

Reflective/exploratory writing, on the other hand, is less involved in the rough-and-tumble of things. It discovers and communicates insights about experience. Accordingly, its usual purpose is to *communicate an experience or an insight* in an effective and pleasing way.

The reflective/exploratory writer expresses opinions, often with great fervor and conviction; but the writer's basic purpose is not so much to persuade you or to present a case, as to make you see and feel what he or she has seen and felt. Hence, the reflective/exploratory essay contributes less to the working order of things than to our intellectual and emotional responses to experience. In this respect it is akin to literature.

Subject matter

The subjects of reflective/exploratory writing are less public and urgent than those of deliberation. The reflective/exploratory writer is free to explore personal experiences, everyday occurrences, out-of-the-way questions—subjects that might seem trivial or bizarre matters for public deliberation. The subject can be as commonplace as tying your shoelaces, as long as your reflection upon the experience is novel or entertaining enough to sustain the interest of a reader. Of course, subjects can be of general, public interest as well. But even so, in this type of writing it is the quality of response and reflection, rather than the validity or persuasiveness of argument, that matters.

Method and form

The usual method of deliberative writing is argumentation—the process of supporting theses with facts, reasoning, and testimony. The usual form of deliberative writing is something approximating the classical scheme of arrangement (see p. 34). Reflective/exploratory writing, on the other hand, is less formal, often favoring special strategies of presentation, particularly narrative. Because this type of essay tries to share experiences and insights, it puts a premium on provocative and stimulating presentation, and it is free to experiment. Some insights are most forcefully communicated, not by demonstrating their validity through argumentation, but by recreating in a reader's mind the process by which you arrived at them.

Style and tone

An essay's *style* is the overall impression it makes through the way it is written. This impression can be controlled by word choice, sentence structure, and the writer's voice and personality projected through the writing. *Tone,* a related and overlapping term, refers specifically to the author's *projected attitude* toward subject and audience. Although both style and tone can vary greatly in all kinds of writing, we can point out some general differences between the style and tone of deliberative writing and the style and tone of reflective/exploratory writing.

Whereas deliberative writing usually cultivates a dignified, public style, reflective/exploratory writing tends to be relaxed, projecting a wide range of attitudes and emotions. In most reflective/exploratory essays there is a strong element of personal expression and a more intimate relationship with the audience. Note the difference in the following opening paragraphs, one from a deliberative essay, the other from a reflective/exploratory essay.

Deliberative essay

> The student legislature has recently proposed a campus-wide referendum on the issue of twenty-four hour visitation in the dormitories. Even though the referendum will be nonbinding, I hope that those students who value their privacy and study time will come out and send student government and the university administration a message by voting NO. Although twenty-four hour visitation in the dorms would be convenient for some individuals at times, it would cause problems that far outweigh these conveniences.—Linda Woolard, (Student Essay)

Reflective/exploratory essay

> One of my amusements, a mournful one I admit, upon these fine spring days, is to watch in the streets of London the young people, and to wonder if they are what I was at their age.
>
> There is an element in human life which the philosophers have neglected, and which I am at a loss to entitle, for I think no name has been coined for it. But I am not at a loss to describe it. It is that change in the proportion of things which is much more than a mere change in perspective, or in point of view. It is that change which makes death so recognizable and too near; achievement necessarily imperfect, and desire necessarily mixed with calculation. . . . All who have passed a certain age know what I mean.—Hilaire Belloc, "The Young People"

Distinctive features of reflective/exploratory writing

These comparisons between deliberative and reflective/exploratory writing, along with your own experience in reading one or two of the essays at the end of this chapter, should give you a fairly accurate notion of the qualities of the reflective/exploratory essay. To summarize, in this type of writing four features are likely to be present:

1. The general purpose, not so much to argue a thesis as to share and reflect upon human experience.
2. The element of personal expression.
3. The relaxed and informal style.
4. The use of special strategies of presentation, particularly narrative.

• Forms for the Reflective/Exploratory Essay

Reflective/exploratory writing is particularly given to special forms of presentation for two reasons. First, it is not bound to factual accuracy or responsible problem solving—it is free to experiment. Second, and more important, special forms like narrative and dramatic monologue are often right for sharing and recreating feelings, insights, or experiences.

All of us have had difficulty trying to explain some striking but subtle flash of insight. Often a better strategy is to recreate the circumstances under which the feeling or insight was generated, leading the reader to experience the feeling or grasp the insight. This process is remarkable because the writer comes to a fuller understanding of the experience in the very act of attempting to communicate it. Perhaps you have experienced this already. The reflective/exploratory essay, as its name indicates, is intrinsically a medium of exploration and discovery.

The following are some of the forms characteristically taken by reflective/exploratory essays.

Straightforward presentation

Straightforward presentation comes closest to the usual, "expository" form of deliberative writing. The writer explains or presents things directly to an audience, making logical connections from one point to the next. But the reflective/exploratory essay differs in tone and style, which are more casual and intimate. It hardly ever comes close to "classical arrangement" (see Chapter 2), which is usual for deliberation. The course that a reflective/exploratory essay takes from beginning to end is much less predictable.

The following passage, from an essay by Charles Lamb, illustrates the highly individual, expressive, and rambling character of *straightforward presentation* as found in the reflective/exploratory essay.

> I have an almost feminine partiality for old china. When I go to see any great house, I enquire for the china-closet, and next for the picture gallery. I cannot defend the order of preference, but by saying, that we have all some taste or other, of too ancient a date to admit of our remembering distinctly that it was an acquired one. I can call to mind the first play, and the first exhibition, that I was taken to; but I am not conscious of a time when china jars and saucers were introduced into my imagination.—Charles Lamb, "Old China"

Narrative

Narrative, of course, tells a story. It recreates experience, by riveting your reader's attention to a series of events or a course of development, and demonstrating how a certain insight or feeling emerged from important experience.

The following passage has the familiar features of narrative form—action in the past tense, events described in chronological sequence, and dialogue. Note also how the situation is developing into a paradox.

> The best fisherman I ever knew was an old, solitary man named Ray Field Peele. (I think that "Ray Field" is an illiterate, anglicized version of "Raphael," but he always wrote "Ray Field" on the disability checks that I cashed for him.) One day he came into the country store where I worked after school and asked me privately for credit until his next check arrived. When my face clouded he said, "I'll show you the best fishing hole in three counties. Nobody knows it but me."
>
> I took him on, more out of affection than confidence in his story, or even out of any real desire to go fishing with him. But it was the best deal I ever made!

Next Saturday, when I met him in front of the store, I had my old car gassed up and ready to go however far within three counties was required. I was flabbergasted when he announced, "We'll walk. It's just about a half mile from here."

"Are you kidding?" I asked. (I figured I'd been had.)—William Baxter, "King of the Red Fins" (Student Essay)

Dramatic presentation

In a *dramatic presentation* you address the reader as if he or she were actually present, or talk to yourself and pretend that the reader is "listening in." This form creates an impression that is quite different from that of straightforward presentation.

At this moment I, the author, am sitting in a small, air-conditioned office at a public university. It is a pleasant and warm afternoon, and outside there are all sorts of people walking around, playing, or sitting on the grass. But right now I do not see or hear any of this because the door is closed and the shades are drawn. There is perfect silence, except for the whirring motor in the cooling unit above my head. My only company is my yellow writing pad and a batch of books, papers, and styrofoam coffee cups. Now that I think about it, I would rather be outside, chatting with some friends.

If I were writing a reflective/exploratory essay instead of a chapter about the reflective/exploratory essay, I would simultaneously present this situation to you, in the present tense, and share my reflections upon it, perhaps on the paradoxical thought that it is sometimes necessary to isolate yourself from people in order to communicate with them.

In the following passage, the author dramatically presents a scene to lead into his reflections on growing older.

> The sun flares red behind leafless elms and battlemented towers as I come in from a lonely walk beside the river; above the chimney tops hangs a thin veil of drifting smoke, blue in the golden light. . . . I have been strolling half the afternoon along the river bank, watching the boats passing up and down; hearing the shrill cries of coxes, the measured plash of oars, the rhythmical rattle of row-locks, intermingled at intervals with the harsh grinding of the chain ferries. Five-and-twenty years ago I was rowing here myself in one of these boats. . . .—Arthur Christopher Benson, "On Growing Older"

• Themes and Strategies of the Reflective/Exploratory Essay

A reflective/exploratory essay pursues certain *themes* or *intuitions,* often employing provocative, surprising, or humorous strategies of expression and presentation. A number of these are presented and illustrated here.

Paradoxes

A paradox is a statement that appears to contradict itself but which is true in some special or extraordinary sense. For instance, Francis Bacon once remarked that kings are really servants. At first glance that statement seems entirely self-contradictory—kings and servants are at opposite ends of the social scale. But when you reflect on the special burdens and dangers of those in the highest positions of authority—which "lesser" people are free of—the statement begins to make sense.

One of the most widely quoted modern paradoxes is the statement of the comic-strip character Pogo: "We have met the enemy and he is us." The statement doesn't make sense until you think of the ways people are their own worst enemies and how their greatest strengths may also be their greatest weaknesses. The paradoxical statement startles you into a fresh discovery of important truths.

Paradoxes usually involve *opposites.* They are made possible by our tendency to view experience in terms of opposites or what appear to be opposites—youth and age, life and death, male and female, rich and poor. But appearances—the superficial, commonplace perceptions of reality—are not always true, and we are occasionally startled, even mystified, by opposites "coming together."

The following paragraph forms the introduction to an essay which explores a paradox about life and death, particularly as it relates to a friend who has died.

> It was in a Surrey churchyard on a gray, damp afternoon—all very solitary and quiet, with no alien spectators and only a very few mourners; and no desolating sense of loss, although a very true and kindly friend was passing from us. A football match was in progress in a field adjoining the churchyard, and I wondered, as I stood by the grave, if, were I the schoolmaster, I would stop the game just for the few minutes during which a body was committed to the earth; and I decided that I would not. In the midst of death we are in life, just as in the midst of life we are in death; it is all as it should be in this bizarre, jostling world. And he whom we had come to bury would have been the first to wish the boys to go on with their sport.—E. V. Lucas, "A Funeral"

Enigmas and puzzles

Enigma is closely related to paradox, and it may actually involve a paradox. An enigma is something puzzling that resists explanation; it seems contradictory, not in line with the orderly flow of things. An essay based upon an enigma usually states or reveals the situation in which the puzzle became apparent and then attempts to resolve it and reflect upon its significance.

The best scientists, philosophers, and poets have always been people who cultivated the habit of sniffing out a puzzle in whatever they were looking at. The reason they do is that original insights are usually answers to questions that most people wouldn't think to ask. Successful essayists develop a knack for finding these puzzles and apparent contradictions and then explore more deeply to resolve them.

You can discover puzzles of this sort in your own experience, in the academic subjects that you are studying and in the people you know. Your friend Jennifer, for instance, has living and working habits that are sloppy and disorganized, and yet her work is as meticulous and detailed as any you have seen. What is it about her character, or about people in general, that explains this?

This passage is from an essay that explores some perplexing anomalies in the way married couples behave. Note that the puzzle consists of apparent opposites—"simpatico" behavior versus inner incompatibility.

> Every once in a while I observe, at a dinner party, at church, or at some other purely social gathering, a couple who seem to be so happily married that it makes me envious. They are so affectionate, they enjoy and admire each other so much, they are so considerate of one another, that I almost want to cry. Their married relationship is so different from most, and so different from my own, that I can't help wondering how the rest of us went wrong.
>
> Here's the strange part: I have known three such couples in the last three years, and I have envied each couple their really simpatico relationship. And each couple, within six months of my first envying them, has gotten a divorce.
>
> I'm not superstitious, mind you, or given to voodoo. I don't think my envy causes relationships to go haywire. But there has to be *some* connection here, don't you think?—June Yorlig, "So Simpatico!" (Student Essay)

"Reversals" and contrary notions

A reversal runs contrary to commonplace thinking or popular wisdom on a subject. Essays that turn upon reversals of the commonplace are usually appealing because of their element of surprise. They can be edifying as well, since they startle readers into unaccustomed avenues of thought. Sometimes these essays have an element of humor, which works in favor of the author. If the audience realizes that you are only partly serious in presenting something so outlandish or so completely at odds with common sense, you are free to present your insight in an extreme way.

Reversals are possible because very few truths are absolute. For every truth, chances are there is an opposite truth. It may not be an "equal" truth, and it may not be a useful truth; but it may be sobering or intriguing nevertheless. Consider the possibilities that honesty is not always the best policy, that laziness is a virtue, or that it is foolish to plan ahead.

Thinking in this way involves a kind of mental gymnastics, a kind of game-playing. The game may not always produce anything particularly startling, but it can be useful nevertheless. Set aside a day. On this day, whenever anyone utters a generalization, ask yourself if the opposite could also be true. Take a reversal of any thought and see where it leads you, how it relates to your own experience, and the various ways in which it might be true. You may come up with something worth forming into an essay.

As is also the case with paradoxes and puzzles, essays built around reversals usually take one of two different forms. One form is straightforward presentation, which states the reversal and then explores it. The other is narrative form, which tells a story, revealing the reversal in the course of events.

The following passage contains excerpts from Henry David Thoreau's spirited put-down of "philanthropy," in *Walden.* Note that Thoreau is not deprecating philanthropy simply to be clever or contrary—he seriously believes that it is overrated and that it gets in the way of more genuine and useful ways of being "good."

> If I knew for a certainty that a man was coming to my house with the conscious design of doing me good, I should run for my life . . . for fear that I should get some of his good done to me,—some of its virus mingled with my blood. . . . A man is not a good *man* to me because he will feed me if I should be starving, or warm me if I should be freezing, or pull me out of a ditch if I should ever fall into one. I can find you a Newfoundland dog what will do as much. Philanthropy is not love for one's fellow-man in the broadest sense. . . .
>
> Philanthropy is almost the only virtue which is sufficiently appreciated by mankind. Nay, it is greatly overrated; and it is our selfishness which overrates it. A robust poor man, one sunny day here in Concord, praised a fellow-townsman to me, because, as he said, he was kind to the poor, meaning himself. The kind uncles and aunts of the race are more esteemed than its true spiritual fathers and mothers.—Henry David Thoreau, *Walden*

Emblems

An emblem is an object, scene, or act which symbolizes or suggests some larger idea or experience. Emblems can be powerful devices of exploration and reflection, because they are integral to the way the human mind absorbs, interprets, and retains experience.

First of all, we have a strong tendency to interpret things according to their resemblances to other things. In trying to understand new concepts, we make analogies—we look for likenesses to things we already know about. It may help a child to understand the nature of sedimentary rocks, for example, if you explain that they are like the fragments of a birthday cake that Mom has made over into a pudding. Analogies can be instruments of discovery as well as of teaching, and a number of great ideas and scientific theories have their origins in a momentary flash of insight, some suddenly perceived likeness between different things or fields of experience—a connection that no one had thought of before.

Poets have recognized and used analogies as instruments of reflection and exploration. You can see the process of analogy at work in the following short poem by Walt Whitman, in which the action of the spider becomes an emblem for—and a way of understanding—an important human experience.

A Noiseless Patient Spider

A noiseless patient spider,
I mark'd where on a little promontory it stood isolated,
Mark'd how to explore the vacant vast surrounding,
It launch'd forth filament, filament, filament, out of itself,
Ever unreeling them, ever tirelessly speeding them.

And you O my soul where you stand,
Surrounded, detached, in measureless oceans of space,
Ceaselessly musing, venturing, throwing, seeking the spheres to
connect them,
Till the bridge you will need be form'd, till the ductile anchor hold,
Till the gossamer thread you fling catch somewhere, O my soul.

—From *Leaves of Grass*

Emblems also reflect the devices of memory. We instinctively remember things by connecting them to sensory images, particularly visual images. Everyone has had the experience of running across an old photograph or sweater that releases a flood of memories, sometimes in vivid detail, about experiences and feelings long forgotten. We "attach" memories to objects, investing them with earlier thoughts and feelings. And we attach sentimental value to them, as ways of preserving something out of the flow of time. We hate to see old buildings or streets torn up, because we have memories stored in them.

These images can be powerful instruments of reflection because we can tap them for lost memories; they can lead us to new insights about ourselves, as we relive crucial moments. The best way of communicating such insights is by letting readers in on the process, developing the emblem—the scene, place, or incident—in a narrative, revealing its significance. In this autobiographical passage, a clump of trees on the prairie symbolizes something important about the author's youth.

> Far away on the almost bare line of the prairie horizon a group of trees used to show. There was a tall one, and a short one, and then a tallish crooked one, and another short one. And to my childish eyes they spelled l-i-f-e, as plainly as any word in my reader was spelled. They were the point that most fascinated me as

> I knelt at the upstairs window, with my elbows on the sill and my chin on my folded arms. I don't know when I first noticed them, for they had been there always, so far as I could remember, a scanty little bit of fringe on a horizon that was generally clear and bare. There were tips of other woods farther to the south, woods that were slightly known to me; but this group of trees at the very limit of seeing appeared to lie beyond the knowledge of anyone. . . .
>
> I suppose the fact that the trees were evidently big and old—ours were still young and small—and perhaps a part of some woods, was their greatest interest to me. For no one can picture what the woods mean to the prairie child. They are a glimpse of dream things, an illustration of poems read, a mystery of undefined possibilities.—Margaret Lynn, *A Stepdaughter of the Prairie*

Characters

The *character* is one of the oldest reflective strategies. It pieces together a portrait—either of a distinct individual or of a composite, generalized figure—for the purpose of revealing, criticizing, or praising certain personality traits. The portrait can be satirical, deriving its humor as well as its message from the fact that the character is not only objectionable or laughable but also the embodiment of some fad or folly.

Essays devoted to characters can use either straightforward presentation or narrative. The former discusses the character's traits openly, giving concrete examples of each; the latter puts together a story in which the character is revealed through appearance, actions, and words. The following passage on the character of "the bore" is excerpted from an essay by Theophrastus, the Greek philosopher/scientist who is credited with inventing the "character" essay. This essay, which was probably composed in the fourth century B.C., illustrates the "straightforward" technique of describing the character trait in question and then following up with examples.

> We may define a bore as a man who cannot refrain from talking. A bore is the sort of fellow who, the moment you open your mouth, tells you that your remarks are idle, that he knows all about it, and if you'll only listen, you'll soon find out. As you attempt to make answer, he suddenly breaks in with such interruptions as: "Don't forget what you were about to say"—"That reminds me"—"What an admirable thing talk is!"—"But, as I omitted to mention"—"You grasp the idea at once"—"I was watching this long time to see whether you would come to the same conclusion as myself." In phrases like this he's so fertile that the person who happens to meet him cannot even open his mouth to speak.—Translated by Charles E. Bennett and William A. Hammond

The following excerpt is from a narrative essay which centers on the character of an old man named Washington Woodward. The passage contains one of the many examples that the author uses to build and explore the ethics of a character who is absorbed in activity but oblivious of its effects or usefulness.

By the time he was twenty-five, he had repaired or built everything but a locomotive. Give him a forge and some scraps of old iron, my grandfather said, and he could make a locomotive too. I knew him to shoe a horse, install plumbing, dig a well, make a gun, build a road, lay a dry stone wall, do the foundation and frame of a house, invent a new kind of trap for beavers, manufacture his own shotgun shells, grind knives and turn a baseball bat on a lathe. The bat was made out of rock maple, and so heavy that I could barely lift it to my shoulders when he made it for my thirteenth birthday. The trouble was that he was incredibly slow. He was not interested in your problems, but in the problems of the job itself. He didn't care if it took him five weeks to shingle an outhouse that plumbing was going to outmode in a year. This was one outhouse that would *stay* shingled, although the shingles might protect only the spiders and the mother cat.—Donald Hall, "A Hundred Thousand Straightened Nails"

Irregular arts

Essays based upon "irregular arts" are usually humorous because they describe activities that most of us wouldn't think of as "arts" at all. They often have titles like, "The Art of ____." The activities they describe are often wiley, mischievous, and anti-social, although not seriously evil:

- The Art of Bluffing Your Way Through a Course
- The Art of Conning Your Roommate
- Backing Down with Dignity
- Psychological Tennis
- The Art of Pretending to Be Well Informed

Do essays based on irregular arts have any serious point? Sometimes not, but there are at least three ways in which their purpose gets beyond that of entertainment alone. First, they often have a satiric intent—they uncover the guiles and deceptions that are a part of most human activity. Second, in describing an irregular art, the essayist functions as a kind of amateur psychologist or sociologist, formulating a theory about some unstudied aspect of human behavior, and reflecting upon it. Finally, there is a point to be made about the amazing subtlety and delicacy of human interactions, even under inglorious or mischievous circumstances. Essays based on irregular arts are often good-natured celebrations of human ingenuity, as well as works of satire.

The following passage is from a book by the British literary scholar and humorist Stephen Potter, on one aspect of what he calls "gamesmanship." The book is really a series of essays on "The Art of Winning Games Without Actually Cheating."

The great second axiom of gamesmanship is now worded as follows: THE FIRST MUSCLE STIFFENED (in his opponent by the Gamesman) IS THE FIRST POINT GAINED. Let us consider some of the processes of Defeat by Tension.

The standard method is known as the "flurry".

The "flurry" is for use when changing in the locker-room before a rackets match, perhaps, or leaving home in your opponent's car for, say, a game of lawn tennis. The object is to create a state of anxiety, to build up an atmosphere of muddled fluster.

Supposing, for instance, that your opponent has a small car. He kindly comes along to pick you up before the game. Your procedure should be as follows: (1) Be late in answering the bell. (2) Don't have your things ready. Appearing at last, (3) call *in an anxious or "rattled" voice* to wife (who need not, of course, be there at all) some taut last-minute questions about dinner. Walk down path and (4) realise you have forgotten shoes. Return with shoes; then just before getting into car pause (5) *a certain length of time* (see any threepenny edition of Bohn's *Tables*) and wonder (i) whether racket is at the club or (ii) whether you have left it "in the bath-room at top of the house".

Like the first hint of paralysis, a scarcely observable fixing of your opponent's expression should now be visible. Now is the time to redouble the attack. Map-play can be brought to bear. On the journey let it be known that you "think you know a better way", *which should turn out, when followed, to be incorrect and should if possible lead to a blind alley.*

Meanwhile, time is getting on. Opponent's tension should have increased.
—Stephen Potter, *The Complete Upsmanship*

Personal experiences

Essays about personal experiences may be humorous or somber, whimsical or meditative in tone. What they all share is the situation in which authors gain distinctive viewpoints through experiences—some way (or place) they lived, some way they were brought up, or some position they attain. The authors reflect on the experiences, gain some useful or intriguing insights and use the medium of the essay to share those experiences and the insights.

Reflective/exploratory essays make use of both the extraordinary and commonplace experiences. *Extraordinary* experiences involve out-of-the-ordinary circumstances. You had an "out-of-body" experience, crossed the Atlantic in a sailboat, or attended a cock-fight. Perhaps you grew up on a South Sea island or are the child of a movie star. Because most people will never have these experiences or be in these positions, they are eager to know what they are like and to share in the insights of those who relate them in an entertaining way.

A word of caution—extraordinary experiences are automatically interesting, at least at the beginning. But if you rely on this automatic interest alone, your essay may fall flat. You should develop some central point or insight out of the special point of view that your experience has afforded you. If that insight embodies one or more of the other strategies—a paradox, an enigma, an emblem or an analogy—then so much the better. George Orwell's "Shooting an Elephant," at the end of this chapter, is a classic example of an essay that relates an extraordinary experience and draws from that experience an intriguingly paradoxical insight.

Commonplace experiences are just the opposite of extraordinary ones. These are experiences that most people have in their lifetimes—growing into and out of adolescence, having children, having a job for the first time, and experiencing the deaths of loved ones.

Even though commonplace experiences are not automatically interesting in the way that extraordinary experiences are, they have immense potential as subjects. Many of these experiences are pivotal in individual human lives; they generate powerful emotions, and the fact that many people have these same emotions increases their power. Moreover, even though many people have these experiences, they have them at different states of their lives and in ways that reflect their own personalities. The interest or beauty of an essay may lie in its highly individual response to a commonplace experience.

Finally, even though pivotal experiences provide us with moments of deep emotion and insight, these emotions and insights are fleeting. They get lost in the hubbub of commonplace activity. The essay, in its attempt to recall and recount the experience, becomes an instrument of exploration and recovery for both author and reader. In the following passage, the author recounts and reflects upon a commonplace experience—going back to the place where one grew up.

> Sometimes I think that those of us who are now in our thirties were born into the last generation to carry the burden of "home," to find in family life the source of all tension and drama. I had by all objective accounts a "normal" and a "happy" family situation, and yet I was almost thirty years old before I could talk to my family on the telephone without crying after I had hung up. We did not fight. Nothing was wrong. And yet some nameless anxiety colored the emotional charges between me and the place that I came from. The question of whether or not you could go home again was a very real part of the baggage with which we left home in the fifties; I suspect that it is irrelevant to the children born of the fragmentation after World War II. A few weeks ago in a San Francisco bar I saw a pretty young girl on crystal take off her clothes and dance for the cash prize in an "amateur-topless" contest. There was no particular sense of moment about this, none of the effect of romantic degradation, of "dark journey," for which my generation strived so assiduously. What sense could that girl make of, say, *Long Day's Journey into Night?* Who is beside the point?—Joan Didion, "On Going Home"

EXERCISE 7.1

Reflective/exploratory essays are often thought of as "poems in prose" because their forms and thematic strategies are often identical to the forms and thematic strategies of lyric poetry.

Several well-known poems are reprinted here. For each, name the form that it uses (see pp. 189–191) and the theme or strategy (or combination of themes and strategies) that the poem uses (see pp. 191–199).

A. THE WORLD IS TOO MUCH WITH US

The world is too much with us; late and soon,
Getting and spending, we lay waste our powers;
Little we see in Nature that is ours;
We have given our hearts away, a sordid boon!
This Sea that bares her bosom to the moon;
The winds that will be howling at all hours,
And are up-gathered now like sleeping flowers;
For this, for everything, we are out of tune;
It move us not.—Great God! I'd rather be
A Pagan suckled in a creed outworn;
So might I, standing on this pleasant lea,
Have glimpses that would make me less forlorn;
Have sight of Proteus rising from the sea;
Or hear old Triton blow his wreathed horn.

William Wordsworth

B. MY MISTRESS' EYES ARE NOTHING LIKE THE SUN

My mistress' eyes are nothing like the sun;
Coral is far more red than her lips' red;
If snow be white, why then her breasts are dun;
If hairs be wires, black wires grow on her head.
I have seen roses damasked red and white,
But no such roses see I in her cheeks;
And in some perfumes is there more delight
Than in the breath that from my mistress reeks.
I love to hear her speak, yet well I know
That music hath a far more pleasing sound;
I grant I never saw a goddess go:
My mistress, when she walks, treads on the ground.
And yet, by heaven, I think my love as rare
As any she, belied with false compare.

William Shakespeare

C. I SAW IN LOUISIANA A LIVE-OAK GROWING

I saw in Louisiana a live-oak growing,
All alone stood it and the moss hung down from the branches,
Without any companion it grew there uttering joyous leaves of dark green,
And its look, rude, unbending, lusty, made me think of myself,

But I wonder'd how it could utter joyous leaves standing alone there without its friend near, for I knew I could not,
And I broke off a twig with a certain number of leaves upon it, and twined around it a little moss,
And brought it away, and I have placed it in sight in my room,
It is not needed to remind me as of my own dear friends,
(For I believe lately I think of little else than of them,)
Yet it remains to me a curious token, it makes me think of manly love;
For all that, and though the live-oak glistens there in Louisiana solitary in a wide flat space,
Uttering joyous leaves all its life without a friend a lover near,
I know very well I could not.

Walt Whitman

• 312 Topics!

The following list of topics is reprinted from an appendix to a textbook and anthology, William M. Tanner's *Modern Familiar Essays.* As you read through the list, try to envision which particular theme or strategy (or combination) seems to be implied or invited by the topic. You may draw a blank on some of these because a list of themes and strategies is by no means exhaustive. In these cases, try to come up with a phrase or sentence that describes the *type* of theme that might be represented by the topic. And don't forget that this list might provide an idea for your next essay!

1. The Joy of Being Envied
2. On Weighing in Public
3. How the Animals Must Pity Us!
4. On Knowing "Just Enough to Get By"
5. My Imaginary Obligations
6. The Stupidity of Good People
7. Where but in College?
8. On Complimenting Nature
9. The Pleasing Torture of Being in Love
10. Some Pleasures of Ignorance
11. On Being a Confidante
12. The Gentle Art of "Passing the Buck"
13. My First Appearance on the Stage
14. On Saying It with Flowers
15. Our "Utmost" Age
16. The Ignominy of Being Genteel
17. On Being a Minister's Son (Daughter)
18. Coddled Intellects
19. "These Terrible Young People"
20. The Embarrassment of Being Civilized
21. How to Lose One's Friends
22. On Being a Foreigner
23. Buying Discontent
24. On Developing a Complex
25. Pollyannaism and Peterpantheism
26. Burdensome Leisure
27. On Being a Misfit

28. The Perils of Literacy
29. The Horrible Fact
30. On Being One of the Public
31. Too Much Sprawl
32. Fashions in Faces
33. "Suppressed Desires"
34. On Being Original
35. If the Truth Must Be Told
36. "And Everything"
37. On Giving the Public What It Wants
38. The Sweetness of Romantic Sorrow
39. Prairie Thoughts
40. Mountain Reflections
41. On Being Ordinary
42. The Taste of Life
43. Between Acts
44. On a Feeling of Superiority
45. The Attraction of Fresh Paint
46. On Being a "Beauty Contestant"
47. Grandmother's Grandchildren
48. Expressive Hands
49. On Avoiding the Subject
50. While Waiting for the Curtain to Rise
51. Silent Facial Communication
52. On Stepping Aside to Let the World Pass
53. Freckle Cures
54. The Trials of an Only Son (Daughter)
55. On Carrying an Umbrella
56. Traveling by Night in a Day Coach
57. My Eternal Question
58. On Being Found Out
59. Bluff and Bluffers
60. The Ills We Have
61. On Being Thought Odd
62. Color Personalities
63. The Perils of Being Thought Clever
64. Loud Speakers
65. On Knowing the Difference
66. Mental Poverty
67. Acting Up
68. On Being *There*
69. Artificial Enthusiasms
70. Rich in Knowledge, Poor in Wisdom
71. On Being an "Advanced Thinker"
72. Intellectual Servility
73. On Laughing at Myself
74. As Others Think Me
75. On Keeping Open-House
76. Presenting the Real Me
77. On Standing By
78. "Just Fishing"
79. That Well-Dressed Feeling
80. On Coming Across
81. Reflections of a "Stylish Stout"
82. On Weighing What You Should Weigh
83. The Goat Impulse in People
84. On Keeping Up
85. Personality in Hats
86. On Carving at the Table
87. Signing on the Dotted Line
88. Old-Furniture Sensations
89. On Sunday Night Suppers
90. The Folly of Being Too Wise
91. On Going to Church
92. My Motley Personality
93. Our Serious Teens
94. On Being Grown-up All the Time
95. The Gentle Art of Sneezing
96. Childish Things
97. Why Owls Are Considered Wise
98. On Anticipating the Worst
99. Sympathy for the Uninitiated
100. Woman's Latest Embellishment
101. A Plea for More Color in Man's Apparel
102. Sunday Evening Sounds
103. Dog Language
104. Our Bird Neighbors
105. "Mental Second Wind"
106. The Simple Truth

107. On Putting on a Brave Front
108. The Joys of Whitewashing
109. "Not That I Am Superstitious"
110. On Being Psychoanalyzed
111. The Tyranny of Tradition
112. My First Proposal
113. On Choosing a Necktie
114. "And All That Sort of Thing"
115. Fallacies We Live By
116. On Going to the Ant
117. "If You Know What I Mean"
118. On Keeping Abreast of the Times
119. Exaggeration in Advertising
120. Uses of Perversity
121. On Writing for Publication
122. Convenient Deafness
123. Easy-Chair Types
124. The Tyranny of Trifles
125. On Buying Social Standing
126. Rediscovering Rural Life
127. Frost Pictures
128. A Cure for Insomnia
129. On Writing at the Top of One's Voice
130. Jargon and Jazz
131. Wood-Fire Magic
132. "Shockingly Vulgar"
133. Frenzied Fiction
134. On Being an Immigrant
135. The Pleasures of Home
136. Springtime Musings
137. The Summer-Vacation Habit
138. On Mooning
139. The Tourist Instinct
140. Music Moods
141. Haunting Melodies
142. Oriental-Rug Magic
143. On Closing One's Mind
144. Radio Widows
145. Mental Shoddiness
146. A Forgetting System
147. On Apologizing
148. Personality in Stationery
149. If I Were Janitor
150. Janitorial Affability
151. Janitorial Tyranny
152. On Eating Crow
153. A Defense of College Slang
154. Calling on the Dean
155. My Taste in Murders
156. Glass Houses
157. On Being a Specimen
158. Space Reserved
159. Thin Ice
160. On Having One's Fortune Told
161. "People Like That"
162. Borrowed Social Capital
163. Inflated Social Values
164. The Relative Proportion of Things
165. On Keeping Quiet
166. Protective Coloring among Teachers
167. Human though Educated
168. Radiomania
169. Wood Smoke
170. Too Much Personality
171. Counting Calories
172. Indoor Botany
173. Antiques Old and New
174. On Nursing a Grouch
175. Personality in Houses
176. Literary Sediment
177. By Candlelight
178. That Haunting Odor
179. By-Products of Gardening
180. On Being Thought Stupid
181. Torches and Firebrands
182. On Taking Thought of One's Stature
183. Calories and Vitamines
184. Weather Moods
185. Museum Types
186. On Secret Drawers
187. The Fad of Collecting
188. My First Poem
189. On Preserving the Past
190. Holding Up Father
191. Fashions in Hair
192. The Necessity of Growing a Moustache

193. American Profiles
194. On Being a Model Young Person
195. Styles in Necklaces
196. Museum Romances
197. Love's Minor Fictions
198. "Did I Ever Look Like That?"
199. Front-Door Beggars
200. Eyes of Youth
201. A Long, Long Thought
202. Beyond Earth
203. A Dip into Astronomy
204. On Wearing Colored Glasses
205. Speed Mania
206. Music with Meals
207. Next to Reading Matter
208. A Plague of Holidays
209. Personality in Musical Instruments
210. Horse Sense
211. A Defense of Routine in Work
212. Deformed Spelling
213. Idealizing the Past
214. The Oblivescence of the Disagreeable
215. Autumn Joys
216. The Passing of Privacy
217. A Plague of Optimism
218. The Utmost in Superlatives
219. On Being Interviewed
220. The Pleasure of Reading Essays (Poetry)
221. Animal Communication
222. Seriousness in Comedians
223. Voices and Gestures
224. The Odor of Sanctity
225. Sawdust
226. Brownies and Pixies
227. Thrill Chasers
228. The Mating Season in College
229. On Opening the Summer House
230. Volsteading Literature
231. The Main-Street Mind
232. Stage Banquets
233. Why Is a Best-Seller?
234. Individuality in Hens
235. The Promise of the Garden
236. The Chaotic School of Writers
237. The Curse of "Confessions" in Modern Literature
238. Our Clever Young Journalists
239. Confessions of a "Column Conductor"
240. Our Mania for "Exposing" People
241. On Easy Writing
242. Sentimental Americans
243. The Narcotic School of Writers
244. On Being an Habitual Objector
245. Subjective Aristocracy
246. American Humor
247. Tides of the Mind
248. On Apologizing for Nature
249. American Laughter
250. Vicarious Reading
251. Barnyard Aristocrats
252. Senior Indifference
253. On Defending Nature
254. Evening Moods
255. The Tyranny of an Economical Mind
256. Our Passion for Perpetuation
257. On Playing a Saxophone
258. Aviation Fancies
259. The Literature of Advertising
260. Conventionality in Epitaphs
261. Guest Towels
262. Choice Sentiments
263. The Passing of Family Kitchens
264. Clerks and "Salespeople"
265. The "Ye Shoppe" Epidemic
266. Too Much Improvement
267. American High-Lustre Finish
268. First-Year Tragedies (Comedies)
269. The Tumultuous Privacy of City Life
270. Individuality of the Days of the Week
271. On Keeping Time
272. The Superiority Complex
273. On Exulting in Vulgarity

274. "Without a Single Redeeming Fault"
275. On Not Being Appreciated
276. The Humor of Being Serious
277. Paramount Trifles
278. Over the Dishpan
279. Silver Days
280. Echoes and Shadows
281. The Passing of Wonder
282. Musical Antipathies
283. On Going to the Dogs
284. Compensations of College Life
285. Pleasure Madness
286. Sincerity and Superlatives
287. Bovine Temperaments
288. Excess Knowledge
289. On Living Up to My Name
290. Intelligence Tests
291. On Becoming Platitudinous
292. Some Ludicrous Self-Deceptions
293. On Surviving a Reputation
294. What My Dog Must Think of Me!
295. Education for "Success"
296. "Intellectual Cafeterias"
297. The Anecdotic Mind
298. Emotional Mass Production
299. The "Bigness" of the American Manner
300. On Being a Victim of One's Self
301. My Mental Insides
302. Eating and Dining
303. On Being a Self-Starter
304. "One Crowded Hour of Glorious Life"
305. The Magic of Seed Catalogues
306. The Gentle Art of Purring
307. On Having Fun with One's Mind
308. The Tyranny of a "Color Scheme"
309. Perambulator Days
310. From Measles to Matrimony
311. On Reading the *Atlantic Monthly* in Public
312. The Smell of Books

ESSAY ASSIGNMENTS

1. Write a narrative essay in which some incident or development in your experience revealed an important insight, perhaps in the form of a paradox, perhaps as the answer to some puzzle or enigma. (George Orwell's "On Shooting an Elephant" is an example, pp. 207–212).

2. Write an essay based upon a character (from your own experience) whose life presents an interesting puzzle or paradox. (Steve Anderson's "Grandpa Anderson: A Pretty Successful Flop," is a response to this assignment, pp. 220–221.)

3. Write an essay, in either narrative or straightforward form, based upon a character whose actions or attitudes annoy you, particularly since they are "typical" in some way—they represent some general set of attitudes or values that you distrust. (Kay Leigh Ferguson's "Guests, Manners, and Organic Bigotry," is a response to this assignment, pp. 221–223.)

4. Write an essay that recreates and explores some incident or scene or place, as an emblem of some general truth or larger set of circumstances.

5. Write an essay based upon any of the 312 topics listed on pp. 201–205. Make certain that the topic suggests not merely some subject that stirs your interest but also some specific theme or strategy such as those discussed on pp. 191–199 of this chapter.

6. Write a humorous or satirical essay based upon an "irregular art" that you have practiced or noticed others practicing. (Joe Pawlosky's "On the Ancient, But Now Sadly Neglected, Art of Leaning," is an example of this type of essay, pp. 216–219.)

7. Begin with some physical object or scene that intrigues you—a painting, a new invention, a panoramic view. Describe the object or scene, and explore your own reasons for being intrigued or moved by it. What to you is its special significance?

Essays for Analysis

Shooting an Elephant

by George Orwell

Best known as the author of two famous novels, 1984 *and* Animal Farm, *George Orwell is also one of this century's most accomplished essayists.*

1 In Moulmein, in lower Burma, I was hated by large numbers of people—the only time in my life that I have been important enough for this to happen to me. I was sub-divisional police officer of the town, and in an aimless, petty kind of way anti-European feeling was very bitter. No one had the guts to raise a riot, but if a European woman went through the bazaars alone somebody would probably spit betel juice over her dress. As a police officer I was an obvious target and was baited whenever it seemed safe to do so. When a nimble Burman tripped me up on the football field and the referee (another Burman) looked the other way, the crowd yelled with hideous laughter. This happened more than once. In the end the sneering yellow faces of young men that met me everywhere, the insults hooted after me when I was at a safe distance, got badly on my nerves. The young Buddhist priests were the worst of all. There were several thousands of them in the town and none of them seemed to have anything to do except stand on street corners and jeer at Europeans.

2 All this was perplexing and upsetting. For at that time I had already made up my mind that imperialism was an evil thing and the sooner I chucked up my job and got out of it the better. Theoretically—and secretly, of course —I was all for the Burmese and all against their oppressors, the British. As for the job I was doing, I hated it more bitterly than I can perhaps make clear. In a job like that you see the dirty work of Empire at close quarters. The wretched prisoners huddling in the stinking cages of the lock-ups, the grey, cowed faces of the long-term convicts, the scarred buttocks of the men who had been flogged with bamboos—all these oppressed me with an intolerable sense of guilt. But I could get nothing into perspective. I was young and ill-educated and I had had to think out my problems in the utter silence that is imposed on every Englishman in the East. I did not even know that the British Empire is dying, still less did I know that it is a great deal better than

the younger empires that are going to supplant it. All I knew was that I was stuck between my hatred of the empire I served and my rage against the evil-spirited little beasts who tried to make my job impossible. With one part of my mind I thought of the British Raj as an unbreakable tyranny, as something clamped down, in *saecula saeculorum,* upon the will of prostrate peoples; with another part I thought that the greatest joy in the world would be to drive a bayonet into a Buddhist priest's guts. Feelings like these are the normal by-products of imperialism; ask any Anglo-Indian official, if you can catch him off duty.

3 One day something happened which in a roundabout way was enlightening. It was a tiny incident in itself, but it gave me a better glimpse than I had had before of the real nature of imperialism—the real motives for which despotic governments act. Early one morning the sub-inspector at a police station at the other end of the town rang me up on the phone and said that an elephant was ravaging the bazaar. Would I please come and do something about it? I did not know what I could do, but I wanted to see what was happening and I got on to a pony and started out. I took my rifle, an old .44 Winchester and much too small to kill an elephant, but I thought the noise might be useful *in terrorem.* Various Burmans stopped me on the way and told me about the elephant's doings. It was not, of course, a wild elephant, but a tame one which had gone "must." It had been chained up, as tame elephants always are when their attack of "must" is due, but on the previous night it had broken its chain and escaped. Its mahout, the only person who could manage it when it was in that state, had set out in pursuit, but had taken the wrong direction and was now twelve hours' journey away, and in the morning the elephant had suddenly reappeared in the town. The Burmese population had no weapons and were quite helpless against it. It had already destroyed somebody's bamboo hut, killed a cow and raided some fruit-stalls and devoured the stock; also it had met the municipal rubbish van and, when the driver jumped out and took to his heels, had turned the van over and inflicted violences upon it.

4 The Burmese sub-inspector and some Indian constables were waiting for me in the quarter where the elephant had been seen. It was a very poor quarter, a labyrinth of squalid bamboo huts, thatched with palm-leaf, winding all over a steep hillside. I remember that it was a cloudy, stuffy morning at the beginning of the rains. We began questioning the people as to where the elephant had gone and, as usual, failed to get any definite information. That is invariably the case in the East; a story always sounds clear enough at a distance, but the nearer you get to the scene of events the vaguer it becomes. Some of the people said that the elephant had gone in one direction, some said that he had gone in another, some professed not even to have heard of any elephant. I had almost made up my mind that the whole story was a pack of lies, when we heard yells a little distance away. There was a loud, scandalized cry of "Go away, child! Go away this instant!" and an old woman with a switch in her hand came round the corner of a hut, violently shooing away a crowd of naked

children. Some more women followed, clicking their tongues and exclaiming; evidently there was something that the children ought not to have seen. I rounded the hut and saw a man's dead body sprawling in the mud. He was an Indian, a black Dravidian coolie, almost naked, and he could not have been dead many minutes. The people said that the elephant had come suddenly upon him round the corner of the hut, caught him with its trunk, put its foot on his back and ground him into the earth. This was the rainy season and the ground was soft, and his face had scored a trench a foot deep and a couple of yards long. He was lying on his belly with arms crucified and head sharply twisted to one side. His face was coated with mud, the eyes wide open, the teeth bared and grinning with an expression of unendurable agony. (Never tell me, by the way, that the dead look peaceful. Most of the corpses I have seen looked devilish.) The friction of the great beast's foot had stripped the skin from his back as neatly as one skins a rabbit. As soon as I saw the dead man I sent an orderly to a friend's house nearby to borrow an elephant rifle. I had already sent back the pony, not wanting it to go mad with fright and throw me if it smelt the elephant.

5 The orderly came back in a few minutes with a rifle and five cartridges, and meanwhile some Burmans had arrived and told us that the elephant was in the paddy fields below, only a few hundred yards away. As I started forward practically the whole population of the quarter flocked out of the houses and followed me. They had seen the rifle and were all shouting excitedly that I was going to shoot the elephant. They had not shown much interest in the elephant when he was merely ravaging their homes, but it was different now that he was going to be shot. It was a bit of fun to them, as it would be to an English crowd; besides they wanted the meat. It made me vaguely uneasy. I had no intention of shooting the elephant—I had merely sent for the rifle to defend myself if necessary—and it is always unnerving to have a crowd following you. I marched down the hill, looking and feeling a fool, with the rifle over my shoulder and an ever-growing army of people jostling at my heels. At the bottom, when you got away from the huts, there was a metalled road and beyond that a miry waste of paddy fields a thousand yards across, not yet ploughed but soggy from the first rains and dotted with coarse grass. The elephant was standing eight yards from the road, his left side towards us. He took not the slightest notice of the crowd's approach. He was tearing up bunches of grass, beating them against his knees to clean them and stuffing them into his mouth.

6 I had halted on the road. As soon as I saw the elephant I knew with perfect certainty that I ought not to shoot him. It is a serious matter to shoot a working elephant—it is comparable to destroying a huge and costly piece of machinery—and obviously one ought not to do it if it can possibly be avoided. And at that distance, peacefully eating, the elephant looked no more dangerous than a cow. I thought then and I think now that his attack of "must" was already passing off; in which case he would merely wander harmlessly about until the mahout came back and caught him. Moreover, I did not in the least

want to shoot him. I decided that I would watch him for a little while to make sure that he did not turn savage again, and then go home.

7 But at that moment I glanced round at the crowd that had followed me. It was an immense crowd, two thousand at the least and growing every minute. It blocked the road for a long distance on either side. I looked at the sea of yellow faces above the garish clothes—faces all happy and excited over this bit of fun, all certain that the elephant was going to be shot. They were watching me as they would watch a conjurer about to perform a trick. They did not like me, but with the magical rifle in my hands I was momentarily worth watching. And suddenly I realized that I should have to shoot the elephant after all. The people expected it of me and I had got to do it; I could feel their two thousand wills pressing me forward, irresistibly. And it was at this moment, as I stood there with the rifle in my hands, that I first grasped the hollowness, the futility of the white man's dominion in the East. Here was I, the white man with his gun, standing in front of the unarmed native crowd —seemingly the leading actor of the piece; but in reality I was only an absurd puppet pushed to and fro by the will of those yellow faces behind. I perceived in this moment that when the white man turns tyrant it is his own freedom that he destroys. He becomes a sort of hollow, posing dummy, the conventionalized figure of a sahib. For it is the condition of his rule that he shall spend his life in trying to impress the "natives," and so in every crisis he has got to do what the "natives" expect of him. He wears a mask, and his face grows to fit it. I had got to shoot the elephant. I had committed myself to doing it when I sent for the rifle. A sahib has got to act like a sahib; he has got to appear resolute, to know his own mind and do definite things. To come all that way, rifle in hand, with two thousand people marching at my heels, and then to trail feebly away, having done nothing—no, that was impossible. The crowd would laugh at me. And my whole life, every white man's life in the East, was one long struggle not to be laughed at.

8 But I did not want to shoot the elephant. I watched him beating his bunch of grass against his knees, with that preoccupied grandmotherly air that elephants have. It seemed to me that it would be murder to shoot him. At that age I was not squeamish about killing animals, but I had never shot an elephant and never wanted to. (Somehow it always seems worse to kill a *large* animal.) Besides, there was the beast's owner to be considered. Alive, the elephant was worth at least a hundred pounds; dead, he would only be worth the value of his tusks, five pounds, possibly. But I had got to act quickly. I turned to some experienced-looking Burmans who had been there when we arrived, and asked them how the elephant had been behaving. They all said the same thing: he took no notice of you if you left him alone, but he might charge if you went too close to him.

9 It was perfectly clear to me what I ought to do. I ought to walk up to within, say, twenty-five yards of the elephant and test his behavior. If he charged, I could shoot; if he took no notice of me, it would be safe to leave him until the mahout came back. But also I knew that I was going to do no

such thing. I was a poor shot with a rifle and the ground was soft mud into which one would sink at every step. If the elephant charged and I missed him, I should have about as much chance as a toad under a steam-roller. But even then I was not thinking particularly of my own skin, only of the watchful yellow faces behind. For at that moment, with the crowd watching me, I was not afraid in the ordinary sense, as I would have been if I had been alone. A white man mustn't be frightened in front of "natives"; and so, in general, he isn't frightened. The sole thought in my mind was that if anything went wrong those two thousand Burmans would see me pursued, caught, trampled on and reduced to a grinning corpse like that Indian up the hill. And if that happened it was quite probable that some of them would laugh. That would never do. There was only one alternative. I shoved the cartridges into the magazine and lay down on the road to get a better aim.

10 The crowd grew very still, and a deep, low, happy sigh, as of people who see the theatre curtain go up at last, breathed from innumerable throats. They were going to have their bit of fun after all. The rifle was a beautiful German thing with cross-hair sights. I did not then know that in shooting an elephant one would shoot to cut an imaginary bar running from ear-hole to ear-hole. I ought, therefore, as the elephant was sideways on, to have aimed straight at his ear-hole; actually I aimed several inches in front of this, thinking the brain would be further forward.

11 When I pulled the trigger I did not hear the bang or feel the kick—one never does when a shot goes home—but I heard the devilish roar of glee that went up from the crowd. In that instant, in too short a time, one would have thought, even for the bullet to get there, a mysterious, terrible change had come over the elephant. He neither stirred nor fell, but every line of his body had altered. He looked suddenly stricken, shrunken, immensely old, as though the frightful impact of the bullet had paralysed him without knocking him down. At last, after what seemed a long time—it might have been five seconds, I dare say—he sagged flabbily to his knees. His mouth slobbered. An enormous senility seemed to have settled upon him. One could have imagined him thousands of years old. I fired again into the same spot. At the second shot he did not collapse but climbed with desperate slowness to his feet and stood weakly upright, with legs sagging and head drooping. I fired a third time. That was the shot that did for him. You could see the agony of it jolt his whole body and knock the last remnant of strength from his legs. But in falling he seemed for a moment to rise, for as his hind legs collapsed beneath him he seemed to tower upward like a huge rock toppling, his trunk reaching skywards like a tree. He trumpeted, for the first and only time. And then down he came, his belly towards me, with a crash that seemed to shake the ground even where I lay.

12 I got up. The Burmans were already racing past me across the mud. It was obvious that the elephant would never rise again, but he was not dead. He was breathing very rhythmically with long rattling gasps, his great mound of a side painfully rising and falling. His mouth was wide open—I could see far

down into caverns of pale pink throat. I waited a long time for him to die, but his breathing did not weaken. Finally I fired my two remaining shots into the spot where I thought his heart must be. The thick blood welled out of him like red velvet, but still he did not die. His body did not even jerk when the shots hit him, the tortured breathing continued without a pause. He was dying, very slowly and in great agony, but in some world remote from me where not even a bullet could damage him further. I felt that I had got to put an end to that dreadful noise. It seemed dreadful to see the great beast lying there, powerless to move and yet powerless to die, and not even to be able to finish him. I sent back for my small rifle and poured shot after shot into his heart and down his throat. They seemed to make no impression. The tortured gasps continued as steadily as the ticking of a clock.

13 In the end I could not stand it any longer and went away. I heard later that it took him half an hour to die. Burmans were bringing dahs and baskets even before I left, and I was told they had stripped his body almost to the bones by the afternoon.

14 Afterwards, of course, there were endless discussions about the shooting of the elephant. The owner was furious, but he was only an Indian and could do nothing. Besides, legally I had done the right thing, for a mad elephant has to be killed, like a mad dog, if its owner fails to control it. Among the Europeans opinion was divided. The older men said I was right, the younger men said it was a damn shame to shoot an elephant for killing a coolie, because an elephant was worth more than any damn Coringhee coolie. And afterwards I was very glad that the coolie had been killed; it put me legally in the right and it gave me a sufficient pretext for shooting the elephant. I often wondered whether any of the others grasped that I had done it solely to avoid looking a fool.

FOR DISCUSSION

1. At the beginning of the essay, Orwell describes his former attitude as one of puzzlement or contradiction. He hated British colonialism, and yet he also despised the Burmese natives. Does the incident of shooting an elephant carry Orwell beyond this contradictory set of attitudes? In what way?

2. The central insight of this essay is a paradox. What is it? What particular set of opposites is involved?

3. The theme of this essay is colonialism, specifically the relationship between colonial "masters" and the native peoples that they have subjugated. What does Orwell do in the first two paragraphs, even as he is discussing his own personal feelings and reactions, to let us know that the purpose of the essay is to explore and reflect upon this theme?

4. Orwell describes at great length and in painstaking detail the shooting and the slow dying of the elephant. Why do you think he does so? Does this particular scene (paragraphs 10–13) possibly function as an emblem (see pp. 194–196 above) in some way?

On Morality

by Joan Didion

Joan Didion, contemporary novelist and journalist, has produced two excellent volumes of essays: Slouching Towards Bethlehem, *from which "On Morality" is taken, and* The White Album. *This essay first appeared in* The American Scholar.

1 AS IT HAPPENS I am in Death Valley, in a room at the Enterprise Motel and Trailer Park, and it is July, and it is hot. In fact it is 119°. I cannot seem to make the air conditioner work, but there is a small refrigerator, and I can wrap ice cubes in a towel and hold them against the small of my back. With the help of the ice cubes I have been trying to think, because *The American Scholar* asked me to, in some abstract way about "morality," a word I distrust more every day, but my mind veers inflexibly toward the particular.

2 Here are some particulars. At midnight last night, on the road in from Las Vegas to Death Valley Junction, a car hit a shoulder and turned over. The driver, very young and apparently drunk, was killed instantly. His girl was found alive but bleeding internally, deep in shock. I talked this afternoon to the nurse who had driven the girl to the nearest doctor, 185 miles across the floor of the Valley and three ranges of lethal mountain road. The nurse explained that her husband, a talc miner, had stayed on the highway with the boy's body until the coroner could get over the mountains from Bishop, at dawn today. "You can't just leave a body on the highway," she said. "It's immoral."

3 It was one instance in which I did not distrust the word, because she meant something quite specific. She meant that if a body is left alone for even a few minutes on the desert, the coyotes close in and eat the flesh. Whether or not a corpse is torn apart by coyotes may seem only a sentimental consideration, but of course it is more: one of the promises we make to one another is that we will try to retrieve our casualties, try not to abandon our dead to the coyotes. If we have been taught to keep our promises—if, in the simplest terms, our upbringing is good enough—we stay with the body, or have bad dreams.

4 I am talking, of course, about the kind of social code that is sometimes called, usually pejoratively, "wagon-train morality." In fact that is precisely what it is. For better or worse, we are what we learned as children: my own childhood was illuminated by graphic litanies of the grief awaiting those who failed in their loyalties to each other. The Donner-Reed Party, starving in the

Sierra snows, all the ephemera of civilization gone save that one vestigial taboo, the provision that no one should eat his own blood kin. The Jayhawkers, who quarreled and separated not far from where I am tonight. Some of them died in the Funerals and some of them died down near Badwater and most of the rest of them died in the Panamints. A woman who got through gave the Valley its name. Some might say that the Jayhawkers were killed by the desert summer, and the Donner Party by the mountain winter, by circumstances beyond control; we were taught instead that they had somewhere abdicated their responsibilities, somehow breached their primary loyalties, or they would not have found themselves helpless in the mountain winter or the desert summer, would not have given way to acrimony, would not have deserted one another, would not have *failed.* In brief, we heard such stories as cautionary tales, and they still suggest the only kind of "morality" that seems to me to have any but the most potentially mendacious meaning.

5 You are quite possibly impatient with me by now; I am talking, you want to say, about a "morality" so primitive that it scarcely deserves the name, a code that has as its point only survival, not the attainment of the ideal good. Exactly. Particularly out here tonight, in this country so ominous and terrible that to live in it is to live with antimatter, it is difficult to believe that "the good" is a knowable quantity. Let me tell you what it is like out here tonight. Stories travel at night on the desert. Someone gets in his pickup and drives a couple of hundred miles for a beer, and he carries news of what is happening, back wherever he came from. Then he drives another hundred miles for another beer, and passes along stories from the last place as well as from the one before; it is a network kept alive by people whose instincts tell them that if they do not keep moving at night on the desert they will lose all reason. Here is a story that is going around the desert tonight: over across the Nevada line, sheriff's deputies are diving in some underground pools, trying to retrieve a couple of bodies known to be in the hole. The widow of one of the drowned boys is over there; she is eighteen, and pregnant, and is said not to leave the hole. The divers go down and come up, and she just stands there and stares into the water. They have been diving for ten days but have found no bottom to the caves, no bodies and no trace of them, only the black 90° water going down and down and down, and a single translucent fish, not classified. The story tonight is that one of the divers has been hauled up incoherent, out of his head, shouting—until they got him out of there so that the widow could not hear—about water that got hotter instead of cooler as he went down, about light flickering through the water, about magma, about underground nuclear testing.

6 That is the tone stories take out here, and there are quite a few of them tonight. And it is more than the stories alone. Across the road at the Faith Community Church a couple of dozen old people, come here to live in trailers and die in the sun, are holding a prayer sing. I cannot hear them and do not want to. What I can hear are occasional coyotes and a constant chorus of

"Baby the Rain Must Fall" from the jukebox in the Snake Room next door, and if I were also to hear those dying voices, those Midwestern voices drawn to this lunar country for some unimaginable atavistic rites, *rock of ages cleft for me,* I think I would lose my own reason. Every now and then I imagine I hear a rattlesnake, but my husband says that it is a faucet, a paper rustling, the wind. Then he stands by a window, and plays a flashlight over the dry wash outside.

7 What does it mean? It means nothing manageable. There is some sinister hysteria in the air out here tonight, some hint of the monstrous perversion to which any human idea can come. "I followed my own conscience." "I did what I thought was right." How many madmen have said it and meant it? How many murderers? Klaus Fuchs said it, and the men who committed the Mountain Meadows Massacre said it, and Alfred Rosenberg said it. And, as we are rotely and rather presumptuously reminded by those who would say it now, Jesus said it. Maybe we have all said it, and maybe we have been wrong. Except on that most primitive level—our loyalties to those we love—what could be more arrogant than to claim the primacy of personal conscience? ("Tell me," a rabbi asked Daniel Bell when he said, as a child, that he did not believe in God. "Do you think God cares?") At least some of the time, the world appears to me as a painting by Hieronymous Bosch; were I to follow my conscience then, it would lead me out onto the desert with Marion Faye, out to where he stood in *The Deer Park* looking east to Los Alamos and praying, as if for rain, that it would happen: "*. . . let it come and clear the rot and the stench and the stink, let it come for all of everywhere, just so it comes and the world stands clear in the white dead dawn.*"

8 Of course you will say that I do not have the right, even if I had the power, to inflict that unreasonable conscience upon you; nor do I want you to inflict your conscience, however reasonable, however enlightened, upon me. ("We must be aware of the dangers which lie in our most generous wishes," Lionel Trilling once wrote. "Some paradox of our nature leads us, when once we have made our fellow men the objects of our enlightened interest, to go on to make them the objects of our pity, then of our wisdom, ultimately of our coercion.") That the ethic of conscience is intrinsically insidious seems scarcely a revelatory point, but it is one raised with increasing infrequency; even those who do raise it tend to *segue* with troubling readiness into the quite contradictory position that the ethic of conscience is dangerous when it is "wrong," and admirable when it is "right."

9 You see I want to be quite obstinate about insisting that we have no way of knowing—beyond that fundamental loyalty to the social code—what is "right" and what is "wrong," what is "good" and what "evil." I dwell so upon this because the most disturbing aspect of "morality" seems to me to be the frequency with which the word now appears; in the press, on television, in the most perfunctory kinds of conversation. Questions of straightforward power (or survival) politics, questions of quite indifferent public policy, questions of

almost anything: they are all assigned these factitious moral burdens. Thei is something facile going on, some self-indulgence at work. Of course we woul all like to "believe" in something, like to assuage our private guilts in publi causes, like to lose our tiresome selves; like, perhaps, to transform the whit flag of defeat at home into the brave white banner of battle away from home. And of course it is all right to do that; that is how, immemorially, things have gotten done. But I think it is all right only so long as we do not delude ourselves about what we are doing, and why. It is all right only so long as we remember that all the *ad hoc* committees, all the picket lines, all the brave signatures in *The New York Times,* all the tools of agitprop straight across the spectrum, do not confer upon anyone any *ipso facto* virtue. It is all right only so long as we recognize that the end may or may not be expedient, may or may not be a good idea, but in any case has nothing to do with "morality." Because when we start deceiving ourselves into thinking not that we want something or need something, not that it is a pragmatic necessity for us to have it, but that it is a *moral imperative* that we have it, then is when we join the fashionable madmen, and then is when the thin whine of hysteria is heard in the land, and then is when we are in bad trouble. And I suspect we are already there.

FOR DISCUSSION

1. Review briefly the section, "Forms for the Reflective/Exploratory Essay," in this chapter (pp. 189–191). Which of the forms is represented by this essay? What do you think the author gains by casting this particular essay in this particular form?

2. Didion uses the scenes and incidents immediately surrounding her to reflect upon the abstract term "morality." What is the illuminating feature that these scenes and incidents share?

3. How would you define what Didion calls "wagon train morality" (paragraph 4)? How does it differ from what she later calls the "ethic of conscience"? Why is one to be preferred over the other?

On the Ancient, Now Sadly Neglected, Art of Leaning

by Joe Pawlosky

This essay first appeared in 1979, in The Greensboro Sun, *one of the nation's finest occasional newspaper/literary reviews.*

1 Of all the skills once thought so necessary for surviving the scourge of work, none has fallen to more serious, and sad, neglect than "the lean"—that singular ability to be entirely at one's ease (to be loafing, in other words) while maintaining the appearance of being feverishly at work. I am not suggesting,

of course, that workers are no longer given to relaxing on the job—God knows, there are as many patent leaners around today as there ever were—, but rather that they have somehow lost the *art* of the lean. On a recent, random tour of our county, for example, I observed a number of various work crews—road repairment, landscapers, construction workers and the like—, and, I am grieved to report, that of all the leaners I saw, not one appeared to be doing anything other than leaning.

2 Like any other of the high and civilizing arts, leaning is, when carried to the height of its perfection, a thing of beauty to behold and admire. It is also, to continue the comparison, an art whose execution is far more difficult and complex than its appearance would lead one to believe.

3 I was first made aware of this a number of years ago by a gentleman named Lowell Glendon, whose legendary leans are still talked about by those who remember him as an asphalt-slinger for the Massachusetts Highway Department. I was, when I came under the great man's tutelage, about to go to work for the Birmingham Landscaping Company. It is possible, I suppose, that I might have survived the ordeal without Lowell's incomparable assistance, but I would have to have done it by actually working for my wages, a degradation that no self-respecting leaner, however desperate, would consider doing. As part of my indoctrination, Lowell took me around to some various road and building construction sites so that I might see, firsthand, some truly great leaners in action.

4 What I saw, I admit, didn't much impress me at the time, but it was certainly to have a profound impact upon my later life of employment. The first exhibit was that of a seemingly ordinary crew of ditch diggers, nine hands in all, and each appearing grimmer and grundgier than the next.

5 "All right," Lowell said after we had spent a few minutes observing them, "what are they doing?"

"Digging a ditch," I replied.

"Okay, that's good for a starter. But now, take a closer look and tell me, what are they *really* doing?"

6 I saw immediately what he was driving at: of that whole gang of cutthroats, all of them leaning on various implements of their trade—picks, shovels, adzes—, not one of them was even moving, much less digging a ditch. In fact, upon closer inspection, it became obvious that the ditch had been dug, probably hours ago, by the idle backhoe standing off in the distance. But even for a leaner as accomplished as Lowell, there was something here to inspire awe and wonder. "Usually," he said, "you'll find one or maybe two such talented leaners on any given job. But the whole crew! My God, it's like seeing an All-Star game."

7 From there we drove to another project, a road construction crew which, by coincidence also had nine men on the job. That was about all they had in common, though, for here the whole gang was working at a feverish clip. Or so it seemed.

8 "All right," Lowell quizzed, "which of those fellows would you say is working the hardest?"

"That's easy," I answered, "the guy over there by the hydrant, the one wearing the blue shirt and yellow bandanna."

9 "You really think so," Lowell smiled with a faint air of superiority. "Well why don't you, just for the fun of it, take out your watch and see just how much work he actually does in the next 15 minutes."

10 Well sir, you talk about object-lessons. I mean that that guy, for all that he moved, could easily have been in a Wax Museum. For fifteen minutes he just stood there, leaning on his shovel and staring down at a pot hole, as if trying to decide whether to approach the cavity from the left, or from the right, or even possibly, from straight on. But so serious and intent was his stare that, even after realizing that he was only loafing, I would still have sworn that he had been working himself to a frazzle. We clocked him for another 30 minutes, and not once did he so much as quiver.

11 "God, can that sucker lean!" Lowell exclaimed as we drove away, "and you, if you have any hope of making it as a landscaper, are going to have to be able to do the same thing."

12 It was, as I say, my innocent, neophytic impression that all I would have to do was go out on the job and start into leaning with the best of them. I wasn't so entirely naive, of course, as not to realize that I would have to do *some* work to sort of establish a reputation for myself, but after that I could just slide into my choicest lean and then hold it for the rest of the day. (I should point out that while it is usually helpful to have a tool or a piece of machinery to lean on, it isn't always necessary. Your true leaner can appear busy under any circumstances, even in the middle of an empty field without so much as a toothpick to assist him. Indeed, I once saw a world-class leaner prop himself up in a hammock, a can of Schlitz nearby, and, with just the right cast of eye, appear far busier than his neighbor who happened just then to be hacking away at a field of ironweed and quackgrass.

13 My first week on the job was an unqualified disaster. After a paltry 30 seconds into my first lean I was cruelly interrupted by Joe Riley, the foreman. "What the hell's the matter," he said, "you got paralysis or something? Get to work." All week long I kept trying, over and over again, to assume a proper and respectable lean, but always kept getting the same discouraging response: "Damnit, Buddy, you wanna goof off, go do it someplace else, okay?" "Hey, whadya think this is, some kind of picnic or something?" Things like that.

14 After that first disheartening encounter with work I knew that if I didn't do something, and fast, I'd probably soon be out looking for another job. Seeking out the sagacious Lowell, I explained to him what had happened.

15 "It's obvious," he said after listening to my lament, "that you still haven't got the hang of it. You're just standing around, that's all, not leaning, and there's a whole world of difference between them." With his accustomed generosity, Lowell gave up his entire Saturday afternoon to work with me on

my leans. He showed me what I was doing wrong and coached me on my stance and my gaze. (It should be noted that the gaze is everything; without it, the whole lean is nothing more than an ambitious slouch.)

16 It was a grueling afternoon, but one that I have since come to value beyond estimation. Oh, I didn't become an overnight success at leaning or anything like that, and the ever-watchful Riley didn't entirely desist from his reminders that I was supposed to be working, but I did make progress. In no time at all I was sliding into one respectable lean after another and holding each for upwards of five or six minutes at a crack. Then, my concentration would flag and my intensity melt and I'd once again be informed that if I liked standing around so much, maybe I ought to do it down at the Unemployment Office where they gave out modest weekly allowances for just such activities.

17 I didn't give up though. Ride me as he would, neither Riley nor anyone else was going to stop *me* from becoming a leaner, not after what I'd put into it. Every chance I got I practiced my stance and worked to perfect and intensify my gaze, which, I should explain, is the art of staring humidly at the work one is *supposed* to be doing. Then, one day in mid-October, it happened.

18 We were working a playground at one of the local elementary schools, getting it ready for spring seeding. There were five of us on the job. Tony and Freeman were on the far side digging a drainage ditch. Willie Jackson was working the smooth grade on the other side of the building and Riley, as usual, was on the tractor, working the rough grade. I don't recall exactly what it was I was supposed to be doing, but at about 11:00 A.M. I decided it was time to put my lean to the acid test and try pulling it off right in front of good ol' Riley. I grabbed a rake and, not ten yards from that whipping tractor, commenced to lean with such inspired vehemence that it made my ears pop. After he had been watching me for some 20 minutes, Riley finally cut off the tractor and came striding up to where I was still holding onto that teeth-clenching lean. "Joe," he said, without the slightest trace of irony, for Riley was definitely not a man given to ironic touches, "Joe, when you get finished with that, I wish you'd go over and give Tony and Freeman a hand with that ditch. At the rate those two goof-offs are going, we'll be here to midnight." Right then I realized I had arrived. I was no longer just your ordinary stander-arounder, but an honest-to-goodness, bona fide leaner. On with the job.

FOR DISCUSSION

1. What specifically is the source of the humor in this essay?
2. This essay does not discover or develop a paradoxical insight, but it could be said to involve a paradox. What is it?
3. What would appear to be the key to learning the art of leaning? Does this have any parallel in learning other arts?

Student Essay: Grandpa Anderson—A Pretty Successful Flop

by Steven Anderson

1 On December 19, 1979, Carl Anderson, my grandfather, will have survived 78 very tough years. Born and raised on a ranch in Colorado, he decided to quit school in the eighth grade because he felt an eighth grade education was all that was necessary to run a successful ranch—which he planned to do for the rest of his life. But even much better educated men than my grandfather failed to predict the Great Depression, and Grandpa Anderson suffered other calamities to boot.

2 After my great-grandfather died, Grandpa got married and took over the ranch, struggling to keep it going through the depression years. All things considered, things were going reasonably well—the crops were good, and they had a son, my father. But a year after my father's birth Grandpa had a hunting accident, which left him with a severed left hand. All the jobs on the ranch—fence mending, cattle roping, cow milking—he now had to do with one hand and a hook. Not to be outdone by mere human disorder, nature also took a turn at Grandpa Anderson. Twice in the next decade his crops were totally destroyed, once by a freak hail storm and again by swarms of grasshoppers.

3 Somehow they survived. And by the time my father was old enough to do a good deal of the ranch work, things were beginning to look brighter, and they began to nurture great hopes for the future of the ranch. But Uncle Sam had different plans. When my father left for the Korean battlefields, Grandpa decided that the game was up. He sold the ranch, and he and my grandmother moved to Denver, where they purchased some apartment buildings with the money from the ranch. But life in Denver turned out to be no easier and no more successful. Grandpa had to spend 14-hour days doing everything from replacing broken water heaters to painting rooms. Before long he realized that he was spending more on up-keep than he was taking in in rent. He decided to sell out, and he started looking for work.

4 Work was hard to find in a big city like Denver, especially for a one-armed man with an eighth grade education. He finally landed a job as a shoe salesman. Incredibly, he and my grandmother managed to get by and even to save some money, and this, added to what was left over from the apartment house disaster, gave them a nest-egg for retirement. But once again disaster struck. Soon after Grandpa retired (settling, ironically, in a high rise constructed on the exact location of the failed apartment building), the corporation in which he had invested most of their retirement money went absolutely bankrupt. Now my grandparents are almost totally dependent upon Social Security.

5 By every external standard, Grandpa was a loser. Nothing worked for him; failure and calamity followed him like a shadow. The amazing thing is

that Grandpa has always been, and is now, one of the happiest men I have ever seen. What's more—although in certain ways his happiness seems to have come *in spite of* his various disasters, there are other ways in which it seems to have come *because of* of these disasters.

6 I really think that the most fulfilling part of Grandpa's life has resulted from his worst setback—the loss of his hand. After moving to Denver he started visiting the hospital to talk to people whose limbs had been amputated. There were many patients that could not be persuaded by doctors and therapists that they could lead normal lives again. Grandpa would visit these patients and give them living proof that life didn't end when they lost an arm or a leg. He would tell them how he had adjusted to his loss and had learned to operate heavy farm machinery, saddle break horses, use farm tools, and even become an excellent hunter again.

7 The hospital counseling has led to other things. Since his retirement Grandpa has also been working in a mission two days a week. At the mission, Grandpa and other volunteers help alcoholics get a new start in life. Grandpa hardly misses a chance to help another man who is in trouble. It's a great knack he has, and his teacher was his own trouble.

8 Another thing that Grandpa learned from his hardship is that happiness doesn't come from a large bank balance but rather from living cheerfully and generously in whatever situation you are in. Maybe people who do have large bank balances know this too, but I've seen a lot of people in the middle—people who have had "normal" luck—who haven't had the good fortune.

FOR DISCUSSION

1. The author of this essay discovers not only a particular paradox about his grandfather but also a more general one about life. State both of them in your own words.
2. Identify the two or three sentences in this essay which most effectively convey its message.

Student Essay: Guests, Manners, and Organic Bigotry

by Kay Leigh Ferguson

1 Recently, I found myself in a situation where I needed to entertain, in my own little home, a guest who drove me crazy. It's true, I admit it right from the beginning—what this woman managed to accomplish in the brief span of 48 hours is really no mammouth task. Circumstances were in her favor, not the least of which was my own highly flammable personality. I must admit that I thrive on enemies, that enemies are essential to my daily diet. Given a

shortage, I grow my own, chew them up and am renewed. Usually they, the enemies, never know the sustenance they have provided. I do have manners after all.

2 Now that she's gone of course, I feel guilty. It's my duty as an American woman to feel guilty for not liking my guest. It's also good manners. Perhaps a scented note card would soothe my prickling conscience.

Darling,

It was so lovely to have you here. I'm sorry things were so hectic and that you were so obnoxious . . .

No, that won't do. The effort, however, reveals the true motives of my reflection. Forgive me Abby, Forgive me Gloria, Forgive me Mother, but when it really gets right down to it—I would much rather figure out what was wrong with her than me. I'll call it "An Organic Examination of Contemporary American Manners" or "Take Your Whole Wheat Goodness and . . ." Well, there are bounds.

3 I need to examine this thing logically. I'm sure it's more than a matter of different lifestyles. What were her particular skills? How could she so quickly set my pot 'a boiling when I had decided in advance to like her? She's potential family yet, and I had already satiated my enemy quota before she arrived.

4 First she had the skills of inflection down to a science. Can you hear it? "Oh," those skilled in this art usually begin. A little "Oh" as if their delicate sensibilities were suddenly caught in their panties or in the case of my guest, as if someone has just offered her a coke and a hot dog. "Oh, you wear *heels.*" The surprise carries the voice through the observation. It is merely an observation. I do in fact wear *heels.* I like to be taller than everybody if at all possible. Also I have the legs of a German farm girl, and heels help create the illusion instead of a Marguax Hemingway type American girl. Big and healthy. She, of course, is a wisp. Her shoes, of course, are flat and practical—more practical than mine, and better. She doesn't say this. She doesn't have to. Her inflection is so polished it isn't necessary. The "you" is drawn long enough to be exclusive. "Heels" circles back to the startled surprise note of "Oh." By the time it leaves her unpainted mouth and reaches my *heels,* it is a perfect circle. Complete. Observation as unspoken insult. "Oh, I see you use *sugar.*" "Oh, *gazpacho,* I made that *once.*"

5 The second skill of which my fine guest demonstrated mastery was the skill of personal information. Here again, exclusiveness is the vital distinction between your average, "I've been using this really great cook book" and "If you would only read this." If I would only read this cook book, which being of the organic variety is not a cook book at all, but a bible, a philosophy of life and womanhood in disguise—then I would not have the flu, be exhausted,

and have violent emotional reactions. "Laurel's Kitchen" the cover says in earth tones. Beneath the title there is a picture of three women at an antique wooden kitchen table, without *heels.*

6 "Oh, I envy you," I say, attempting to be reasonable. "I have never had the time to really learn what I'm doing with this vegetarian thing." I haven't eaten meat for eight years; she stopped six months ago. Her zealotry has the strength of youth.

7 "Laurel says that there is really no reason for a woman to work," she answers. "This kind of cooking keeps you busy, and you save money in the long run by staying at home, not eating out and stuff."

8 She and her man have been living on a very low budget to prepare for the traveling that has brought them here. Already my kitchen is overrun with their coolers, special bowls, cannisters of protein yeast, etc. I have suggested we go out to dinner. I have been busy working, and I have no intention of cooking, no matter what Laurel says. My guest, of course, doesn't want to spend the money. She spends a great deal of time the second day of her visit calculating aloud how much money they have spent. Five dollars a day is way off the budget. "We've got to get out of here," she cries as if my thoughts had power. I am busy preparing a dinner party for six, with no ingredients from the coolers on which I keep stumping my toes. Even barefoot, so there.

9 I suppose there is really no need to go into the skill of the turning eyes. This one takes a partner and my dear visitor never lets hers out of her carrot juice sharpened sight. She is his rib and he her organic mission. When I smoke, her eyes seek his. When I refuse to cook or puff a drug or paint my face, her eyes seek his. She cannot bear to watch my suicide. I cannot bear her wholesome bigotry. . . .

10 But that's enough. I am feeling better already. My cigarette and coke sustain me. My enemy is described, and I am victorious.

FOR DISCUSSION

1. How would you describe the tone of this essay? What image of the author is conveyed?
2. This essay is based upon a "character" (see pp. 196–197 above). Describe in your own words the type of character that is portrayed here.
3. In addition to being based upon a "character," this essay describes, to some extent, an "irregular art" (see pp. 197–198). What name would you give this art?

Informative Writing

Overview

This chapter introduces some of the situations, functions, and strategies of informative writing—writing whose purpose is not to support a thesis but to organize and communicate information. Like other kinds of writing, informative writing has a number of specifically related purposes, settings, strategies, and styles.

- **What Is Informative Writing?**
  - **Information is in everything**
  - **Everything requires an organizing perspective**
  - **Nothing is completely neutral**
- **The Compass of Information: Types and Situations**
  - **Knowledge**
  - **Action**
  - **Public concern, evaluation, decision making**
  - **Entertainment and vicarious experience**
- **Sorting and Organizing Information**
  - **Writing about a problem**
  - **Writing about a controversy**
  - **Writing about events, discoveries, or developments**
  - **Writing about an item, place, or thing**
  - **Writing about a concept, movement, or institution**
  - **Writing about a person**
  - **Writing about a process, method, or procedure**
- **Strategies for Conveying Information Effectively**
  - **Facts and examples**
  - **Descriptive detail**
  - **Definition**
  - **Comparison and contrast**
  - **Causal and logical explanation**
  - **Analogy**
  - **The hypothetical case**
  - **Pictures, charts, and diagrams**

- Beginnings and Endings
  - The framing function
  - Ways to begin
  - Ways to conclude
- Style: Formality, Informality, and the Authorial "I"
  - Levels of formality
  - The authorial "I"
- Essay Assignments
- Essays for Analysis

• What Is Informative Writing?

Informative writing is commonly thought of as the easiest kind of discourse to define and understand—writing whose chief purpose is not to argue a thesis but to present information. This definition would help you identify almost any piece of informative writing. However, there are three points—three complicating factors—that will lead to a deeper and more precise understanding of what informative writing is and how it operates in society.

Information is in everything

A confusing factor in understanding informative writing is that all types of writing contain information. Information is in all discourse. In fact, sometimes we get better information, and more of it, from a deliberative essay—one that argues for or against a thesis—than from an informative essay on the same subject. The difference between informative writing and deliberative or argumentative writing lies not so much in the amount or quality of information as in its *purpose.*

In deliberative writing, information is presented for the purpose of supporting a thesis—to confirm an argument or support a point of view. In informative writing, on the other hand, the primary function is to convey information, even though there may be secondary evaluative or directive functions. Informative writers do express opinions and come to conclusions, but they do not argue the point. And they generally avoid expressing opinions that are controversial.

Everything requires an organizing perspective

A second complicating factor is that there are very few cases in which you can simply present the facts. If you write a recipe for party punch, you can get by with a simple presentation of details: 1 cup of apple juice, 2 cups of cheap champagne, etc. But most matters worth writing about require more explaining and organizing. A good informative writer not only lists facts but also provides a set of explanations, framing generalizations, and organizing perspectives in order to develop the facts into a coherent, overall picture. The problem is that different organizing perspectives often involve different or competing understandings of the subject.

One example is this textbook. It is presented as informative discourse, yet it incorporates a distinctive organizing perspective. Its perspective is basically traditional but differs markedly from the organizing perspective of other rhetoric texts. Scholars in the field of rhetoric and composition engage in *deliberative* discourse about the merits of different organizing perspectives, and this textbook takes a stand on a number of questions, by the fact of presenting the material in a certain way. However, the book does not argue points about the merits of its organizing perspective, and it does not arrange material so as to support any particular argument.

This makes a big difference. For the deliberative writer, the organizing perspective helps support a thesis. For the informative writer, on the other hand, the organizing perspective orders and clarifies the material. The presentation itself is not designed to support a conclusion.

Nothing is completely neutral

People expect the writers of informative discourse to be objective and unbiased. The whole point is to provide information, which helps readers form opinions. We feel betrayed when we find that an author pretends to be a broker of information but is underhandedly trying to persuade us. We sense that the writer is not playing by the rules.

Both readers and writers of informative discourse must be sensitive to ways in which bias and persuasive appeals can slip into informative discourse. At the same time, it is a mistake to think that information can be absolutely neutral or that informative discourse does nothing but satisfy human curiosity. This unrealistic view of information overlooks two important facts. First, *writers of information are selective in what they write.* Publications that claim to present "just the facts" neglect to point out that there is no way that they could present *all* the facts. The very act of choosing a subject—or of choosing to emphasize one subject over another subject—involves a commitment to that subject, a decision that it merits more attention.

Second, *writers of information have different motives, and readers have different needs.* Sometimes writers choose subjects just because they think an audience is curious about them. But in many cases, information can fulfill more specific purposes. For example, organizations like the Audubon Society sponsor and publish informative essays on American wildlife because they value it and want to protect it. They hope that, by knowing it better, others will value it also. And newspapers occasionally devote whole pages to information about civic events, such as downtown arts festivals, because they wish to promote these activities and encourage people to participate in them.

These are just two examples of informative writing for specific purposes. We will explore these more systematically later in this chapter. For now, keep in mind that the definition and place-in-society of informative discourse is more complex that it might at first appear.

EXERCISE 8.1

Listed below are some specific instances of informative discourse. For each instance, what secondary or covert purposes might be involved?

A. A detailed, factual article on the causes, cures, and prevention of venereal disease, written by a leading health official, is published in a magazine read widely by females, age eleven to twenty.

B. A free-lance writer is commissioned to write a feature article on Alaska's delicate ecological balance. The article is paid for by one of the larger oil corporations and published in a quarterly magazine sponsored by the corporation. It is accompanied by beautiful, full-page photographs of the Alaskan landscape.

C. A feature article on the ten most scenic vacation spots in the world appears in the magazine you find tucked into the seat of a commercial airplane.

D. A weekly news magazine decides that for the next fifty weeks it will publish a feature article on the people and customs of every state in the Union.

E. A nuclear physicist writes an article which explains in everyday language how nuclear reactors work, how hazardous nuclear wastes are formed, and how scientists are trying to solve the problem.

• The Compass of Information: Types and Situations

The primary purpose of informative writing is to present, clarify, and organize a subject. However, there are many different types and situations of informative writing. These types function in different ways and they fulfill different secondary purposes. Although it would be impossible to present a list of all types, it may be useful to think of any particular instance of informative writing as "leaning" in one of a few basic directions, in the manner of a compass (see chart). We can relate many of the common types of informative writing to one or more of these "directions."

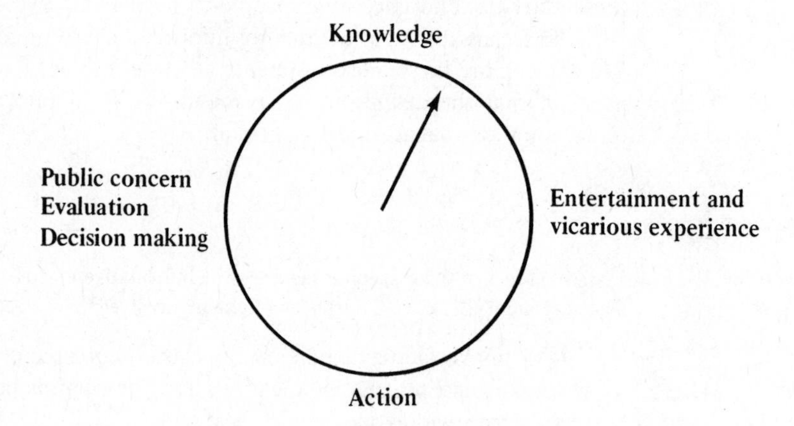

Knowledge

One point on the compass is *knowledge*—information whose chief purpose is to gather, organize, and communicate what is known about a subject, primarily as a matter of reference, without regard for how the information is used. The clearest examples of this type are the encyclopedia essay and the kind of "research report" that is often assigned to students in college courses. (See Appendix 1, pp. 291–300). This type of writing should be thorough, clear, concise, and balanced in its presentation of facts and of differing views or theories.

Action

Opposite knowledge is *action,* —information for guiding or assisting people in performing operations or jobs, or in achieving goals. The clearest example of this type is the "How-To" article—"How to Tune Your Car," or "How to develop Black and White Photographs." Obviously, one of the most important qualities of this type of writing is clarity. Many a frustrated do-it-yourselfer can testify that informative writers do not always achieve clarity in their instructions.

Also leaning in the direction of *action* is writing that offers advice on attaining certain goals—"How to Win Friends and Influence People," or "How to Succeed in College." Because such writings deal with the decisions people make in their lives, decisions subject to radical differences of opinion, this type of information readily spills over into other types of writing.

Public concern, evaluation, decision making

Informative writing leans in this direction when it treats subjects of *public concern* or controversy. Although this type of informative essay does not take sides, its author should be aware that because the information relates to a subject of concern, readers might make choices or evaluations on the basis of the information presented.

Several types of informative writing lean in this direction. One is the "background report" on a current problem or controversy—on a rash of violent crimes in the region, for instance, and what citizens are trying to do about them. A related type is the "inside report"—an account, for instance, of the behind-the-scenes actions that led to some important action or decision. Three important abilities are necessary in these types of informative writing. First is the ability to discover and organize information, through research and interviews. Second is the ability to translate specialized information and concepts into everyday language, and third is the ability to maintain a balanced viewpoint—to put aside prejudices and convictions for the sake of objective presentation.

Another type of informative writing leans in the direction of *public concern* and *evaluation* because it gives publicity to its subject and invites public assessment. Feature articles and "profiles" devoted to people who have achieved distinction or notoriety in politics, science, or the arts sometimes fit into this category. Although the purpose of such writing is not to give an opinion, its effect is often either to heighten or diminish the public esteem in which its subject is held.

Entertainment and vicarious experience

At the fourth point on the compass of information is *entertainment and vicarious experience.* Informative writing that leans in this direction aims at an entertaining, readable style, and at graphic description and narration, more than at thoroughness or balance. Familiar examples of this type of informative writing are travelogue articles and feature articles on unusual people and events. Most sports and entertainment features also fit into this category.

EXERCISE 8.2

Different instances of informative writing can have one of the following characteristics: 1) They can lean heavily in one of the directions indicated by the "compass of information"; 2) they can lie somewhere between two directions, or shift back and forth between two directions; or 3) they can remain indeterminate, not leaning one way or another. Discuss the "leanings" of each of the instances listed below.

A. An essay on how to install a shower in an old bathroom.

B. An essay on how to make money in the stock market.

C. An essay on how to get ahead by intimidating your fellow workers.

D. A feature on the newly appointed president of your college or university.

E. An article chronicling your six-week journey down the Nile river.

F. An essay explaining how a local controversy over a book-banning in the public schools got started, what the arguments on both sides are, and how the controversy relates to national trends in this area.

G. A feature on the American bald eagle.

H. A report translating into layman's language the findings of a recent study in cell biology.

I. A report condensing and summarizing the findings of a recently appointed commission on child abuse.

J. A report condensing and summarizing the arguments of a recent book calling for a total ban on nuclear power plants.

EXERCISE 8.3

Turn back to the specific instances listed in Exercise 8.1 (p. 229). Discuss the "leanings" of these specific instances, just as you did in the preceding exercise.

• Sorting and Organizing Information

Whatever the particular "leaning" of your own informative essay, you face the important pre-writing task of gathering and organizing material. For almost any essay, the three most important sources of information are your own memory, interviews, and written materials. You will find a guide to sources of information in Appendix 1 of this book, "The Research Report," pp. 291–300. However, it is unrealistic to think you can simply gather information from various sources and then organize it. You must begin to sort and organize information while you are gathering it. Otherwise, you will have no way of distinguishing what is useful from what isn't; you probably won't get through it all, and there may be important segments that you miss entirely. Remember that the amount of potential information on any given subject is staggering. You must devise a method of sorting it, of making sure you cover the most important aspects, and of rejecting irrelevant or redundant material.

In some circumstances your information gathering may be guided by one question from the beginning. What were Abraham Lincoln's attitudes toward black people? Or what caused America's recent population shift from the North and Midwest to the South and West? Here you know exactly what you are looking for. On other occasions, however, you may have a subject but no specific guidance. Your goal (or your assignment) may be to do a report or get a story on a particular subject. The best way of establishing a method of investigation is to develop a short list of the most important questions that might be asked about the subject, and then to organize your search around the categories of information that these questions provide.

It is impossible to predict what the most important questions will be for a particular situation. However, a match of typical writing situations with some relevant questions could be useful. Not all of the questions in any particular set below will be relevant to your subject and purpose, but using the set of questions can at least insure that you examined most of the angles.

Writing about a problem

For this kind of topic, the problem-solving model presented in Chapter 3 of this book (p. 75) can be an excellent tool for discovery. It generates the following questions:

1. What exactly is the problem? What undesirable condition or conflict exists?
2. What are the causes of the problem? Is it a new problem or an old problem? Are there other problems like it, or is it unique?
3. How serious is the problem?
4. What are the separate components of the problem? Is it part of some larger problem?
5. What goals and values must be met and adhered to by any solution that is offered?
6. What are some possible solutions to the problem?
7. What further problems might be caused by the particular solutions? What objections have been raised to particular solutions?
8. What is the outlook for solving the problem?

Writing about a controversy

1. How did the controversy begin? How did it develop from that point?
2. Who are the major disputants? What different philosophical, social, or national viewpoints do they represent?

3. What exactly is at issue in the controversy? Does it center on a question of policy, of value, or of understanding?
4. What is the significance of the controversy? What larger questions are brought up by the controversy?
5. What is the outlook for resolving the controversy?

Writing about events, discoveries, or developments

Reporters ask *Who, What, When, Where,* and *Why.* The following set of questions is really an elaboration of this device.

1. What has happened or developed? Who was involved? What was the sequence of events?
2. What are the causes and background of the event or development? What might have prevented it? What human motives or conflicts were involved.
3. Are the current sources of information reliable? What myths or misconceptions exist about the event? Are there differing versions of what happened?
4. What *kind* of thing has happened or developed? Does the event belong to some larger category of events?
5. What is it like? How does it compare and contrast with other events?
6. What is the significance of the event? How will it affect the lives of the people for whom you are writing? What does it reveal about the people involved?

Writing about an item, a place, or "thing"

1. Is it natural or man-made?
2. What are its distinguishing characteristics—shape, color size, etc.?
3. What myths or misconceptions exist about it?
4. What other things is it similar to? How does it differ from similar things?
5. What is its structure? How do its parts fit or work together?
6. What is its history? How might it develop in the future?
7. What is its significance?

Writing about a concept, movement, or institution

1. What are the commonplace or popular meanings of the term? What myths or misconceptions about the term exist? What is the "proper" meaning of the term, or the meaning that you wish to focus upon?
2. What are the essential features of the concept?
3. Does the concept name a single notion or experience, or does it apply to a broad range or class of ideas?

4. What are the range and limits of the concept? How much variation is possible?
5. What is its history and development? What important people or groups of people have been associated with it, past and present?
6. How is it similar to or different from other ideas, concepts, or movements?
7. What is its significance? What controversies or criticisms has it aroused?

Writing about a person

1. What is of particular interest to you or to your audience about the person?
2. What myths, misconceptions, or controversies exist about the person?
3. What is the person's background and development? What important changes occurred in the person's life?
4. What is the person's essential character or achievement?
5. What incidents, actions, sayings, or writings best illustrate the person's essential character or achievement?
6. What puzzles or unanswered questions remain about the person?

Writing about a process, method, or procedure

1. What are the component elements or materials involved in the process?
2. What is the sequence of operations in the process?
3. What things can go wrong in the process?
4. What important changes occur during the process?

EXERCISE 8.4

The preceding sets of questions could not possibly cover every specific situation that calls for informative writing. Studying them, however, can give you a sense of how to ask questions on your own for specific subjects. Make a list of questions for one or more of the specific situations listed below.

A. The health department announced that last year there was a dramatic increase in reported cases of child abuse. Your job is to write a background report on this problem.

B. Last year a group of people started publishing a small magazine on matters of interest to people in your city. The magazine has been a success and you are to write an informative essay on it.

C. Your assignment is to write a report on the contents and impact of a successful recent book on the subject of crime in America.

• Strategies for Conveying Information Effectively

Every informative writer faces two kinds of problems. The first is finding the crucial questions that need to be answered about a topic. The second is identifying those elements that, for a particular audience, require special explanation and clarification. Remember that a primary function of informative writing is to present and explain things clearly and fully to an audience that knows less than you do.

- What can I do to help my audience understand this more clearly?
- What aspects of this material are potentially confusing?
- What aspects of this material require special explanation?

The following seven strategies are the most important for dealing with problems of clear and effective presentation.

Facts and examples

In any kind of presentation, you must make generalizations and characterizations. However, unless your readers are already familiar with the topic, generalizations don't mean very much unless you support them, clarify them, and fill them in with facts and examples. Facts and examples give your reader a specific and graphic hold on the subject. It's possible, of course, to overload your writing with detail, but this is hardly ever a problem with inexperienced writers.

The passage that follows begins with a generalization and backs it up with a series of examples.

> When a word may be applied in two possible ways, one favorable or complimentary and the other reverse, it is extremely likely that it will specialize in the less desirable sense. Thus, *suggestive* is likely to mean only "evilly suggestive," though it *may* still mean "informative" or "illuminating," and though the noun *suggestion* has escaped any such specialization—just as the verb *to harbor* is limited to unworthy or illegal concealment (as in "harboring a criminal" or "harboring thoughts of revenge"), while the noun *harbor* retains the old broad and literal meaning of "haven." *Asylum,* through association with the idea of "refuge for the insane," has followed a course like that of the verb *harbor.* A *libel,* in Middle English and early Modern English, was simply a "brief bit of writing" (from Lat. *libellum,* little book); now it is definitely limited to something malicious or defamatory. *Doom* once meant "judgment"; now it means only "condemnation." *Reek,* as we have seen, can now stand only for unpleasant distillations; *stink* and *stench* have specialized in the same way from a formerly neutral meaning, and *smell* and even *odor* seem likely to follow their lead. A *smirk* was once merely a smile, without the suggestion of affection. One could

formerly *resent* benefits as well as injuries, and *retaliate* for favors as well as slights; compare with the present meanings of these words the ordinary implications of the phrase "get even with" or "get square with."—Stuart Robertson and Frederic G. Cassidy, *The Development of Modern English*

EXERCISE 8.5

Construct a paragraph of 50–100 words using the strategy of *facts and examples.* Use one of the following sentences as a "lead" or "topic" sentence. Or construct a lead sentence of your own.

A. For most college students the pace of life begins to quicken dramatically about the third week into the semester.

B. In recent years Americans have learned the hard way that natural resources are not unlimited.

C. Most of us have developed a fairly sophisticated set of strategies for putting off the act of writing.

Descriptive detail

Closely related to the strategy of *facts and examples* is that of *descriptive detail.* Particularly if your subject is a place, event, item, or product, general statements like "It is a breathtaking scene," or "It was a violent encounter," are going to fall flat without lots of supporting detail. What exactly is there? What exactly took place? What exactly was said? How does it look? Make your reader see the scene, event, or item as vividly and as concretely as possible.

In the passage that follows, the writer has captured the style and method of the great baseball pitcher, Bob Gibson:

> The pitch, as I have said, shot across the plate with a notable amount of right-to-left (from Gibson's vantage point) action, and his catchers sometimes gave the curious impression that they were cutting off a ball that was headed on a much longer journey—a one-hundred-foot fastball. But with Gibson pitching you were always a little distracted from the plate and the batter, because his delivery continued so extravagantly after the ball was released that you almost felt that the pitch was incidental to the whole affair. The follow-through sometimes suggested a far-out basketball move—a fast downcourt feint. His right leg, which was up and twisted to the right in the air as the ball was let go (all normal enough for a right-handed pitcher), now continued forward in a sudden sidewise rush, crossing his planted left leg, actually stepping over it, and he finished with a full running step toward the right-field foul line, which wrenched his body in the same direction, so that he now had to follow the flight of the ball by peering over his *right* shoulder. Both his arms whirled in the air to help him keep his balance during this acrobatic maneuver, but the key to his overpowering speed and stuff

was not the strength of his pitching arm—it was the powerful, driving thrust of his legs, culminating in that final extra step, which brought his right foot clomping down on the sloping left-hand side of the mound, with the full weight of his body slamming and twisting behind it. . . .

All in all, the pitch and its extended amplifications made it look as if Gibson were leaping at the batter, with hostile intent. He always looked much closer to the plate at the end than any other pitcher; he made pitching seem unfair.
—Roger Angell, "The Sporting Scene"

EXERCISE 8.6

Construct a paragraph of 50–100 words using the strategy of *descriptive detail.* Use one of the following sentences as a "lead" or "topic" sentence. Or construct a lead sentence of your own.

A. At first glance Magnolia Mall looks like any other giant, enclosed shopping center.

B. Playing this pinball machine is a dazzling experience.

Definition

The information writer should always clarify the meanings of any terms the audience might not know; when your subject involves abstract concepts or different ideological perspectives on the same experience, definition can be crucial. In defining a term, you are concerned with four basic things:

1. The *class* of items or concepts to which a term belongs.
2. The characteristics that *distinguish* a particular item from other members of the same class.
3. The way in which a particular item or concept *differs* from or is similar to other items or concepts.
4. The *special meanings and emotional connotations* that a term has acquired in a particular context.

The first three of these things are present in the following example, an explanatory definition of "figures of speech." The author begins by placing the term in a general category. He then lists the term's characteristics by giving examples. Finally, he sharpens the definition by comparing the term with a closely related one.

Images become involved in our thinking (for better or for worse) when they enter into what are commonly called *"figures of speech."* A figure of speech consists in a comparison between two things, which we may label "X" and "Y." Generally one of the things, say X, is the one we are saying something about, and the X-term (or primary term) denotes the thing *to which* some other thing is compared. In a figure of speech we say something about X by comparing Y *to* it; the Y-term (or secondary term) denotes the thing which is compared to X. In "love is blind," "love" is the primary term and "blind (person)" is the secondary term. Or when H. G. Wells says that the brain of man is a "food-getting instrument, like the snout of a pig," "brain" is the primary term and "snout of a pig" is the secondary term. When the figurative statement is elliptical, we have to supply part of the terms ourselves.

All figures of speech are comparisons, but not all comparisons are figures of speech. To begin with a simple example, we may say that "James was as angry as a hornet" is figurative, but that "James was angry as John" is *not.* It is not hard to see that there is a difference here, but it is impossible to state the difference exactly without using highly technical language. James and John are evidently much more alike than James and the hornet, for James and John both belong to the same biological species. Thus James and John can *both* be angry, in the same sense of the word. But James and the hornet *cannot* both be angry in the same sense of the word: the hornet doesn't feel the same way, and he doesn't behave the same way. He can't get red in the face or stamp his feet with rage: he can only zoom, buzz, and sting.—Monroe Beardsley, *Thinking Straight*

EXERCISE 8.7

Construct a paragraph of 50–100 words using the strategy of *definition.* Use one of the following sentences as a "lead" or "topic" sentence. Or construct a lead sentence of your own.

A. Apart from compassion, the quality most admired in Abraham Lincoln is that of integrity.

B. Few concepts in American political life arouse more controversy, indignation, and confusion than that of "welfare."

Comparison and contrast

Comparison and contrast play a role in definition. However, they are also useful in explaining the exact nature of a particular item or concept. One of the best ways of clarifying the presentation of a complex or unfamiliar item is to show how it differs from (or is similar to) related items.

In the example that follows, the author helps us understand a modern problem by comparing two dissimilar situations—ancient and modern.

Among preliterate peoples adolescence frequently does not cause the amount of trouble it does with us. From an early age the boy is in almost constant association with his father and learns almost all his skills and attitudes from him. With us, however, an adolescent boy is educated more by other associations in the community than by his father. Furthermore, among many primitives, boys and girls at about the time of puberty are inducted into manhood and womanhood or at least take their first step toward that goal. Initiation rites and impressive ceremonies mark a definite change in their status, and they acquire new rights and freedom, though new responsibilities as well. In our own society, however, there is no social recognition of new status when adolescence comes on. The boy becomes a young man physiologically, but he is still treated as a child and does not attain his majority till he is twenty-one. He is like a child who has outgrown his clothes and toys but is not given any others. This is at the root of his rebellion, when it comes to such a pass. His parents still try to dominate him in all his behavior—in his choice of clothes, work, friends, recreation, and even bedtime. In other words, the parent-child relationship continues long after it should have changed to a parent-adult relationship. The youth resents this, and the fight is on.—Ray E. Baber, *Marriage and the Family*

EXERCISE 8.8

Construct a paragraph of 50–100 words using the strategy of *comparison and contrast.* Use one of the following sentences as a "lead" or "topic" sentence. Or construct a lead sentence of your own.

A. Actually being at a baseball game is a very different experience from seeing it on television.

B. We can clarify the notion of a "healthy sense of pride," by comparing it with the related notion of "arrogance."

Causal and logical explanation

Informative writing sometimes fails by leaving the reader puzzled, asking, "How can that be?" or "How could that have happened?" The writer, who may understand these things perfectly well, has forgotten that the reader is not familiar with the subject. The writer has left holes in the story or contradictions in the explanation.

The remedies for these faults are *causal explanation* and *logical explanation.* Causal explanation clarifies some aspect of a subject by explaining its background, indicating what factors made it possible and shaped its development. Logical explanation, on the other hand, can dispel confusion about some statement that might seem hard to believe. You show it really is true, in spite of the fact that it may seem unbelievable or incompatible with things you've already said.

The first passage below, from an article on "bird aerodynamics," is a causal explanation:

> Of all the powers of birds in the air probably none has caused more wonder than their soaring ability. To see a bird rise in the air and sail on motionless wings into the distance until at last it disappears from sight gives one a sense of magic. We now know how it is done, but it is still difficult to realize what is happening as we watch it.

Actually the bird is coasting downhill in relation to the flow of air. It rises because it is riding a rising current of air which is ascending faster than the bird is sinking in the current.—"Bird Aerodynamics," *Scientific American*

This next passage is a logical explanation. The author first presents a generalization that seems rather extraordinary. He then tells why, and in what way, it is true:

> Not every human being can play the violin, do calculus, jump high hurdles, or sail a canoe, no matter how excellent his teachers or how arduous his training—but every person constantly creates utterances never before spoken on earth. Incredible as it may seem at first thought, the sentence you just read possibly appeared in exactly this form for the first time in the history of the English language—and the same thing might be said about the sentence you are reading now. In fact, if conventional remarks—such as greetings, farewells, stock phrases like *thank you,* proverbs, clichés, and so forth—are disregarded, in theory all of a person's speech consists of sentences never before uttered.
>
> A moment's reflection reveals why that may be so. Every language groups its vocabulary into a number of different classes such as nouns, verbs, adjectives, and so on. If English possessed a mere 1,000 nouns (such as *trees, children, horses*) and only 1,000 verbs *(grow, die, change),* the number of possible two-word sentences, therefore, would be 1,000 × 1,000, or one million. Of course, most of these sentences will be meaningless to a speaker today—yet at one time people thought *atoms split* was a meaningless utterance. The nouns, however, might also serve as the objects of these same verbs in three-word sentences. So with the same meager repertory of 1,000 nouns and 1,000 verbs capable of taking an object, the number of possible three-word sentences increases to 1,000 × 1,000 × 1,000, or one billion. These calculations, of course, are just for minimal sentences and an impoverished vocabulary. Most languages offer their speakers many times a thousand nouns and a thousand verbs, and in addition they possess other classes of words that function as adverbs, adjectives, articles, prepositions, and so on. Think, too, in terms of four-word, ten-word, even fifty-word sentences—and the number of possible grammatical combinations becomes astronomical. One linguist calculated that it would take ten trillion years (two thousand times the estimated age of the earth) to utter all the possible English sentences that use exactly twenty words. Therefore, it is improbable that any twenty-word sentence a person speaks was ever spoken previously—and the same thing would hold true, of course, for sentences of greater length, and for most shorter ones as well.
> —Peter Farb, *Word Play: What Happens When People Talk,* 1973

EXERCISE 8.9

Construct a paragraph of 50–100 words using either a *causal* or a *logical* explanation. Use one of the following sentences as a "lead" or "topic" sentence. Or construct one of your own.

A. Cows keep on chewing long after they have stopped eating.

B. It's natural for people to get wrinkles as they grow older.

C. Most people know more about child rearing than they think they do.

Analogy

One of the best ways of explaining the complex or the unfamiliar is by analogy —showing how an item or experience is similar in certain respects to a more familiar item or experience. Highly theoretical subjects, in fact, seem almost to require analogical presentation, as in the explanation of photosynthesis in the example below:

> Light, in the latest theory, is not waves in a sea of ether, or a jet from a nozzle; it could be compared rather to machine gun fire, every photo-electric bullet of energy traveling in regular rhythm, at a speed that bridges the astronomical gap in eight minutes. As each bullet hits an electron of chlorophyll it sets it to vibrating, at its own rate, just as one tuning fork, when struck, will cause another to hum in the same pitch. A bullet strikes—and one electron is knocked galley west into a dervish dance like the madness of the atoms in the sun. The energy splits open chlorophyll molecules, recombines their atoms, and lies there, dormant, in foods.—Donald C. Peattie, *Flowering Earth*

EXERCISE 8.10

Construct a paragraph of 50–100 words in which you use the strategy of analogy to describe or explain one of the following. Or choose an item of your own.

A. Chemical compounding

B. Writing an essay

C. Static electricity

D. Taking the SAT

The hypothetical case

A hypothetical case is an example, usually an extended one, that doesn't exist but which neatly illustrates a principle, a concept, or a process. There are two advantages to this kind of strategy. You can think up a situation that is easily understandable to your audience, and you can tailor the details of the situation so as to exemplify complexities of the experience.

In the following passage, the author uses a detailed hypothetical case to show how a language changes over time:

Imagine a village of a thousand people all speaking the same language and never hearing any language other than their own. As the decades pass and generation succeeds generation, it will not be very apparent to the speakers of the language that any considerable language change is going on. Oldsters may occasionally be conscious of and annoyed by the speech forms of youngsters. They will notice new words, new expressions, "bad" pronunciations, but will ordinarily put these down to the irresponsibility of youth, and decide piously that the language of the younger generation will revert to decency when the generation grows up.

It doesn't revert, though. The new expressions and the new pronunciations persist, and presently there is another younger generation with its own new expressions and its own pronunciations. And thus the language changes. If members of the village could speak to one another across five hundred years, they would probably find themselves unable to communicate.

Now suppose that the village divides itself and half the people move away. They move across the river or over a mountain and form a new village. Suppose the separation is so complete that the people of New Village have no contact with the people of Old Village. The language of both villages will change, drifting away from the language of their common ancestors. But the drift will not be in the same direction. In both villages there will be new expressions and new pronunciations, but not the same ones. In the course of time the language of Old Village and New Village will be mutually unintelligible with the language they both started with. They will also be mutually unintelligible with one another. —Paul Roberts, *Understanding English*

EXERCISE 8.11

Construct a paragraph in which you build a *hypothetical case* to illustrate one of the following principles or ideas. Or choose an idea of your own.

A. There is some danger in pushing a child into music lessons too soon.

B. In training an animal to do anything, there is no substitute for the method of positive reinforcement.

Pictures, charts, and diagrams

Much of the informative writing published today makes use of *pictures, charts, or diagrams.* In popular information, the pictures function mainly as attention grabbers. But graphic representations can be useful explanatory devices, and there are some subjects for which they are almost indispensable. If a graphic device can help clarify some aspect of your topic, you should use it, provided you have technical means to produce it.

In this textbook there are explanatory diagrams on pages 48 and 230.

• Beginnings and Endings

The framing function

In all kinds of writing, we use introductions to grab the reader's attention and focus it on our subject. We use conclusions to summarize main points, to speculate about the subject, and to create a satisfying sense of an ending. However, in informative writing, introductions and conclusions have the special function of *framing* the information—giving it a context and tying it together into a unified whole.

In informative writing, facts and explanations do not support a thesis; they are there for their own sake. Consequently, even when it is very orderly, the presentation needs some kind of frame, something to make it a whole thing and not just a collection of separate things. In informative writing, introductions and conclusions perform this framing and unifying function.

As an example of the framing function, see the opening of "A Sears Suit," presented on pp. 4–5. The essay's purpose is to present information about an important legal action brought against the government by the Sears, Roebuck and Company. Here's the way the essay begins:

> Normally, companies are on the receiving end of lawsuits about discrimination against workers on the basis of sex and race. But last week Sears, Roebuck, the world's largest retailor (annual sales: more than $17 billion), reversed the pattern.
>
> In a sweeping class action filed in the Washington, D. C. Federal District Court, Sears blamed the Government for whatever employment imbalances exist in the retail industry.

In this introduction the author moves directly to the specific event, the actual lawsuit; but at the same time he attaches the event to a generalization that tells us something about its significance and why we might be interested in it. The generalization not only attracts interest; it provides a frame for the information that follows.

After presenting some facts and details about the case, the article explains that the company instituted the suit primarily as a "public relations gesture," calling attention to contradictions and inconsistencies in the federal regulations. It then concludes with a generalization and a quotation:

> A good many businessmen would agree with Sears Chairman Edward Telling when he says that his suit is a needed effort "to cut through conflicting regulations and to force a clarification of irreconcilables."

This generalization supplements the introductory generalization, so that together they make a unifying frame for the information—one that emphasizes the social and political significance of a legal action. The quotation adds authenticity to the framing generalization and helps create a satisfying sense of an ending.

Some critics would maintain that the amount of framing generalization is out of proportion to the amount of information presented and that there is a bias in favor of the plaintiff in the suit. This criticism is a fair one, touching on a problem with popular reporting in the weekly news magazines and on television. Framing very meager sets of facts with unifying generalizations leads to vapid editorializing.

The cause of whatever bias exists in this article is not that the author has gone too far but that he has not gone far enough. He needed a framing generalization for the information, and it was proper to look for one. But he grabbed what was closest at hand, instead of examining the case in depth. Superficiality, more than an underhanded attempt to persuade, is the spoiler of informative writing.

Ways to begin

The introduction to an informative essay should:

1. arouse the reader's interest;
2. focus the reader's attention on a specific event, question, or aspect of the subject; and
3. provide, or begin to provide, a unifying frame for the information to be presented.

An introduction cannot always do all of these things at once, and it may not need to do them all. Arousing interest is less important, for instance, in research or reference writing than in popular reporting or feature writing. The unifying frame is less important in the simple reporting of news than in the longer essay which provides background and detail. As with any writing, you should consider the needs of the situation, examine your options, and use common sense.

Some common openers for informative writing are described and illustrated here.

Framing generalization. This strategy provides a general statement which "includes" the information to be presented, builds a context for it, and says something about its significance. The quotation from "A Sears Suit" is an example. This quotation also illustrates a trick that informative writers use to arouse interest—The **X but Y** pattern. It begins with a statement or generalization, and follows it with a statement that seems to contradict it or to take off in a different direction, using such connectives as *but, nevertheless, however, on the other hand.* This creates an "edge," a sense of disjunction that arouses the reader's interest.

Corrective assertion. This strategy calls attention to some popular misconception or erroneous opinion about a subject, and then sets the record straight. This strategy also provides an attention-getting edge, and it usually involves use of the **X BUT Y** pattern.

> Even though it is generally recognized that meanings change, many people still cling, curiously enough, to the quite contradictory notion that words all have 'true' meanings, that changes somehow take us away from the 'true' meaning, and that the way to find out what a word 'really means' is to find out what it once meant. . . . A little reflection should show that an appeal to etymology in order to establish the present meaning of the word is as untrustworthy as an appeal to spelling in order to establish its present pronunciation.—Stuart Robertson, *The Development of Modern English*

Framing question. This opener confronts the reader directly with the question, or the set of questions, that your essay is designed to answer. In addition to providing a partial frame, this device also serves to arouse and focus interest.

> To what extent did Agrippina control her son Nero? How did she do so, and what was the nature of the relationship between them? Was she for a time, as is often suggested, the true emperor of Rome? These questions come to the mind of any person who studies Nero's life and rule as emperor.—Jenny Maxwell, "Agrippina, Rome's Most Influential Woman" (Student Research Report)

Background lead. This opener leads the reader into your subject with some of its historical background and development. It not only gives the reader information necessary for understanding the subject, it also builds a context for your essay, indicating why the subject is important and timely.

> Heart disease continues to take a heavy toll of human life, being responsible for nearly a million deaths a year in the U.S. alone. The toll has been reduced somewhat by improved medical procedures, new drugs and pacemakers, and it could be reduced far more if individuals assumed greater responsibility for controlling such proved risk factors as smoking, inadequate exercise, high blood pressure, obesity and excessive stress. In this arsenal of therapy and prevention an additional weapon may soon be available: the total artificial heart.—Robert K. Jarvik, "The Total Artificial Heart"

Focusing event. This opener is used in a great deal of informative writing because it is such an attractive attention-getter. Begin by describing a particular event or circumstance, sometimes in the form of a story. This event either illustrates some aspect of your subject or brings out the larger questions that your essay is intended to explore.

> One summer evening in the late eighteenth century, a British professor of rhetoric and "political philosophy" stepped out into his garden, clad only in a nightshirt, for a breath of air. He fell into a reverie about economic theory and proceeded to go for a stroll. Only after he had travelled fifteen miles down a country lane did he "come to" and remember why he had stepped outside in the first place. The professor was Adam Smith, author of *The Wealth of Nations,* the classic treatment and defense of free-market economics.
>
> This charming incident may be irrelevant to the substance of Smith's political thought, but it does stand as a reminder of its quality—particularly its speculative, abstract dimension. Like the physicists of his time, Smith saw the world as basically self-governing. Left to its own devices, the market system produced its own admirable order, unneedful of government. This one principle, more than any other, shaped Smith's views on the role of government in human affairs.—June Yorlig, "Adam Smith on the Role of Government" (Student Research Essay)

Focusing or framing quotation. This opener uses a quotation, usually from an authority or from someone you have interviewed in the process of gathering information. The quotation serves either as a "framing generalization," as part of a "focusing event," or as a thought-provoking sample of opinion on a subject, as in the following example.

> "Physicians are becoming a social problem. Twenty percent of all treatment given in hospitals is the wrong treatment. Physicians are the highest paid profession in the world. Unnecessary surgery is ripping off Americans." With these inflammatory words a sociology professor began a course in medical problems two semesters ago. Students in the course were not long into the reading list before discovering that not all sociologists agree with this professor's judgment, and more surprisingly, that not all physicians completely disagree. The very severity of the professors remarks, however, inspires some penetrating questions: What exactly is "unnecessary surgery?" Is it a severe problem in the United States today? And if so, how has it come to be a problem?—Penelope Nance, "Too Much Surgery?" (Student Essay)

Provocative or surprising statement. This opener is a come-on, a blatant attention-grabber, and often very effective. The trick is to catch your readers with some astonishing fact or outrageous-sounding generalization.

> Our planet has the wrong name. Our ancestors named it Earth, after the land they found all around them. So far as they thought about the planet as a whole,

they believed for centuries that its surface consisted almost entirely of rocks and soil, except for some smallish bodies of water like the Mediterranean Sea and the Black Sea. They knew about the Atlantic, of course, but they regarded it as a relatively narrow river running around the rim of the world. If the ancients had known what the earth was really like, they undoubtedly would have named it Ocean after the tremendous areas of water that cover 70.8 per cent of its surface. —Leonard Engel, *The Sea*

In the time it takes to read this sentence, 8 acres of forest will disappear. —"Vanishing Forests," *Newsweek*

Mystery/intrigue. This opener, like the previous one, is an attention-grabber that works best when the subject matter justifies it.

Something peculiar has been going on in science for the past 100 years or so. Many researchers are unaware of it, and others won't admit it even to their own colleagues. But there is a strangeness in the air.

What has happened is that biologists, who once postulated a privileged role for the human mind in nature's hierarchy, have been moving relentlessly toward the hard-core materialism that characterized 19th-century physics. At the same time, physicists, faced with compelling experimental evidence, have been moving away from strictly mechanical models of the universe to a view that sees the mind as playing an integral role in all physical events. It is as if the two disciplines were on fast-moving trains, going in opposite directions and not noticing what is happening across the tracks.—Harold J. Morowitz, "Rediscovering the Mind"

Ways to conclude

After you've presented your information, what's left to do? When informative writers fail to find a satisfying answer to this question, their essays either end too abruptly or limp along as the author gropes for something that sounds like an ending. Here are some ways of finding a satisfying ending for your essay:

- Look for a concluding generalization, one that summarizes your main points and says something about the significance of the information.
- Write about the possible implications of your information. What further questions or problems does it suggest? What questions might it answer?
- Reflect upon possible future directions that the people or problems described in your essay might take.
- Look for a lesson or conclusion that arises out of your presentation. (Be careful not to push into a controversial thesis.)
- Make an evaluation of the situation you presented or of some aspect of it. Although you are writing an informative essay, not an argumentative one,

it is sometimes appropriate to conclude with an evaluative point—especially if the point emerges clearly out of the material and it is not controversial.

- Look for a concluding example, focusing event, or quotation that illustrates your main point in a striking or provocative way. (It could be used with a concluding generalization or question.)

Because they grow distinctly out of the subjects of individual essays, conclusions are more difficult to exemplify in isolated passages than introductions. Three of many possibilities are described and illustrated here.

Drawing a conclusion or making an evaluation. This type of closing actually draws a conclusion or makes an evaluation. It need not amount to arguing a case or taking sides on a controversy. At its best, it is an intelligent judgment that arises out of a judicious examination of the subject. The following closing is from an informative essay on present and future sources of water.

> Although the projected global demand for water will remain well below the total amount potentially available for many years to come, the global surplus offers no consolation to those countries and regions facing a chronic water shortage. For such areas only two strategies are available: to increase the supply by investing in dams and other measures for the control of the water cycle, and to manage the demand, so that the available water is applied to the most urgent needs and utilized with optimum efficiency. Both approaches may be necessary, but with the increasing cost of investment capital, particularly for the developing countries, the latter approach is becoming the more attractive one.—Robert P. Ambroggi, "Water"

Remaining questions or problems. This conclusion looks beyond the confines of the present or of this report, pointing to questions that still need to be answered, or problems that still need to be solved. The following closing is from an article on construction of an artificial heart.

> It should be evident from this account that substantial technical problems remain to be solved before a total artificial heart can be routinely utilized in human patients. Ethical, social and economic considerations must also be dealt with. When the artificial heart has been perfected, it must be made available in sufficient quantity to serve a large number of people. The criteria for selecting recipients must be defined clearly and objectively to ensure a short period of hospitalization and a rapid recovery for a high percentage of the recipients. Patients will need sociological and psychological counseling to help them adapt to a situation new in human experience. Nowhere else will the dependence of life on technology and machines be more apparent.

> If the artificial heart is ever to achieve its objective, it must be more than a pump. It must also be more than functional, reliable and dependable. It must be forgettable.—Robert K. Jarvik, "The Total Artificial Heart"

Future directions or implications. This conclusion also looks beyond the present, this time to conclude something about future developments or problems. The closing below is from a report on the present state of solar technology for private homes.

> For the immediate future, it seems that the rate of growth in solar applications to individual houses will depend on a number of political and economic factors. How much "seed" money will the government be willing or able to commit to basic research? Will the price of conventional fuels level off in the next decade, or will they continue to rise? Will the synthetic fuels industry become so successful as to divert attention away from solar power?
>
> These factors are likely to control the next decade. However, as we look into the distant future, it seems likely that fewer and fewer conventional homes will be built, while more and more solar homes will be constructed.—William Baxter, "Solar Homes: An Answer for the Future?" (Student Research Essay)

• Style: Formality, Informality, and the Authorial "I"

Style is the overall impression a piece of writing makes, through its particular words and phrases and sentence structures, as well as the author's projected voice and attitude. Like most kinds of writing, informative writing permits a great deal of variation in style; there is no right or wrong set of choices. The writer must find the most appropriate choices for a particular situation, subject, and audience.

Levels of formality

A good deal of stylistic variation can be described in terms of *formality* and *informality.* These qualities are easier to recognize than to define or describe; however, if you think of "formal" and "informal" as naming two extremes of presentation, with gradations in between, their differences become clear.

Highly formal writing diverges widely from the language of ordinary, casual conversation. Word choice is learned, precise, and often literary; sentence structure is relatively complex. Very little of the writer's own voice, feelings, or personality is projected.

Highly informal writing is just the opposite, approximating casual conversation. Its words are simple and casual, perhaps including slang; its sentences are shorter and less complex. The author's personality is apparent.

Several levels of style are illustrated in the following passages.

Highly formal style

Most philosophers have been led by the argument from illusion, by the causal argument, or by the introspective analysis advocated in the sense-datum theory to conclude that our immediate awareness in perception is not, as direct, or common-sense realism claims, of material objects (of distinct, external physical entities perceptible by different persons at once) but of sensa (private, transitory, probably mental existents that may also be called sensations, sense data, ideas, representations, or impressions).—R.J. Hirst, "Phenomenalism"

Moderately formal or "middle" style

Even though many writers do not want to be concerned with punctuation, capitalization, and spelling, they have to be because the reader cannot easily do without them. All of the mechanics are signals of one kind or another. Sending out the wrong signals is misdirecting the reader or, more often, momentarily delaying the decoding process. Readers don't like obstacles. Even though mechanics are certainly not the most important thing in the world of writing, they are certainly obvious when they are misused. And when they are misused they create an impression of illiteracy more readily than almost any other element of writing. The public at large seems not to regard diction, structure, and style to the extent that it regards mechanics, possibly because the accurate use of mechanics seems the most elementary.—William F. Irmscher, *Teaching Expository Writing*

Informal style

This may sound absurd, but gliders do fly without engines and model airplanes do fly without pilots. As for the insides of an airplane, they are disappointing for they are mostly hollow. No, what keeps an airplane up is its shape—the impact of the air upon its shape. . . .

This—that its shape is what counts—is what makes the airplane so beautiful. It also makes it easy to understand. You don't have to open it up and look at "the works" inside as one has to do with a watch, a refrigerator or an automobile. An airplane's outside appearance is its "works." If you want to understand it, simply have a look.

Look at the wing. It holds the airplane up entirely by its shape. A wing is nothing but an air deflector . . .—Wolfgang Langewiesche, "Why An Airplane Flies"

Highly informal style

So what?

I mean, I go down to a place like Logan's, say, or the Hilton Underground or Toby's Red Hat, or even JJs, and here are these people—and I mean ANYBODY—crowding around, lining up, PACKING the place. They're not talking to anybody much. They're just standing there pumping quarters into these idiotic machines which celebrate their loss of two bits with a chintzy light show and a few bells. No, they're not just standing there, they're having FITS, they're WHACKING the blasted things, getting ALL WORKED UP! And it's the ones who get most worked up who stay there longest.

So what's the big pay-off? You get a little three-ounce polished steel ball to dance and carom around awhile, you light a few lights, drop targets pop up, the thing clunks into a little scoring saucer and then pops out again, activates a rollover button or two until finally it disappears into the nothingness at the bottom of the sloping cabinet.

You get five balls, you lose a quarter.

And people are lining up for this!—D. Hand, "As the World Tilts"

No passage is good or bad just because of its style. What counts is appropriateness to subject, audience, and situation. The first passage here is very complex and difficult to read. But the author is writing to an audience of professional scholars, and he is trying to do justice to a complex subject in short space.

The style of the second passage is most appropriate for informative writing for general audiences, and for topics that are not very technical or specialized. The tone is relaxed but not as conversational as that in the passage on airplanes following it. The vocabulary is educated but not obscure or technical. The author does not shrink from complex sentence structure, but he doesn't overload it with subordinating and parenthetical constructions. And he mixes up the length of his sentences.

The style of the third passage is more conversational than the second, but certainly not as breezy and excited as the last one. Its style is effective for its purpose—to convey a principle of aerodynamics to a popular audience, and to be entertaining.

The style of the final passage would be inappropriate to the subjects and audiences of any of the other three. However, it *is* good for what it's meant for—a freewheeling, entertaining feature on an amusing topic, where the accuracy or integrity of information is not really an issue.

EXERCISE 8.12

Rewrite the "highly informal" passage, p. 251. Retain as much of the content as possible, but change the style to "formal" or "moderately formal."

EXERCISE 8.13

Rewrite the "moderately formal" passage, p. 251. Retain as much of the content as possible, but change the style to "very informal."

The authorial "I"

One of the most difficult questions that student writers ask is whether or not to use "I," and more generally, whether or not to inject themselves into their writing. The question is tricky for the informative essay. In the *deliberative* essay, in which you argue a thesis, it is often useful to identify a viewpoint as your own and to argue the case in your own voice, using "I." In the *reflective/exploratory* essay, the "I" is almost indispensable, since the usual objective is to share and explore your own feelings and experiences. But *informative* writing is difficult to generalize about. Here is some advice.

1. Injecting yourself into the informative essay can detract from your subject matter and undermine the sense of balance and objectivity that readers expect. In general, don't do it unless there is a good reason (see 2, 3, and 4 below).
2. Don't hesitate to use the "I" when avoiding it would make your presentation stuffy or awkward.
3. If your subject involves you, then you probably *should* include yourself in the presentation. It would be less than candid not to do so.
4. If something from your own experience can add interest, clarity or depth to your presentation, you should consider including it, in the first person, except under the most formal circumstances.

ESSAY ASSIGNMENTS

1. Write a background report on a local problem or controversy, presenting a balanced view of all sides. Assume that your audience is directly affected by the problem or controversy.

2. You have been hired as a writer for a project to publish a pamphlet consisting of a series of reports on small, limited-circulation magazines. Write a report on a magazine that is published in your town or state. (Consult the periodicals librarian in your library for a list of other interesting possibilities). Be sure to devise a set of questions to guide you in organizing material for your report.

3. Write a summary report based on a recent nonfiction book, a substantial essay on an important and timely subject, or a commission report. Your purpose is to publicize this information and present it in everyday language.

4. Write an informative essay based on your interviews with a person in your town or on your campus who has achieved some distinction or notoriety. Be sure to acquaint yourself with the specific area in which this person has attained distinction.

5. Write a report describing some intriguing situation that you know about. You could use the form of a narrative, including dialogue, involving yourself as an observer or one of the participants. Without using overt generalizations, communicate something of the significance of the situation.

Essays for Analysis

An Eastern Toe in the Stream of Consciousness

by Daniel Goleman

Daniel Goleman is a senior editor for Psychology Today. *In this essay he uses his own knowledge, his reading, and interviews with several people as sources of information about an interesting trend in a specific field. This essay was published in January, 1980.*

1 "Buddhism will come to the West as a psychology," according to Chogyam Trungpa, the controversial lama who is one of the most important spokesmen for Buddhism in America.

It may come as a surprise to most Americans that Asian religions like Buddhism contain elaborate psychologies, theories of the mind that are quite distinct from religious rituals. Many who were attracted to Zen in the fifties, lured by the work of such popularizers as D. T. Suzuki and Alan Watts, saw in its gentle paradoxes a means of escaping stress in their lives. The massive number of young people who explored Oriental religions and meditative techniques in the sixties found helpful insights and at least a fleeting peace of mind. As a graduate student in psychology at Harvard in the sixties, like many in my generation, I meditated, attended talks by visiting gurus, read Eastern spiritual texts; later, I spent two years studying Asian psychology in India and Sri Lanka.

2 The wave of interest in Oriental religions peaked in the seventies. But now they seem to be making gradual headway as psychologies, not as religions. There is a small but growing number of American psychologists and psychiatrists interested in possible therapeutic applications of Asian psychologies—particularly the Buddhist brand. Last April, for example, the annual meeting of the Western Psychological Association featured a symposium on Buddhism as psychology. The following month the American Psychiatric Association convention had a panel called "Applying Ways of the East to Western Psycho-

therapy." In June, the Blaisdell Institute, a center for the study of culture and religion affiliated with Claremont Graduate School in California will hold a conference for therapists on Buddhist psychology. Some popular current textbooks in psychology, such as *Personality and Personal Growth* by Robert Frager and James Fadiman, devote chapters to Eastern psychologies. Frager and Fadiman are on the faculty of the California Institute for Transpersonal Psychology, one of the few institutions that offer a Ph.D. in the study of Eastern psychologies.

3 In Boulder, Colorado, Chogyam Trungpa has founded the Naropa Institute, a center of Buddhist religion and psychology that is currently seeking accreditation for its graduate program and has just launched its own *Journal of Psychology.* Trungpa, 41, is a highly respected Buddhist lama who fled his Tibetan homeland after the Chinese invasion of 1959. He has studied at Oxford and has written several scholarly books on Buddhism. In this country he has gained prominence as the founder of a chain of meditation centers, as well as a certain amount of unwelcome attention from journalists critical of what they describe as his arbitrary and autocratic personal style.

4 The director of the Naropa Institute's graduate program in psychology is Edward Podvoll, a psychiatrist with impeccable credentials. Before going to Naropa, Podvoll was director of training at the Austen Riggs Center in Stockbridge, Massachusetts, a prestigious psychoanalytic clinic which included Erik Erikson among its regular staff. Podvoll first became interested in Buddhist psychology in 1974, after visiting a nearby meditation center. His instruction in Buddhist meditation, he recalls, "immediately made sense as a next step to take in looking closely at the mind. I felt confident I had gone as far as you could go through an interpersonal relationship with a therapist. But looking into the nature of the mind with the rigor of meditation was something I hadn't heard about, something I realized I was starved for. It was a far subtler level of observation of the mind than I'd ever encountered in training."

5 Buddhist meditation, which had such a powerful effect on Podvoll, differs markedly from most other forms of meditation common in America. Transcendental meditation (TM), for example, is essentially a form of passive concentration; meditators bring their focus back to a mantra whenever their attention wanders. The most widespread form of Buddhist meditation, called "mindfulness," requires that meditators witness their stream of awareness with an even attentiveness, noting each sequence of thought from beginning to end. In meditations like TM, whatever thoughts cross one's mind are regarded as irrelevant distractions, while mindfulness makes those thoughts themselves the object of awareness.

The reason for attending to such thoughts is that according to a basic tenet of Buddhism, there is no "self" per se. That is, our personal sense of an ongoing identity is an illusion. By observing and categorizing experience into its component emotions, thoughts, and sensations, a person can see his or her own experience as a set of impersonal processes which comprise the sense of self.

6 This Buddhist sense of identity presents a direct challenge to Western psychology's notion of the ego. While there are various definitions of ego, Western psychologists since Freud have tended to see it as the bulwark of mental health. Some therapists encourage building "ego strength"; others, "ego integrity." Erikson's influential theory of human development plots in detail the nuances of developing "ego identity."

7 Buddhist psychologists, on the other hand, see the ego as itself pathological, and some therapists have begun to adopt that view in dealing with their patients. Podvoll, who is also a psychiatrist in private practice, says: "Patients assemble a whole story line, a whole personal mythology or belief system about how they became what they are. They construct a history to explain the predicament they're in. But the Buddhist perspective sees that history—and in fact all the ego—as a fiction the person constructs."

8 He continues: "Freud had that same insight in his *Interpretation of Dreams.* He referred to dreams as a defensive structure to rationalize 'the beloved ego.' He seemed to glimpse that the ego was a fiction, at least in his early writings. Twenty years later that view was gone."

9 Podvoll does not see his pursuit of Buddhist psychology as a break with the psychoanalytic lineage, but rather as a means of following the implications of analysis to their logical end: "Freud urged the analyst to cultivate what he called a 'freely hovering attention,' the ability to be in another person's world, but not of it. To do this the analyst has to keep his own projections and defenses in abeyance, and keep a mirrorlike awareness. Freud never really was able to offer a technique for doing it effectively. Besides self-analysis—and that's a heroic task—no other tool in Western psychology is designed for it." In Podvoll's opinion, Buddhist meditation is that tool.

10 According to Buddhist psychological theory, meditation will eventually lead the sense of personal identity, or ego, to wither away, leaving in its stead an impersonal blend of mental processes. The specifics of that blend are spelled out in the "Abhidharma," an analysis of the nature of experience that is found among the various schools of Buddhism. Abhidharma is a theory of perception and cognition, on the one hand, and a theory of psychopathology, on the other. It embodies a precise, accountant's view of the mind in operation.

11 Abhidharma reached its fullest development about the fifth century A.D. and has been preserved largely unchanged since then. Its formulators were rather obsessive chroniclers of the stream of consciousness. Through introspection, they hit on a list of 53 "properties of mind" which, in differing combinations, characterize any given moment of experience. (The number 53 is arbitrary; in some branches of Buddhism, the list goes up to 175.) Every moment of awareness, according to Abhidharma, is characterized by a subset of these properties. In an unpleasant moment, for example, agitation, envy, and avarice may predominate. In a more pleasant moment, zest, composure, and proficiency may hold sway.

12 In its most practical application, Abhidharma defines mental health. Of the 53 properties, 14 are labeled unhealthy; a contrasting 14 are called healthy.

For the most part, the lists are compatible with Western psychology: the unhealthy properties include anxiety, worry, and torpor; the healthy list includes confidence, composure, and adaptability. Almost everyone experiences the full range of healthy and unhealthy states of mind from time to time, Abhidharma acknowledges. The theory posits that the only route to full health is through the practice of Buddhist "mindful" meditation, which creates a distance in the meditator's mind between an ongoing absorption in plans, memories, hopes, and fears, and a part of awareness that simply watches the mental flow without getting immersed in it. By achieving a detached awareness of mental processes, the meditator gains insights that eventually lead to mental health. Buddhists recognize that complete accomplishment of such careful self-observation requires years of meditation.

13 In the hands of a professional, the method can be therapeutic. Gary Deatherage, a psychotherapist in British Columbia, has used mindfulness meditation as a self-treatment regimen in his private practice. In an article published in the *Journal of Transpersonal Psychology,* Deatherage wrote: "The first goal of mindfulness training is to begin to show the client the workings of his own mental processes. . . . He will then quickly discover a rather complicated but comforting situation where there is one aspect of his 'mental self' which is calm and psychologically strong, and which can watch, label, and see the melodramas of the other 'selves' which get so involved in painful memories of the past or beautiful and escapist fantasies of the future. By helping the patient to identify for a time with the strong and neutral 'watcher self," there begins to develop within him the strength, motivation, and ability to fully participate in and benefit from whatever other forms of psychotherapy are being provided."

14 Deatherage reports on the use of mindfulness meditation techniques with a suicidal divorcée suffering from recurring depression, anxiety, inability to concentrate, and "loss of interest in life." He gave her the assignment of sitting quietly and watching the second hand of a clock, attending fully to its sweeping movements. Whenever she noticed her concentration breaking, she was to label the interruption. She found that the same thoughts kept racing through her mind, mainly regrets about her misfortunes with her ex-husband. This exercise, Deatherage concludes, "seemed to cause this young woman to withdraw some of her involvement in those depressing thoughts of the past, and to give her the realization that there was more than just those thoughts present in her mind. . . . She learned to identify herself as the objective watcher of her disturbing thoughts instead of the depressed thinker, and she began to feel relief from her psychiatric complaints."

15 Not all students of Buddhist psychology are comfortable with Deatherage's use of mindfulness as therapy. Psychologist Daniel Brown, an instructor in the department of psychiatry at Harvard Medical School, is thoroughly familiar with Buddhist psychology (he wrote his dissertation on a classical Tibetan text on meditation) but his approach as a therapist remains psychoanalytic. "The more I study both traditions," Brown contends, "the more

I see them as miles apart. When I do therapy, I practice conventional methods. That's what people come to me for. The two have very different goals and very different methods. Therapy aims for self-awareness or adjustment. Buddhist meditation aims for liberation through a new perception of reality."

16 In a recent issue of the *American Journal of Psychiatry,* Roger Walsh, a psychiatrist at the University of California, Irvine's medical school suggests that Asian psychologies present a threat to Western psychologists because of their radically different assumptions about human nature—for example, their negative stance toward the ego. Western psychologists, he writes, have sometimes reacted with name-calling—using psychiatric labels to discredit opposing views. In the 1930s, for example, psychoanalyst Franz Alexander described Buddhist meditation as "artificial catatonia"; more recently, a report by the Group for the Advancement of Psychiatry concluded that the effects of spiritual disciplines such as Buddhism border on the psychotic.

17 What might be gained by giving more credence to the theories of Buddhist psychology? Walsh points out that it "forces us to look at our own psychological ethnocentrism, to see the limits implicit in our paradigms. Western psychologies are by and large oriented toward pathology. Eastern psychologies offer road maps and tools for cultivating high levels of well-being."

18 Advocates of Buddhist psychology like to cite an old Tibetan prophecy: "When the iron bird flies, the Teachings will go to the West." Airplanes now fly; and Buddhist psychology has indeed come to the West. But it has yet to make itself known to most working psychologists here. If it is to become anything more than a novelty, it will have to prove itself, on pragmatic grounds, better suited than traditional psychology for some therapeutic chores. Such are the demands of the psychological marketplace.

19 But Buddhist psychology is a relatively recent arrival, and it has not had time to prove its value, nor has it yet been submitted to careful scientific tests. It is one of very few new strains since psychoanalysis to be introduced to American psychology from abroad. How it will fare remains to be seen. It does, however, display one trait American psychologies are short on: longevity. Buddhist psychology has a proven life span of more than two millennia. Behaviorism should live so long.

FOR DISCUSSION

1. The introductory paragraphs of this essay produce a focusing generalization with an "*X BUT Y*" pattern (see p. 245). Identify this generalization.
2. Identify the methods of presentation in paragraphs 5, 6–7, 10, and 13.
3. What paragraph or paragraphs constitute the conclusion of this essay? What does Goleman do in the conclusion?

The Chemistry of Acupuncture

by the editors of *Scientific American*

In every issue of Scientific American *there is a section called "Science and the Citizen," consisting of short reports which summarize and explain the contents of recent scientific studies. Topics are chosen on the basis of their general public interest. The summary report reprinted here first appeared in July, 1979.*

1 Acupuncture, the ancient Chinese art of relieving pain by inserting fine needles at specific points and depths on the surface of the body, has attracted much attention outside China in recent years. Some non-Chinese physicians have applied the technique and have maintained that they get similar results; others have speculated on how such effects could be explained, if not by hypnotic suggestion, then by known principles of nerve physiology. Now a Chinese investigator, Chang Hsiang-tung of the Shanghai Institute of Physiology, surveys acupuncture in the light of the newest findings in the physiology of pain.

2 Writing in *Chinese Medical Journal,* Chang describes how in China until quite recently the pain-suppressing effects of acupuncture were explained only according to the metaphysical tenets of traditional Chinese medicine. This view holds that pain and disease result from a disruption or blocking in the circulation of vital energy through 12 hypothetical meridians (channels) in the body, each of which is associated with a particular organ system. By inserting acupuncture needles at certain points in the meridians (which are not correlated with specific anatomical structures) the blocked channels can be cleared and the healthy state of energy flow restored.

3 Attempts by both non-Chinese and Chinese investigators to relate the empirical practice of acupuncture to modern physiology were initially based on the observation that many acupuncture points lie close to clusters of nerve endings, suggesting that the flow of energy through the hypothetical meridians might be analogous to the functioning of the nervous system and the various chemical systems that mediate its regulation and control. The obvious question then arose of how needles inserted into the body at specific points could activate the nervous system to yield analgesia in distant parts of the body. Also to be explained was the fact that the analgesia takes about 20 minutes to develop and persists for some time after the needles have been withdrawn.

4 It has long been known that there are two major classes of nerve fibers that carry pain information from the peripheral pain receptors to the spinal cord: the low-threshold *A-delta* fibers, which give rise to sharp, mild pain, and the high-threshold *C* fibers, which give rise to severe, burning pain. Chang suggests that mild stimulation of the acupuncture needles (traditionally ac-

complished by twirling the needles) selectively activates the low-threshold fibers in the deep tissues underlying the acupuncture points. The resulting impulses are transmitted to relays in the spinal cord and the brain, where they interfere with the transmission of messages from the high-threshold fibers, so that severe pain is kept from reaching conscious awareness. This "gate" hypothesis is supported by a number of experimental findings. For example, if a local anesthetic is injected into the tissues under an acupuncture point, it completely abolishes both the characteristic mild discomfort caused by the needle and the remote analgesic effect.

5 The specificity of acupuncture points, writes Chang, seems to lie in the segmental organization of the spinal cord: each segment of the cord innervates a particular region of the trunk and the limbs. The acupuncture points on the arms are usually stimulated to relieve pain in the head and the upper body, and those on the legs are stimulated to relieve pain in the lower body. This observation suggests that the low-threshold pain impulses generated by acupuncture needling travel to the spinal cord and block the transmission of severe-pain messages entering the same segment of the cord or adjacent segments.

6 Chang points out that although the specific nerve-cell interactions that give rise to acupuncture analgesia are not well understood, there has been much interest in the involvement of certain neurotransmitters: the chemicals that carry excitatory and inhibitory messages between nerve cells at relay centers in the spinal cord and the brain. Experiments on monkeys and human beings have demonstrated that the analgesic effect of acupuncture can be appreciably reduced by the administration of the drug naloxone, which blocks the action of morphine. This finding has been interpreted to mean that acupuncture triggers the release in the central nervous system of morphinelike peptide molecules: the short chains of amino acids called enkephalins and the longer chains called endorphins. Indeed, enkephalin and another peptide, substance P, have been implicated in pain perception, substance P with the transmission of pain-related impulses and enkephalin with their suppression.

7 The rapid and transient action of a neurotransmitter such as enkephalin is hard to reconcile, however, with the slow induction and lingering action of acupuncture. It is therefore unlikely that enkephalin alone is responsible for the analgesic effect. Indeed, B. Sjölund and his colleagues in Sweden have shown that during acupuncture there is an increase in the concentration in the spinal fluid of a class of endorphins designated Fraction I, which are distinct from enkephalin. The rise in Fraction I endorphins in the spinal fluid is localized mainly at the level of the spinal segments receiving input from the needled acupuncture point. It therefore seems that acupuncture triggers the liberation in the spinal cord (and possibly in the brain as well) of long-lasting morphine-like peptides that suppress the transmission of pain impulses. These peptides do not appear to be released into the bloodstream, however, because

elevated levels of endorphins in the blood after acupuncture have not been detected.

8 Chang cites the work of investigators in China indicating that acupuncture causes an increase in the amount of the neurotransmitter serotonin in the brain. Selective destruction of the serotonin-containing cells in the brain stem of experimental animals reduces the analgesic effect of acupuncture, whereas electrical stimulation of these cells enhances the effect. How serotonin might interact with the endorphins, however, is not yet understood.

9 Such inquiries into the physiology of acupuncture, Chang writes, have already resulted in important modifications of the technique. Many Chinese physicians now choose acupuncture points on the basis of the segmental-innervation theory rather than the traditional meridian theory. A large number of acupuncture points have been shown to be redundant or superfluous, and they have been omitted without sacrificing the analgesic effect. The resulting simplification of the technique has saved patients unnecessary discomfort from the repeated insertion of needles. Electrical rather than mechanical stimulation of the needles is also gaining ground, since it reduces the danger of contamination of the operation field by the acupuncturist and minimizes the tissue damage caused by needling. Finally, drugs that enhance the effectiveness of acupuncture (including many drugs that by themselves are not analgesics) are coming into clinical use. Some Chinese physicians are also experimenting with "acupressure," the application of finger pressure to acupuncture points, which in some cases has been shown to be as effective as needling in relieving pain.

10 Chang observes that since acupuncture does not entail the hazardous and unpleasant side effects of anesthetic agents and opiate drugs its potential value in analgesia and anesthesia is clear. He concludes: "This age-old Chinese healing art is now already placed on a solid scientific basis and is indeed rejuvenated and revitalized. There is no doubt that acupuncture will become a new addition to the world medical armamentarium for combating pain."

FOR DISCUSSION

1. What type of introduction does this essay use? What type of conclusion?
2. In preparing this report, the author apparently limited his viewpoint through one or two questions. What are these questions? Given more time and space, what other questions might the author have asked?
3. This article was written for an audience of educated people who have some knowledge of and interest in science. If you were asked to rewrite the article for a popular audience—the audience of *Reader's Digest,* for example—what changes, omissions, or additions would you make?

In Celebration of Life: Dr. Lewis Thomas Has More Good News About the Human Condition

by Paul Gray

This essay is an example of a feature article which publicizes the work and life of someone who has achieved distinction in a certain field—in this case the unlikely combination of literature and medical research. The occasion was the publication of Thomas' second book of essays, The Medusa and the Snail. *The essay appeared in* Time *in May, 1979.*

> *There is nothing at all absurd about the human condition. We matter. It seems to me a good guess, hazarded by a good many people who have thought of it, that we may be engaged in the formation of something like a mind for the life of this planet. If this is so, we are still at the most primitive stage, still fumbling with language and thinking, but infinitely capacitated for the future. Looked at this way, it is remarkable that we've come as far as we have in so short a period, really no time at all as geologists measure time. We are the newest, the youngest, and the brightest things around.—Lewis Thomas*

1 Who is this man, and why is he saying all those nice things about the human race? The first question is simpler than the second. Lewis Thomas, 65, is a doctor and an administrator (currently president and chief executive officer of the Memorial Sloan-Kettering Cancer Center in New York City). He is a biologist, a researcher and a professor. He is a published poet and, quite possibly, the best essayist on science now working anywhere in the world.

2 This last accomplishment has brought Thomas more attention than all the others put together. A collection of 29 of his essays was published in 1974 under the title *The Lives of a Cell: Notes of a Biology Watcher.* No one expected much, least of all the author. For one thing, most Americans escape from the study of biology as fast as their teachers will let them; if they think of the subject at all, they are likely to remember rubbery dead frogs and the smell of formaldehyde. For another, Thomas made few concessions to the ignorance of laymen. He certainly did not obfuscate, but he gave complex matters the taxonomic precision they required: "It has been proposed that symbiotic linkages between prokaryotic cells were the origin of eukaryotes, and that fusion between different sorts of eukaryotes (*e.g.,* motile, ciliated cells joined to phagocytic ones) . . ." Such is not the stuff that bestsellers are made of, but that is precisely what Thomas' book became. Novelist Joyce Carol Oates found the essays "remarkable . . . undogmatic . . . gently persuasive." John Updike praised Thomas' "shimmering vision." Reviewers picked up the applause; so did more and more readers. The book has now sold over 300,000 copies in hardback and paperback and has been translated into eleven languages. *The Lives of a Cell* was given a National Book Award in April 1975, but not in the category of science. It was honored as a contribution to the field of arts and letters.

3 Which is what it was. And so is *The Medusa and the Snail* (Viking; 175 pages; $8.95), a collection of 29 more Thomas essays to be published this month. If anything, the new book is better than its predecessor. Thomas' prose seems firmer, his conclusions surer, his voice more resonant. He ranges farther and farther away from the laboratory, and devotes his attention to larger chunks of society as well is to bacteria and viruses. Taken together, his two books form an extended paean to this, the best of all possible worlds.

4 That is the second riddle about Thomas and his philosophy. He bears no resemblance to the fatuous Dr. Pangloss, who chirped about this best world while stumbling through a series of catastrophes. Voltaire's doctor was an *a priori* optimist, and nothing that he saw or experienced could rattle his foolhardy faith. Thomas reverses this procedure and writes about things he has observed, grounding his conclusions in the tiniest material details that the world can provide. Because he has peered at nature's building blocks more closely than anyone but fellow biologists, and because he can translate his visions more gracefully than anyone but fellow writers, Thomas' good news about the human race is practically unique. Given the pessimistic tenor of our age the good doctor and his message could not have come along at a better time.

5 What in the world can he find to be hopeful about? As it turns out, almost everything. Most simply, Thomas argues that the overwhelming tendency in nature is toward symbiosis, union, harmony. The post-Darwinian view of life as a constant, murderous struggle, Tennyson's personification of nature "red in tooth and claw," do not match the facts that Thomas has seen. Even what looks like random slaughter may be the opposite.

6 Take, Thomas suggests, the case of the nudibranch (a sea slug) and the medusa (a jellyfish) that live in the Bay of Naples. The slug lives with a tiny fragment of the medusa permanently and parasitically attached near its mouth. The vestigial jellyfish apparently is still able to reproduce; its offspring swim off and become normal adult jellyfish. The slug also produces larvae, but these are rather quickly trapped and subsumed by the new jellyfish. Aha, one would think, the jellyfish are getting back at the slugs for prior mutilations. No such thing. "Soon the snails," Thomas writes, "undigested and insatiable, begin to eat, browsing away first at the radial canals, then the borders of the rim, finally the tentacles, until the jellyfish becomes reduced in substance by being eaten, while the snail grows correspondingly in size." At the end, the jellyfish are once again tiny parasites, and the whole cycle begins anew. Which one is the predator, then, and which one the prey? This underwater dance lends Thomas' new book its title and occupies the first essay; its implications echo through all that follows. Life may not be a matter of eat or be eaten; it may boil down to eating *and* being eaten.

7 This may seem cold comfort to some, but it is not the only one that Thomas offers. Other happy refrains are sounded and re-sounded as the essays (averaging only 1,200 words long) tumble forth. He seems bemused by the phenomenon of healthy hypochondriacs. Americans, for example, are need-

lessly "obsessed with Health." Thomas wonders why, particularly at a time when "we are free of the great infectious diseases, especially tuberculosis and lobar pneumonia, which used to cut us down long before our time." Humans are not frail organisms coveted by every death-dealing microbe in the world, as so much pop medicine would have it. Quite the contrary: "We are in real life, a reasonably healthy people. Far from being ineptly put together, we are amazingly tough, durable organisms, full of health, ready for most contingencies."

8 Similarly, Thomas suggests that death may not be the rattling, agonized event that humans fear. He is no stranger to the spectacle of death and its ravages. But he cites interesting evidence gathered from people who have slipped toward death before being rescued. Their testimony suggests a peaceful experience. When death is imminent, the brain apparently realizes that pain can no longer be useful as an alarm to spur escape. So the pain is turned off and replaced by a kind of blissful surrender. Thomas writes: "If I had to design an ecosystem in which creatures had to live off each other and in which dying was an indispensable part of living, I couldn't think of a better way to manage."

9 One of the charms of boarding Thomas' train of thought is the puckish delight he takes in turning beliefs or assumptions upside down. The current to-do about the likelihood of cloning humans? Not worth worrying about, Thomas says, and impossible besides. But (and most of his essays pivot merrily on that word) he has a suggestion for those who cannot resist tinkering: "Set cloning aside, and don't try it. Instead go in the other direction. Look for ways to get mutations more quickly, new variety, different songs." Continued genetic errors, after all, enabled the primeval strand of DNA to diversify into the vast spectrum of life. Humans have mimed this sloppy but productive process; "the capacity to leap across mountains of information to land lightly on the wrong side represents the highest of human endowments." With tongue in cheek, Thomas hails the arrival of the computer age; he looks forward to the bigger mistakes that the programming of bigger computers will make.

10 He believes that certain attempts to pierce the mystery of things are conducted backward: "Instead of using what we can guess at about the nature of thought to explain the nature of music, start over again. Begin with music and see what this can tell us about the sensation of thinking." He recommends an experiment, enlisting Johann Sebastian Bach to support his hypothesis: "Put on *The St. Matthew Passion* and turn the volume up all the way. That is the sound of the whole central nervous system of human beings, all at once."

11 Such imaginative leaps are typical throughout *The Medusa and the Snail.* Though the book is about science, its form is a demonstration of art. In fact, a Thomas essay blooms organically in much the same manner as a romantic ode or sonnet. A receptive mind encounters something in nature; the object out there is gradually drawn into the thinking subject; reflection occurs, hypotheses are put forward and tested, a pulse of excitement becomes audible; suddenly, everything coalesces, time stands still for a moment, an image is born

out of matter and spirit. If Wordsworth had gone to medical school, he might have produced something very like the essays of Lewis Thomas.

12 What Thomas does is extraordinarily rare. It is hard enough to explain specialized scientific findings to scientists in other fields, and harder still to get it right and still hold the attention of untutored novices. Add touches of poetry, joyful optimism and an awe-inspired mysticism, and the job becomes impossible. Except that the impossible, like so many of the natural phenomena that Thomas describes, happens.

13 The doctor's prose and insights are unassailably his own, but the roll of physician-writer is nearly as old as the art of healing. St. Luke was probably a physician. One of Alexander Pope's close friends was Dr. John Arbuthnot, who dabbled in literature himself. A more modern roster includes serious practitioners like Anton Chekhov and William Carlos Williams, as well as others who had some medical training: Arthur Conan Doyle, Somerset Maugham and Walker Percy. In recent years, onetime doctors have turned to go-go careers on the edges of literature: Michael Crichton, from novels into film writing and directing *The Great Train Robbery;* Jonathan Miller, from comedy in *Beyond the Fringe* to medical reporting on the BBC's *The Body in Question;* Graham Chapman, into satire and lunacy as a member of *Monty Python's Flying Circus.* None of this surprises Thomas, as he told TIME Correspondent Peter Stoler last week: "The physician for quite a long time was quite well educated; in fact, he was often the best, sometimes the only, educated person in the community." The mere fact of literacy made those who possessed it writers. Thomas adds: "Doctors are trained to observe, and to express their ideas precisely. Medical training is good training for a writing career." True, but Thomas remains slightly beyond the circle of all the luminous names who have been taught medicine and also made up stories. When he began writing consistently, at the age of 57, he did not turn to plays, novels or poems. He wrote about what he knew: science.

14 It had been familiar to him since childhood. Medicine was in the family bloodline; his father was a general practitioner who later specialized in surgery. Some of Thomas' earliest memories are of traveling with his father in the family's Franklin: "When we made most house calls, we'd park right in front of the house. When he called on Christian Scientists, it was understood that he'd park his car a block away and walk to the house, so that no one would know that they were seeing a doctor." His father's job looked like fun to young Lewis, and he pointed himself in the same direction. After graduating from a private day school in Manhattan he entered Princeton. His interest in medicine flagged for a time; exposure to the poems of T.S. Eliot and Ezra Pound inspired him to try his own hand. He published works in the college magazine, but a senior-year course in advanced biology redirected him toward medicine.

15 He moved easily through Harvard Medical School, surprised at how little doctors in the 1930s actually knew about the illnesses they treated: "Doctors were never really taught to or expected to cure diseases. We were

taught to learn the names of the diseases and make accurate diagnoses, so we could make accurate prognoses." After graduation, Thomas interned at Boston City Hospital, becoming especially interested in meningitis infections of the brain. He also continued writing poems; one of his works composed during this period was published in the *Atlantic Monthly.*

16 After Boston, he did his residency at the Neurological Institute in New York City. In 1941 he married Beryl Dawson, a Vassar girl he had met at a college dance; they were wed about a year when Thomas, then at the Rockefeller Institute, was called for service in the Navy. Lieut. Commander Thomas waded ashore during the dramatic invasion of Okinawa and collected a lifelong memory: "I went over the side of a troop transport with a case on my shoulder containing 50 white mice, bedded on white toilet paper. One soldier who watched me wade ashore with this load said, 'Now I've seen everything.' " Thomas' burden was not a secret weapon but a collection of research animals; the Navy feared that troops on Okinawa would be endangered by a disease called scrub typhus, and Thomas' assignment was to study the dangers. That threat never materialized, so Thomas had to make do with an outbreak of Japanese B encephalitis. It was, he remembers, "the only game in town."

17 After the war Thomas became an "academic tramp." His momentum carried him away from the practice of medicine and toward research, teaching and administration. He wound steadily up the helix of professional advancement: research at Johns Hopkins, teaching at Tulane and the University of Minnesota. Back in New York, he moved through lower posts to become dean of the New York University medical school. In 1969 Thomas moved to Yale as a professor and chairman of the medical school's department of pathology; three years later he was named dean of the medical school. He left after a year at that to take charge of the Sloan-Kettering complex in Manhattan, one of the most important cancer research and treatment centers in the world.

18 He also found time to teach medicine and pathology at the Cornell University medical college and to rejoin the faculty at Rockefeller University. Along the way, Thomas and his wife had three daughters. In spite of growing administrative burdens, he had published more than 200 technical articles on infectious diseases and related matters. The corner office, it turns out, was never Thomas' goal: "I made each change because it offered better opportunities for research, because I found the scientific opportunities irresistible."

19 Thomas' career had plotted an impressive arc. Though unknown to the general public, he was a successful and esteemed member of the U.S. medical Establishment; he had taught at the right places and run some of them as well. The rest of his life was his to live out in dignified, influential isolation. There was no reason to believe that any work bearing Thomas' name would ever appear on paperback racks in airports or drugstores. But then, as *The Medusa and the Snail* indicates, there is no reason for expecting many things to happen until they do; only then can the moving forces behind events leap into clarity.

20 Thomas' "error," a word he traces back to an old root meaning "to

wander about, looking for something," occurred in 1970, when he put together a short, casual talk on the phenomenon of inflammation and what it might represent as a biological process. He delivered it at a symposium held at Upjohn Co.'s Brook Lodge in Michigan. A member of the audience passed a copy of the speech to Dr. Franz Joseph Ingelfinger, then the editor of the *New England Journal of Medicine.* Ingelfinger had already roiled the academic waters by warning potential contributors that medical research should be made compatible with good, clear writing. The graceful, straightforward style of Thomas' speech struck the editor as just what he had in mind, and he offered Thomas the chance to write a monthly column for the journal. There were two conditions: the columns could run no longer than one page (about 1,200 words), and they had to be submitted in time to meet deadlines. If these strictures were met, the editor offered a bonus: Thomas' pieces would be printed, with no changes or revisions, exactly as he had written them. "That was irresistible," recalls the columnist. "I had to say yes."

21 Thomas was at Yale at the time and maintained a house in Woods Hole, Mass., where he and his wife retreated on weekends. He used the driving time from New Haven to consider ideas; then he spent the weekends writing his column longhand on ruled pads, finishing it by the time he was ready to drive home on Sunday night. "I wrote three or four pieces this way," says Thomas. "Then I called Ingelfinger and told him that I thought I had done enough. He said that he wanted me to continue and persuaded me that I should, so I did." Very shortly afterward, Thomas' column began attracting a cult of pass-along readers. The evolution that led to *The Lives of a Cell* and *The Medusa and the Snail* had begun.

22 Thomas still writes his monthly column, one job among many in his crowded professional life. He is a familiar figure in the halls at Sloan-Kettering, walking quickly, the tall figure canted slightly forward at the waist, his lab coat billowing out behind him, Groucho-style. He is on the run elsewhere as well, making frequent trips to Washington for committee work and to testify at congressional hearings, and to Cambridge, where he serves on the Harvard Board of Overseers. In his laboratory he continues experimenting, currently studying two microbes that lack cell walls and observing how they interact with the body's immune system. He also reads voraciously, particularly poetry, and is teaching himself Greek so that he can read Homer in the original. The doctor's spare time is not wasted in worry; he smokes a pipe constantly, enjoys a drink before dinner, eats whatever he likes and refuses to undergo annual checkups.

23 After some 45 years in medicine, Thomas remains a carrier of infectious enthusiasm. "It's the greatest damned entertainment in the world," he says of his work. "It's just plain fun learning something that you didn't know . . . There is a real aesthetic experience in being dumbfounded." He is still astonished at things that others, mistakenly, take for granted. Why, he muses in *The Medusa and the Snail,* did people make such a fuss over the test-tube baby in England? The true miracle was, as always, the union of egg and sperm and

the emergence of a cell that can grow into a human brain. "The mere existence of that cell," he writes, "should be one of the greatest astonishments of the earth. People ought to be walking around all day, all through their waking hours, calling to each other in endless wonderment, talking of nothing except that cell." Thomas' pyrotechnic conclusion demands the accompaniment of Bach, with the volume turned way up: "No one has the ghost of an idea how this works, and nothing else in life can ever be so puzzling. If anyone does succeed in explaining it, within my lifetime, I will charter a skywriting airplane, maybe a whole fleet of them, and send them aloft to write one great exclamation point after another, around the whole sky, until all my money runs out."

FOR DISCUSSION

1. Look back at the set of questions for writing about a person (p.235). How many of these questions has the author covered? Is there any order to his presentation of material?
2. The *kind* of publication an informative essay is written for has a good deal to do with what material is included and what is left out. What things are included here that relate chiefly to the fact that *Time* is a "popular" (as opposed to scholarly or specialized) news magazine?
3. Identify the methods of presentation in paragraphs 4, 6, 8, 11, and 22.
4. What secondary or covert motivations might underlie the writing and publication of this essay at the particular time that it was written and published?
5. What were Gray's sources of information for this essay?

Student Essay

Water Babies

by Sandra Andrews

1 Everyone knows that physical fitness is extremely important for a child's physical and mental health, but few realize that physical fitness can and should begin when the child is an infant. One of the most successful physical health programs to have appeared in recent years is the "water-baby" program, in which infants are taught the basic movements for eventually learning to swim.

2 One of the most common misconceptions about the water-baby program is that it was devised by and for swimming enthusiasts, who want to give their children a head start on the sport. It's true that water-baby classes provide an excellent pre-swimming experience, but water-babies is primarily an exercise program. Its immediate goal is not to teach the infant to swim but to pattern the child's muscles for more advanced development as the child grows older. As it turns out, water is an excellent medium for developing strength in the

large muscles. Infants receive very little total body exercise in their daily land experiences; but in the water, children can exercise every part of their bodies without restriction or danger.

3 Water-baby classes are taught primarily in YMCA's and YWCA's, but each child's program actually begins at home, in the bathtub, with mother and child playing together in the water. At this stage the baby learns to enjoy playing in the water, to associate water-play with motherly affection, and to put its face in the water in a playful context.

4 These playful activities continue when formal classes begin—usually at six months but sometimes as early as three—but they are now incorporated into a series of exercises designed to develop specific skills. Although different programs emphasize different kinds and levels of skill, the basic sequence is from kicking and stroking, to floating, and finally to bobbing. At the first stage, infants begin to develop the muscles needed for basic swimming movements; at the second, they learn to keep themselves afloat in the water, on both their backs and tummies; and finally, they learn to go entirely under water (with mother holding on, of course) and bob up to the top.

5 Many adults find it astonishing that infants can be coached in these activities, and they imagine frightful scenes in which parents and instructors bully the babies, kicking and screaming, into the water. Actually, this attitude probably derives from experiences with older children. Water-baby advocates point out that fear of water is not instinctual in children but is a learned behavior that doesn't appear until around three years of age. The whole point of water-babies is to catch the children before anxiety about water has a chance to develop.

6 In the classes I observed as part of a project in my Child Development course, there was indeed some crying and resistance, but not nearly as much as one might expect. And what a sight it was to see children under a year old casually floating on their backs and bobbing up and down in the water!

7 Water-baby supporters like to point out that the program is valuable because it does so many useful things at once: It contributes to the overall physical and emotional development of the child; it teaches basic swimming skills; and it provides important survival skills. (No child can be drown-proofed, but almost all infants can be taught to roll over on their backs or to grasp the side of the pool.) Behavioral studies in Russia have shown some correlation between swim instruction and intelligence, but no causal link has been established.

8 On the negative side, some doctors worry that infants, who are already highly vulnerable to infections, may become even more so in swimming pools surrounded by other infants. Also some Red Cross counselors have cautioned that children and parents can become over-confident, at a time when the children do not really have the ability to survive alone in water.

9 All the same, water-babies programs have gained widespread acceptance since their introduction in the early seventies. In her book, *Your Baby Can Swim,* Bonnie Prudden reports that an early survey of YMCA's and YWCA's

across the country revealed that 52 percent of the organizations were negative in their thinking about water-babies. In a more recent survey of the same institutions, however, 90 percent were positive, 10 percent were mildly positive, and not a single institution remained negative.

10 Water-babies is not the only physical health program for infants, of course, and for any particular baby it may not be the best one. Certainly, anyone considering the program should consult the child's physician and inquire about the quality of whatever local program is offered. However, for large numbers of parents and children, water-babies is making a big splash.

FOR DISCUSSION

1. Where does this essay fit on the "compass of information" (p. 230)? What purpose or purposes might the author have, other than that of simply presenting information?

2. Where might this essay be published? To what group does it seem primarily directed?

3. Construct an outline which reveals the principal questions that this essay answers about the water-baby program. Can you think of other questions the author might have explored?

4. Review the seven "strategies for conveying information effectively," pp. 236–243. Which strategies does the author of this essay use in paragraphs 2, 4, and 5?

5. Counting the first two paragraphs of this essay as its introduction, which methods of introduction do you find combined here?

6. Evaluate the conclusion. Is it too much of a gimmick? Can you think of an alternate way to close the essay?

Part Four

Practical Considerations

Appendix 1

The Research Report

Overview

- Introduction
- Subjects for the Research Report
- Purpose and Audience
- Sources of Information
- Using Source Materials
- Forms for Notes
- Forms for Bibliography or "Works Cited"
- Sample Research Report

• Introduction

Although this appendix contains a guide to research writing in general, it is primarily oriented to the *research* or *term paper* required in many college courses.

Many people have the erroneous notion that the research paper involves a kind of writing different from any other. They get so wrapped up in taking notes and compiling a bibliography that they forget an important fact—*the research paper is an essay,* usually either *deliberative* or *informative.* In order to succeed it must have more than proper documentation; it must have those qualities of a good essay discussed throughout this book. This appendix concentrates on the research report, or documented informative essay, since that is the kind of research paper most often assigned in undergraduate courses.

In a documented research report most of your pre-writing and information-gathering requires research in the library, principally with books and periodicals. You may be expected not only to find out what you need to know about a given subject but also to cover a range of source material, sometimes stipulated by an instructor. As with any informative essay, you still face the tasks of organizing and of discovering focusing questions and generalizations, but you are also responsible for a fuller investigation and for synthesizing a variety of materials into a unified presentation.

The research report also requires you to demonstrate the correctness and authenticity of your information. This is done chiefly through direct reference to authoritative sources with documentation, usually with documentary notes. In other respects, the research report is an informative essay. The various pre-writing and organizing procedures outlined in Part 3, "Informative Writing," should help you compose it.

• Subjects for the Research Report

Subjects for research reports usually develop out of the material you study in a course. Your instructor may assign your topic, or you may be asked to develop a topic out of your own interests. In either case, you should take care from the beginning to narrow your topic to a manageable size. You cannot write effectively on "The Civil War," or "The Women's Movement," or "The English Language," or "John Stuart Mill." These topics are much too broad. Look for a *single question* or a *single set of questions* that your report can be designed to answer about your topic. Instead of "John Stuart Mill," concentrate on a specific direction of questioning. What was Mill's role in early women's movements, and how has he influenced later movements?

Sometimes an instructor will narrow the topic for you by casting the research assignment in the form of a question. What was the Populist Tom

Watson's attitude toward blacks? How did it differ from that of other Southern political leaders in his age? Was it entirely consistent with his other attitudes? Did it change over time?

If a topic is not assigned to you in this way, you need to work through the narrowing process yourself. Even after you have arrived at a potentially manageable question or set of questions about your subject, you should confer with your instructor, who can tell you whether you're on a reasonable course and can make further suggestions.

• Purpose and Audience

It is easy to locate the place of the research report on the "compass of information" (see p. 230). Its purpose is to organize and communicate *knowledge* about a subject. Clarity, organization, and thoroughness are very important, and the style of the essay tends to be more in the direction of formality than of informality.

Because of the artificiality of the situation in which many research reports are written, *audience* is difficult to assess. It is often apparent that the audience of your essay is none other than your instructor, and that the purpose in assigning it is to see how well you can master a subject and make a coherent, interesting presentation. That's just part of the way schooling works.

However, you will always do a better job if you write your essay *as if it were an act of communication to a real audience,* rather than a demonstration of your scholarly abilities. Make it interesting. In your introduction and conclusion try to point out some possible contexts for the information—why, for instance, someone interested in the general subject should be interested in the specific question or set of questions that you are attempting to answer, or why the question came up in the first place. This is not merely a gimmick; it builds a place for your essay in some larger search or enterprise. It builds a potential audience for your essay. And it will probably help keep you on track as you compose the essay.

• Sources of Information

For any subject there are basically two sources of information—*primary* and *secondary.*

Primary sources include artifacts or actual examples of the items or ideas you are studying, interviews or correspondence with the person you are studying, the actual works of literature you are studying, and historical documents, such as letters, official records, and diaries.

Secondary sources are written works, usually books or essays, that compile information, analyze and organize it, and develop arguments and generalizations about it. This section will deal almost exclusively with finding secondary source materials.

Usually, by the time you have settled on a topic, read a few things about it, and discussed it with a few people (including your instructor), you will already have a partial—and sizable—list of books and articles. This early "hatching" or incubation period can be quite valuable to you. People mention titles to you; your instructor gives you a short list. You find several interesting items in the bibliography of a textbook, and the footnotes in one book or article lead you to several more items. You might find a number of interesting-looking titles in the card catalogue of your library, and the reference librarian may suggest several more. You will probably find some of your best sources this way.

At some point, however, you are going to need to conduct a more formal, organized search for sources. The best way of getting at this is through standard reference works, bibliographies, and periodical indexes. Your instructor may recommend a particular bibliography or index that is especially useful for your subject. The following list is a general one.

General encyclopedias

Encyclopedias are not generally the best references, because the articles in them are usually short, highly generalized, and often derivative from better, more detailed sources. However, a general encyclopedia is often a good place to start. It can acquaint you with the subject, introduce you to some of the special vocabulary associated with the subject, and lead you to a short list of books and articles. Consult the index (in the first volume) as well as the alphabetically arranged titles of articles.

Do not spend a lot of time going through encyclopedias. The two best for most general purposes are the following:

Encyclopaedia Britannica
The most recent edition is divided into a *Micropaedia,* which contains short, generalized articles and an index, and a *Macropaedia,* which contains longer, more detailed articles, with short bibliographies. The *Macropaedia* articles are more useful.

Encyclopedia Americana

Specialized encyclopedias and dictionaries

The specialized encyclopedias in various scholarly fields contain articles on topics that you will not always find in the general encyclopedias. Dictionaries in this category provide short articles on the specialized vocabularies of various fields of study. Your reference librarian is the best person to help you find a specialized encyclopedia or dictionary.

Art:

Encyclopedia of Painting (1955)
Encyclopedia of World Art (1959–68)

Education:

A Cyclopedia of Education, ed. Paul Monroe (5 vols., 1911–1913)
Encyclopedia of Educational Research (4th ed., 1969)

Folklore and mythology:

Funk and Wagnalls Standard Dictionary of Folklore, Mythology, and Legend (2 vols., 1949–50)

New Larousse Encyclopedia of Mythology (rev. ed., 1969)

History:

An Encyclopedia of World History, ed. William L. Langer (5th ed., 1972)

The Cambridge Ancient History, ed. John B. Bury, et al. (12 vols., 1923–1939; 3rd ed., 1970–)

Encyclopedia of American History, ed. Richard B. Morris and Henry Steele Commager (rev. ed., 1970)

Dictionary of American History, ed. James T. Adams (6 vols., 1940–63)

Literature:

The Oxford Companion to American Literature, ed. James D. Hart (4th ed., 1965)

The Oxford Companion to English Literature, ed. Sir Paul Harvey, rev. by Dorothy Eagle (4th ed., 1967)

The Oxford Companion to the Theatre, ed. Phyllis Hartwell (3rd ed., 1967)

Music:

The Harvard Dictionary of Music, ed. Willi Apel (2nd ed., 1969)

International Cyclopedia of Music and Musicians, ed. Oscar Thompson (10th ed., 1975)

Natural sciences and mathematics:

The Encyclopedia of the Biological Sciences, ed. Peter Gray (1967)

International Encyclopedia of Chemical Sciences (1964)

McGraw-Hill Encyclopedia of Science and Technology (15 vols., 4th ed., 1977)

Universal Encyclopedia of Mathematics (1964)

Philosophy:

The Encyclopaedia of Philosophy, ed. Paul Edwards (8 vols., 1967)

Religion:

Encyclopaedia of Religion and Ethics, ed. James Hastings (13 vols., 1908–26)

Jewish Encyclopedia, ed. Isidore Singer, et al. (12 vols., 1901–06)

The New Catholic Encyclopedia (15 vols., 1967)

The New Standard Jewish Encyclopedia, ed. Cecil Roth (New rev. ed., 1977)

The Oxford Dictionary of the Christian Church, ed. F. L. Cross and Elizabeth A. Livingston (1974)

Social sciences:

Encyclopedia of the Social Sciences (15 vols., 1930–35)

International Encyclopedia of the Social Sciences (17 vols., 1968)

Biographical sources

Current Biography (1940–)
[Published monthly; has an annual index.]

Dictionary of American Biography (20 vols., supplements, 1928–50)

Dictionary of National Biography (22 vols., supplements (1908–)
[British biography.]

Who's Who in America (2 vols., 1899–)
[Published every two years.]

Current events, facts, statistics

Facts on File and *Facts on File Yearbook* (1940–)
[Published weekly.]

Information Please Alamanac (1947–)
[Published annually.]

World Almanac and Book of Facts (1868–)
[Published annually.]

Periodical indexes

For many topics, particularly if they are narrow, your best sources are articles in magazines and scholarly journals. There are a number of general indexes to periodical literature, arranged usually by subject and author, and there are many specialized indexes. For specialized indexes see your reference librarian or the reference catalogue of your library. The most important general indexes are the following:

Reader's Guide to Periodical Literature (1900–)

International Index (1907–65)

[Indexes articles in the social sciences and humanities. See items below for continuations.]

Social Sciences and Humanities Index (1965–1974)
[Continuation of *International Index* (above).]
Humanities Index (1974–)
[Continuation of the *Social Sciences and Humanities Index.*]
Social Sciences Index (1974–)
[Continuation of the *Social Sciences and Humanities Index.*]
The New York Times Index (1913–)

Bibliographies

A bibliography is a list of books and articles on a given topic. There are literally thousands of bibliographies, many of which make large volumes in themselves. Some bibliographies in scholarly disciplines are compiled and published annually.

Your best guide to specialized bibliographies is your instructor, your reference librarian, or the reference catalogue in your library. For a general guide to bibliographies and other reference materials, see *Guide to Reference Books,* Winchell, Constance M. (9th ed., 1976)

• Using Source Materials

Reasons for using reference notes

Reference notes serve three purposes in a research report:

1. verifying the accuracy or authority of your information;
2. giving credit to the author whose investigations and ideas you are drawing from;
3. providing a body of reference for readers who may want to follow up with investigations of their own.

In many instances reference notes serve all of these purposes at once. The following examples illustrate them separately:

Verifying the accuracy or authority of a statement:

Social customs and religious beliefs in underdeveloped countries do not present insurmountable obstacles to population control. E. A. Wrigley, a leading student of population, cites a number of cases in which high fertility does not appear to be prized among families in underdeveloped countries. He concludes that "If the surveys and other evidence can be taken at face value, there is a general desire to keep families small in most developing countries."[1]

---

[1] Population and History (New York: McGraw-Hill, 1969), p. 218.

Giving credit:

Another striking feature of American frontier speech is the creation of rollicking, high-sounding words, using suffixes like -acious, -iferous, and -ticate. Some prominent examples are "kankarriferous," "rambunctious," "angeliferous," and "splendiferous."[1]

---

[1] Albert H. Marckwardt, American English (New York: Oxford Univ. Press, 1958), p. 100.

Providing follow-up reference:

Modern literary critics have been especially fascinated by the phenomenon of metaphor, a figure of speech embodying an implied comparison between two fields of reference.[1]

---

[1] For a good general introduction to issues and problems, see Terence Hawkes, Metaphor (London: Methuen, 1972); see also Owen Thomas, Metaphor and Related Subjects (New York: Random House, 1969).

The best way of assuring complete and accurate references is to keep records of essential bibliographical information, on note cards, for all the books and articles you consult. (Forms for bibliographical entries are given on pp. 287–290.) Take notes from your reading on the same size cards and keep separate stacks of cards for each source, each stack headed by a bibliography card. Later, when you refer directly or indirectly to a particular source, you can go back to the cards for exact information to be used in the report, along with exact publication information and page references for notes. Finally, when putting together the bibliography page or "Works Cited" for your report, you can simply stack the relevant bibliography cards in alphabetical order and type them.

Sample bibliography card:

PE
1072
M28

Marckwardt, Albert H.
American English
New York; Oxford Univ. Press
1958

Sample note card:

Frontier Speech — Marckwardt

p. 100 Another feature is high-sounding words with suffixes like -acious, -iferous, -ticate, etc.

Examples. "kankarriferous," "rambunctious," "splendiferous"

Direct quotation

There are two ways of bringing information and ideas from your research into the body of your report—direct quotation and paraphrase. Don't rely too heavily on direct quotation. Limit it to situations in which direct quotation seems especially warranted. Generally, if a passage is of manageable length, you should consider quoting it directly under the following conditions:

- if the passage is from a work of literature;
- if the passage is phrased in a way that is especially succinct or eloquent;
- if quoting the passage directly will lend authority to your report;
- if the passage itself is part of the subject of your investigation.

Usually, when quoting a source directly, you should identify the author (and sometimes the title of the publication) in the body of your report. Your reader should not have to consult the notes for this essential information. Notes for quotations should serve to provide details of the source's publication. If a quotation is long enough to take up more than three or four lines on a page, it should be separated from the text and "blocked"—indented five spaces from both the left and right margins.)

Example #1:

Herman Melville wastes no time at all in signalling to his readers that Moby Dick is a book about man's spiritual crisis. In the very first paragraph his hero, Ishmael, describes himself in terms that reveal a state of spiritual death, a crisis that the upcoming whaling voyage must somehow resolve:

> Whenever I find myself growing grim about the mouth; whenever it is a damp, drizzly November in my soul; whenever I find myself inadvertently pausing before coffin warehouses, and bringing up the rear of every funeral I meet . . . then I account it high time to get to sea as soon as I can. This is my substitute for pistol and ball.[1]

---

[1] Ed. Harrison Hayford and Hershel Parker (New York: W. W. Norton, 1967), p. 12.

Note that, since the author and title of the reference are given in the text, they are not repeated in the note. Note also that the quoted sentence is shortened to manageable length by the ellipsis.

Example #2:
Sometimes you can make a quotation more manageable by using only an essential clause or phrase incorporated into the structure of your sentence.

As a populist leader, Meary Lease was apparently somewhat deficient in her understanding of the movement and its true goals; nevertheless, the historian William George Clugston has concluded that "in personality, and in force of character, she overshadowed any man-figure the state produced during her generation."[1]

---

[1] Rascals in Democracy (New York: Richard R. Smith, 1940), p. 92.

Paraphrase

A good quotation, strategically placed, can add just the note of authority and liveliness that a research report needs. Over-quoting, however, has just the opposite effect—the report becomes tedious, and it may appear directionless. Inexperienced writers tend to use too many direct quotations, sometimes giving their reports the appearance of anthologies of quoted passages, loosely strung together. Unless a particular passage from your source meets one of the conditions mentioned in the section on "Direct Quotation," you should use paraphrase—a restatement in your own words, usually with some compression, of the information or idea in your source.

In fact you should already have paraphrased and summarized material from your source in the process of note-taking. Writing long passages verbatim on note cards is very wasteful, both of time and note cards. Copying passages rather than paraphrasing and condensing simply postpones the necessary task of synthesizing and compressing your material.

Consider, for instance, the following passage from Thoreau's "Civil Disobedience":

> It is not a man's duty, as a matter of course, to devote himself to the eradication of any, even the most enormous wrong; he may still properly have other concerns to engage him; but it is his duty, at least, to wash his hands of it, and, if he gives it no thought longer, not to give it practically his support.

Paraphrased, the idea might appear in the following form:

Thoreau's position, as stated in "Civil Disobedience," is that passive resistance to evil is a human obligation. A person is not obligated to oppose the evil actively, because he may be involved in other, equally important pursuits. But he is obligated to deny it any kind of practical support.[1]

---

[1] The Variorum Civil Disobedience, ed. Walter Roy Harding (New York: New York Univ. Press, 1958), p. 36.

• Forms for Notes

Methods of documentation and forms for notes vary from discipline to discipline. The forms presented below are those prescribed by the Modern Language Association. (See *MLA Handbook for Writers of Research Papers, Theses, and Dissertations,* New York: Modern Language Association, 1977, the most widely used guide for documentation in the humanities.)

General format

The practice of typing footnotes at the bottom of the page has now been mercifully abandoned for research papers. The usual practice now is to put all the notes, in numbered sequence, in a special section at the end of the essay. The following rules of general format apply:

1. Within the text, a note is indicated by an arabic numeral placed after the material cited and raised slightly above the line.
2. Notes are numbered consecutively throughout the text.
3. On a separate page at the end of the essay the notes appear with their numbers. Double-space within and between them. (See "Notes" in the **Sample Research Report,** p. 298.)
4. If you give the title of the work or the author's name in your text, you need not repeat it in the note. Omitting both, however, would be confusing. (See the note for William George Clugston's *Rascals in Democracy,* p. 282.)

Sample notes—first references

The first time you refer to a source in the notes, include all publication information not actually mentioned in the text of your report. The special forms for this information are represented in the following samples. (The types of publications most commonly cited in research reports are represented here. For other types, see the *MLA Handbook.*)

Book with a single author:

[1] Albert H. Marckwardt, American English (New York: Oxford Univ. Press, 1958), p. 100.

Book with two or more authors:

[2] René Wellek and Austin Warren, Theory of Literature, 3rd ed. (New York: Harcourt, 1962), pp. 89-90.

[Note the inclusion of the edition number of a book.]
[The form for names is the same for articles as for books.]

Edition of a literary work:

[3] Herman Melville, Moby Dick, ed. Harrison Hayford and Hershel Parker (New York: Norton, 1967), p. 12.

Book with an editor:

[4] The American Writer and the Great Depression, ed. Harvey Swados (Minneapolis, Minn.: Bobbs-Merrill, 1966), p. xiii.

Book with a translator:

[5] Suetonius, The Twelve Caesars, trans. Robert Graves (New York: Penguin, 1957).

Book published in more than one volume:

[6] Reinhold Niebuhr, The Nature and Destiny of Man (New York: Scribner's, 1941), II, 98.

[Note that when a volume number is used the abbreviation for "page" or "pages" is omitted.]

Book published in a series:

[7] Louis I. Bredvold, The Intellectual Milieu of John Dryden, University of Michigan Publications in Language and Literature, No. 12 (Ann Arbor, Mich.: Univ. of Michigan Press, 1934), pp. 18-19.

Article in a journal with continuous pagination throughout the annual volume:

[8] Richard Hoggart, "Humanistic Studies and Mass Culture," Daedalus, 99 (1970), 455.

[Note that when a volume number is used, the abbreviation for "page" is omitted.]

Article from a journal that pages each issue separately:

[9] Nathan Glazer, "Black English and Reluctant Judges," The Public Interest, No. 62 (1981), p. 41.

Article from a weekly magazine or weekly newspaper:

[10] Ann Berk, "Modern Woman's Double Life," Newsweek, 29 Sept. 1980, p. 17.

[If the article is unsigned, begin with the title.]

Article from a monthly magazine:

[11] Daniel Goleman, "An Eastern Toe in the Stream of Consciousness," Psychology Today, Jan. 1980, p. 84.

Article from a daily newspaper:

[12] Jane E. Brody, "Cold Hands and Feet of Raynaud's Disease," New York Times, 7 Jan. 1981, Sec. 1, p. 15, col. 1.

[If the article is unsigned, begin with the title.]

Unsigned editorial:

[13] "Werner von Braun," Editorial, Washington Post, 23 June 1977, Sec. A, p. 24, col. 1.

Article from an encyclopedia:

[14] Chaim Perelman, "Rhetoric," New Encyclopaedia Britannica: Macropaedia, 1974 ed.

[Volume and page numbers are not necessary. If the article is unsigned, begin with the title. *Britannica* articles are initialed; full names are listed in the first volume, *Propaedia.*]

Article from an edited collection of articles:

[15] Roderick M. Chisolm, "Austin's Philosophical Papers," in Symposium on J. L. Austin, ed. Ted Honereich (New York: Humanities Press, 1969), p. 124.

Article from a collection of articles by the same author:

[16] Walter J. Ong, "Memory as Art," in his Rhetoric, Romance and Technology: Studies in the Interaction of Expression and Culture (Ithaca, N.Y.: Cornell Univ. Press, 1971), p. 110.

Book review:

[17] J. Jeffrey Auer, rev. of The Language of Modern Politics, by Kenneth Hudson, Quarterly Journal of Speech, 66 (1980), 463.

[If a review is unsigned, begin with the words "Rev. of." If the review is titled, use the form in the following sample.]

[18] Peter S. Prescott, "Mean Streets in Moscow," rev. of Gorky Park, by Martin Cruz Smith, Newsweek, 6 April 1981, p. 100.

The Bible:

It is not necessary, under most circumstances, to document information about editions and translations of The Bible. Nor are notes generally necessary. Indicate the exact source by chapter and verse (John 3: 16) in the text of your report.

Personal interview or telephone interview:

[19] Personal interview with President Ronald Reagan, 15 Jan. 1981.

[20] Telephone interview with President Ronald Reagan, 15 Jan. 1981.

Sample notes—second references

The first time a source is cited in the notes, publication information should be complete, as in the previous examples. Subsequent references to the same source can be considerably shortened, as in the following examples. (Sources cited are from the sample notes in the preceding section.)

Book or article:

[13] Marckwardt, p. 102.

[The author's last name and the page reference are all that is needed.]

Different volume:

[14] Niebuhr, I, 132.

[Include the new volume number.]

More than one title by the same author:

[15] Marckwardt, American English, p. 83.

[Add a shortened version of each title.]

• Forms for Bibliography or "Works Cited"

The Bibliography or Works Cited is the last section of a research report, providing an alphabetical listing of every item used in the report. It provides complete bibliographical information for all source materials and also presents the reader with an overview of the range of sources covered in the report. With some types of documentation, particularly those used in the social sciences, the bibliography is essential because the forms for footnotes do not require complete bibliographical information. With the method of documentation presented in this book, a bibliography or "list of references" is not absolutely essential, since complete information is required in the notes. Bibliographies are especially convenient, however, for readers who intend to follow up your research with investigations of their own. Follow your instructor's advice on whether to include a bibliography.

General format

The bibliography comes at the end of the research report, beginning a new page, after the notes. The following rules of format apply:

1. Entries are listed alphabetically and are *not* numbered. Alphabetization is by the last names of authors. If an entry has no author, use the first word (other than *a, an,* or *the*) in the title.
2. Entries are double-spaced, with double-spacing between entries.
3. The first line of each entry begins at the left-hand margin, but each additional line is indented 5 spaces.

4. Multiple titles by a single author are alphabetized by the first words in titles. After the first entry by an author, substitute 10 hyphens followed by a period (----------.) for the author's name.
5. Forms for bibliographical entries differ in both arrangement and punctuation from those for notes. See the sample forms below.

For the general appearance of the bibliography section, see the **Sample Research Report,** p. 300.

Sample Bibliographical Entries

The following bibliographical entries are for the same sources, and in the same order, as those for **Sample Notes,** p. 283.

Book with a single author:

Marckwardt, Albert H. American English. New York: Oxford Univ. Press, 1958.

Book with two or more authors:

Wellek, René, and Austin Warren, Theory of Literature. 2nd ed. 3rd ed. New York: Harcourt, 1962.

[Note that the second name is not inverted.]

Edition of a literary work:

Melville, Herman. Moby Dick. Ed. Harrison Hayford and Hershel Parker. New York: Norton, 1967.

Book with an editor:

Harvey Swados, ed. The American Writer and the Great Depression. Minneapolis, Minn.: Bobbs-Merrill, 1966.

Book with a translator:

Tranquillus, Gaius Suetonius. The Twelve Caesars. Trans. Robert Graves. New York: Penguin, 1937.

Book published in more than one volume:

Niebuhr, Reinhold. The Nature and Destiny of Man. 2 vols. New York: Scribner's, 1941.

Book published in a series:

Bredvold, Louis I. The Intellectual Milieu of John Dryden. University of Michigan Publications in Language and Literature, No. 12. Ann Arbor, Mich.: Univ. of Michigan Press, 1934.

Article in a journal with continuous pagination throughout the annual volume:

Hoggart, Richard. "Humanistic Studies and Mass Culture." Daedalus, 99 (1970), 451-472.

Article from a journal that pages each issue separately:

Glazer, Nathan. "Black English and Reluctant Judges." The Public Interest, No. 62 (1981), pp. 40-54.

Article from a weekly magazine or weekly newspaper:

Berk, Ann. "Modern Woman's Double Life." Newsweek, 29 Sept. 1980, pp. 17.

Article from a monthly magazine:

Goleman, Daniel. "An Eastern Toe in the Stream of Consciousness." Psychology Today, Jan. 1980, pp. 84, 86-87.

Article from a daily newspaper:

Brody, Jane E. "Cold Hands and Feet of Raynaud's Disease." New York Times, 7 Jan. 1981, Sec. 1, p. 15, cols. 1-6.

[If the article is unsigned, begin with the title and alphabetize.]

Unsigned editorial from a daily newspaper:

"Werner von Braun." Editorial. Washington Post, 23 June 1977, Sec. A, p. 24, col. 1.

Article from an encyclopedia:

Perelman, Chaim. "Rhetoric." Encyclopaedia Britannica: Macropaedia. 1974 ed.

Article from an edited collection of articles:

Chisolm, Roderick M. "Austin's Philosophical Papers." In Symposium On J. L. Austin. Ed. Ted Hondereich. New York: Humanities Press, 1969.

Article from a collection of articles by the same author:

Ong, Walter J. "Memory as Art." In his Rhetoric, Romance, and Technology: Studies in the Interaction of Expression and Culture. Ithaca, N. Y.: Cornell Univ. Press, 1971, pp. 104-112.

Book review:

Rev. of The Language of Modern Politics, by Kenneth Hudson. Quarterly Journal of Speech, 66 (1980), 463-65.

Prescott, Peter S. "Mean Streets in Moscow." Rev. of Gorky Park, by Martin Cruz Smith, Newsweek, 6 (April 1981), p. 100.

Personal interview or telephone interview:

President Ronald Reagan. Personal interview. 15 Jan. 1981.

President Ronald Reagan. Telephone interview. 15 Jan. 1981.

• Sample Research Report

The following research report was written in a second-semester freshman composition course at the University of North Carolina at Greensboro. The reading matter for the course was a group of books, articles, and literary works on the subject of the Roman emperors and their families. The purpose of the research report was to provide detailed information, to the instructor and to other members of the class, on a topic that could only be touched upon in classroom discussions and in the basic readings.

The overall format of the essay, including conventions for title and pagination, is the one recommended by the *MLA Handbook.*

Jenny Maxwell

Professor Griffith

English 102

November 20, 1981

Agrippina, Rome's Most Influential Woman

To what extent did Agrippina control her son Nero? How did she do so, and what was the nature of the relationship between them? Was she for a time, as is often suggested, the true emperor of Rome? These questions come to the mind of any person who studies Nero's life and rule as emperor. Agrippina's extraordinary relationship with her son is not only fascinating as a personal history; it is a dramatic account of how political power was won and exercised and lost in the late Roman Empire.

To consider Agrippina's influence on Nero, we must consider Agrippina herself. Tacitus tells us that Agrippina was a woman who "to this day remains unique as . . . the sister, wife, and mother of emperors."[1] We can assume that this heritage was a major factor in molding her personality, for, according to historian Bernard W. Henderson, she was a proud, arrogant, and stubborn person.[2] She was also noted for being energetic, a quality that she must have relied on greatly in her efforts to make Nero emperor of Rome. She must have possessed a good deal of charm as well. Agrippina managed to marry her uncle, Claudius, in order to persuade him to adopt Nero as a son and thus to secure

Nero's succession, even though Claudius had a son of his own. This accomplishment seems even more remarkable when we consider the further information, from Tacitus, that this was "the first known adoption into the patrician branch of the Claudii."[3] Agrippina had the pride and arrogance we associate with a powerful person. She had the energy and determination and charm needed to acquire that power. Perhaps this is why she felt that she deserved it.

No one seems to know whether Agrippina felt a mother's love for Nero. She seems to have been more concerned with Nero's usefulness in her own effort to gain power, accustomed as she was to ruling totally those around her.[4] One historian has concluded that Agrippina's motive for bringing Nero to power was personal ambition, not maternal ambition, and that she intended from the beginning to exercise power in Nero's name.[5] She was certainly reluctant to surrender her power while Nero was emperor, and this reluctance tends to confirm the belief that personal ambition was her motive.

Though Nero may have been more important to Agrippina as a means of gaining power, it is possible that she loved him, too. Will Durant writes that Seneca often complained of Agrippina's interference in his attempts to teach her son. Nero would go to his mother whenever he had been reprimanded for anything, certain that she would comfort and excuse him.[6] Whether this is a sign of Agrippina's love, her cunning, or simply an inconsistent, doting foolishness, it is difficult to say.

But there are clearer signs of her affection: In one incident, as related by Dio Cassius, Agrippina is supposed to have said, on hearing that Nero would murder her after becoming emperor, "Let him kill me, if only he shall rule."[7] Guglielmo Ferrero believes that Agrippina, who was young, beautiful, and rich, and who probably attracted the interest of many handsome young men, sacrificed her own happiness for that of her son when she married Claudius, an old and sickly man.[8] In Ferrero's view, Agrippina considered herself solely a means for the advancement of her son, and she married Claudius for this end. If these stories and claims are accurate, then perhaps Agrippina had motives other than personal gain in securing the throne for her son.[9]

However, Agrippina's drive for personal power stands out prominently in her story. In his book, Nero: Reality and Legend, B. H. Warmington tells how Agrippina constantly goaded the leisurely and retiring boy into "ceaseless activity," so that she could exercise "power behind the scenes." Warmington points out that Romans were opposed to the submission of men to women in government and that this was precisely why Agrippina needed Nero. She could act in the name of Nero, easily, since she was so adept at controlling him.[10]

The degree to which Agrippina actually influenced Nero and the degree to which she actually wielded power in his name are matters of some dispute. Roman coinage of the time reveals that Agrippina did exercise some influence. Michael Grant points out that Agrippina was the only woman in the history of the Empire to be "openly declared superior to the emperor."[11] Grant refers to the coins produced at the beginning of Nero's reign. Agrippina appeared on the front of these coins, facing Nero, with the emperor's title reserved for the reverse side of the coin.

But coinage was only a symptom of her influence. Agrippina is known to have listened to meetings of the Senate, carried on government correspondence, considered and decided questions of state, and issued orders.[12] While concluding that the first months of the principate seemed to crown Agrippina's ambitions, Warmington warns that opinions on the extent of Agrippina's actual influence vary.[13] We should look carefully at the available facts, keeping in mind that writers tend to enjoy portraying the influential and power-hungry woman in any age.

The most sensational of the stories about Agrippina is that she committed incest with her son in order to increase her power over him. There is no clear indication that there is any truth in it. Dio tells us that it was common knowledge in Rome that Nero had a mistress who closely resembled his mother, and that, when speaking of the affair to others he would joke that he was "having intercourse with his mother."[14] Grant believes that the tradition is "so persistent that there is probably something in it."[15]

If we accept the view that their relationship was incestuous, we have to wonder which of them desired it and sparked it--Agrippina,

Nero, or both of them? Tacitus gives us two opinions: According to Cluvius Rufus, Agrippina, in her passion to retain power, would appear before her son "decked out and ready for incest."[16] Fabius Rusticus, on the other hand, reports that the desire was Nero's, not Agrippina's.[17] There is, of course, no solid evidence that Nero committed incest with his mother, though the stories are persistent and come from a variety of sources. Warmington seems to grasp the significance of the tradition, in speculating that, however true or false the stories may be, they indicate an "uneasy relationship" between the two.[18]

This uneasy relationship did not improve with time. Nero, frustrated by his mother's domination, removed her bodyguards and finally sent her away from the palace. His own resentful feelings were reflected when Agrippina's name and portrait ceased to appear on Roman coins. Grant confirms that the change was seen and noted, and meant to be noted.[19]

There are three possible explanations for the ill-feelings between the two. Some feel that Acte, an ex-slave and Nero's mistress, created the final break. Bernard Henderson believes that this relationship, which he terms "the most harmless and most sentimental episode in Nero's life," completed the breach begun by Agrippina's overweening desire for power.[20] Ferrero claims that the "definitive break" came when Nero left Acte for Poppea Sabina, the woman he later married.[21]

Both of these women are supposed to have encouraged Nero to assert his independence, and Agrippina was no doubt angered by it all.

The third and most likely reason for their disaffection is that Nero became increasingly frustrated by his mother's constant demands and attempts to place restrictions on his behavior. Though Acte and Poppea Sabina may have increased his awareness of the situation, it seems certain that his frustration at being so closely controlled drove him from his mother. According to Suetonius, the "over-watchful, over-critical eye of Agrippina . . . proved more than he could stand."[22] At one point she threatened to replace Nero with Britannicus, Claudius' natural son. Nero became convinced that she was sneering at his artistic endeavors and was secretly plotting his downfall. Aware that her influence was weakening, Agrippina displayed hysterical fits of ill-temper.[23] Finally, terrified by her threats and her violent behavior, Nero decided that Agrippina must die.

Nero attempted several times to murder Agrippina. On the several occasions when he tried to poison her she had taken the antidote in advance! He then arranged a boat collision, replacing her boat with one of his own, a collapsible contraption in which he hoped his mother would either drown or be crushed to death. When she swam to safety, Nero decided to employ an outright and violent murder. To her villa he sent men who brutally stabbed and beat her to death. What drove him to it? Some say the women in his life, but a more plausible explanation is that Nero was desperate to find a way to free himself from his mother's psychological domination.[24]

Even after Agrippina's death, Nero remained under her influence. He was never able to free his conscience from guilt, and he believed that her spirit haunted him.[25] He indulged himself in even more intense sexual pleasures after Agrippina's death, but still he felt his mother's disapproval. Curiously, though it is considered the distinguishing mark of Nero's reign, this matricide had little effect on his standing in Rome.[26] And even though it is the action for which Nero "has been pilloried throughout the ages,"[27] there were no demonstrations by the people at the time of its occurrence.

Was Nero, the matricide, the true emperor of Rome or was Agrippina, his victim, the person in power? Though Agrippina literally gave her son the world, she was reluctant to allow him to enjoy it. She seems to have been determined to control Nero, and to a large extent she succeeded, even after she was dead. We cannot be certain that she actually ruled Rome, from "behind the scenes." It seems reasonable to say that Agrippina did not actually rule but that she held Nero so closely under her influence that things went her way more often than not.

Notes

[1] Publius Cornelius Tacitus, The Annals of Imperial Rome, trans. Michael Grant (New York: Penguin, 1971), p. 271.

[2] The Life and Principate of the Emperor Nero (Philadelphia: Lippincott, 1903), p. 57.

[3] Tacitus, p. 263.

[4] Jacob Abbott, History of Nero (New York: Harper and Brothers, 1881), p. 151.

[5] Abbott, p. 141.

[6] Caesar and Christ (New York: Simon and Schuster, 1944), p. 274.

[7] Cassius Dio Cocceianus, Dio's Rome, trans. Herbert Baldwin Foster (Troy, N.Y.: Pafraets Book Co., 1906), p. 5.

[8] The Women of the Caesars (New York: Century Co., 1911), p. 276.

[9] Ferrero, p. 276.

[10] (London: Chatto and Windus, 1969), p. 13.

[11] The Twelve Caesars (New York: Scribner's, 1975), p. 1952.

[12] Abbott, p. 145.

[13] Warmington, p. 43.

[14] Dio, p. 15.

[15] Grant, p. 160.

[16] Tacitus, p. 313.

[17] Tacitus, p. 313.

[18] Warmington, p. 47.

[19] Grant, p. 284.

[20] Henderson, p. 61.

[21] Ferrero, p. 320.

[22] Gaius Suetonius Tranquillus, The Twelve Caesars, trans. Robert Graves (New York: Penguin, 1957), p. 227.

[23] Grant, p. 153.

[24] Grant, p. 162.

[25] Suetonius, p. 228.

[26] Warmington, p. 46.

[27] Grant, p. 162.

Bibliography

Abbott, Jacob. *History of Nero*. New York: Harper and Brothers, 1881.

Cocceianus, Cassius Dio. *Dio's Rome*. Trans. Herbert Baldwin Foster. Troy, N.Y.: Pafreats Book Co., 1906.

Durant, Will. *Caesar and Christ*. New York: Simon and Schuster, 1944.

Ferrero, Guglielmo. *The Women of the Caesars*. New York: Century, 1911.

Grant, Michael. *History of Rome*. New York: Scribner's, 1978.

Henderson, Bernard W. *The Life and Principate of the Emperor Nero*. Philadelphia: Lippincott, 1903.

Tacitus, Publius Cornelius. *The Annals of Imperial Rome*. Trans. Michael Grant. New York: Penguin, 1971.

Tranquillus, Gaius Suetonius. *The Twelve Caesars*. Trans. Robert Graves. New York: Penguin, 1937.

Warmington, B. H. *Nero: Reality and Legend*. London: Chatto and Windus, 1969.

Appendix 2 Logic and Logical Fallacies

Overview

- Introduction
- Common Fallacies

  Narrow Sampling

  Big Numbers

  False Cause

  Begging the Question

  Red Herring

  False Analogy

  Arguing to the Crowd

  Arguing to the Person

  Appeal to Ignorance

  Either/Or

• Introduction

A fallacy is an illogical or misleading argument. Sometimes people commit fallacies on purpose, hoping to deceive an audience; but most of the time people simply fall into them through carelessness or misjudgment.

In argumentation, as in anything else, there are dozens of ways to go wrong. Some of these are discussed in the six chapters of Part I, Deliberative Writing. For the most part, however, these chapters deal with ways to find good arguments rather than with ways to avoid bad ones.

There are good reasons, though, for devoting some formal study to bad arguments. First, it sharpens the skills you already gained, by teaching you to avoid fallacies, or at least to edit them out of your own writing. But just as important, it teaches you to recognize them in the writing of others—an important skill, since most deliberative writing requires that you deal with arguments already put forward by others. Finally, the ability to detect bad arguments could actually increase your opportunities for engaging in deliberative writing. Many essays are responses to the errors and bad reasoning in other essays.

Arguments go wrong by departing from the principles of sound reasoning, by misusing key terms, or by replacing reasoning and evidence with emotional come-ons and scare tactics. (Bad arguments can still be persuasive to the unsuspecting, of course, as advertisers and political propagandists know too well.) The following are the most commonly committed fallacies.

• Common Fallacies

Narrow sampling

Any generalization should be based on a sample of evidence that is large enough to assure that what is true of the individuals or individual items studied is true of the group as a whole. The conclusion that your student body opposes intercollegiate athletics, based on conversations with three or four people in one of your classes, is an obvious case of inadequate sampling.

In addition to being large enough, a sample of evidence should be representative, assuring that the generalization applies to the whole group and not just a particular segment of it. A survey meant to be representative of your student body but which asked questions only of freshman and sophomore women would be grossly unrepresentative. No sample of evidence can be perfectly representative, of course, but common sense should tell you that the more diverse something is, the more care you should take to assure that all parts are examined.

Most racial and ethnic prejudice exemplify the fallacy of narrow sampling. The actions or habits of a small and sometimes isolated minority are assumed to be those of the group as a whole.

Big numbers

This fallacy is closely related to "narrow sampling" because it calls attention to the sheer size of the sample without mentioning what proportion of the whole the sample actually represents. "Any nation that spends fifty million dollars a year on cat food must be immoral." This impressive sounding argument can't be judged unless we know the size of the nation's economy. The fact that two hundred thousand citizens of Utopia favor a different form of government may or may not be significant. What is the population of Utopia?

False cause

A number of the pitfalls of causal reasoning are discussed in Chapter 6. The most common of these bears the Latin title, *post hoc, ergo propter hoc:* "after this, therefore because of this." The mere fact that Event B occurred after Event A does not make A the cause of B. The Great Depression occurred after Herbert Hoover was elected President, but that fact does not make Hoover or his election responsible for the Great Depression. Whenever anyone implies a causal relationship by saying something like, "It was not too long after X occurred that Y occurred," you have a right to ask, "But what is the exact linkage between these two events?"

Begging the question

Begging the question is a type of circular reasoning in which the conclusion is assumed from the beginning. This reasoning is often heard in popular advertising: "The Fiasco widget is the best widget money can buy—you can be sure because it's made by Fiasco." The statement, of course, begs the most important questions—what are the qualities of a good widget, and how does the Fiasco widget exhibit these qualities?

Another way to beg the question is to load the assertion with *evaluative* terms that pretend to be *descriptive* (see Chapter 5, pp. 131–133). The statement, "Such pornographic works as *The Catcher in the Rye* should of course be banned from the school library," slips in an unsubstantiated evaluation, begging the question of what constitutes pornography and the question of how the book fits the definition.

Arguing to the crowd *(ad populum)*

This fallacy is closely related to question-begging. It uses emotionally charged and value-laden terminology designed to appeal to popular fears and prejudices. Unsubstantiated verbal identifications with such universally approved notions as Americanism, patriotism, the family, and motherhood often substitute for evidence and reasoning; as do identifications with such feared and vilified concepts as godlessness, cowardice, Communism, creeping socialism, facism, or McCarthyism. Quite understandably, this fallacy often goes by the name of *Name-Calling.*

Arguing to the person *(ad hominem)*

This kind of desperate counter-attack is described in Chapter 5, p. 136—arguing "to the man" instead of "to the issue." Instead of answering a charge or accusation directly, the arguer attacks the person or group who made it: "The people who made this charge are simply trying to cover up their own incompetence" or "The man who has accused my client is himself an alleged embezzler." Such attacks, even if true, do not face up to the question of whether the original accusations or complaints were valid.

Ad hominem arguments can have a positive cast as well: "My client would not commit such an act as this. He has always been a good citizen, a church leader, and a strong family man." The real question, of course, is whether or not he committed the act.

Red herring (arguing off the point)

Related to the *ad hominem* argument is the *red herring,* the introduction of any consideration that sidetracks the discussion from the particular point at issue. (This diversionary tactic gets its name from the practice of dragging a smoked herring across the path of chase dogs, to take them off the scent.) A United States senator, for instance, once defended government subsidies to a group of his own constituents, with a long speech on how hard-working and patriotic these constituents were. Many in the audience recognized this argument as a "red herring" and wished inaudibly that he would "get to the point."

False analogy

For general discussions of the uses of analogy in argument, see Chapter 4, p. 97 and Chapter 5, p. 134. In general, analogy is a weak (though often appealing) form of argument. Because no analogy can be exact, analogy is never safe from the charge of distortion. A *false analogy* is one that links things or experiences that are not fundamentally similar. Attempts to identify current American discrimination against its ethnic minorities with Nazi Germany's annihilation of Jews, for instance, ignore vast differences of motive and effect.

Appeal to ignorance
(argumentum ad ignorantiam)

This is the trick of claiming to have proved your point because no one else can prove you wrong. For instance: "There are no scientific studies that prove that angels do not exist"; or "Opponents of this tax legislation have failed to show that it will not bring prosperity to the economy." These arguments are fallacious in two ways. First, they offer no evidence or reasoning on behalf of their claims; and second, they unfairly shift the burden of proof away from the proposers of new ideas or policies to those who are properly skeptical of them. For this reason the *appeal to ignorance* is sometimes also known as *shifting the burden of proof.*

Either/or

This is the fallacy of oversimplifying an issue by reducing it to just two conflicting alternatives. The notion that we must either increase military spending or lose our national security is just as much of an oversimplification as the notion that we must either reduce military spending or wreck the domestic economy and risk world war. In a complex world there are more options than these arguments allow for. Careful debaters do not allow themselves to get caught between two conflicting alternatives. You can defeat this reasoning by calling attention to the real complexity of things.

EXERCISE

Identify the fallacies, or the combinations of fallacies, in the following arguments.

A. Joe: Rembrandt's *The Night Watch* is a truly great painting.
Moe: How so?
Joe: Rembrandt is one of the greatest painters of all time.

B. The choice is ours: Are we going to give businesses more freedom from strangling regulation, or are we going to continue to go down the road of Communism?

C. How long are we going to continue social welfare for America's fighting class by approving huge military budgets?

D. The depression years following the stock market crash of 1929 were years of rich literary activity in America. Great literature needs to be nourished by hard times.

E. No political organization can survive without a single leader who has complete authority. Without a captain at the helm, the ship of state will drift along the shore and crash on the rocks.

F. There is no hard evidence to support the claim that Laetrile is ineffective in fighting cancer.

G. Smith certainly deserves to be promoted ahead of Jones. She came from a relatively poor family and had to work hard for everything, whereas Jones has had a fairly easy time of it.

H. Over five million Americans are now in prison—a sign of the lawlessness which has gripped our nation.

I. Congressman Day's proposal to turn all golf courses into public parks is a very bad idea. The reason he proposed it in the first place is that, when he was a child, his father neglected him by playing golf all the time; and now, in his own neurotic way, Congressman Day is trying to get even with his father.

J. Students are clearly more ignorant than they used to be. I met three students just this week who couldn't identify the author of the line, "Forever wilt thou love and she be fair!"

Appendix 3 Editing and Proofreading

Overview

- Introduction
- Correct Construction
- Readable and Effective Style
- A Short Guide to Punctuation
- A Short Glossary of Usage

• Introduction

The medium of writing requires and repays special care. If you haven't edited your essay you haven't finished composing it. Editing means going back over what you have written, making sure that it is as clear, correct, readable, and effective as you can make it. In the process, you discover new ways of saying things and new things to say.

Don't be overly concerned about editorial problems when composing the first draft of an essay. It's difficult enough just getting thoughts organized and stated coherently. Different people do compose in different ways, and many writers do a fair amount of editing as they go along. But the process of writing usually presents too many little decisions of form and usage for anyone to make at once. No one gets everything right the first time. All writing, even that of accomplished writers, needs editing.

Every piece of writing is unique in some ways, and not all editorial problems can be predicted. Those that can (leaving aside spelling errors) fall into three groups—*correct construction, readable and effective style,* and *usage.* Punctuation is not really a separate category, since it is involved in both construction and style. However, for the sake of convenience, a separate guide to punctuation is included here.

• Correct Construction

Sentence fragment

Edited written English requires each sentence to be a complete, independent clause. A *phrase* (not containing both subject and verb) or a *dependent clause* (introduced with a subordinating word, such as *that, which, when, where, although, unless*), punctuated as a complete sentence, is a *fragment.*

The requirement of complete sentences is not absolute, and accomplished writers do occasionally use sentence fragments. Like this one. However, the use of unintentional sentence fragments among inexperienced writers is such a widespread problem that most students should be wary of them.

Correct a sentence fragment by joining it to an adjacent sentence or by re-writing it to make an independent clause.

Faulty: Many physicians are reluctant to report cases of suspected child abuse. Perhaps because they are afraid of lawsuits.

Analysis: "Perhaps because they are afraid of lawsuits" is not a complete sentence but a dependent clause. (The subordinating word "because" is the key.)

Edited: **Perhaps because they are afraid of lawsuits, many physicians are reluctant to report cases of suspected child abuse.**

Faulty: I have a number of friends who commute to campus. Some who drive their own cars and some who don't.

Analysis: The second sentence is not an independent clause.

Edited: **I have a number of friends who commute to campus, some who drive their own cars and some who don't.**

OR

I have a number of friends who commute to campus. Some of them drive their own cars and some don't.

Comma splice/run-on sentence

A comma splice or run-on sentence is two independent clauses joined by a comma or simply run together.

Correct a comma splice or run-on sentence by making two sentences, by joining the sentences using a proper conjunction, by making one of the sentences a dependent clause, or by inserting a semicolon.

Faulty: At 55 miles per hour, driving is absolutely monotonous, falling asleep is a real possibility.

Analysis: Two independent clauses joined by a comma.

Edited: **At 55 miles per hour, driving is absolutely monotonous, and falling asleep is a real possibility.**

OR

At 55 miles per hour, driving is absolutely monotonous; falling asleep is a real possibility.

OR

Because driving is absolutely monotonous at 55 miles per hour, falling asleep is a real possibility.

Subject-verb agreement

Singular subjects require the singular form of the verb, usually with the *-s* ending. Plural subjects require the plural form of the verb. Most errors of subject-verb agreement occur when the writer forgets the number (singular or plural) of the subject and matches the number of the verb to some word that has come between subject and verb. Another cause of error is that writers often forget that singular indefinite pronouns—*any, each, either, neither, one, none*—require the singular form of the verb, even when they are followed by compound subjects.

Correct an error of subject-verb agreement either by changing the form of the verb to agree with the subject, or by changing the number of the subject.

Faulty:	Neither of these construction projects were delayed by anti-nuclear demonstrations.
Analysis:	The writer has made the verb agree with the closest noun, "projects." But "Neither" is the real subject of the sentence, and it requires a singular verb.
Edited:	**Neither of these construction projects was delayed by anti-nuclear demonstrations.**
Faulty:	A riot-control alert is called any time a large crowd gather near the entrance of the compound.
Analysis:	In American (as opposed to British) English, collective nouns, such as *group, team, band, committee,* and *jury,* are considered singular.
Edited:	**A riot-control alert is called any time a large crowd gathers near the entrance of the compound.**

Pronoun-antecedent agreement

The antecedent of a pronoun is the word to which it refers. A pronoun should agree with its antecedent in gender (masculine, feminine, neuter) and in number (singular or plural).

Errors of pronoun-antecedent agreement usually occur when the writer forgets either the number of the antecedent or the antecedent itself. An additional problem is that edited written English lacks a completely acceptable singular pronoun to agree with a singular indefinite antecedent. *They, them, their (Everyone should take off their coat),* which have developed as singular indefinites in spoken English, are not yet accepted in edited written English. And the generic use of *he, him, his (Everyone should take off his coat)* is often regarded as sexist.

Correct a faulty agreement of pronoun and antecedent by changing the number of the pronoun to agree with the antecedent, or by changing the number of the antecedent. When forced to choose between singular indefinite they, them, their *and generic* he, him, his, *change the antecedent to plural, or avoid the issue entirely by re-wording the sentence.*

Faulty:	Everyone should bring their coat.
Analysis:	"Everyone" requires a singular pronoun in edited written English.
Edited:	**All students should bring their coats.**
	OR
	Everyone should bring a coat.

Faulty: Neither Bill nor Gary was able to drive their own car.

Analysis: When parts of an antecedent are linked by *nor* or *or,* the pronoun should agree in gender and number with second part.

Edited: **Neither Bill nor Gary was able to drive his own car.**

Faulty: Neither Bill nor Mary was able to drive their own car.

Analysis: As phrased, with *neither . . . nor,* this sentence presents a problem that is unsolvable in English.

Edited: **Both Bill and Mary were unable to drive their own cars.**

Vague or ambiguous pronoun reference

Edited written English requires that pronouns have definite and unmistakable antecedents, usually in the same sentence or in the sentence just preceding. The most common instances of faulty pronoun reference involve the vague use of *which, this, they, you,* and *it,* and pronouns for which there are two possible antecedents.

Correct an error of pronoun reference by changing the sentence so that the pronoun refers to one antecedent only, by inserting a definite antecedent for the pronoun, or by finding a definite substitute for which, this, you, it, *or* they.

Faulty: She sits in front of the television when she does her work, which annoys me.

Analysis: The sentence contains no precise referent for the relative pronoun *which.*

Edited: **It annoys me that she sits in front of the television when she does her work.**

Faulty: After talking to Marlow over the telephone, Bill knew that he had no chance of getting the job.

Analysis: It is not clear whether Marlow had no chance or Bill had no chance.

Edited: **After talking to him over the telephone, Bill knew that Marlow had no chance of getting the job.**

OR

Bill knew that he had no chance of getting the job, after talking to Marlow over the telephone.

Faulty: In the Scout camps they try to make conditions as sanitary as possible.

Analysis: There is no antecedent for the pronoun.

Edited: **In the Scout camps every effort is made to keep conditions sanitary.**

OR

The administrators of the Scout camps try to make conditions as sanitary as possible.

Dangling or misplaced modifiers

Edited written English requires modifying phrases to have definite and unmistakable *referents*—words that they modify—within the same sentence. Because the placement of modifying phrases varies, writers sometimes produce combinations that either distort the relationship between a modifier and its referent or leave the modifier without any referent at all.

A *dangling modifier* is a phrase that does not really modify any word or phrase in the sentence, because the modified element has been left out or stated indirectly. A *misplaced modifier* is one that appears to modify a word other than the one intended.

Correct a dangling or misplaced modifier by changing the sentence so that the modified word stands next to the modifier, by making sure that the sentence has a direct (rather than implied) referent for the modifier, or by changing the phrase to a subordinate clause.

Faulty: As a saccharine user, these are frightening facts.

Analysis: The modifier "as a saccharine user" has no direct referent in the sentence.

Edited: **As a saccharine user, I find these facts frightening.**

Faulty: Once published on the front page in bold letters, many people in town became aware of my grandfather's "crime."

Analysis: The phrase, "once published . . ." seems to modify "many people" rather than its real referent, "my grandfather's 'crime.' "

Edited: **Once published on the front page in bold letters, my grandfather's "crime" became known to many people in town.**

OR

Many people in town became aware of my grandfather's "crime," once it was published on the front page in bold letters."

Faulty: By combining all the scientific research and knowledge gained so far, perhaps the unnecessary duplication of tests can be prevented.

Analysis: The sentence contains no logical subject for the participle, "combining."

Edited: **If scientists could combine all the scientific research and knowledge gained so far, perhaps the unnecessary duplication of tests could be prevented.**

OR

Perhaps by combining all the scientific research and knowledge gained so far, scientists could prevent the unnecessary duplication of tests.

Mixed constructions

Sometimes writers shift grammatical or logical gears in the middle of a sentence, beginning a thought with one type of construction, but concluding with part of another. The following sentence contains a mixed construction:

> Although welfare payments have increased dramatically in the last decade does not mean that there are more poor people in this country.

A complete sentence could have followed the opening clause (which begins with "Although"), or a subject clause could have preceded the predicate (which begins with "does not"). But this sentence has the head end of one type of construction and the tail end of another.

> *Correct a mixed construction by changing one of the parts so that it conforms grammatically or logically to the other.*

Faulty: Although welfare payments have increased dramatically in the last decade does not mean that there are more poor people in this country.

Edited: **Although welfare payments have increased dramatically in the last decade, the number of poor people in this country has not necessarily risen.**

OR

The fact that welfare payments have increased dramatically in the last decade does not mean that there are more poor people in this country.

Faulty: Henderson hoped that by returning all the money would restore his credibility in the congregation.

Analysis: The main clause "Henderson hoped that . . ." needs to be followed by a clause; or the predicate "would restore . . ." needs to be preceded by a phrase functioning as subject.

Edited: **Henderson hoped that by returning all the money he would restore his credibility among the congregation.**

OR

Henderson hoped that returning all the money would restore his credibility among the congregation.

EXERCISE

Correct the faulty constructions in the following sentences.

A. Many times a student needs to find their advisor and are not able to.

B. The mayor's decision to cancel the rock concert was appropriate. Although I can't say I like it.

C. There is one type of relief that involves no drugs and eases tension and stress, which is meditation.

D. Mr. Lake now lives in London, he left his job with Western Electric to become a legal representative for a chain of hotels.

E. Opening the door, the worst smell I ever encountered came out of the room.

F. A recent survey of six hundred students reveal that the majority oppose fraternities and sororities.

G. At the meeting I attended they failed to inform you that automobiles belonging to students would be towed if not removed after the first day.

H. Although inexperienced students commit construction errors in their writing is not a sign that they don't understand their language.

I. Dr. Minyard's speech was delightful, however, the ideas in it seemed a bit extreme.

J. By typing out address labels beforehand, a great deal of time was saved by the secretaries.

• Readable and Effective Style

A piece of writing can be free of construction errors but still lack readability and effectiveness. Its sentences can be difficult and annoying for a reader to process, or its ideas may be expressed in such a way that the reader must strain to grasp them.

Readability implies ease of processing, but it does not always mean simplicity. One cause of an unreadable style might be unnecessarily complicated syntax or unnecessarily grandiose or specialized word choice. But another cause might be a string of simple sentences, when a single sentence containing several subordinate clauses would provide easier access to the main point. In general, a readable style is one which guides the reader efficiently to the author's ideas, with as few ambiguities and annoyances as possible.

Edit your writing for readability and effectiveness, keeping in mind the following principles.

"Strung out" sentences

Avoid the "strung out" sentence that contains several independent clauses joined by coordinating conjunctions. Prefer the sentence with a single, easily identifiable main clause, modified by subordinate clauses and phrases. Correct a strung out sentence by changing some of the independent clauses to dependent clauses or phrases. Make two separate sentences if necessary.

Faulty: The orientation committee should put aside one afternoon and evening and have a picnic for everyone, and then later those who wanted to play games could, and for those who did not wish to participate there could be a movie provided by the Student Government.

Analysis: The sentence is overloaded with independent clauses and other units joined by coordinating conjunctions. It seems to ramble.

Edited: **The orientation committee should put aside one afternoon and evening for a picnic. Later, those who wish could play games, while others attend a movie provided by the Student Government.**

Faulty: More people live by themselves and more women work and more money is available, and for these reasons one of every three American food dollars now goes to restaurants.

Analysis: There are too many short, independent clauses strung together by conjunctions. The reader is not led directly to the main point.

Edited: **Because more people live by themselves, more women work, and more money is available, one of every three American food dollars now goes to restaurants.**

Choppy sentences

Avoid a string of short, choppy sentences. Combine short, choppy sentences by converting some of them to modifying clauses or phrases.

Faulty: Charles has two main problems. The first one concerns his inability to keep good records. The second one is that he cannot stay awake. He is very fat. He also has high blood pressure. This may be partly responsible for his poor job performance.

Analysis: The reader has to plow through many short, choppy sentences to get to the main point. Combine some of these sentences, condensing the phrasing where possible.

Edited: **Charles' two main problems are his inability to keep good records and his inability to stay awake. His obesity and high blood pressure may be partly responsible for his poor job performance.**

Faulty: Anthony Lewis recently had an essay in the *New York Times.* He said that it was wrong for the CIA to engage in covert operations abroad. It wasn't effective either. The reason is that these operations nearly always backfire. This causes embarrassment for the United States.

Analysis: Too many short, choppy sentences leave the passage without focus. Combining these sentences will lead the reader directly to the main point.

Edited: **In a recent *New York Times* essay, Anthony Lewis claimed that covert operations abroad by the CIA were not only wrong but ineffective as well, since they nearly always backfire, causing embarrassment for the United States.**

Parallel items

Express parallel items or ideas in parallel form. Make compound subjects, objects, or modifying phrases parallel by using the same grammatical construction in each. Subjects and complements joined by the verb *be* should be parallel.

Faulty: Five wrecks have occurred in the past month, all resulting in injury to students and due to the negligence of the bus drivers.

Analysis: The two modifying phrases would be much more effective if made parallel. The second should be changed to a participle phrase like the first.

Edited: **Five wrecks have occurred in the past month, all resulting in injury to students and all caused by the negligence of the bus drivers.**

Faulty: Previously, Charles' principal duties were to keep records and the equipment delivery and pickup of equipment.

Analysis: The phrases that describe Charles' duties should be parallel in form.

Edited: **Previously, Charles' principal duties were to keep records and to deliver and pick up equipment.**

Faulty: The only way to control this campus problem is by establishing much harsher regulations.

Analysis: The subject is stated in the form of an infinitive phrase. The complement would be more effective if stated in the same form.

Edited: **The only way to control this campus problem is to establish much harsher regulations.**

Subject and verb connection

Keep the connections between subjects and verbs as clear as possible. Avoid or re-arrange intervening structures that distort these connections.

Faulty: Teachers who seldom prepare for their classes and who do nothing to help slower students keep pace with brighter ones undermine the system of education.

Analysis: The two long relative clauses between the subject and predicate distort the connection between them.

Edited: **Teachers undermine the system of education when they seldom prepare for their classes and when they do nothing to help slower students keep pace with brighter ones.**

Faulty: To think that a variety of supervisors working out of several different agencies can coordinate the resources needed to solve these problems is a mistake.

Analysis: The long *that*-clause distorts the relationship between simple subject *(to think)* and predicate *(is),* making agreement seem faulty even though it is correct. Solve this problem by moving the main clause to the front of the sentence.

Edited: **It is a mistake to think that a variety of supervisors working out of several different agencies can coordinate the resources needed to solve these problems.**

Modifiers and the words they modify

To keep the connection between modifiers and the words they modify as clear as possible, avoid or re-arrange intervening structures that distort these connections. Avoid ambiguously placed modifiers.

Faulty: Meditation has no harmful side effects, unlike antibiotics and tranquilizers.

Analysis: "Unlike antibiotics and tranquilizers" goes with "meditation," not "side effects."

Edited: **Unlike antibiotics and tranquilizers, meditation has no harmful side effects**

OR

Meditation, unlike antibiotics and tranquilizers, has no harmful side effects.

Faulty: Although these programs have received much attention and support, as they exist today, they do more harm than good.

Analysis: The phrase "as they exist today" was intended to modify the latter clause. But in its present placement, the phrase might at first be taken to modify the first clause.

Edited: **Although these programs have received much attention and support, they do more harm than good, as they exist today.**

OR

These programs have received much attention and support, but as they exist today, they do more harm than good.

Directness

Avoid circumlocutions—round-about ways of saying things. Eliminate unnecessary words and phrases.

Faulty: The Congress has effected the adoption of a very complicated plan in order to fulfill its need of accomplishment at solving a problem which might be dealt with in a more humane and simple manner.

Analysis: The sentence contains a number of unnecessary words and phrases. It says in a complicated way something that could be said more simply.

Edited: **The Congress has adopted a very complicated plan in order to solve a problem that could be solved more simply and humanely.**

Faulty: In Brigid Brophy's essay, "Monogamy," she overlooks the spiritual factors which our country revolves around.

Analysis: There are two problems here. The formula, "In Brigid Brophy's essay . . . she," is awkward; the "she" appears in a possessive form. "Revolves around" is a vague metaphor that complicates the syntax but adds nothing to the meaning of the sentence.

Edited: **In her essay, "Monogamy," Brigid Brophy overlooks our country's spiritual values.**

Redundancies

Avoid redundancies and expressions that repeat what you have already said.

Faulty: These skills enable the reader to interpret the author's meaning by perceiving the unstated themes that are implicit in the reading passage.

Analysis: The following are redundancies: "Unstated themes" are by definition "implicit," and a "passage" is necessarily something to be read—you don't need to say "reading passage."

Edited: **These skills enable the reader to interpret the author's meaning by perceiving the unstated themes in the passage.**

Faulty: Even though I have never seen an accident on the lake, I have read various accounts of accidents both fatal and non-fatal, several of which resulted in deaths.

Analysis: The sentence is highly repetitive. If the accidents were "both fatal and non-fatal," then it stands to reason that some of them resulted in deaths.

Edited: **Even though I have never seen an accident on the lake, I have read various accounts of accidents, several of which were fatal.**

Clarity

In general, use simpler rather than more complex expressions, familiar rather than academic or high-sounding ones, and short ones rather than long ones.

Faulty: With the application of this method of muscle control, a patient possesses the liberty of discretionary exercise intervals, without encountering the necessity of ingesting antibiotics or tranquilizers.

Analysis: This sentence is ludicrously formal and complex. Everything in it can be said in a simpler way, without any loss of meaning.

Edited: **Using this method of muscle control, a patient can exercise whenever he wants to without having to take antibiotics or tranquilizers.**

Faulty: Among educators, there exists a dichotomy of opinion with regard to the effects of television.

Analysis: The phrasing here is too high-sounding and wordy.

Edited: **Educators disagree about the effects of television.**

Active verbs

Whenever possible, use active instead of passive voice; use verbal forms instead of their corresponding nominalizations; use verbs of action instead of verbs of being.

Faulty: In my case, social activities were really hated.

Analysis: The passive voice is unnecessary here and causes excess verbiage.

Edited: **I really hated social activities.**

Faulty: These steps to insure that the adopted child has a good home are taken because agency officials have the realization that adopted children are subject to many unusual problems.

Analysis: The passive construction in the main clause complicates the sentence unnecessarily and muddies the question of who is doing what. "Have the realization" can be readily replaced with the verb, "realize." An active verbal substitute can be found for "are subject to."

Edited: **Because they realize that adopted children face many unusual problems, agency officials take these steps to insure that the child has a good home.**

Faulty: Careful consideration should be given to this problem by college students.

Analysis: "Consideration" should be replaced by the verb, "consider." Passive voice is unnecessary here and distorts the implicit subject/verb connection between "students" and "consider."

Edited: **College students should consider this problem carefully.**

Faulty: There is the unmistakable implication in Dr. Minyard's essay that democracy and excellence are incompatible.

Analysis: The verb of being ("there is . . .") followed by a nominalization ("implication") is wordy and awkward; it also distorts the implicit verb/object connection between "imply" and "that democracy and excellence are incompatible."

Edited: **Dr. Minyard's essay unmistakably implies that democracy and excellence are incompatible.**

Logical connections

Make sure that the connections between words and phrases are logical and precise. Don't make your reader stop to figure out your meaning. Avoid ambiguous and illogical phrasing.

Faulty: The availability of advisors should also be increased.

Analysis: The notion of increasing the availability of advisors is vague and ambiguous. You can make the advisors more *accessible,* or you can increase the *number* of advisors.

Edited: **The number of advisors should also be increased.**

OR

Advisors should also be more accessible.

Faulty: The 55 mile-per-hour speed limit has illustrated many positive results.

Analysis: The speed limit has not "illustrated" anything, including "positive results."

Edited: **The 55 mile-per-hour speed limit has resulted in many benefits.**

EXERCISE

Edit the following sentences to make them more readable and effective.

A. Charles' principal duties were relieved when he began to be very inefficient in his work.

B. There is the need for universities to have policies concerning the continued employment of ineffective employees.

C. A recent survey taken in which sixty freshmen and upperclassmen were interviewed revealed the fact that the majority strongly disfavors "social cliques."

D. A couple of my friends have received unfair treatment, but most of them have been too afraid to complain.

E. Turn on the TV and flip the channel and you will find numerous superstar evangelists delivering their messages, and we can deliver our checks in return.

F. A twi-night double-header is when they have a double-header and one of the games is in the late afternoon and the other game is in the evening.

G. A system of collegiate football playoffs will bring order to the current, haphazard collection of bowl games, will be fairer to all the teams involved, and also college football fans will have a more definite sense of who the national champion is.

H. The most advantageous procedure for the elimination of fleas from the skin and hair of cats is the purchase and installation of a flea collar on same.

I. The argument that a system of collegiate football playoffs will bring order to the present schedule of bowl games, will be fairer to all the teams involved, and will give fans a more definite sense of who the national champion is is wrong.

J. George Will recently had an essay in *Newsweek.* In it he said that nuclear power was more economical than any other source. He also said that it was safer. The article appeared three days before a huge nuclear accident. This was at Three Mile Island, which is in Pennsylvania.

• A Short Guide to Punctuation

This section does not attempt to cover every use of every punctuation mark in written English. It concentrates, rather, on uses that are most likely to cause problems for inexperienced writers.

The period

1. Use a period to end any sentence that is not a direct question, exclamation, or excited command.

The author of this book lives in North Carolina. *(Statement)*

Marilyn asked where the author lived. *(Indirect question)*

Ask Marilyn where the author lives. *(Direction or mild command)*

2. Place periods *inside* quotation marks.

Everyone was now aware of my grandfather's "crime."

Then Ilsa said, "Play it, Sam."

3. If an entire sentence is in parentheses, place the period *inside* the parenthesis. If less than an entire sentence is in parentheses, place the period *outside* the parenthesis.

   Agrippina and Nero have been repeatedly accused of committing incest, in spite of the paltry evidence. (Several ancient sources specifically deny the claim.)

   Several ancient sources specifically deny the claim (Tacitus, for instance).

4. Use periods with abbreviations.

   e.g., Mr., Mrs., etc., cf.

5. Some abbreviations do not require periods.

   USSR (Union of Soviet Socialist Republics)

   USA (United States of America)

   YMCA (Young Men's Christian Association)

The question mark

1. Use a question mark to end a direct question.

   When should one use a question mark?

2. Do not use a question mark to end an indirect question.

   Ilsa asked Rick whether he wanted Sam to play the song again.

   The question is whether she knew the implications of what she was doing.

3. If a question is being quoted directly, place the question mark *inside* the quotation mark. If a question is not being quoted, place the question mark *outside* the quotation mark.

   The steamfitter asked, "How long will we be down here?"

   How could my grandfather have committed such a "crime"?

The exclamation point

1. Use an exclamation point after an interjection, a strong command, or any excited or especially forceful statement.

   When she saw what he had done, she cried, "Oh heavens!"

   Stamp out frisbee-throwers, now!

2. Don't overuse exclamation points to intensify statements. Look instead for alternative phrasing that will express the force of a statement.

3. If an interjection, a strong command, or forceful statement is quoted directly, place the explanation point *inside* the quotation mark. If not, place the exclamation point *outside* the question mark.

When she saw what he had done, she cried, "Oh heavens!"

She hadn't even read "A Good Man is Hard to Find"!

The comma

Because the comma is the most variously used punctuation mark, it presents the most difficulties to inexperienced writers. The treatment that follows concentrates on common uses and misuses.

1. Use a comma before a coordinating conjunction to join independent clauses into a compound sentence.

The leopard cannot change its spots, but man has the power to change his skin.

Jill knew that she was expected to win the contest, and she tried very hard to come up with the right answers.

2. Do not use a comma before a coordinating conjunction to join compound subjects, predicates, or objects.

Faulty: The Jack of Diamonds, and the Ace of Spades bowed before the Queen of Hearts.

Edited: **The Jack of Diamonds and the Ace of Spades bowed before the Queen of Hearts.**

Faulty: Rick crushed his cigarette, and brushed aside a tear.

Edited: **Rick crushed his cigarette and brushed aside a tear.**

3. Do not use a comma to join the subject and predicate of a sentence, even if there would be a pause in speech.

Faulty: Charles' constant drowsiness and his mismanagement of the warehouse, caused his dismissal.

Edited: **Charles' constant drowsiness and his mismanagement of the warehouse caused his dismissal.**

4. Use commas to join a series of closely related short sentences with parallel structure.

We had no money, we had no credit, and we had no friends.

5. Use commas to join words, phrases, or clauses that form a series within the sentence.

A writer needs to consider his purpose, subject, audience, and situation.

The obvious fact is that man is a child of nature, subject to its vicissitudes, compelled by its necessities, driven by its impulses, and confined within the brevity of the years which nature permits.—Reinhold Niebuhr

Marvin understood that there would be no more opportunities to explain himself, that he would continue to be misunderstood, and, in short, that he would have to leave town.—Warren Brevor

6. Use a comma to set off an introductory word, phrase, or clause.

Granted, this project will be expensive.

As for the penguins' eggs, when Cherry Garrard got back to London the first thing he did was to take them to the Natural History Museum.—Nancy Mitford

If you want to raise your children the way you were raised, you have a definite pattern to follow.—Benjamin Spock

Omit the comma from a short introductory element, as long as no confusion results:

Yesterday the entire crew stayed away.

If one baby cries they all start crying.

Faulty: Seated the children became more polite.

Edited: **Seated, the children became more polite.**

7. Use a comma to set off a nonrestrictive modifier. Nonrestrictive modifiers can include appositives, relative clauses, participle phrases, and prepositional phrases.

When a modifier is nonrestrictive, it adds new information to the specific word it refers to, and it often seems to modify the entire sentence more than any specific word. Restrictive modifiers, on the other hand, offer essential identifying information about the items they modify.

Restrictive: The new course *that you mentioned* will be offered next fall.

Nonrestrictive: The new course, *which we actually began to plan three years ago,* will be offered next fall.

Restrictive: That old car *parked in the garage* belongs to my brother.

Nonrestrictive: That old car, *beaten down by years of the worst possible treatment,* miraculously kept on running.

8. Use commas to set off parenthetical or transitional expressions.

Marvin's sister, as it turned out, had never even heard of a Winchester.

Rick was determined, no matter what his feelings told him, to do the honorable thing.

Ilsa, however, would have given up everything.

9. Place commas *inside* quotation marks.

We ended the course with a discussion of Wordsworth's "Resolution and Independence," a poem about artistic inspiration.

"War," he sputtered, "is nature's way!"

The semicolon

1. Use the semicolon to join two or more independent clauses without a conjunction, if the clauses express parallel or contrasting thoughts, in roughly parallel form or close logical relationship.

   In 1917 we had been saving Europe from the Germans; in the forties we had been saving it from the Germans again; we shall presently be returning no doubt . . . to rescue it from the Russians.—Edmund Wilson

   Therefore, just the same, don't you meddle with old unloaded firearms; they are the most deadly and unerring things that have ever been created by man.—Samuel Clemens

2. Use the semicolon before a conjunctive adverb—such as *indeed, nevertheless, moreover, however, therefore, consequently*—to join two related independent clauses.

   Many people in the audience were displeased with the music; indeed, many thought it no music at all.

   A fertilized female tarantula lays from 200 to 400 eggs at a time; thus it is possible for a single tarantula to produce several thousand young.—Alexander Petrunkevitch

3. Use a semicolon to divide a compound sentence if one or both of the independent clauses are long and complex.

   Since the mid-1940's over 200 basic chemicals have been created for use in killing insects, weeds, rodents, and other organisms described in the modern vernacular as "pests"; and they are sold under several thousand different brand names.—Rachel Carson

4. Use semicolons to join items in a series if they are long or already contain commas of their own.

   There is nothing soft or benevolent about the images from the second half of the 60's: the orange glow over the ruins of city slums; the daily dose of maiming and killing from Vietnam on the evening news; the stench of tear gas, vomit and blood in the streets of Chicago at the 1968 Democratic Convention; crippled Vietnam veterans being beaten up for demonstrating against the war.—Susan Jacoby

5. Always place a semicolon *outside* quotation marks. (If a quotation ends in a semicolon, the semicolon is dropped.)

   Harrison's philosophy was to "live and let live"; his brother's was to take what he could get, and damn the consequences.—Wallace Brevor

6. Don't use a semicolon to join a phrase or dependent clause to an independent clause. This produces a sentence fragment.

Faulty: The mayor's decision to cancel the rock concert was justified; although I can't say I liked it.

Edited: **The mayor's decision to cancel the rock concert was justified, although I can't say I liked it.**

The colon

1. Use a colon to introduce a series of items.

Every internal combustion engine has three basic systems: an ignition system, a firing system, and an exhaust system.

2. Use a colon to introduce and call attention to a quotation.

Ardent followers of the Golden Rule should consider George Bernard Shaw's adaptation: "Do not do unto others as you would they should do unto you. Their tastes may not be the same."

Among Hindus the taboo against killing cows does not appear to be absolute. During a drought in 1967, *The New York Times* reported: "Hindus facing starvation in the drought-stricken area of Bihar are slaughtering cows and eating the meat even though the animals are sacred to the Hindu religion."

3. Use a colon to indicate that an explanation or example will follow:

So two cheers for democracy: one because it admits variety and two because it permits criticism. Two cheers are quite enough: there is no occasion to give it three. —E.M. Forster

The wrongs against which we now array ourselves are no common wrongs: they cut to the very roots of human life.—Woodrow Wilson

4. Don't use a colon in the middle of a clause.

Faulty: The three major systems of an internal combustion engine are: the ignition system, the firing system, and the exhaust system.

Edited: **The three major systems of an internal combustion engine are the ignition system, the firing system, and the exhaust system.**

OR

The internal combustion engine has three major systems: the ignition system, the firing system, and the exhaust system.

The dash

1. Use dashes to add emphasis to a parenthetical phrase or clause.

What's good in people—and consequently in the world—is their insistence on creation, their belief in friendship, in loyalty, for its own sake.—E. M. Forster

2. Use a dash to add something to a concept or idea expressed in the main clause of the sentence.

   I would rather live among the modern Barbarians than in a society really dominated by the completely alienated—whether existentialist or beatnik.—Joseph Wood Krutch

   In Moulmein, in Lower Burma, I was hated by large numbers of people—the only time in my life that I have been important enough for this to happen to me.—George Orwell

3. Use a dash to bring the important features of a thought up front, outside the sentence proper.

   The insistence on creation, the belief in friendship, in loyalty, for its own sake—these are the things that are good in people, and consequently in the world.—Paraphrase of E.M. Forster

Quotation marks

1. Use quotation marks with direct quotations, or with any part of a statement that is quoted verbatim.

   George Bernard Shaw wrote: "Do not do unto others as you would they should do unto you. Their tastes might not be the same."

   Ambrose Bierce defined love as "a form of temporary insanity, curable by marriage."

2. Use quotation marks with dialogue. Follow these conventions of punctuation:

   a. Always place periods and commas *inside* quotation marks.
   b. Always place colons and semicolons outside quotation marks.
   c. If a question mark or exclamation point is part of the statement quoted, place it *inside* the quotation mark; if it is not part of the statement quoted, place it *outside* the quotation mark. (See the exclamation point and the question mark for examples.)
   d. In writing dialogue, indicate a change of speaker with a new paragraph.
   e. If the situation calls for quotation marks inside quotation marks, use *single quotation marks* inside.

      "I have to study," she lied. "I'm preparing a report on Flannery O'Connor's 'A Good Man is Hard to Find.' "

   f. If you shorten a quotation by omitting words or phrases, use *ellipsis points* (. . .) to indicate the omission.

Original: It is not a man's duty, as a matter of course, to devote himself to the eradication of any, even the most enormous wrong; he may still properly have other concerns to engage him; but it is his duty, at least, to wash his hands of it, and, if he gives it no thought longer, not give it practically his support.—Henry David Thoreau

Shortened: It is not a man's duty . . . to devote himself to the eradication of any . . . wrong; he may still properly have other concerns to engage him; but it is his duty . . . to wash his hands of it, and . . . not give it practically his support.

3. Use quotation marks to identify the titles of newspaper and magazine articles, poems, short stories, chapters of books, and songs. Use underlining or italics, not quotation marks, for the titles of books, movies, newspapers, radio programs, television programs, and symphonies.

4. Use quotation marks to identify words that are being used in a special sense or whose meaning is being discussed.

By "realism" I do not mean an image or presentation that conforms to the appearances of external reality, but rather a philosophy which holds that words such as "honor," "love," and "duty" name "real" things that have a "real," albeit abstract, existence.

5. Use quotation marks, sparingly, to signal the ironic use of a word.

Only Judge Harrison ever realized the real meaning and purpose of grandfather's "crime."

• A Short Glossary of Usage

Writing is by nature a more formal and careful medium than ordinary conversation, and readers tend to be less tolerant of careless word choice than listeners are. Careful and customary usage is partly a matter of being polite, of showing respect for your audience and their normal expectations. It is also a matter of making what you have to say more acceptable in form, and therefore more persuasive. Careful and appropriate word choice is very often taken as a sign of precise and capable reasoning. Careless or inappropriate usage always damages an author's image.

The glossary that follows concentrates on the most commonly cited problems of *written* usage. It also includes some pairs of words that sound alike in speech and are sometimes confused in writing.

accept, except. Often confused in writing. *Accept* is a verb, meaning "receive, obtain." *Except* is a preposition or conjunction meaning "other than."

affect, effect. Often confused in writing. *Affect* is usually a verb; *effect* is usually a noun.

Taking a composition course did not **affect** his writing.

It had no **effect.**

ain't. Disfavored in edited American English except when used jokingly.

all ready, already. Often confused in writing. *All ready* means "completely ready" or that everyone is ready. *Already* means "by now" or "previously."

all right. Always two words. *Alright* is a misspelling.

almost, most. *Most* is disfavored as a substitute for *almost.*

I write **almost** (not *most*) every day.

a lot, alot. *A lot* is always written as two words. *Alot* is a misspelling. Generally, more precise and formal expressions can be found. See also *lots, lots of.*

among, between. Use *among* for relationships involving more than two items. Use *between* for relationships involving only two items.

Among (not *between*) the employees, Jack's love affair with his secretary was an ill-kept secret.

amount of, number of. Use *amount of* to refer only to things that cannot be counted. Use *number of* with countable items.

Most professors yearn for a larger **number of** (not *amount of*) brilliant students.

and/or. Avoid if possible. This usage has become popular because it sounds scientific. However, it reduces readability by breaking up the flow of a sentence.

as, because. Avoid *as* as a substitute for *because* or *since.*

Marshall was able to work two hours extra, **because** (not *as*) his bus did not leave until midnight.

as, like. In statements that make analogies or comparisons, use *as* or *as if* to join clauses.

After the storm, the pier looked **as if** (not *like*) it had been bombed.

awful, awfully. Avoid as a general intensifier, as in "She was *awfully* nice." More precise expressions can be found.

awhile, a while. Use *awhile* as an adverb, *a while* as a noun phrase.

He stood there **awhile** (not *a while*).

He stood there for **a while** (not *awhile*).

bad, badly. Avoid using the adverb *badly* as an adjective.

She felt **bad** (not *badly*).

beside, besides. Often confused. *Beside* means "next to"; *besides* means "in addition to," or in different contexts, "except."

Besides (not *beside*) this one book, he had no other projects at the moment.

between, among. See *among.*

but, hardly, scarcely. When used as quantifiers, these words are negative in meaning. Therefore, to avoid doubling the negative, avoid using them with *not* or contractions of *not.*

I had **but** (not *I didn't have but*) three dollars in my pocket.

He had **hardly** (not *he hadn't hardly*) finished one book before he began another.

can, may. Most readers will expect you to preserve a distinction between these words. *Can* indicates capacity or ability; *may* indicates permission.

censor, censure. Often confused. *Censor* means "to edit, delete, or ban objectionable material." *Censure* means "to criticize formally."

complement, compliment. Often confused. *Complement* means to go well with, to coordinate smoothly with; *compliment* means to praise.

continual, continuous. Although the distinction between these two words is all but obliterated in speech, there is still a difference in meaning. *Continual* means "over and over again"; *continuous* means "without interruption."

This typewriter breaks down **continually.**

This typewriter vibrates **continuously.**

could of. Often confused with *could have* because the pronunciations are similar.

Marilyn **could have** (not *could of*) had the position if she had wanted it.

criteria, criterion. *Criteria* is plural; *criterion* is singular.

That **criterion** is impossible to meet.

Those **criteria** are impossible to meet.

data, datum. *Data* is plural, meaning "facts." Although the singular *datum* is almost never used, *data* should be used only as a plural in formal writing.

Your professor's data **are** (not *is*) probably incorrect.

different from, different than. Traditionally, the preferred American usage is *different from.* Because it must be followed by a noun phrase which repeats the compared noun, *different from* sometimes leads to wordier constructions.

She sang the aria in a **different** key **from** that which she had used earlier.

She sang the aria in a **different** key **than** she had earlier.

disinterested, uninterested. These two words are synonymous in most speech, but in more educated usage *disinterested* means "impartial, unbiased." Since we already have one word that means "uninterested," the distinction is worth preserving in educated speech and writing.

Many professors appear **uninterested** (not *disinterested*) in the progress of their students.

due to, because of. Traditional educated usage restricts *due to* to constructions with the verb "to be." "Jack's failure was **due to** his incompetence and laziness, nothing else." With other verbs, traditional usage favors *because of:* "Jack was fired **because of** (not *due to*) his incompetence and laziness, nothing else."

effect. See *affect.*

enthused, enthusiastic. Formal usage favors the adjective, *enthusiastic.*

fewer, less. Use *fewer* to refer to countable items. Use *less* only with items that cannot be counted.

We have **fewer** students than last year.

I have **less** energy than you.

flaunt, flout. *Flaunt* means to "display, show off." *Flout* means to "defy, scorn."

good, well. In formal usage, use *good* only as an adjective, *well* only as an adverb.

I feel **good** (not *well*).

The crew performed **well** (not *good*).

had ought. Standard usage prefers *ought* by itself, with no auxiliaries. Avoid *had ought, should ought.*

hanged, hung. *Hanged* is used only in the sense of "execute by hanging." For all other meanings use *hung.*

hardly. See *but, hardly, scarcely.*

hisself. Nonstandard usage for *himself.*

hopefully. Many educated readers still object to the use of this word in the sense of "I hope," or "it is to be hoped that." It should be used only in the sense of "filled with hope."

imply, infer. *Imply* means "suggest"; *infer* means "conclude."

Dr. Minyard **implied** in his speech that democracy and excellence were incompatible.

I **inferred** that he did not believe in democracy.

irregardless. Nonstandard for *regardless.*

its, it's. Often confused in writing because an apostrophe is usual with possessive words. But the pronoun *its* is already the possessive form of *it,* and the apostrophe is unnecessary. *It's* should be used only as a contraction for *it is.*

kind of, sort of. As substitutes for "rather" or "somewhat," these expressions are generally considered too casual for written discourse.

lay. See *lie, lay.*

less. See *fewer, less.*

lie, lay. In formal written usage, try to sort out these confusing verbs. It's easy enough to remember that *lie* is intransitive ("lie down") and *lay* is transitive ("lay the books on the table"). The trouble is in the past tense, where *lay* is the past tense of *lie.* The past tense of *lay* is *laid.*

Marvin **lies** (not *lays*) on the sofa all day.

Yesterday, he **lay** (not *laid*) on the sofa all day.

like, as. See *as.*

literally. This word is too often used to mean its opposite, "figuratively." "He was **literally** scared to death," means he actually did die of fright.

lots, lots of. Too casual for formal writing. Use *a great deal, a great many,* or *much.* See also *a lot.*

may, can. See *can, may.*

media. *Media* is plural and requires the plural form of the verb. The singular form of *media* is *medium* (the *medium* of television).

off of. In writing, leave off the *of.*

The correction fluid **fell off** (not *off of*) the desk.

phenomena, phenomenon. *Phenomena* is plural; the singular form is *phenomenon.*

The roller derby is a curious **phenomenon** of our age.

Scientists try to explain these **phenomena.**

principal, principle. Often confused. *Principal* is either an adjective meaning "main" (the *principal* parts) or a noun referring either to the head of an organization (the *principal* of the school) or to an item in a financial transaction (*principal* and interest). *Principle* is always a noun and means "idea" or "guiding concept" (the *principle* of equality).

quote, quotes. The more formal *quotation, quotations* are favored in writing.

reason is because. Disfavored in formal writing because it creates an unparallel structure, with a noun phrase (*reason*) complemented by subordinate clause (*because*). The *reason is that* is favored.

The reason she didn't go is **that** (not *because*) she was preparing a report.

should of, would of. Often confused with *should have* because the pronunciations are similar.

He **should have** (not *should of*) come to class more often.

that, which. As relative pronouns, these words are sometimes interchangeable, although formal usage favors *that* in restrictive clauses, *which* in nonrestrictive clauses.

The book **that** you are reading was made in America. (restrictive)

This book, **which** was written over a period of two years, will be published in 1981.

their, there, they're. Sometimes confused in writing. *Their* is the possessive form of *they:* "The children returned to **their** homes." *There* is a demonstrative pronoun or expletive: "**There** is my brother's car." *They're* is the contraction of *they are:* "**They're** at the zoo."

thusly, thus. The *-ly* is unnecessary. Use *thus.*

to, too, two. Sometimes confused in writing. *To* is a preposition (*to* the house); *too* is an intensifier (*too* salty) or a synonym of "also" (Sally was there *too*); *two* is a numeral (*two* hands).

which. See *that, which.*

-wise. Much overused as a suffix to make adverbs out of nouns, *-wise* creates imprecise and inelegant expressions. "John was in a precarious situation, *lovelifewise.*" A better phrasing is, "John's love life was precarious."

would of. See *should of, would of.*

Index

Acknowledgments

permission. From "The Grand Inquisitor, Born Again" by Michael Novak, *National Review,* September 14, 1979. Copyright © 1979 by National Review, Inc., 150 East 35th Street, New York, N.Y. 10016. Reprinted by permission. From "TV News and Public Opinion" by Marvin Maurer from *Point Counterpoint: Readings in American Government* by Herbert M. Levine. Copyright © 1979 by Scott, Foresman and Company. Reprinted by permission of the author. **CHAPTER THREE** Adaptation of "Problem-Solving, Composing, and Liberal Education" by Richard L. Larson from *College English,* vol. 33, no. 6, March 1972. Copyright © 1972 by the National Council of Teachers of English. Reprinted by permission of the publisher and the author. **CHAPTER FOUR** From "The Economic Common Sense of Pollution" by Larry E. Ruff. *The Public Interest,* Spring 1970, no. 19, p. 69. Reprinted by permission. From "Spare the Rod, Save the Child" by Nat Hentoff from *Social Policy,* November/December 1979, vol. 10, no. 3, p. 58. Copyright © 1979 by Social Policy Corporation, New York, New York 10036. Reprinted by permission. "A Crash Program for Right to Drive" by Art Buchwald from *The Washington Post,* June 27, 1968. Reprinted by permission of the author. "Let's Not Get Out the Vote" by Robert E. Coulson from *Harper's Magazine,* November 1955, vol. 2111, no. 1266. Copyright © 1955 by Harper & Brothers. Reprinted by permission of the author. **CHAPTER FIVE** From " 'Now Don't Try to Reason with Me!': Rhetoric, Today, Left, Right, and Center" by Wayne C. Booth. Reprinted from *The University of Chicago Magazine,* November–December 1967. Copyright © 1967 by The University of Chicago. Reprinted by permission. From *The Feast of Fools: A Theological Essay on Festivity and Fantasy* by Harvey Cox. Copyright © 1969 by Harvey Cox. Reprinted by permission of Harvard University Press. "Thinking About Equality" by Michael Novak, *National Review,* October 12, 1979. Copyright © 1979 by National Review, Inc. Reprinted by permission. From "The Ploy of Sex" by George Will from *The Washington Post,* January 29, 1974. Copyright © 1974, The Washington Post Company. Reprinted with permission. From "Clark vs. Javits: Battle of Left Jabs" by George Will from *The Washington Post,* October 26, 1974. Copyright © 1974, The Washington Post Company. Reprinted with permission. From "A Village for the Handicapped" by George Will from *The Washington Post,* July 23, 1975. Copyright © 1975, The Washington Post Company. Reprinted with permission. "The Loom Dance" by Sherwood Anderson. Reprinted by permission of Harold Ober Associates Incorporated. Copyright 1930 by The New Republic, Inc. Renewed © 1957 by Eleanor Copenhaver Anderson. **CHAPTER SIX** Excerpt from "Views" by Anthony Brandt from *The Atlantic Monthly,* July 1977, vol. 240, no. 1. Copyright © 1977, by The Atlantic Monthly Company, Boston, Mass. Reprinted by permission of Paul R. Reynolds, Inc. "Who Killed King Kong?" by X. J. Kennedy from *Dissent,* vol. 7, no. 2, Spring 1960. Reprinted by permission. "Joey: A 'Mechanical Boy' " by Bruno Bettelheim from *Scientific American,* March 1959. Copyright © 1959 by Scientific American, Inc. All rights reserved. Reprinted by permission.

PART TWO From "A Step-daughter of the Prairie" by Margaret Lynn from *Atlantic Monthly,* March 1911. Copyright 1911 by the Atlantic Monthly Company, Boston, Mass. Reprinted with permission. From "On Going Home" from *Slouching Towards Bethlehem* by Joan Didion. Copyright © 1967 by Joan Didion. Reprinted by permission of Farrar, Straus and Giroux, Inc. From *Shooting and Elephant and Other Essays* by George Orwell, copyright 1950 by Sonia Brownell Orwell; copyright 1978 by Sonia Pitt-Rivers. Reprinted by permission of Harcourt Brace Jovanovich, Inc., the estate of the late George Orwell and Martin Secker and Warburg. "On Morality" from *Slouching Towards Bethlehem* by Joan Didion. Copyright © 1965, 1968 by Joan Didion. Reprinted by permission of Farrar, Straus and Giroux, Inc. "On the Ancient, but Now Sadly Neglected, Art of Leaning" by Joe Pawlosky from *The Greensboro Sun,* December 15, 1979, vol. 7, issue 6. Copyright © 1979 by Jim Clark. Reprinted by permission.

PART THREE From "The Total Artificial Heart" by Robert K. Jarvik from *Scientific American,* January 1981, vol. 244, no. 1. Copyright © 1980 by Scientific American, Inc. All rights reserved. Reprinted by permission. "Phenomenalism" by R. J. Hirst. Reprinted by permission of the Publisher from *The Encyclopedia of Philosophy,* Paul Edwards, Editor. Volume 6, page 130. Copyright © 1967 by Macmillan, Inc. From "As the World Tilts" by D. Hand from *Greensboro,* February 1977. Copyright © 1977 by Leisure Publishing Company. All rights reserved. Reprinted by permission. "Science and the Citizen: The Chemistry of Acupuncture" from *Scientific American,* July 1979. Copyright © 1979 by Scientific American, Inc. All rights reserved. Reprinted by permission. "In Celebration of Life" by Paul Gray from *Time,* May 14, 1979, vol. 113, no. 20. Reprinted by permission from *Time,* The Weekly Newsmagazine; Copyright Time Inc. 1979.

Additional Acknowledgments Carl Cohen, "Justice Debased: The Weber Decision." *Commentary,* vol. 68, no. 3, September 1979. Judianne Densen-Gerber, "What Pornographers Are Doing to Children: A Shocking Report." *Redbook,* vol. 149, no. 4, August 1977, p. 86. Arthur C. Clarke, "We'll Never Conquer Space." *Science Digest,* June 1960, vol. 47, no. 6. Erich Fromm, "Our Way of Life Makes Us Miserable." *Saturday Evening Post,* July 25–August 1, 1964. Margaret Mead and Rhoda Metraux, *A Way of Seeing.* New York: The McCall Publishing Company, 1961, pp. 74 and 76. Nathan Glazer, "The Issue of Cultural Pluralism in America Today," from *White Ethnics: Their Life in Working Class America,* ed. by Joseph Ryan. Englewood Cliffs: Prentice-Hall, Inc., 1973. Leonard Bloomfield, *Language.* New York: Holt, Rinehart and Winston, 1933, p. 42. Alvin Toffler, *Future Shock.* New York: Random House, 1970, pp. 12–13, 52–53, 134. Eric Hoffer, *The True Believer: Thoughts on the Nature of Mass Movements.* New York: Harper & Row, Publishers, Inc. 1951, pp. 80, 81, 121. Christopher Lasch, *The Culture of Narcissism: American Life in an Age of Diminishing Expectations.* New York: W.W. Norton & Company, Inc., 1979, p. 106. Desmond Morris, *Manwatching: A Field Guide to Human Behavior.* London: Jonathan Cape Ltd., 1977, p. 153. Rollo May, *Love and Will.* New York, W.W. Norton & Company, Inc. 1969. Joseph Pieper, *Leisure the Basis of Culture,* trans. by Alexander Dru. New York: Pantheon Books, Inc., 1952, pp. 50, 56–57. James David Barber, *The Presidential Character: Predicting Performance in the White House.* Englewood Cliffs: Prentice-Hall, Inc., 1972, p. 7. Ramsey Clark, *Crime in America: Observations on Its Nature, Causes, Prevention and Control.* New York: Simon and Schuster, 1970, p. 57. John Kenneth Galbraith, *The Affluent Society.* New York: Houghton Mifflin Company, 1969, pp. 7–8. Milton Friedman, *Capitalism and Freedom.* Chicago: The University of Chicago Press, 1962, pp. 9–10. Arthur Christopher Benson, *From a College Window.* New York: G.P. Putnam's Sons, 1906. Donald Hall, *String Too Short to Be Saved.* New York: Viking Press, 1961, p. 23. Stephen Potter, *The Complete Upmanship.* New York: Holt, Rinehart and Winston, 1970. William M. Tanner and D. Barrett Tanner, *Modern Familiar Essays.* Boston: Little, Brown and Company, 1930. Stuart Robertson, *The Development of Modern English,* second edition, revised by Frederic G. Cassidy. New York: Prentice-Hall, Inc., 1954. Roger Angell, "The Sporting Scene." *The New Yorker,* September 22, 1980, pp. 91, 92. Ray E. Baber, *Marriage and the Family.* New York: McGraw-Hill Book Company, Inc., 1953, p. 313. John H. Storer, "Bird Aerodynamics." *Scientific American,* vol. 186, no. 4, April 1952, p. 28. Peter Farb, *Word Play: What Happens When People Talk.* New York: Random House, 1973, pp. 222–223. Donald C. Peattie, *Flowering Earth.* New York: G.P. Putnam's Sons, 1939, p. 32. Paul Roberts, *Understanding English.* New York: Harper & Row, Publishers, 1958, pp. 305–306. Leonard Engel, "The Matchless Phenomenon of the Sea," *The Sea, Life Nature Library.* New York: Time Inc., 1961. "Vanishing Forests." *Newsweek,* November 24, 1980, p. 117. Harold J. Morowitz, "Rediscovering the Mind." *Psychology Today,* vol. 13, no. 3, August 1980, p. 12. Robert P. Ambroggi, "Water." *Scientific American,* vol. 243, no. 3, September 1980, p. 116. William F. Irmscher, *Teaching Expository Writing.* New York: Holt, Rinehart and Winston, 1979, p. 126. Wolfgang Langewiesche, "Why An Airplane Flies." *Life,* May 17, 1943, vol. 14, no. 20, p. 50.